Jump into JMP® Scripting

Second Edition

Wendy Murphrey
Rosemary Lucas

§sas.

sas.com/books

The correct bibliographic citation for this manual is as follows: Murphrey, Wendy and Rosemary Lucas. 2018. *Jump into JMP® Scripting, Second Edition.* Cary, NC: SAS Institute Inc.

Jump into JMP® Scripting, Second Edition

Contents

About This Book

What Does This Book Cover?

This book shows how to get started using the JMP scripting language (JSL) and explains the fundamental concepts needed to make the most of JSL. It also provides a rich source of example scripts for those who need to accomplish a specific task with scripting. As a bonus, information about helpful tools and advanced concepts has been added to this, the second edition.

Is This Book for You?

If you want to automate JMP analyses that you perform on a regular basis, want to know more about customizing your JMP reports, or need a good source for example scripts, this book is for you.

What Are the Prerequisites for This Book?

This book assumes that you have experience using JMP interactively and are familiar with the JMP menus and toolbars.

What Is the Scope of This Book?

If you do not know anything about JSL and need a quick start, the first three chapters of this book show you how to capture scripts that JMP generates and pull these scripts together into a cohesive program.

From there, a discussion of the fundamental concepts of JSL is provided to help you understand more about the language. Advanced scripting concepts and some useful tools follow to complete section 1.

If you do know a bit about scripting and seek examples of performing specific tasks, the second section of this book provides diverse example scripts. We hope you find this section of the book to be a good reference resource as you continue learning JSL.

If you are looking for complete and comprehensive treatment of JSL syntax, we recommend that you consult the Scripting Index, *Scripting Guide*, and *JSL Syntax Reference*, which are accessed from the Help menu within JMP software.

What's New in This Edition?

Instructions and examples have been updated, using the new and improved features of JMP software and JSL. Three new chapters about JSL fundamentals, advanced concepts, and helpful tools have been added.

How This Book Is Organized

This book is divided into two main parts. The first section is an introduction to JSL, showing how to use JMP to capture scripts and how to make modifications to combine scripts. This section also contains chapters on advanced scripting concepts, as well as introductions to helpful tools for scripting tasks. The second section of this book contains well over 50 example scripts for common scripting tasks. These scripts can be downloaded from the SAS Press website and modified by users for their specific needs.

Typographical Conventions Used in This Book

The following typographic conventions are used in this book:

regular	is used for most text.
italic	*is used for emphasis and object references within text.*
bold	identifies JMP menu and dialog choices and JSL functions. Choices such as **Help ▶ About JMP** mean you select **Help**, and then select **About JMP**.
//	identifies comments within the code.
/* */	delimits lengthy comments within the code.

Interspersed in the chapters are helpful hints, which are denoted with the shaded gray background and the chair icon. So, when you see the chair icon, hold onto your seat because something important is noted here.

Software Used to Develop the Book's Content

JMP PRO 14.1.0 for Windows was used to develop the scripts and create the screen shots for this book. All scripts were tested using JMP PRO 14.1 for both Windows and Macintosh operating systems.

If you are using a Macintosh operating system, you might find that menu items are different from those described in the book. For example, on Windows you would access the log by selecting the **View** menu. However, on Macintosh you would access the log by selecting the **Window** menu. We recommend reviewing the JMP 14 Menu Card and Quick Reference to find the Macintosh equivalent menu and shortcut items. These PDF files are found by selecting **Help ▶ Books ▶ Menu Card** and **Help ▶ Books ▶ Quick Reference**.

Example Code and Data

You can access the example code and data for this book by linking to the author pages here:
support.sas.com/murphrey
support.sas.com/lucas

Acknowledgments

Writing a book requires not only an author, but a whole host of support from many sources. In our case, one very important source of encouragement and support came from our mentor and colleague, Ryan Gilmore. Not only did Ryan teach both of us JMP Scripting Language when we started working in JMP Technical Support years ago, he critiqued the original book while in its infancy and helped guide us to write a better book. Thank you, Ryan.

We would also like to thank former and present members of the JMP Technical Support team for their support, including our managers Eddie Routten and Duane Hayes. Thank you all for your encouragement.

To John Sall who conceived and started JMP software, we are inspired by your enthusiasm and honored to have the opportunity to work with you and the rest of the JMP Division.

Special thanks go to our reviewers extraordinaire, who offered their expertise and advice on our drafts despite full-time duties elsewhere: Mark Bailey, Monica Beals, Justin Chilton, and Adam Morris.

Thank you, Catherine Connolly, our exceptional developmental editor. Many thanks go to Stacy Suggs, Robert Harris, Denise Jones, and Joel Byrd, who took our drafts and created the beautiful finished product. And to Julie Palmieri, SAS Press Editor-in-Chief, we thank you for giving us the opportunity to publish our scripting book.

And finally, we thank our families for their endless support during the writing of this book. Thank you Graham and Walker Murphrey, for your patience and understanding. And last but not least, we especially thank our spouses, Bob Lucas and Britt Murphrey, for taking on extra duties so that we could work on the book.

Section 1

Introduction to JSL

What is JSL? Beginning with the release of JMP 4 in 2000, a scripting language became a key feature of the software. The JMP scripting language, known as JSL, consists of various commands that, when put together appropriately, instruct JMP to perform designated tasks automatically.

What is a JSL script? A JSL script is a program that includes a series of JSL commands that process various tasks during a single execution. JSL offers you the freedom to create scripts from the very simple and specific to the most generic and complex.

The following are examples of actions that can be scripted:

- opening a data table
- adding columns
- selecting rows
- creating subset or summary tables
- performing various analyses
- saving data tables, journals, and more

This list is by no means exhaustive. In fact, it is only the beginning!

It might be best to ignore all thoughts of other programming languages that you are familiar with, because JSL is quite distinctive. Please don't try to figure out what language it is similar to at this point, as it might cause unnecessary frustration and headaches!

Chapter 1: Make JMP Work for You

Overview

Have you ever worried that you will have to write pages and pages of code, and won't know where to start? There's no need to fret, because JMP, the best scripter of all, can write the scripts for you. We're going to show you how.

In this chapter, you will learn about:

- capturing scripts from your analyses
- using scripts from imported data and data manipulations
- creating a combined script composed of two separate captured scripts

Capturing Scripts from Your Analyses

You just created a report that impresses your manager. She likes it so much that she wants the report weekly. So, what to do?

Do not panic. Instead, save the scripts and execute them next week to create your report.

In your report, you might have noticed the red triangle icons, clicked on a few of the icons, and used some of the options in the drop-down menus to modify or customize your analysis. See Figure 1.1 for an example.

Figure 1.1 Bivariate Menu

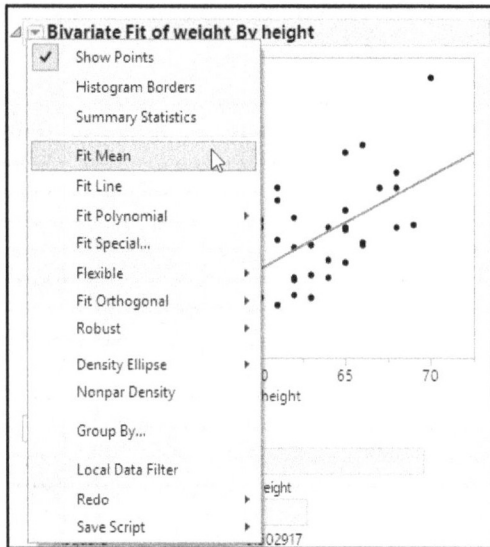

Did you know that you can capture a script of your analysis, plus many of the post-analysis changes you made? While JMP does not record every step you perform interactively, you can reproduce your results with scripting.

In Figure 1.2, notice the last item on the menu is **Save Script**. Selecting it opens a sub-menu that itemizes choices for saving the analysis script to regenerate the report, including most options.

Scripts that are generated by JMP can be captured in a variety of ways using selections in the **Save Script** menu.

Figure 1.2 Save Script Menu

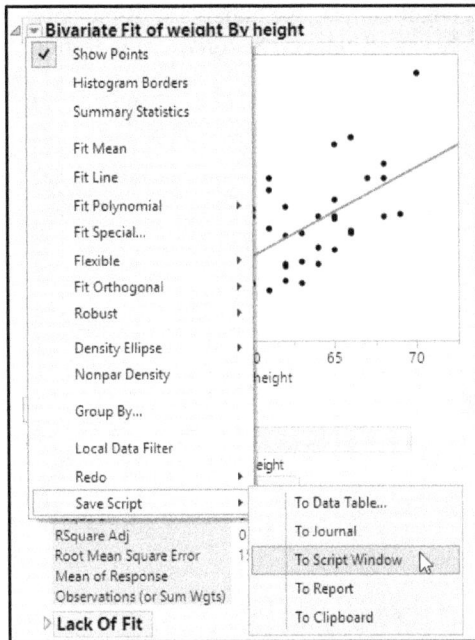

Let's take a look at three of these options.

Saving Scripts to a Data Table

Keeping a script with its associated data is a good idea. The **Save Script ▶ To Data Table** option stores the script as a property of the data table known as a table script. As a table script, it stays with the table until you delete it. You can update or add data to the table, execute the script, and see the results. And when you save the table, you also save the script. So when you give the data table to a colleague, she can open the table, execute the scripts with the data you intended, and view your reports.

After selecting **Save Script ▶ To Data Table**, you are prompted to provide a name for the table script or accept the default. In this dialog, you can also choose to replace an existing table script that has the same name or simply to append a suffix to ensure a unique name is assigned.

Figure 1.3 Table Script Naming

A green triangle icon, sometimes referred to as a *play* button, appears in the table panel beside the new table script. Clicking the green triangle icon runs the script. Right-clicking the table script name opens a menu with several items: **Run Script**, **Edit**, **Delete**, **Group Scripts/Ungroup Scripts**, **Copy**, **Debug Script**, and **Paste**.

Figure 1.4 Table Script Options

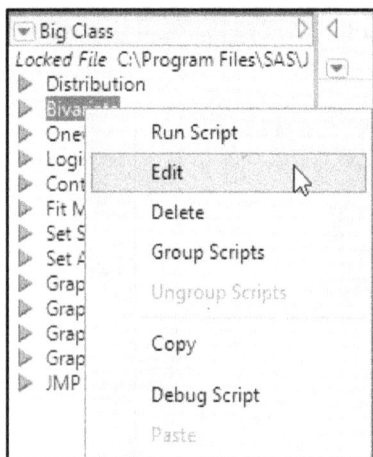

Choosing **Run Script** executes the script. This is the same action as clicking the green triangle icon.

Selecting **Edit** opens a window where you can view and edit the script.

Figure 1.5 Sample Script That Was Saved as a Table Script

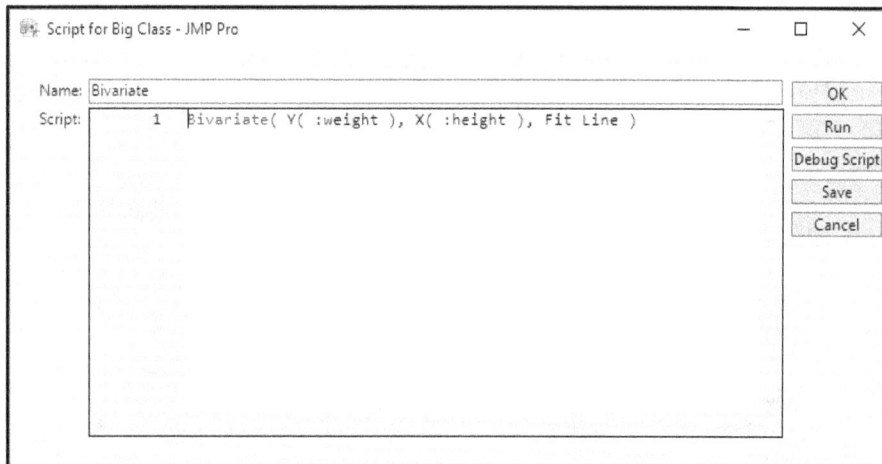

Selecting **Delete** removes all selected table scripts from the data table.

The **Group Scripts** option provides the ability to group selected table scripts. This enables you to organize your table scripts in a manner that makes sense for the data or even your analysis process.

For example, suppose you wanted to arrange the first three table scripts in the Big Class data table as a group called *Basic Analyses*. You would begin by selecting the three table scripts, right-clicking any one of them, and selecting **Group Scripts**.

Figure 1.6 Group Scripts

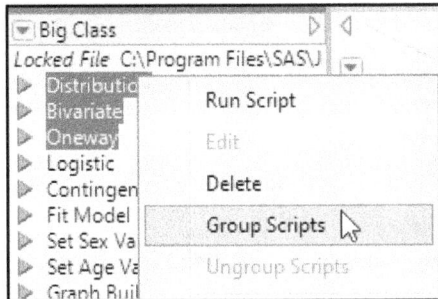

The default name is based upon the name of the first table script and also provides an indication of the number of table scripts included in the group. Simply click the group name once to rename it to something more meaningful. Right-clicking the group and selecting **Run Script** runs each table script in the order in which they appear in the group.

Figure 1.7 Renamed and Run Group Script

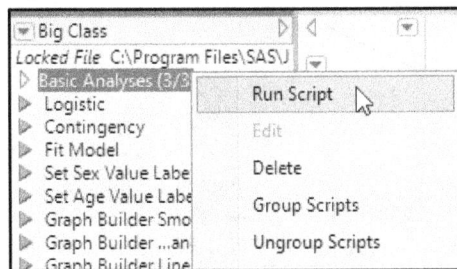

The **Copy** option seems obvious but can be a bit deceiving. In fact, it does more than store the selected table script to your clipboard. The script that is copied includes the entire data table message used to add a new table script, which makes for easy pasting of the table script into a different data table.

To see what we mean, suppose you saved a script in your data table named *Distribution of height*. Selecting **Copy** would place the following code on your clipboard:

```
Add Properties to Table(
    {New Script(
        "Distribution of height",
        Distribution( Continuous Distribution( Column( :height ) ) )
    )}
)
```

If you only wanted the contents of the table script, you have the following options:

1. Paste the preceding code into your main script and delete the unwanted options.
2. Select **Edit,** and then select and copy the desired section of the script.

Selecting the **Debug Script** option opens the JSL Debugger. The details and usage of the JSL Debugger are discussed in chapter 5.

Finally, the **Paste** option is another one that seems straight forward but has a little twist. When you select the **Paste** option, JMP actually just runs the script that is on your clipboard.

For example, if you had the entire **Add Properties to Table()** script, as shown above, stored on your clipboard, the script would be executed and the new table script would appear in the table panel.

On the other hand, if you only had the **Distribution()** code on your clipboard, then the Distribution report would appear and no new table script would be added to the table panel.

> Did you know that many of the sample data tables in your JMP installation include scripts that have already been saved? Right-click the green triangle icon to the left of a script that interests you, and then select **Edit** to display a ready-made script.

Figure 1.8 Table Panel with Saved Scripts

Saving Scripts to a Script Window

The **Save Script ▶ To Script Window** option places your script into a window named Script Window. This window is a script editor where you can edit your saved script. If this window is kept open, you can accumulate scripts from additional analyses by issuing the **Save Script ▶ To Script Window** command from those reports.

It is easy to save your script as a script file from this window. Select **File ▶ Save As**, and then select **Save As Type, JMP Scripts (*.jsl)**.

Figure 1.9 Script Window with Bivariate Script

Saving Scripts to the Clipboard

This is an easy one. The **To Clipboard** option places the script on the clipboard, and then you can paste the script wherever you need it.

Capturing Scripts from Imported Data

Importing data from various sources can be a tedious, arduous task. For the data types used most often, you can extract the script from JMP after importing the data using interactive methods.

The resulting JMP table automatically includes a table script named **Source**. This table script contains the JSL needed to import the data again using the same settings.

Figure 1.10 Text Import Table

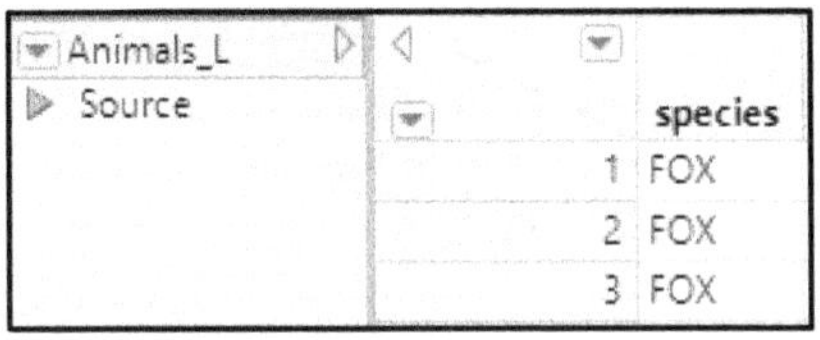

To see the code that JMP generated to reproduce the import of the data, right-click the green triangle icon next to **Source**, and select **Edit**. Notice in the following figure that the code consists of an **Open** statement with all possible settings needed to import the Excel file.

Figure 1.11 Source Script for Excel Import

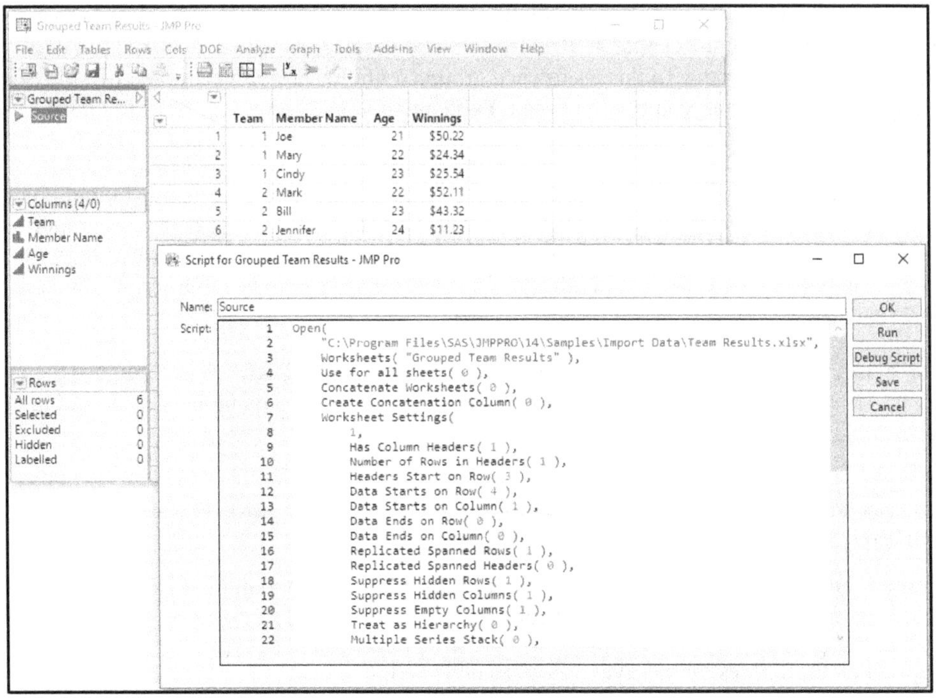

Using **File ▶ Open,** you can choose to open a variety of file types. Of the file formats supported by default, **Source** table scripts are included when any of the following data files are imported:

- Excel files
- text files
- SAS data sets

A new feature for JMP 14 is the ability to import multiple text data files. By accessing this feature from the **File ▶ Import Multiple Files** menu, you can choose to import text files stored in a variety of formats from a single directory. This feature allows you the flexibility to specify all the files in the directory or to narrow the list by specifying the file types, characters in the name, range of file sizes, or a range of file modified dates. For unstructured file types, there are options for how the data should be imported. There are also options to stack files that have a similar format into a single data table or to open each file in separate data tables. You can also add columns to the resulting data table that identify the name, size, and modified date of the source file.

This handy new feature is already popular with users. Just like other imported data, the resulting JMP data tables will have a **Source** table script containing the code to perform the import with the same settings again. A second table script called **Files** contains a list of files that were imported.

In the **File ▶ Database** menu, there are two options to import data from a database. The **Query Builder** enables you to build complex SQL queries without having to write the SQL statements. Upon running the query, the resulting JMP data table contains a **Source** table script. Passwords are masked by the code % _PWD_%.

The **Open Table** option is the traditional method for connecting to an ODBC data source, which is frequently used to import data using less complicated SQL statements. With default preference settings, the resulting table contains a **Source** table script with the password clearly visible. If you do not see any table scripts in the resulting table, select **File ▶ Preferences** and deselect the check box beside **ODBC Hide Connection String** found in the Tables preference group. With this preference turned off, the **Source** table script will appear the next time you use the **Open Table** method to import data from an ODBC database.

Using **File ▶ SAS**, you can connect to SAS installed on your local machine or SAS that is running on a server. The **Browse Data** option enables you to navigate your libraries to select the data to be imported. The SAS Query Builder is similar to the SQL Query Builder in appearance and functionality, except it is specifically used for importing SAS data. With either of these methods a **Source** table script is included in the resulting JMP data table.

Finally, the **File ▶ Internet Open** menu enables you to import data from a URL. When you use the **Open as Data** option, the data selected from the URL is imported into a new JMP data table. The resulting table contains a **Source** table script.

Capturing Scripts from Data Manipulations

Just as you captured scripts from importing data, you can perform some data manipulation tasks through the interactive menus, and JMP will save the script for you.

Almost every option on the **Tables** menu saves a **Source** table script.

Figure 1.12 Tables Menu

The exceptions are **Anonymize** and any of the other options that enable you to replace or update the existing table.

For example, suppose you wanted to sort the Fitness sample data table by name. You would select **Tables** ▶ **Sort** and cast Name as the By column.

Figure 1.13 Sort by Name

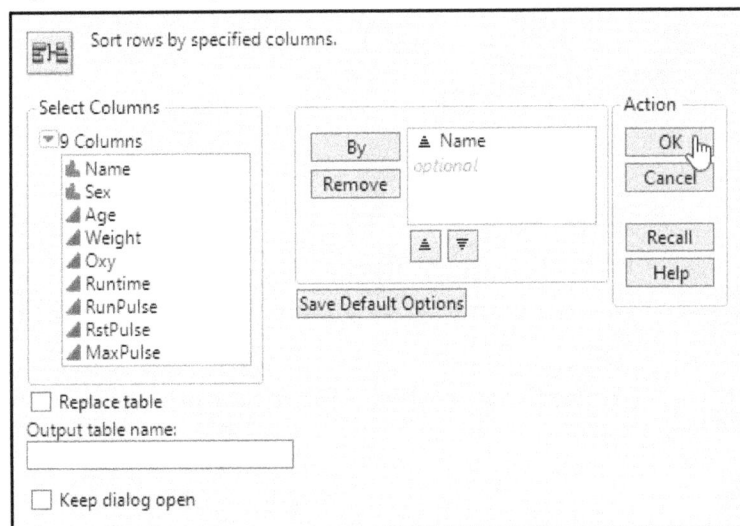

If you click **OK** at this point, a new data table is generated with a **Source** table script that provides you with the code to sort the original data table by the Name column. However, if you select the **Replace table** option, then the data is sorted in place, and no **Source** table script is added to the original table. If you do want the table replaced, copy the **Source** script and add a comma plus the option **Replace Table,** as shown below:

```
Data Table( "Fitness" ) << Sort(
    By( :Name ),
    Order( Ascending ),
    Replace Table
)
```

Compare Data Tables is special in that it does not generate a new data table unless requested. In some ways, it is more like an analysis. There is a **Save Script** red triangle option in the results window. If you select **Save Differences Summary** from the red triangle, a new data table appears with a **Source** table script that contains the JSL script to re-create the Compare Data Tables report.

Another type of data manipulation where you can extract the script is **Cols ▶ Recode**.

Figure 1.14 Recode Menu with Column Selected

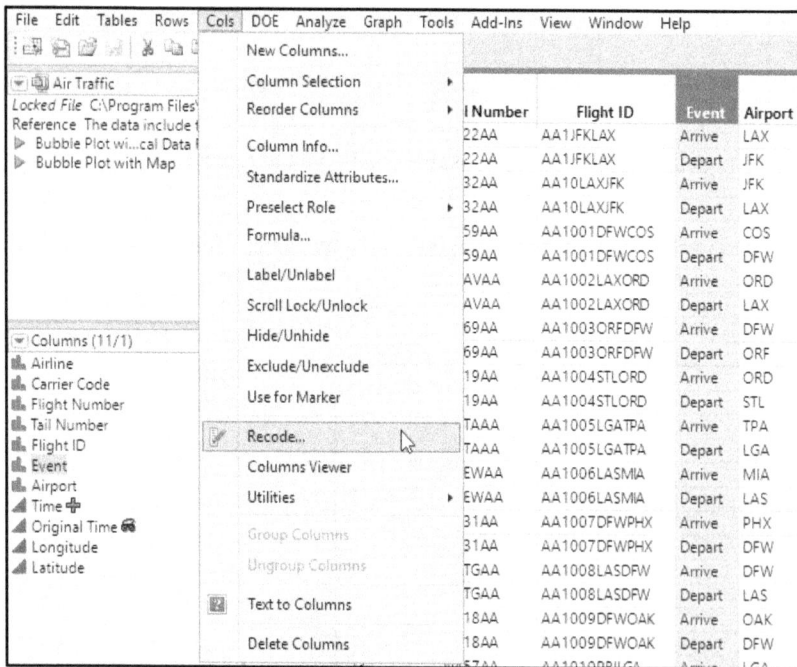

The key is to extract the script using the red triangle before you dismiss the window. In Figure 1.15, the script was saved for recoding the Event column in place by selecting **Script ▶ Save to Script Window** from the red triangle. You can also save the script for recoding to a new column or a new formula column.

Figure 1.15 Save Recode Script to Script Window

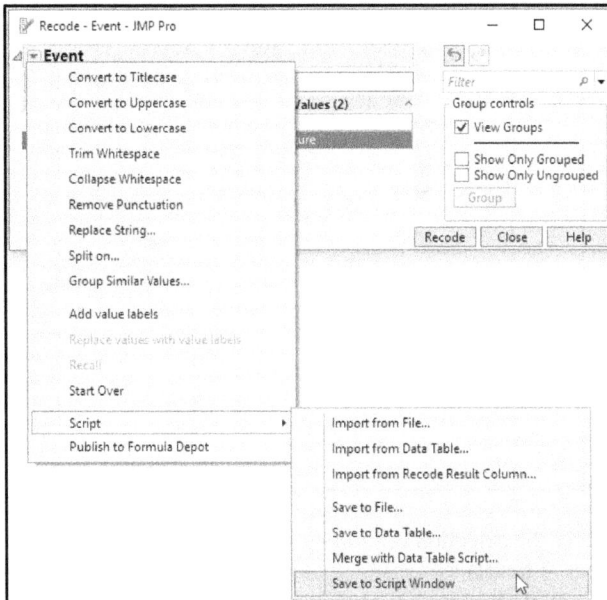

Figure 1.16 Saved Script for Recode

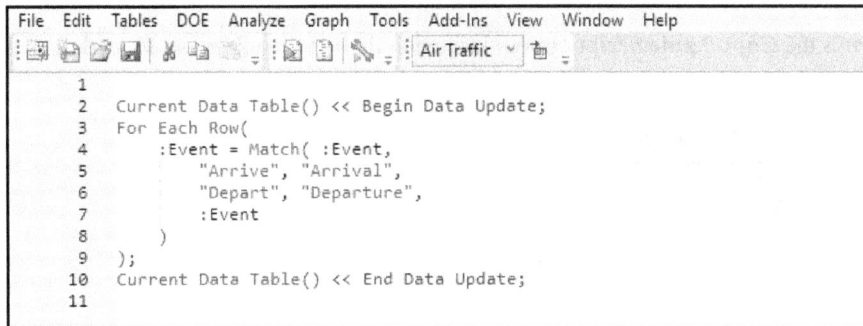

The data filter for the data table, **Rows ▶ Data Filter**, gives users the ability to create complex data subsets, as well as options to hide and exclude portions of data from plots and analyses. After you have done all that hard work to make the perfect filtering setup for your table, you can easily save a script of the data filter for the next time. Click the red triangle icon next to **Data Filter** and select **Save Script ▶ To Data Table,** where it will be conveniently stored with the table. Or you can select one of the other options from the **Save Script** submenu, such as the **To Script Window**, to incorporate the data filter script into a custom script of your design.

Figure 1.17 Data Filter Save Script Menu

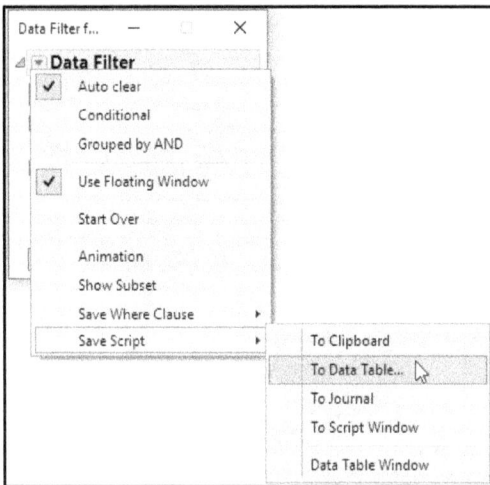

The **Data Filter** option also enables you to capture the selection criteria by selecting **Save Where Clause** from the red triangle menu. The result is a **Select Where()** expression that you could use in a main script. However, unlike other scripts that we have shown you, this code cannot be run as it is. We will demonstrate **Select Where()** in further detail in chapter 7. For now, we just want to point out that you can save the selection criteria.

Another useful feature is the **Copy Table Script** option, located in the red triangle menu to the left of the table name:

Figure 1.18 Copy Table Script Menu Item

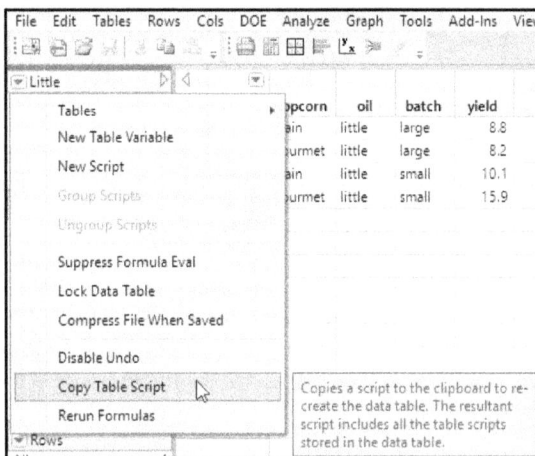

By selecting this option, you can create a script that makes an exact duplicate of your data table. Keep in mind that the JMP application does not record all of your changes and actions made to the data table. Rather, the **Copy Table Script** option captures the current state of the data table in a script when selected.

Why use this option? Capturing a script of your table is a great method for showing you how features are scripted in your table. Want an easy way to capture a script of those formulas or column properties you painstakingly created interactively? Use **Copy Table Script** and paste the captured script into a Script window, where you can locate and extract those portions of the script for use elsewhere.

> Keep in mind that **Copy Table Script** places all of the values in each row and column on your clipboard. If your table is rather large, copying and pasting the script will be slower than for smaller data tables.

Figure 1.19 Table Script

```
File  Edit  Tables  DOE  Analyze  Graph  Tools  Add-Ins  View  Window  Help

                                              Little          v

 1   New Table( "Little",
 2       Add Rows( 4 ),
 3       New Column( "popcorn",
 4           Character( 7 ),
 5           "Nominal",
 6           Use Value Labels( 1 ),
 7           Set Values( {"plain", "gourmet", "plain", "gourmet"} ),
 8           Set Display Width( 58 )
 9       ),
10       New Column( "oil",
11           Character( 6 ),
12           "Nominal",
13           Use Value Labels( 1 ),
14           Set Values( {"little", "little", "little", "little"} ),
15           Set Display Width( 51 )
16       ),
17       New Column( "batch",
18           Character( 5 ),
19           "Nominal",
20           Value Labels(
21               {"l" = "large",
22                "s" = "small"}
23           ),
24           Use Value Labels( 1 ),
25           Set Values( {"l", "l", "s", "s"} ),
26           Set Display Width( 51 )
27       ),
28       New Column( "yield",
29           Numeric,
30           "Continuous",
31           Format( "Fixed Dec", 6, 1 ),
32           Set Values( [8.8, 8.2, 10.1, 15.9] ),
33           Set Display Width( 51 )
34       )
35   )|
```

Creating a Combined Script

Now that you've seen how easy it is to capture scripts, we are going to show you something a little more interesting. Remember that your manager wants the report generated each week? We will show you how easy it is to create a script that imports the data *and* makes the report.

In this sample, we put together a script that does the following:

- imports some text data
- creates a Distribution analysis

Importing the Text Data

Let's begin by importing the Bigclass_L.txt file.

1. Select **File ▶ Open**. You can find this file in the Sample Import Data folder. For a typical JMP or JMP Pro 14 Windows installation, you would find the file in this directory:

   C:\Program Files\SAS\JMP\14\Samples\Import Data\
   C:\Program Files\SAS\JMPPRO\14\Samples\Import Data\

   Bigclass_L.txt is a tab-delimited file. If you use the **Data, using Text Import preferences** option as shown in Figure 1.20, tab must be specified as an End of Field option in your text import preferences (this is a default setting).

Figure 1.20 Open Text File for Windows

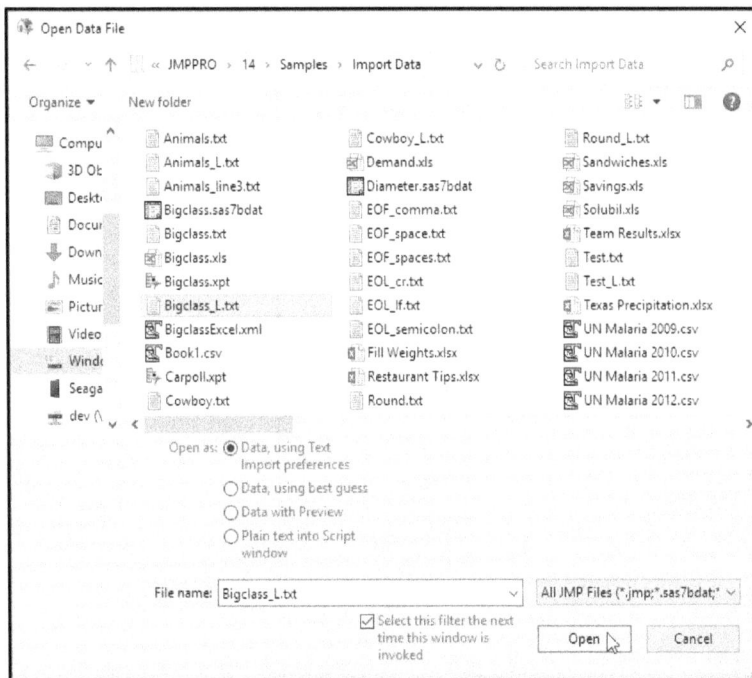

2. After the data file is imported into JMP, right-click the green triangle icon beside **Source** and select **Edit**.
3. In the resulting window, select the entire script and copy it by right-clicking the selected text and selecting **Copy**.

Figure 1.21 Copy of Source Script

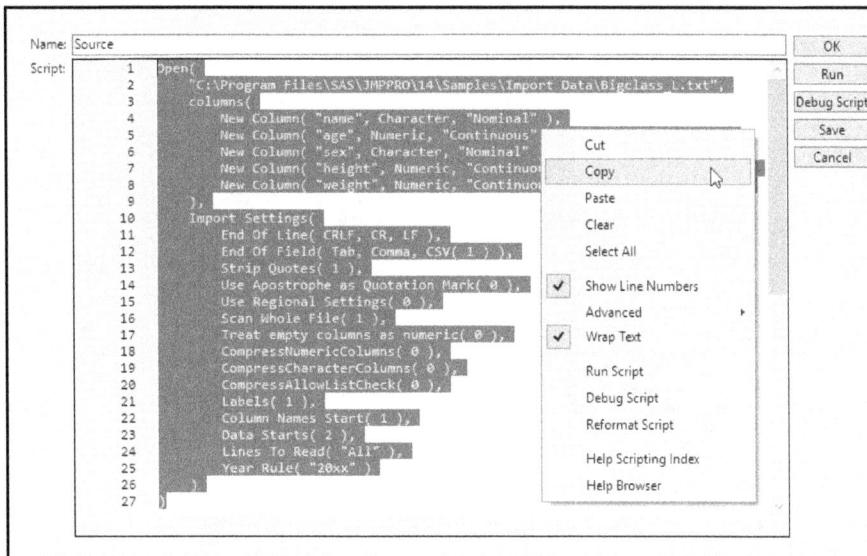

4. Click **OK** to dismiss the Source Table Script window.
5. From the **File** menu, select **New ▶ Script**.
6. Paste the script by clicking the **Edit** menu and selecting **Paste**.
7. Add a semicolon after the last closing parenthesis, because you will be adding more code.

The semicolon, known as the **Glue** operator, is necessary in this case because it tells JMP to expect further JSL statements. Additional details about the **Glue** operator can be found in chapter 4.

Figure 1.22 Paste of Import Code

```
File   Edit   Tables   DOE   Analyze   Graph   Tools   Add-Ins   View   Window   Help
                                                      Bigclass_L
1    Open(
2        "C:\Program Files\SAS\JMPPRO\14\Samples\Import Data\Bigclass_L.txt",
3        columns(
4            New Column( "name", Character, "Nominal" ),
5            New Column( "age", Numeric, "Continuous", Format( "Best", 12 ) ),
6            New Column( "sex", Character, "Nominal" ),
7            New Column( "height", Numeric, "Continuous", Format( "Best", 12 ) ),
8            New Column( "weight", Numeric, "Continuous", Format( "Best", 12 ) )
9        ),
10       Import Settings(
11           End Of Line( CRLF, CR, LF ),
12           End Of Field( Tab, Comma, CSV( 1 ) ),
13           Strip Quotes( 1 ),
14           Use Apostrophe as Quotation Mark( 0 ),
15           Use Regional Settings( 0 ),
16           Scan Whole File( 1 ),
17           Treat empty columns as numeric( 0 ),
18           CompressNumericColumns( 0 ),
19           CompressCharacterColumns( 0 ),
20           CompressAllowListCheck( 0 ),
21           Labels( 1 ),
22           Column Names Start( 1 ),
23           Data Starts( 2 ),
24           Lines To Read( "All" ),
25           Year Rule( "20xx" )
26       )
27   );
```

8.   Press the **Enter** key a couple of times to move the cursor down a few lines.

Creating a Distribution Analysis

So far, we have pasted the script to import a text file into a Script window. Now, we will create a Distribution analysis and save its script.

1.   From the **Analyze** menu, select **Distribution**.

2.   Cast **age** in the **Y, Columns** role and click **OK**.

Figure 1.23 Distribution Launch Window

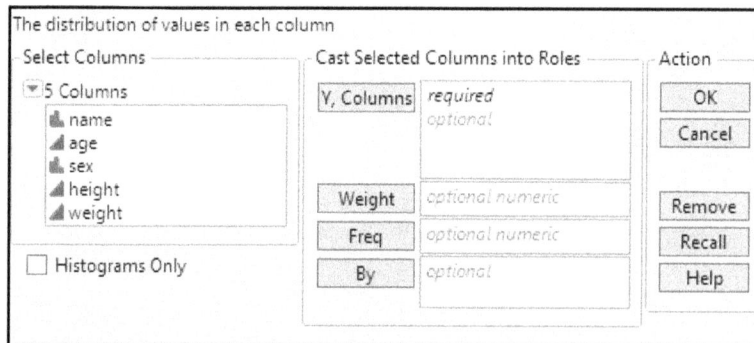

3.   In the Distribution analysis window, capture the script by clicking the uppermost red triangle and selecting **Save Script ▶ To Clipboard.**

Figure 1.24 Copy Script to Clipboard

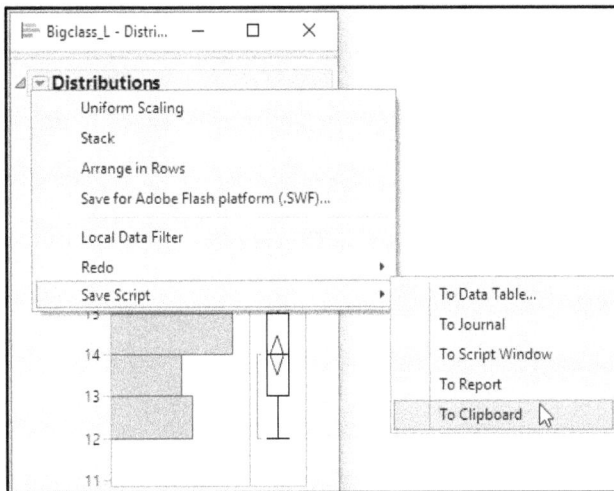

This action saves the **Distribution** script onto the clipboard.

Now return to the Script window that contains the text import script, and place the cursor in the space below the semicolon, near the bottom of the window.

Figure 1.25 Placing the Cursor

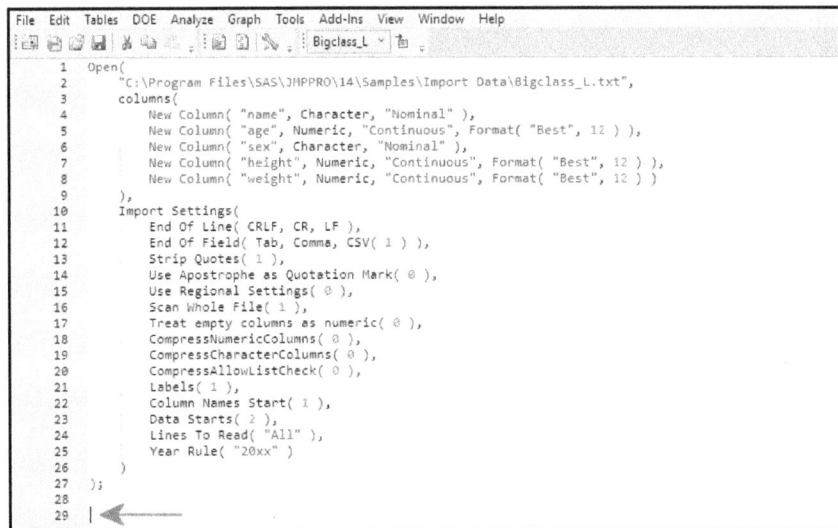

4. To paste the **Distribution** script from the clipboard into the Script window, select **Edit ▶ Paste**.

5. Add a semicolon after the last closing parenthesis in case you later decide to add code and because this is a good programming practice.

Figure 1.26 Script Window with Distribution Script Pasted

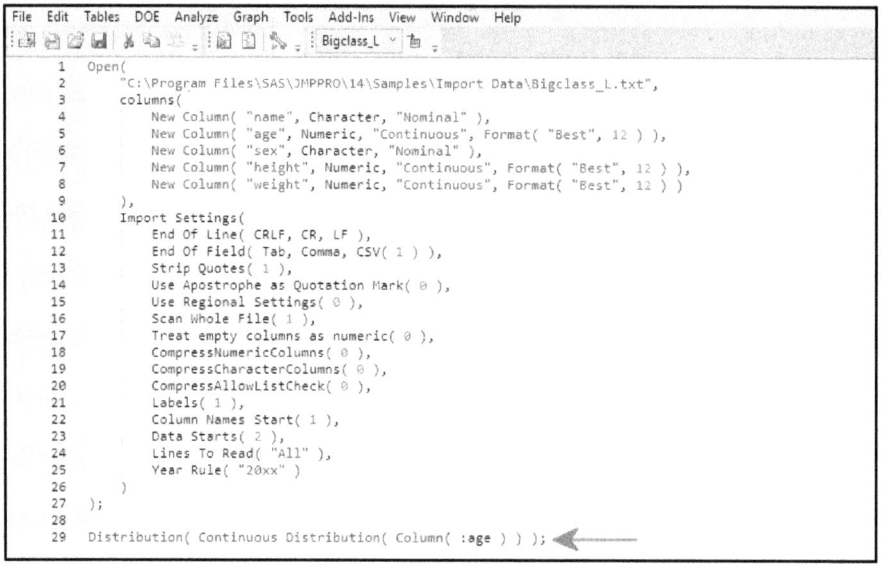

```
File  Edit  Tables  DOE  Analyze  Graph  Tools  Add-Ins  View  Window  Help
                                        Bigclass_L
 1  Open(
 2      "C:\Program Files\SAS\JMPPRO\14\Samples\Import Data\Bigclass_L.txt",
 3      columns(
 4          New Column( "name", Character, "Nominal" ),
 5          New Column( "age", Numeric, "Continuous", Format( "Best", 12 ) ),
 6          New Column( "sex", Character, "Nominal" ),
 7          New Column( "height", Numeric, "Continuous", Format( "Best", 12 ) ),
 8          New Column( "weight", Numeric, "Continuous", Format( "Best", 12 ) )
 9      ),
10      Import Settings(
11          End Of Line( CRLF, CR, LF ),
12          End Of Field( Tab, Comma, CSV( 1 ) ),
13          Strip Quotes( 1 ),
14          Use Apostrophe as Quotation Mark( 0 ),
15          Use Regional Settings( 0 ),
16          Scan Whole File( 1 ),
17          Treat empty columns as numeric( 0 ),
18          CompressNumericColumns( 0 ),
19          CompressCharacterColumns( 0 ),
20          CompressAllowListCheck( 0 ),
21          Labels( 1 ),
22          Column Names Start( 1 ),
23          Data Starts( 2 ),
24          Lines To Read( "All" ),
25          Year Rule( "20xx" )
26      )
27  );
28
29  Distribution( Continuous Distribution( Column( :age ) ) );  ◄————
```

6. Close the Distribution analysis window that we created interactively, and then close the data table, Bigclass_L, leaving only the Script window open.

7. Finally, let's look at the different methods we can use to initiate script execution and then run the script to verify that it produces the expected results.

Executing a Script

There are several ways to execute a JSL script:

- From the **Edit** menu, select **Run Script**.

- Click the **Run Script** button on the toolbar.

- Right-click anywhere in the Script Editor window, and select **Run Script** from the pop-up menu.

- Use the keyboard shortcut for this same action: **CTRL+R**.

- Double-click a JSL file from a file browser.

> To *execute* or *run* a script means the same thing, and we might use the terms interchangeably throughout this book.

For this case, we will use the first method. From the **Edit** menu, select **Run Script**.

Now you will see that the text was imported into a data table, and the Distribution analysis was created from that data.

Figure 1.27 Results of Executing Combined Captured Scripts

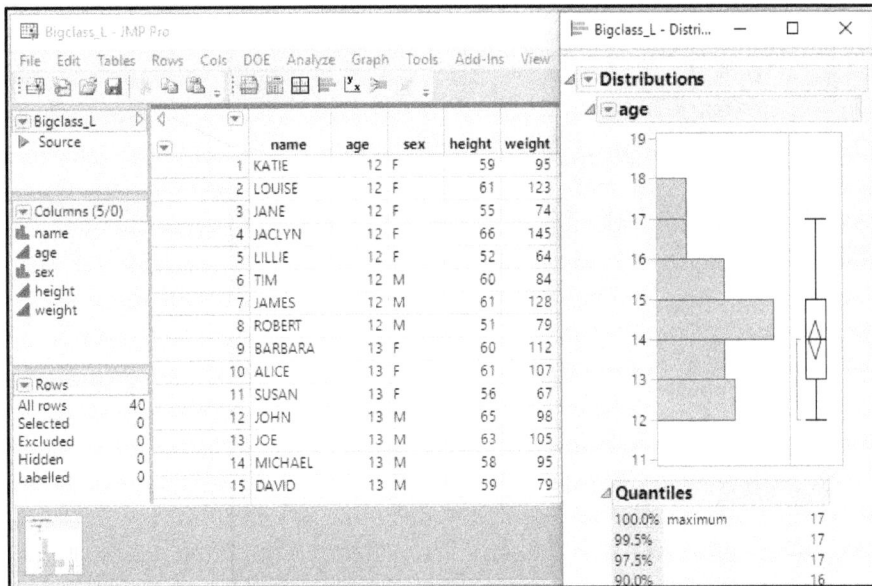

Checking the Log

The Log window is where the code that you executed is displayed, along with any messages JMP has returned. If you have not already done so, display the Log window by clicking the **View** menu, and then selecting **Log**.

You can either leave the Log window as a separate window, or you can embed it into your Script window. To embed the Log into the Script window, right-click anywhere inside the script, and then select **Show Embedded Log**.

The Log window is also a Script Editor, which means that you can select code and execute it directly from within the log.

Figure 1.28 Log Window Showing Code

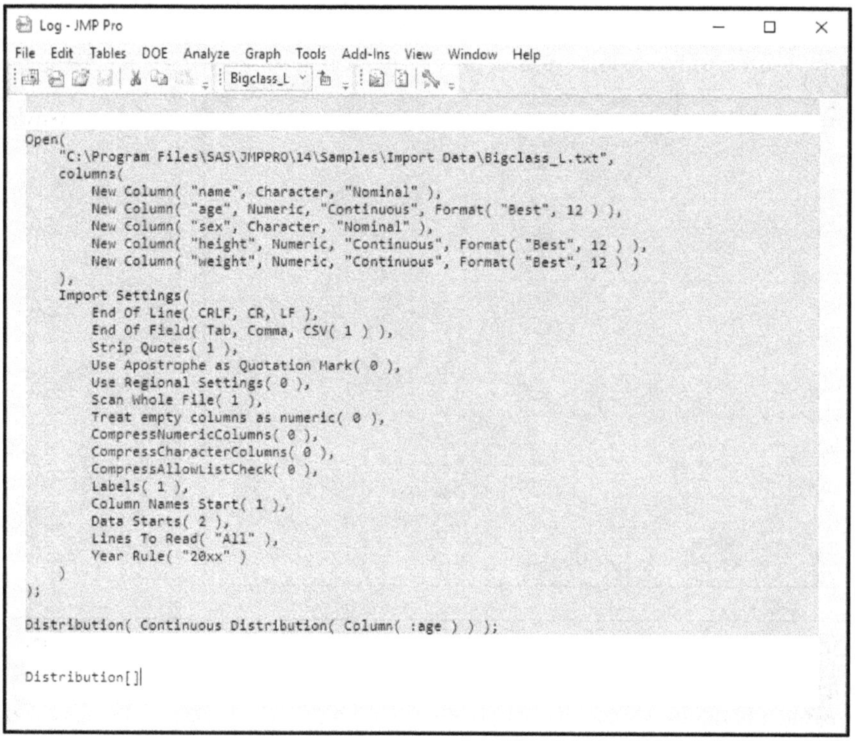

The **Distribution[ ]** shown at the bottom of the log represents the Distribution object that is returned by the Distribution platform. This is simply the return value from running the **Distribution()** script.

Saving a Script

Let's save the script, because we will be coming back to it later.

1. Bring the script that we created to the forefront of the JMP application by selecting **Window ▶ Script**.
2. On the **File** menu, select **Save As**.
3. Navigate to a convenient, yet memorable, location, and name the script **Sample1.JSL**.
4. Click the **Save** button.

Figure 1.29 Save Sample1.JSL

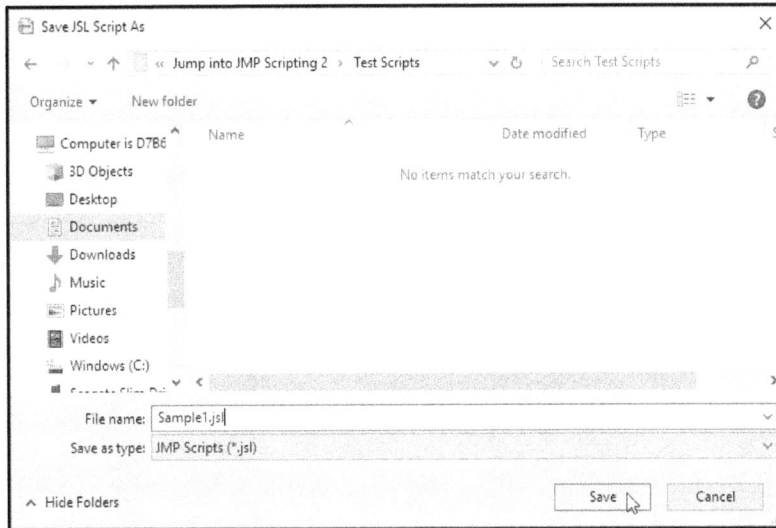

You are finished! You have put together an entire script that will do the following:

- import text data
- create a Distribution report

Summary

Now you've learned how JMP can work for you by extracting scripts of your reports, your imported data, and some data manipulations.

What's next? It's time to roll up your sleeves, because in the next chapter we will show you how to stitch together multiple scripts using the Script Editor.

Chapter 2: Stitching It Together

Overview

After reading chapter 1, you should know how to get scripts from JMP and combine them into a single Script window. In this chapter, we show you how to stitch the individual scripts together with a few JSL tricks, so that a single script will complete a variety of tasks for you at the click of a button.

In this chapter, you will learn about the following:

- stitching together a Summary table and one analysis
- stitching together the import of Excel file data, a Summary table, and two analyses
- creating a custom add-in that will execute a script

Stitching Saved Scripts Together

Your manager is thrilled with the information that you have been giving her. Now, in addition to what you have already been producing weekly, she wants the data summarized, along with some further analysis.

In the previous chapter, you learned how to make JMP write the scripts for you. You also learned how to put two independent scripts together so that they are executed consecutively.

Now, we will continue to show you how easy it is to combine multiple scripts. However, this time you will have to do a small amount of coding to ensure that the scripts will run together successfully.

Combining Summary Data with an Analysis

In this exercise, we create each of the following interactively, and then capture scripts that JMP generates for us:

- summary table from the original data
- Graph Builder Line Chart

Interactive Steps

Our first task is to use the Excel Wizard to import an Excel file containing data about a class of students. Next, we summarize the data by creating a Summary table that produces the mean height for each age by gender.

1. We first check the Excel import preferences to ensure that the Excel Wizard will be invoked when opening an Excel file. Select **File ▶ Preferences**. Select **General** in the left panel. Set the **Excel Open Method** to **Use Excel Wizard**. Set the **Use Excel Labels as Heading** to **Use best guess**. Click **OK** to apply and close the Preferences window.

Figure 2.1 Excel Preferences

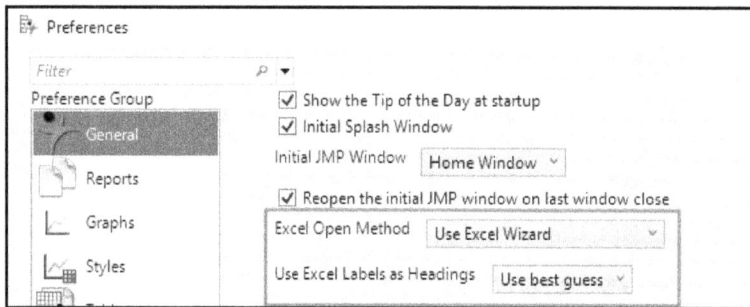

2. From the **Help** menu, select **Sample Data**.

Figure 2.2 Access Sample Data Index

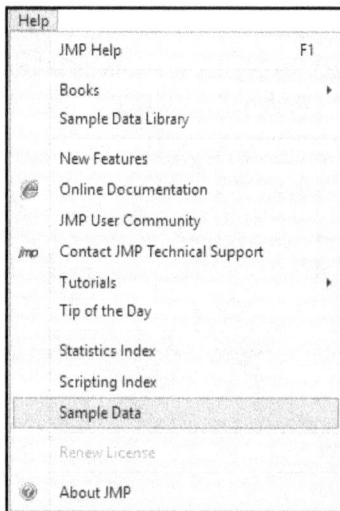

3. Click the **Open the Sample Import Data Directory** button in the Sample Data Index window.

Figure 2.3 Sample Import Data Directory Selection

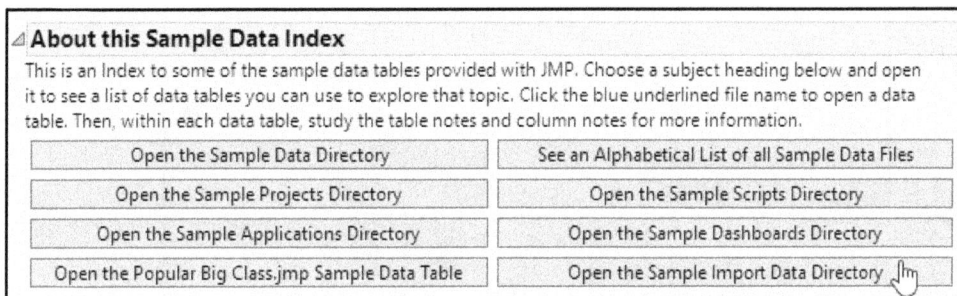

△ **About this Sample Data Index**

This is an Index to some of the sample data tables provided with JMP. Choose a subject heading below and open it to see a list of data tables you can use to explore that topic. Click the blue underlined file name to open a data table. Then, within each data table, study the table notes and column notes for more information.

Open the Sample Data Directory	See an Alphabetical List of all Sample Data Files
Open the Sample Projects Directory	Open the Sample Scripts Directory
Open the Sample Applications Directory	Open the Sample Dashboards Directory
Open the Popular Big Class.jmp Sample Data Table	Open the Sample Import Data Directory

4. In the Open window, select the **Bigclass.xls** file, and then click **Open** to open the data table.

Figure 2.4 Select and Open the Bigclass.xls file

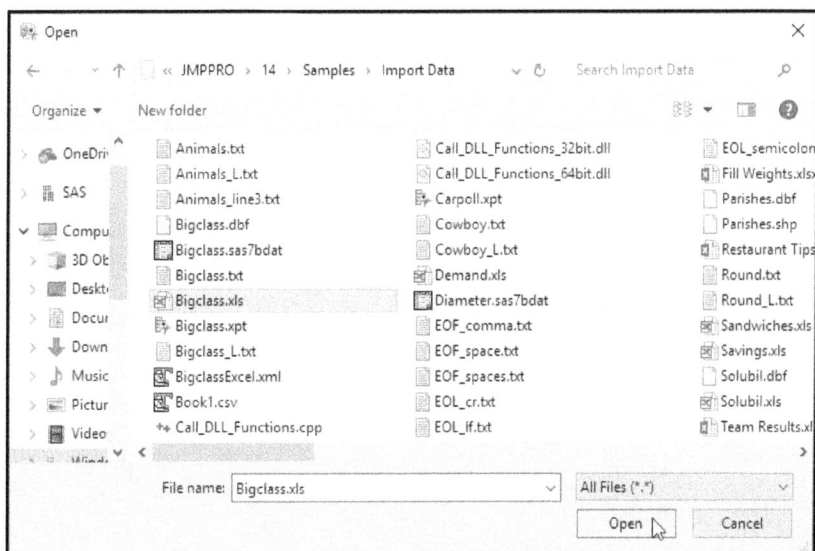

5. The Excel Import Wizard window opens. Change the **Individual Worksheet Settings** to match those in Figure 2.5, if necessary, and then click the **Import** button.

Figure 2.5 Excel Import Wizard Window

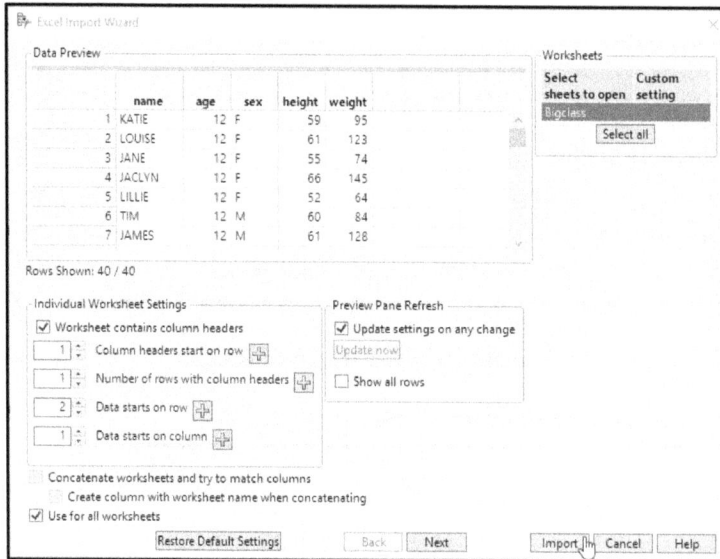

6. The Bigclass table will open, as shown in Figure 2.6.

Figure 2.6 Bigclass Data Table

7. Close the Sample Data Index window.
8. From the **Tables** menu, select **Summary**.

Figure 2.7 Select Summary Table

9. In the resulting window:
    a. Select the **height** column.
    b. Click the **Statistics** button, and then select **Mean**.
    c. Select the **age** column, and then click the **Group** button.
    d. Select the **sex** column, and then click the **Subgroup** button.
    e. Click **OK**.

Figure 2.8 Summary Window

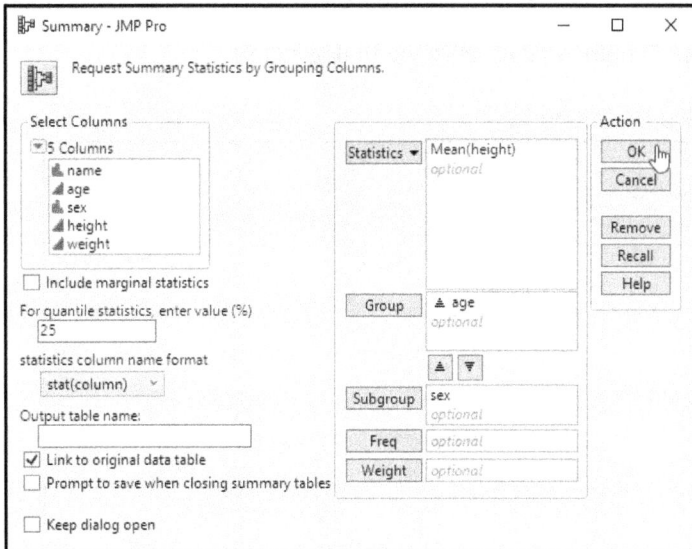

10. The summary table named Bigclass By (age) is created.

Figure 2.9 Bigclass By (age) Summary Table

		age	N Rows	Mean(height, F)	Mean(height, M)
	1	12	8	58.6	57.333333333333
	2	13	7	59	61.25
	3	14	12	62.6	65.285714285714
	4	15	7	63	65.2
	5	16	3	62.5	68
	6	17	3	62	69

File · Edit · Tables · Rows · Cols · DOE · Analyze · Graph · Tools · Add-Ins · View · Window

▼ Bigclass By (age)
▷ Source

▼ Columns (4/0)
◢ age
◢ N Rows
◢ Mean(height, F)
◢ Mean(height, M)

Next, we create a Graph Builder Line Chart with connected lines to identify any trends.

11. With the Bigclass By (age) data table as the active table, select **Graph ▶ Graph Builder**.

Figure 2.10 Graph Builder Menu Selection

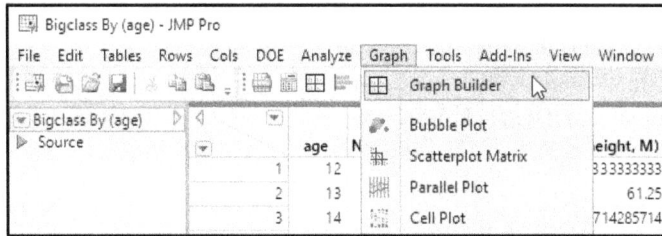

Bigclass By (age) - JMP Pro

File · Edit · Tables · Rows · Cols · DOE · Analyze · Graph · Tools · Add-Ins · View · Window

Graph Builder
Bubble Plot
Scatterplot Matrix
Parallel Plot
Cell Plot

12. In the resulting Graph Builder window, click the **Dialog** button.

Figure 2.11 Selecting the Dialog Option

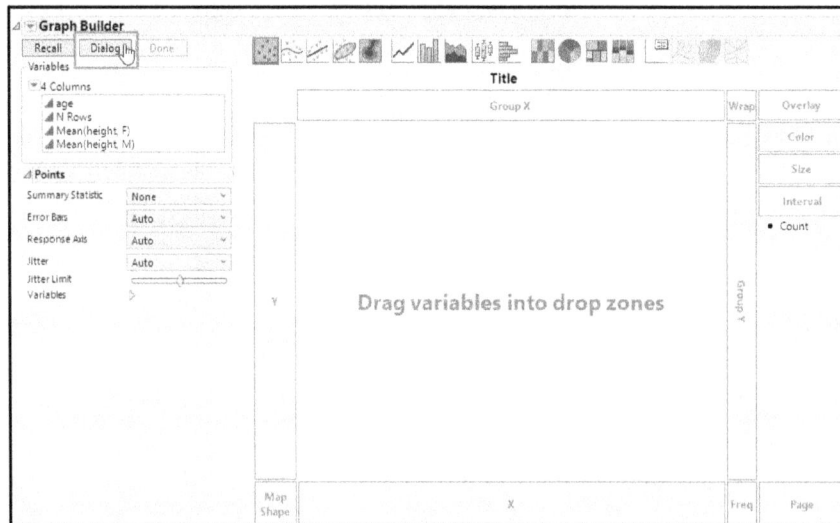

13. In the Dialog window:
    a. Select the **Mean(height, F)** and **Mean(height, M)** columns.
    b. Click the **Y** button.
    c. Select the **age** column, and then click the **X** button.
    d. In the **Options** panel, select **Points** and **Line**.
    e. Click **OK**.

Figure 2.12 Graph Builder Dialog Window

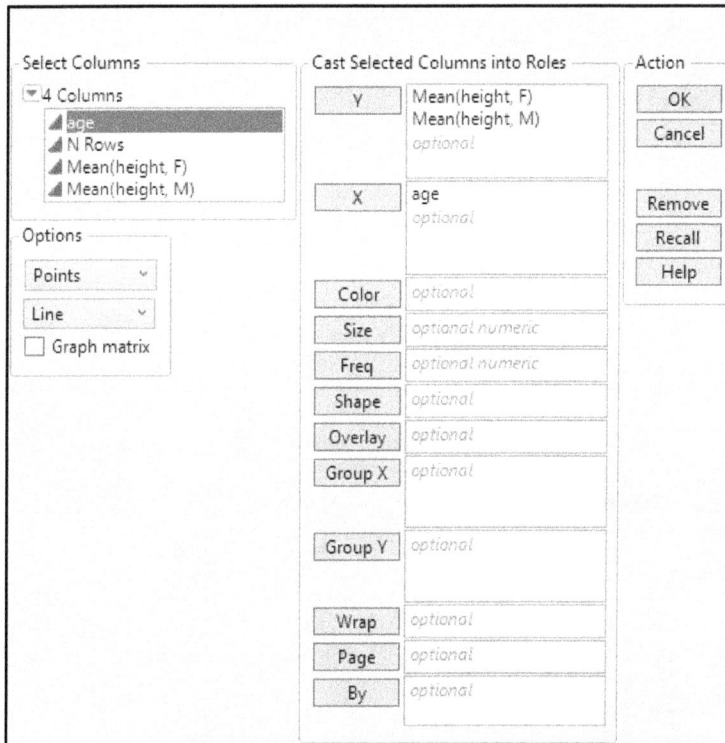

14. When the Graph Builder Line Chart appears, click the **Done** button.

Figure 2.13 Click Done Button

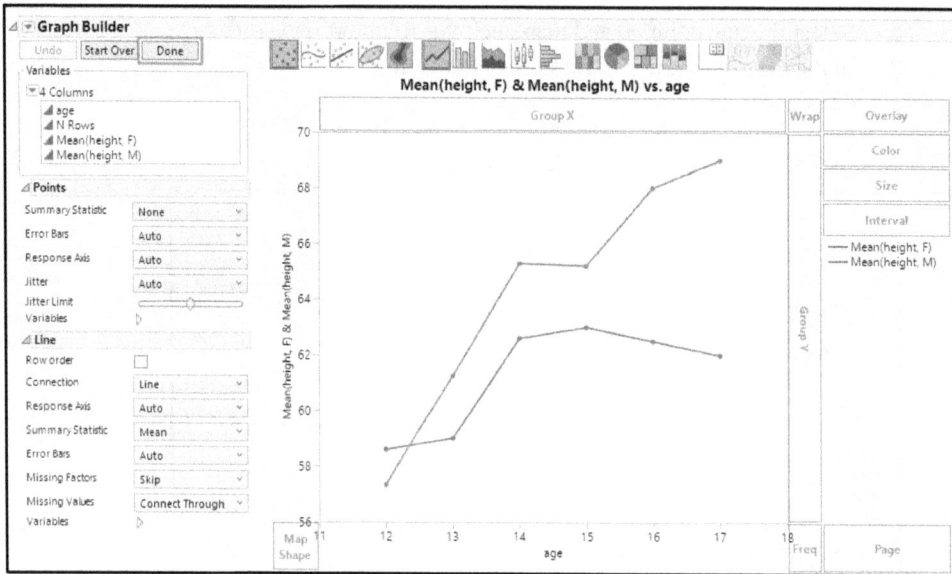

Now, we have created the Summary table and the Graph Builder Line Chart.

Figure 2.14 Summary Table and Graph Builder Line Chart

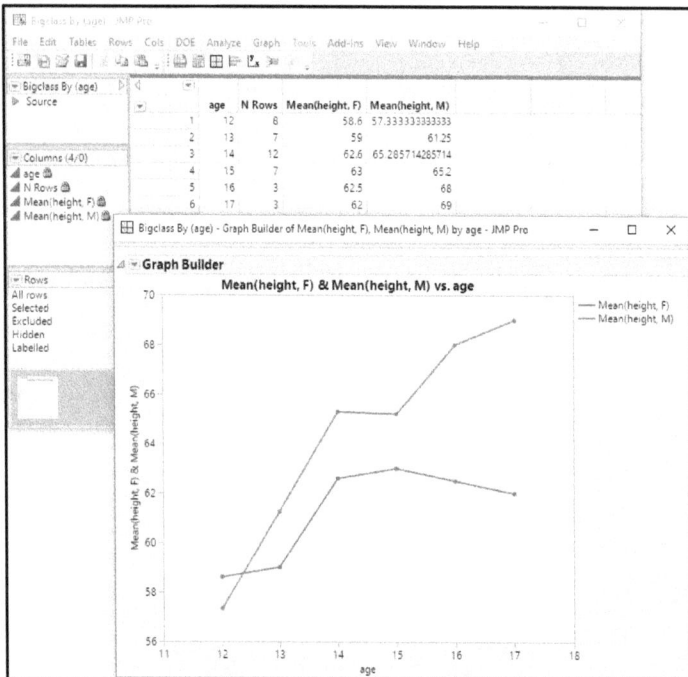

Next, we will extract the scripts that JMP generated for us and combine them in a single script.

Extracting the Scripts

As you saw in chapter 1, table scripts are a bit different in that you cannot simply save the script to a Script window like we could if we were saving the script from an analysis. Therefore, we need to open a new Script window where the scripts can be pasted.

1. From the **File** menu, select **New ▶ Script**.
2. From the **Window** menu, select **Bigclass By (age)** to locate the Summary table.
3. When the Summary data table is in view, open the **Source** table script by right-clicking the green triangle, and then selecting **Edit**.

Figure 2.15 Edit Summary Source Script

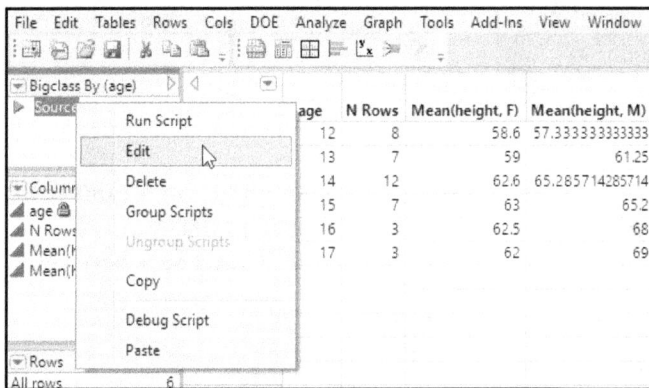

4. In the resulting window, select the entire script and copy it by right-clicking the script and selecting **Copy**.

Figure 2.16 View of Summary Source Script

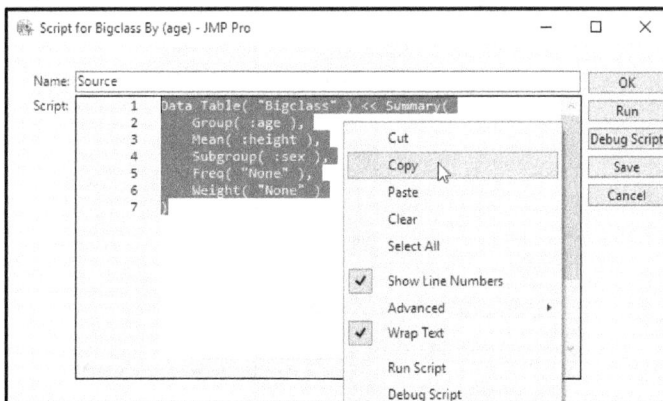

5. Click **OK** to dismiss the Source Table Script window.
6. From the **Window** menu, select **Script** to locate your new Script window.

7. Paste the script by clicking the **Edit** menu and selecting **Paste**.
8. Add a semicolon after the last closing parenthesis.

Figure 2.17 Pasted Summary Script

```
File  Edit  Tables  DOE  Analyze  Graph  Tools  Add-Ins  View  Window  Help
                                            Bigclass By (age)

1    Data Table( "Bigclass" ) << Summary(
2        Group( :age ),
3        Mean( :height ),
4        Subgroup( :sex ),
5        Freq( "None" ),
6        Weight( "None" )
7    );
8
```

> Notice that the previous Script window displays line numbers. You can turn on the line numbers option by right-clicking the Script window and selecting **Show Line Numbers** from the context menu.

Next, we copy the Graph Builder Line Chart script.

1. From the **Window** menu, select **Bigclass By (age)- Graph Builder of Mean(height, F), Mean(height, M) by Age** to locate the Graph Builder Line Chart report.
2. In the Graph Builder window, click the red triangle, and then select **Save Script ⊠ To Clipboard.**

Figure 2.18 Copy Graph Builder Line Chart script

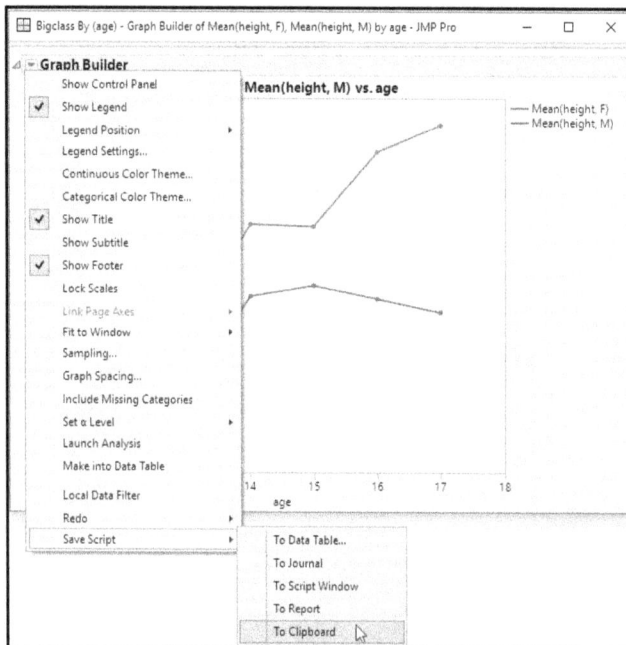

3. Go back to the Script window and press the **Enter** key a couple of times to move the cursor down a few lines.
4. Paste the script into the Script window by selecting **Edit ▶ Paste**.

Figure 2.19 Paste Graph Builder Line Chart Script

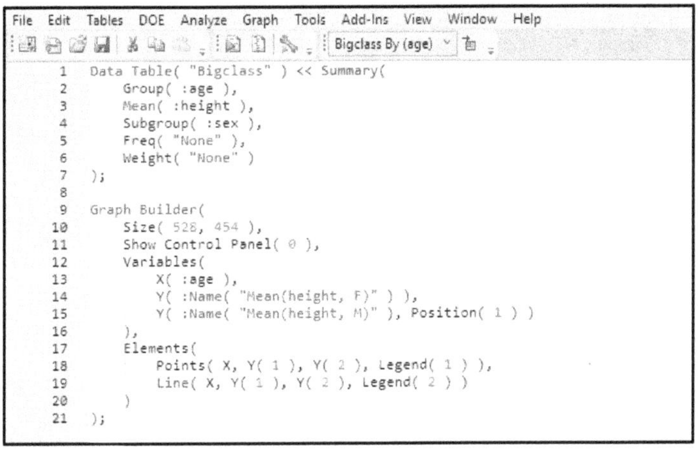


```
Data Table( "Bigclass" ) << Summary(
	Group( :age ),
	Mean( :height ),
	Subgroup( :sex ),
	Freq( "None" ),
	Weight( "None" )
);

Graph Builder(
	Size( 528, 454 ),
	Show Control Panel( 0 ),
	Variables(
		X( :age ),
		Y( :Name( "Mean(height, F)" ) ),
		Y( :Name( "Mean(height, M)" ), Position( 1 ) )
	),
	Elements(
		Points( X, Y( 1 ), Y( 2 ), Legend( 1 ) ),
		Line( X, Y( 1 ), Y( 2 ), Legend( 2 ) )
	)
);
```

5. Add a semicolon after the last closing parenthesis.
6. Use the **Window** menu to locate the **Bigclass By (age)- Graph Builder of Mean(height, F), Mean(height, M) by Age** report window, and then close it. Repeat these steps to locate and close the **Bigclass By (age)** data table.

Coding Changes

Now this script looks pretty good, but there is a potential problem. This code depends on the current data table being the Summary table. Although this example script might run without error, in real life, JMP will probably be doing more in the background, which could cause a change in the current data table. We will discuss background tasks in more detail as we go along.

If the current data table gets changed and you run this code, JMP will return error messages to the log as shown here.

```
Specified Column not found in data table. in access or evaluation of 'Y' , Y(
:Name( "Mean(height, F)" ) ) /*###*/


Exception in platform launch in access or evaluation of 'Graph Builder' , Graph
Builder(/*###*/Size( 528, 454 ),
    Show Control Panel( 0 ),
    Variables(
           X( :age ),
           Y( :Name( "Mean(height, F)" ) ),
           Y( :Name( "Mean(height, M)" ), Position( 1 ) )
    ),
    Elements(
           Points( X, Y( 1 ), Y( 2 ), Legend( 1 ) ),
           Line( X, Y( 1 ), Y( 2 ), Legend( 2 ) )
    )
```

```
)

In the following script, error marked by /*###*/
Graph Builder(
    Size( 528, 454 ),
    Show Control Panel( 0 ),
    Variables(
            X( :age ),
            Y( :Name( "Mean(height, F)" ) ) /*###*/,
            Y( :Name( "Mean(height, M)" ), Position( 1 ) )
    ),
    Elements(
            Points( X, Y( 1 ), Y( 2 ), Legend( 1 ) ),
            Line( X, Y( 1 ), Y( 2 ), Legend( 2 ) )
    )
)
```

What does all that mean?

These error messages indicate that JMP cannot find the columns **Mean(height, F)** and **Mean(height, M)**. These columns are not found because JMP is looking at the original Big Class data table, rather than at the Summary table.

How do we correct this?

First, we assign a name (you can think of it as a nickname) to the Summary table using an assignment statement. This name is also known as a *global variable*. Global variables are references you assign that remain throughout the JMP session. A discussion of global and local JSL variables is covered in chapter 4.

> Unlike other languages, JMP does not require that you first declare the global variable. Simply assign it to an object, such as a data table, and start using it!

1. In the script, set the Summary table name to be **sumDT**, as shown in Figure 2.20.

Figure 2.20 Data Table Name Assignment

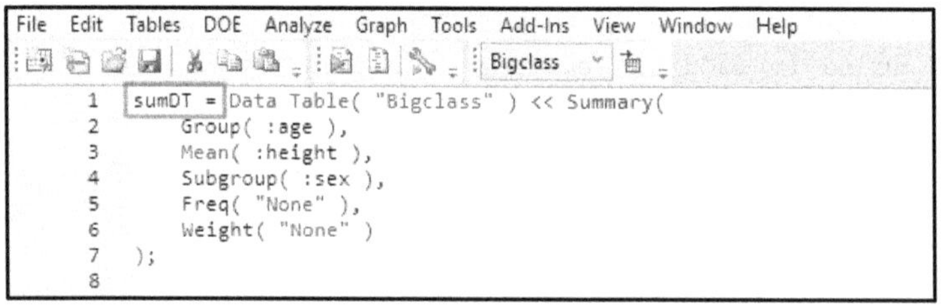

In this example, **sumDT** will continue to represent the **Bigclass By (age)** Summary table until the data table is closed, **sumDT** is redefined, or you close JMP.

Next, we tell JMP that the Graph Builder Line Chart should be created using the data stored in the Summary table rather than in the original **Bigclass** data table.

In order to accomplish this task, it is important to understand that JSL is a powerful language that is built upon the concept of *sending* messages to JMP objects in order to tell them what to do.

Here is the basic form of a JSL statement:

```
object << Message( Argument );
```

where `<<` is the send operator.

1. In the script, send the Graph Builder message to the Summary data table by adding **sumDT** (as the object) and the send operator (<<), as shown in Figure 2.21. You can assign a reference to the Graph Builder output here, as well. This is helpful if you need to reference the Graph Builder object later in your script.

Figure 2.21 Data Table Specified

```
File  Edit  Tables  DOE  Analyze  Graph  Tools  Add-Ins  View  Window  Help

1    sumDT = Data Table( "Bigclass" ) << Summary(
2        Group( :age ),
3        Mean( :height ),
4        Subgroup( :sex ),
5        Freq( "None" ),
6        Weight( "None" )
7    );
8
9    gb = sumDT << Graph Builder(
10       Size( 528, 454 ),
11       Show Control Panel( 0 ),
12       Variables(
13           X( :age ),
14           Y( :height ),
15           Y( :weight, Position( 1 ) )
16       ),
17       Elements(
18           Points( X, Y( 1 ), Y( 2 ), Legend( 1 ) ),
19           Line( X, Y( 1 ), Y( 2 ), Legend( 2 ) )
20       )
21   );
```

It is an important scripting habit to be what we call *data-table specific* in your scripts. By sending platform messages to a specific data table reference, you ensure that JMP always looks for the data in the table specified.

After making these changes, the code will run successfully.

1. From the **Edit** menu, select **Run Script**.

Figure 2.22 Sample 2 Results

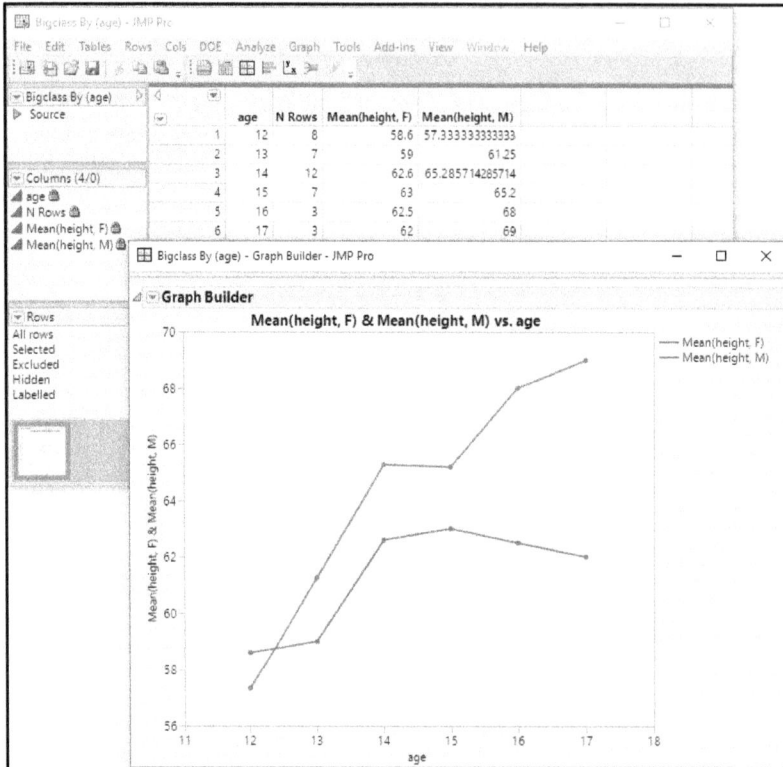

2. With the Script window active, click the **File** menu, and then select **Save As**.
3. Navigate to the same location as the previous example, name the script **Sample2.jsl**, and then click **Save**.

Figure 2.23 Save Sample2.jsl

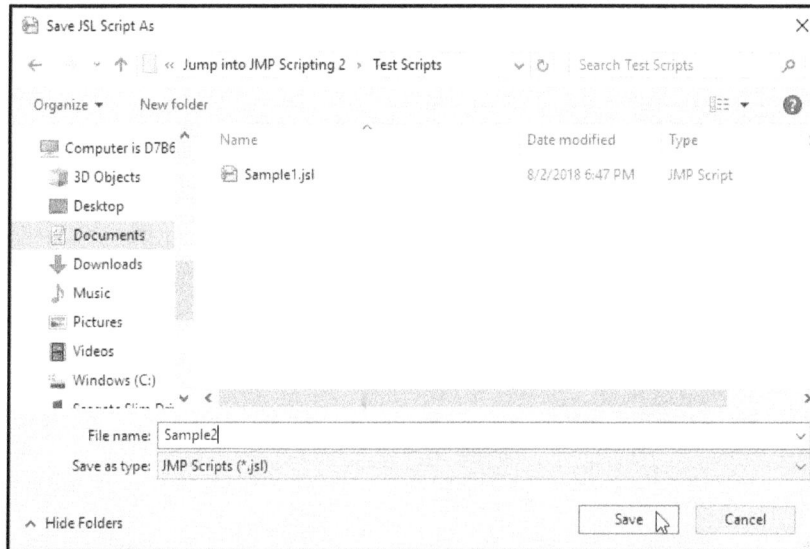

Combining Data Import, Summary, and Two Analyses

Now that you've seen how easy it is to combine scripts of various tasks into one script, we are going to show you something a little more interesting. In this sample, we put together a script that brings in elements from the two scripts that you previously saved.

> If you are following along from the previous sample, close all open analyses, and close the Script window. To do this, click the **Window** menu, and then select **Close All**.

Extracting the Scripts

Because we are bringing in scripts that we stored in JSL files, there won't be any scripts to capture interactively from JMP. Instead, we will open Sample1.jsl and Sample2.jsl and extract the desired sections of code in order to build the new script.

To begin, open a new Script window by clicking on the **File** menu and selecting **New ▶ Script**. This is where we will build the main script.

Next, extract the code from the Sample1.jsl file:

1. From the **File** menu, select **Open**.
2. Ensure the **Files of type** field is set to *All JMP Files*.
3. Navigate to the location where you saved the Sample1.jsl file, and then select the file.
4. Click **Open**.
5. Select the entire script, and then copy it by right-clicking and selecting **Copy** from the menu.

6. Go back to your main Script window by selecting **Window ▶ Script.**
7. Paste the script by selecting **Edit ▶ Paste.**

Figure 2.24 Paste Sample1.jsl

```
File  Edit  Tables  DOE  Analyze  Graph  Tools  Add-Ins  View  Window  Help

    1   Open(
    2       "C:\Program Files\SAS\JMPPRO\14\Samples\Import Data\Bigclass_L.txt",
    3       columns(
    4           New Column( "name", Character, "Nominal" ),
    5           New Column( "age", Numeric, "Continuous", Format( "Best", 12 ) ),
    6           New Column( "sex", Character, "Nominal" ),
    7           New Column( "height", Numeric, "Continuous", Format( "Best", 12 ) ),
    8           New Column( "weight", Numeric, "Continuous", Format( "Best", 12 ) )
    9       ),
   10       Import Settings(
   11           End Of Line( CRLF, CR, LF ),
   12           End Of Field( Tab, Comma, CSV( 1 ) ),
   13           Strip Quotes( 1 ),
   14           Use Apostrophe as Quotation Mark( 0 ),
   15           Use Regional Settings( 0 ),
   16           Scan Whole File( 1 ),
   17           Treat empty columns as numeric( 0 ),
   18           CompressNumericColumns( 0 ),
   19           CompressCharacterColumns( 0 ),
   20           CompressAllowListCheck( 0 ),
   21           Labels( 1 ),
   22           Column Names Start( 1 ),
   23           Data Starts( 2 ),
   24           Lines To Read( "All" ),
   25           Year Rule( "20xx" )
   26       )
   27   );
   28
   29   Distribution( Continuous Distribution( Column( :age ) ) );
```

4. Locate and close the Sample1 Script window by selecting **Window ▶ Sample1**. Then from the **File** menu, select **Close**.

So far in the script, we have instructed JMP to import a text file and create a Distribution analysis from it. Next, we will paste in the script from Sample 2 at the end of our current script.

1. From the **File** menu, select **Open**.
2. Ensure the **Files of type** field is set to *All JMP Files*.
3. Navigate to the location where you saved the Sample2.jsl file, and then select the file.
4. Click **Open**.
5. Select the entire script, then copy by right-clicking and selecting **Copy** from the menu.
6. Go back to your main Script window by selecting **Window ▶ Script**.
7. Press the **Enter** key a couple of times to move the cursor down a few lines below the Distribution.
8. Paste the script by selecting **Edit ▶ Paste.**

Figure 2.25 Paste Sample2.jsl

```
31  sumDT = Data Table( "Bigclass" ) << Summary(
32      Group( :age ),
33      Mean( :height ),
34      Subgroup( :sex ),
35      Freq( "None" ),
36      Weight( "None" )
37  );
38
39  gb = sumDT << Graph Builder(
40      Size( 528, 454 ),
41      Show Control Panel( 0 ),
42      Variables(
43          X( :age ),
44          Y( :Name( "Mean(height, F)" ) ),
45          Y( :Name( "Mean(height, M)" ), Position( 1 ) )
46      ),
47      Elements(
48          Points( X, Y( 1 ), Y( 2 ), Legend( 1 ) ),
49          Line( X, Y( 1 ), Y( 2 ), Legend( 2 ) )
50      )
51  );
```

9. Locate and close the Sample2 Script window by selecting **Sample2** from the **Window** menu. Then from the **File** menu, select **Close**.

Coding Changes

Now, once again we have created a script that looks good but will not run successfully.

Why not? The messages in the log provide a significant hint, as shown here:

```
Cannot locate data table in access or evaluation of 'Data Table' , Data
Table/*###*/("Bigclass")
```

And farther down you can locate the error by the **/*####*/** marks.

```
sumDt = Data Table/*###*/("Bigclass") << Summary(
    Group( :age ),
    Mean( :height ),
    Subgroup( :sex ),
    Freq( "None" ),
    Weight( "None" )
);
```

> If your Log window is closed, you can view it by selecting **Log** from the **View** menu.

The problem in this example is that the data table that we want to create our Summary table from is not named Bigclass, but rather Bigclass_L. There are a couple of ways to correct this problem.

- Use the exact table name by specifying it in the **Data Table()** argument:

```
sumDt = Data Table( "Bigclass_L" ) << Summary(
    Group( :age ),
    Mean( :height ),
```

```
    Subgroup( :sex ),
    Freq( "None" ),
    Weight( "None" )
);
```

- Assign a variable to the data table when it is imported, and use the variable name in place of the **Data Table()** function. This option might require slightly more coding, but actually allows for greater flexibility. See Figure 2.26.

Figure 2.26 Final Script

```
dt = Open(
    "C:\Program Files\SAS\JMPPRO\14\Samples\Import Data\Bigclass_L.txt",
    columns(
        New Column( "name", Character, "Nominal" ),
        New Column( "age", Numeric, "Continuous", Format( "Best", 12 ) ),
        New Column( "sex", Character, "Nominal" ),
        New Column( "height", Numeric, "Continuous", Format( "Best", 12 ) ),
        New Column( "weight", Numeric, "Continuous", Format( "Best", 12 ) )
    ),
    Import Settings(
        End Of Line( CRLF, CR, LF ),
        End Of Field( Tab, Comma, CSV( 1 ) ),
        Strip Quotes( 1 ),
        Use Apostrophe as Quotation Mark( 0 ),
        Use Regional Settings( 0 ),
        Scan Whole File( 1 ),
        Treat empty columns as numeric( 0 ),
        CompressNumericColumns( 0 ),
        CompressCharacterColumns( 0 ),
        CompressAllowListCheck( 0 ),
        Labels( 1 ),
        Column Names Start( 1 ),
        Data Starts( 2 ),
        Lines To Read( "All" ),
        Year Rule( "20xx" )
    )
);

dist = dt << Distribution( Continuous Distribution( Column( :age ) ) );

sumDT = dt << Summary(
    Group( :age ),
    Mean( :height ),
    Subgroup( :sex ),
    Freq( "None" ),
    Weight( "None" )
);

gb = sumDT << Graph Builder(
    Size( 528, 454 ),
    Show Control Panel( 0 ),
    Variables(
        X( :age ),
        Y( :Name( "Mean(height, F)" ) ),
        Y( :Name( "Mean(height, M)" ), Position( 1 ) )
    ),
    Elements(
        Points( X, Y( 1 ), Y( 2 ), Legend( 1 ) ),
        Line( X, Y( 1 ), Y( 2 ), Legend( 2 ) )
    )
);
```

After making the changes noted in Figure 2.26, run your script to see the results.

Figure 2.27 Final Results

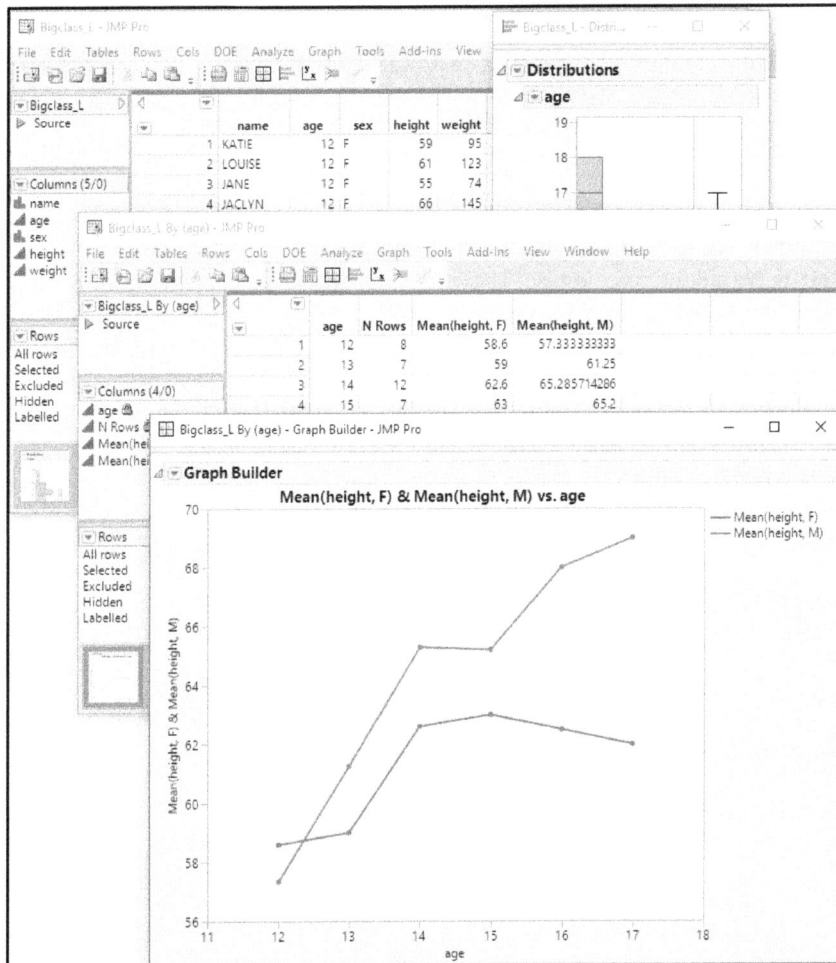

Now that you have a script that does everything your manager wants, save the script to your desired location, and name it **WeeklyReport.jsl**.

You are finished! You have put together an entire script that will do the following:

- import text data
- create a Distribution of the data
- summarize the data
- create a Graph Builder Line Chart from the summarized data

And all of this has been done with very little code written by you!

Saving the Analysis Script to an Add-In

You could keep your **WeeklyReport** script as a JSL file, because JSL files are a great place to store scripts so that they can be opened and executed in the future.

Or perhaps you would rather click a menu item and have JMP perform all those tasks for you at once. This is possible by adding your script as an item in the **Add-Ins** menu.

In this section, we demonstrate how you can save your script as a JMP add-in. In fact, you could share the JMP add-in with your manager and co-workers so that they will be able to run their own reports.

To create and save the add-in, follow these steps:

1. From the **File** menu, select **New ▶ Add-In**.
2. Select the **General Info** tab.
    a. Enter an **Add-In Name** for your add-in. This name will appear in the **View ▶ Add-Ins** window. We will use **My Weekly Report** as the name.
    b. Enter an **Add-In ID,** which is a unique string that starts with a character; is no longer than 64 characters; consists only of letters, numbers, periods, and underscores; and has no spaces. The format recommended as shown in Figure 2.28 is called reverse-DNS. Using this format ensures that the Add-In ID is unique. We will use com.ABCcompany.myaddin.
    c. Enter the version of the add-in.
    d. Enter the minimum JMP version that the add-in works on.
    e. Select whether your script runs on Windows, Macintosh, or both JMP operating systems.
    f. The **Uninstall before reinstalling** box should remain selected. This will prevent multiple copies of the same add-in.
    g. As the title suggests, checking the **Install after save** box instructs JMP to install the add-in after you save it. If this box is not selected, then the add-in will not be accessible from the **Add-Ins** menu until you install it.

Figure 2.28 General Tab

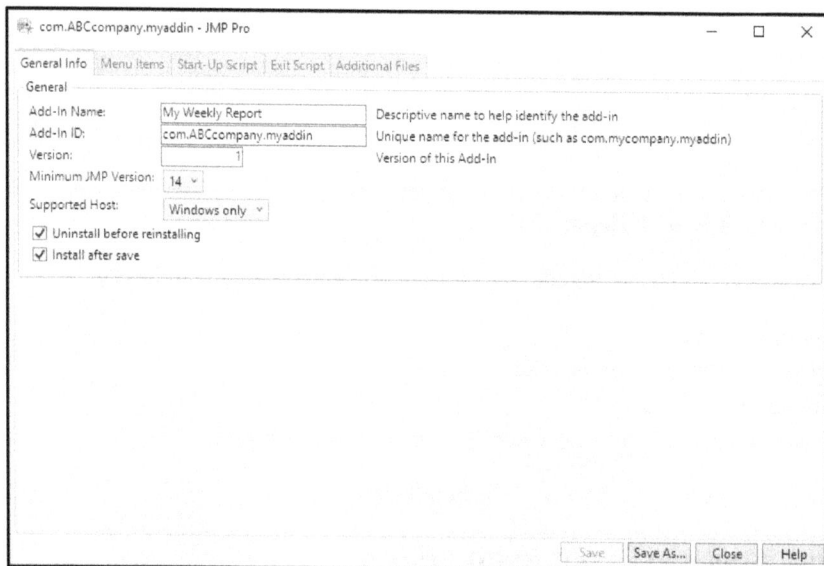

3. Click the **Menu Items** tab.
4. Click the **Add Command** button.

There are four areas under **Details** that affect your menu item:

- **General**
  - ○ Enter the **Menu Item Name** as you wish for it to appear in the **Add-In** menu. We selected **My Weekly Report** as the menu item name.
  - ○ The **Tooltip for menu item** enables you to specify some additional detail about the menu item in a pop-up tooltip. This field is optional.
- **Action**
  - ○ Next, you have the option of copying and pasting your script into the **Run this JSL** window or selecting **Run JSL in this file** and browsing to select your script file. To ensure there are no accidental copy or paste errors, click the button for **Run JSL in this file,** and then click the **Browse** button. Locate your WeeklyReport.jsl file and click **Open.**
  - ○ The check box for using the "Here" namespace is optional. We recommend leaving the default check in place to keep all of your JSL variables local to the script. Again, we will discuss global and local variables in chapter 4.
- **Icon**
  - ○ This optional setting enables you to specify an icon that will appear next to your menu item. For this example, we will not use an icon.
- **Shortcut**
  - ○ The **Shortcut** setting enables you to specify a keyboard shortcut that will invoke the menu item. For this example we will not specify a shortcut.

To continue creating and saving the add-in, follow the next steps:

1. Click **Save As**, and then navigate to a location of choice to save the **.jmpaddin** file**.**
2. Click **Close** to dismiss the Add-In window**.**

Figure 2.29 Menu Items Tab

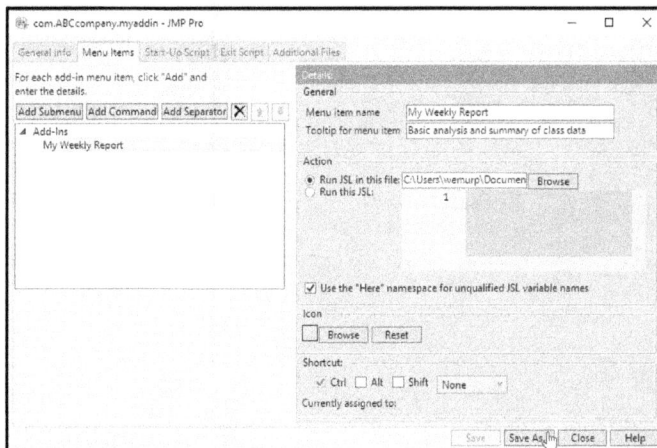

The add-in for running the WeeklyReport.jsl file is set up and saved.

Now, test it to be sure it works properly.

- Make sure you have closed all the open data tables in reports by clicking the **Window** menu and selecting **Close All**.
- From the **Add-Ins** menu, select **My Weekly Report** (you might have named your add-in differently).

Figure 2.30 Add-Ins Menu Item Selection

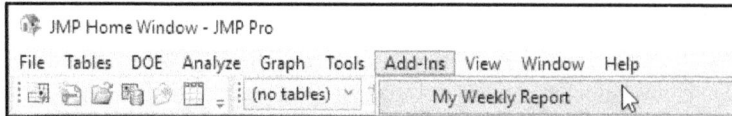

The results should be the same as when you run the WeeklyReport.jsl by selecting **Edit ▶ Run Script**, but the menu item makes the process much easier now.

Figure 2.31 Weekly Report Results Using Add-In

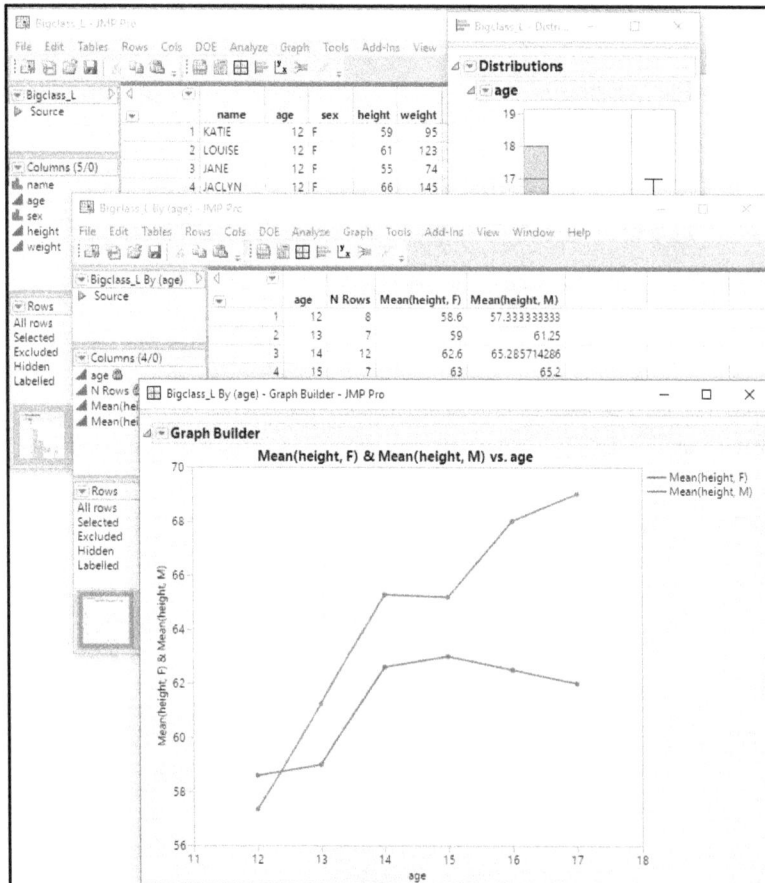

Summary

These are the basics that should enable you to start scripting very quickly. Keep the following key points in mind:

- Perform your analysis interactively first.
- Extract scripts from JMP as the foundation for your script.
- Stitch the scripts together by assigning variable names to objects such as data tables and reports.
- Don't forget to add semicolons between statements.

Chapter 3: The Double Layer Cake

Overview

You now have the script to import your data and create your report. Once again, your manager says she wants you to add a few refinements, maybe add a few items, and delete some others. In order to manipulate the elements of a report, you need to understand how it is constructed. In this chapter, you will learn about the following:

- folding back the layers of the results
- the analysis layer
- the report layer

Folding Back the Layers of the Results

JMP creates a platform object when you launch any platform from the **Analyze** or **Graph** menus. When developing scripts, it is important to understand how the platform object is constructed in order to customize it using JSL. Think of the platform object as consisting of two layers, similar to a double layer cake:

- The analysis layer provides access to all the options available through the red triangle menus.
- The report layer provides access to all the options available through context menus. In other words, these are the options that are available when you right-click within the platform results.

Let's consider each level, starting with the analysis layer.

The Analysis Layer

The options for the analysis layer can be viewed in the red triangle icon drop-down menu of the report. For example, after you launch the Distribution platform and create a report, click the red triangle icon to the left of the response variable, and you will see a menu with a number of options that can be turned on and off, as designated by the presence or absence of checkmarks.

This example assumes that the distribution platform has the default preferences in place.

Figure 3.1 Menu That Shows the Platform Options for Distributions

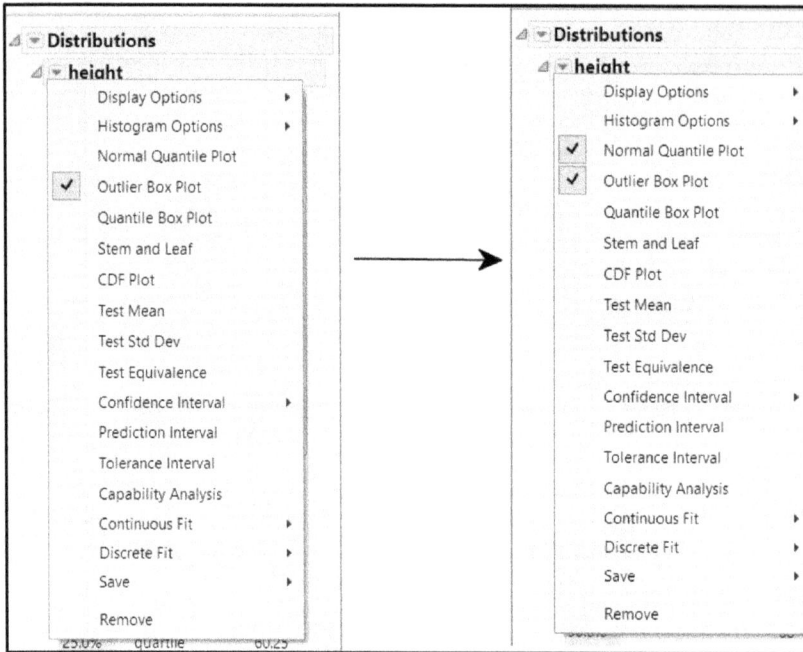

As you know, when you select an option that was not previously selected, more information is added to the report. In this example, a Normal Quantile plot was requested.

Figure 3.2 The Normal Quantile Plot Is Added

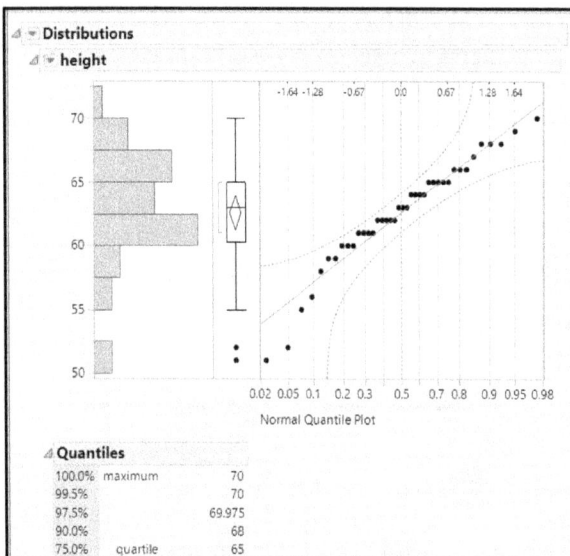

The same options that you select or deselect interactively in the red triangle icon menu can also be applied in JSL.

There are two methods for including platform options in JSL.

- You can specify the options *in* the platform launch:

```
dist = dt << Distribution(
        Y( :height ),
        Normal Quantile Plot( 1 ),
        Outlier Box Plot( 0 )
);
```

- Or you can send messages to the platform object *after* the launch:

```
dist << Normal Quantile Plot( 1 );

dist << Outlier Box Plot( 0 );
```

The options can be turned on by using "1" as the argument, and turned off by using "0" as the argument.

In JSL, using "1" in an argument indicates "true" and turns an option on, and using "0" in an argument means "false" and turns an option off.

Figure 3.3 Menu and Script

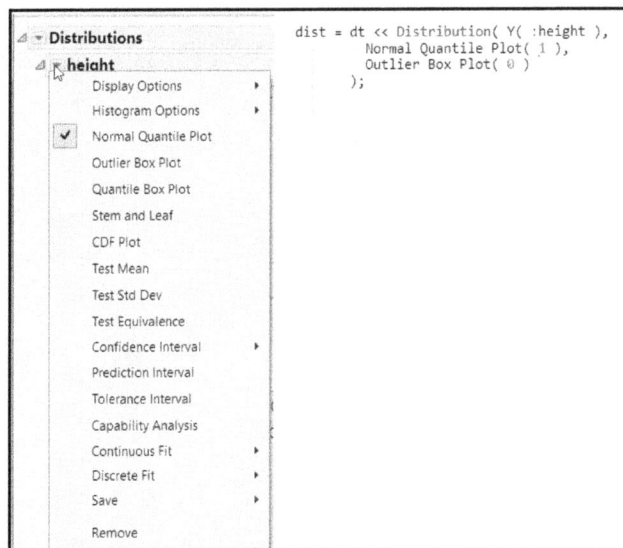

Besides looking at the drop-down menus, how can you find out all the options available for a platform object? One method is to execute a **Show Properties** command and view the log for the details:

```
dist = dt << Distribution( Y( :height ) );
Show Properties( dist );
```

Figure 3.4 The Log Window

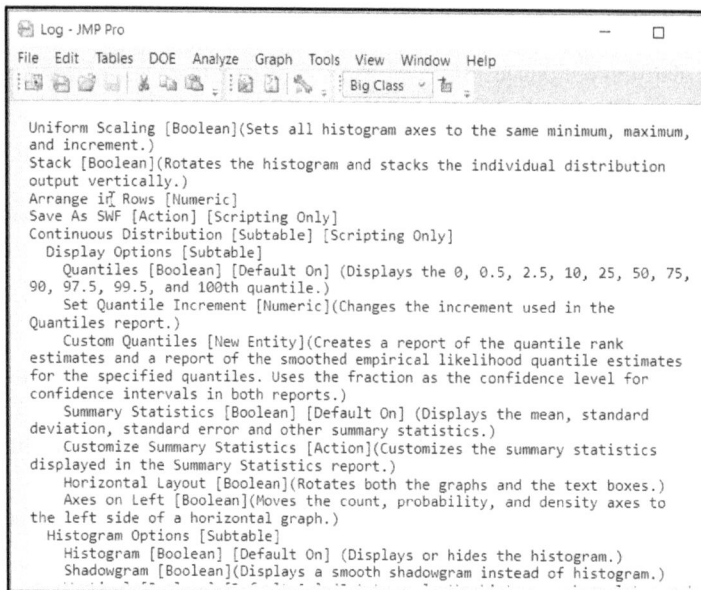

Figure 3.4 shows the Log window that results after you perform the **Show Properties** command on the **Distribution** reference. This output is handy, but a little difficult to read.

We highly recommend becoming familiar with the Scripting Index, accessed from the **Help** menu. We will cover the Scripting Index with more detail in chapter 5.

Select **Help ▶ Scripting Index**, and then click the **All Categories** button and select **Objects** from the drop-down menu.

Figure 3.5 Selecting Objects in the Scripting Index

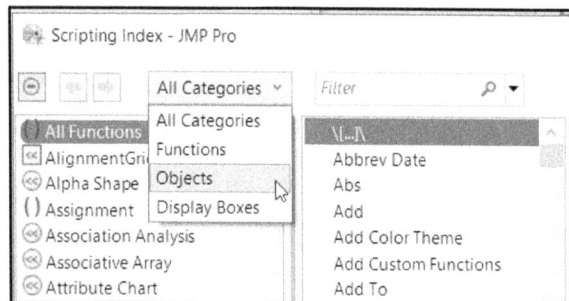

Scroll down the column on the left side of the Scripting Index and select the **Distribution** platform object from the list (see Figure 3.6).

Figure 3.6 Highlighting of Distribution in the Object Scripting Index

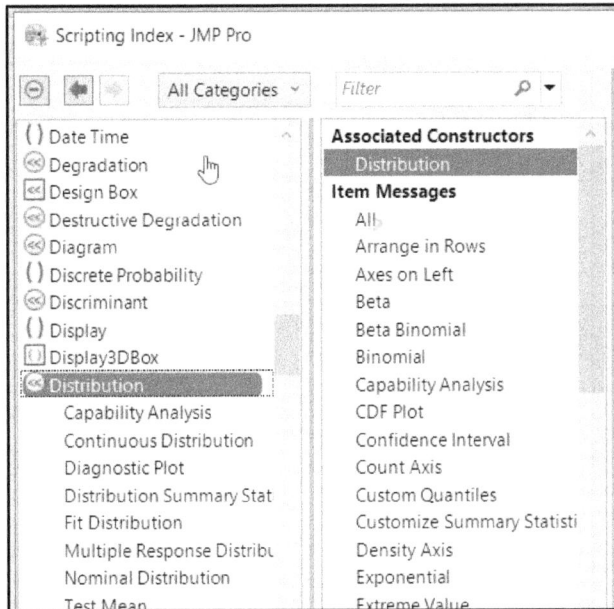

As Figure 3.6 shows, when you highlight **Distribution** in the **Objects** category, the messages that are available for that platform object are displayed.

Note that some options in the Show Properties Log windows are followed by the designation **[Scripting Only]**. This designation means that the option is available only through scripting, and you cannot access it through the interactive interface. Therefore, it is to your advantage to review the details for an object either through the **Show Properties** command or through the Scripting Index. Otherwise, you might miss something that could be useful for your scripting project.

The Report Layer

The report layer consists of presentation options and display boxes. Let's look at each of these items in detail.

Presentation Options

Interactively, you can make changes to the report layer by right-clicking and selecting options from the context menu. For example, you can add a legend or change the background color.

Figure 3.7 Context Menu Launched from a Bivariate Plot

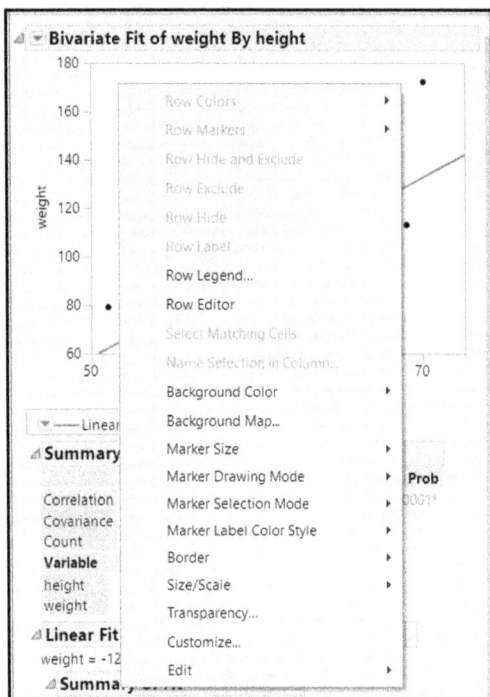

How do you access these same options using JSL?

Earlier in this chapter, you used the platform object when accessing the analysis layer. To do the same for the report layer, you need to send the **Report** command to the platform object. Let's look at two methods for performing this task.

In the following code, a reference is first created for the Bivariate results that we arbitrarily named **biv**.

```
biv = dt << Bivariate( Y( :weight ), X( :height ) );
```

To access the report layer:

- One method is to send the **Report** message to the Bivariate reference and name it **repBiv**:

  ```
  repBiv = biv << Report;
  ```

- You can also wrap the **Report()** function around the platform reference:

  ```
  repBiv = Report( biv );
  ```

Now we have the first step in accessing the report layer. However, before we can send messages with the report reference, we must understand how the report is organized and constructed.

Display Boxes

The basic building blocks of any JMP report are the display boxes. There are many types of display boxes, and each has its own set of messages. How do you know which display boxes are used in a report? And if there is more than one of that type of display box, how do you know which one to reference? You might not be able to determine this by looking at the report.

JMP actually has a built-in feature that shows the arrangement of the display boxes. To view this feature, right-click the topmost gray disclosure icon in a report. From the drop-down menu, select **Edit ▶ Show Tree Structure**.

Figure 3.8 Tree Structure of a Bivariate Report

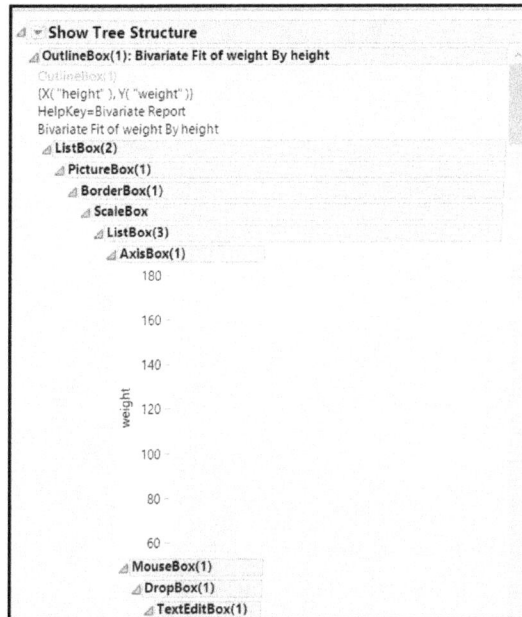

JMP draws a diagram showing the hierarchical organization of the different display boxes that make up the report. If you scroll down in the report, you will see the OutlineBox, AxisBox, FrameBox, and PictureBox. These are basic display boxes found in most reports, and there is a number associated with each one. Knowing the type and number of the display box enables you to reference individual display boxes in a JMP report. Let's explore using some of the common types of display boxes.

FrameBox

Suppose you want to enlarge your Bivariate plot. To change the size of the graph interactively, you could right-click the plot and select **Size/Scale ▶ Frame Size** in the context menu (see Figure 3.9).

Figure 3.9 Accessing the Frame Size Interactively

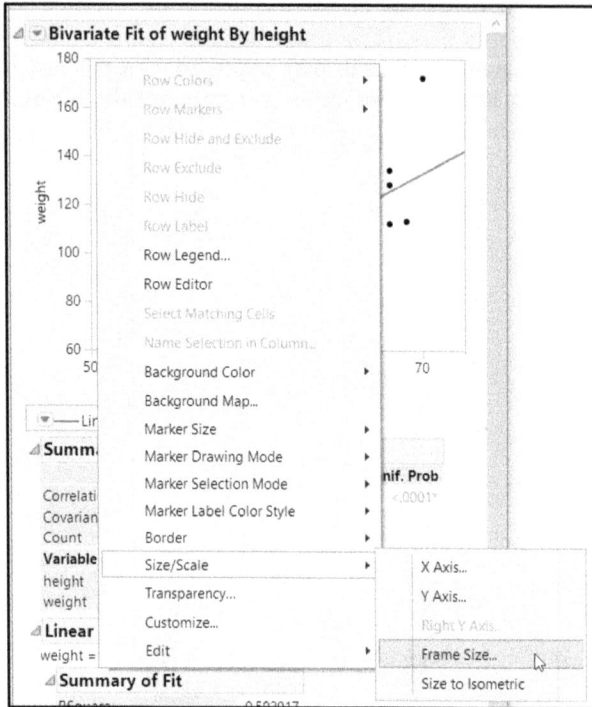

A window appears where you can specify the horizontal and vertical size of the plot in pixels.

Figure 3.10 The Frame Size Window

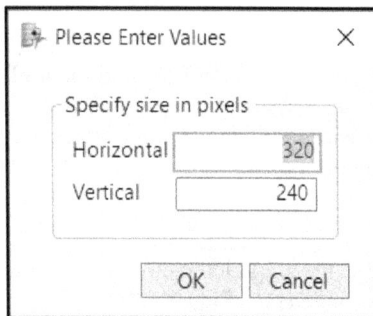

To perform this same action in JSL, first determine what type of display box you need to reference. In the display tree, the display box that holds the plot is the FrameBox, and it is the first FrameBox created in the report. Therefore, it is referenced as FrameBox(1).

Figure 3.11 Display Tree of the Bivariate Report

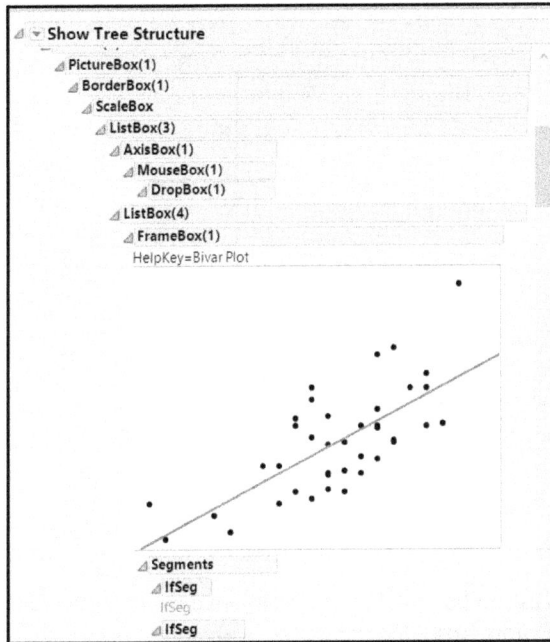

To determine what message to send to this FrameBox, go to the Display Box Scripting Index by selecting **Help ▶ Scripting Index.** In the Scripting Index window, click the **All Categories** button and select **Display Boxes** in the drop-down menu.

Figure 3.12 Selecting the Display Boxes Index Option

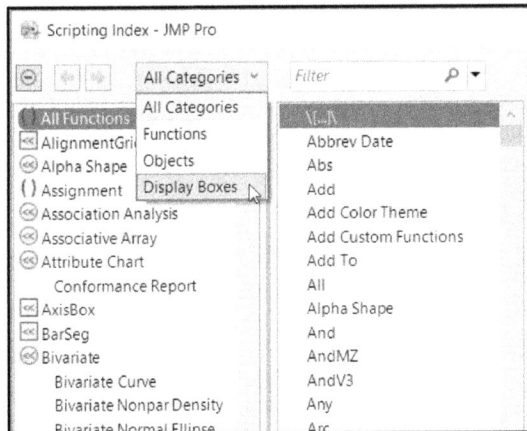

Scroll down to and select **FrameBox** in the left column.

Figure 3.13 Messages for FrameBox

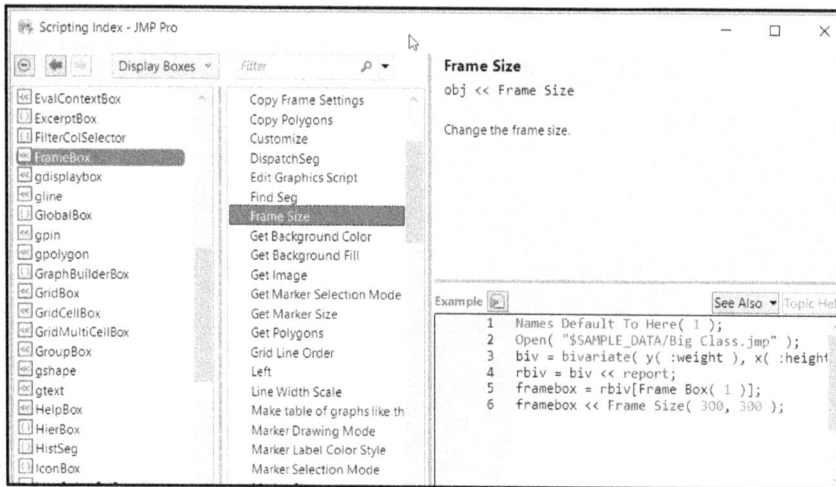

Note that many of the options have the same names as can be found on the interactive menu. In the list of available messages for FrameBox, there is one for **Frame Size**, under the **Size/Scale** topic. Note also, on the far right of the Scripting Index window, a section that shows syntax, and below it, one or more examples where the syntax is used. These are important features that are discussed in chapter 5.

The following scripting statements are needed to create the plot and change the frame size of the Bivariate plot:

```
biv = dt << Bivariate( Y( :weight ), X( :height ) );
repBiv = biv << Report;
repBiv[FrameBox( 1 )] << Frame Size( 250, 400 );
```

When you see square brackets in a script in the context of a report, it means that something is being subscripted. In the preceding example, we are navigating the report layer by referencing the first FrameBox within the report. We will discuss Display Boxes in more detail in chapter 7.

Figure 3.14 The Results of Executing the Script

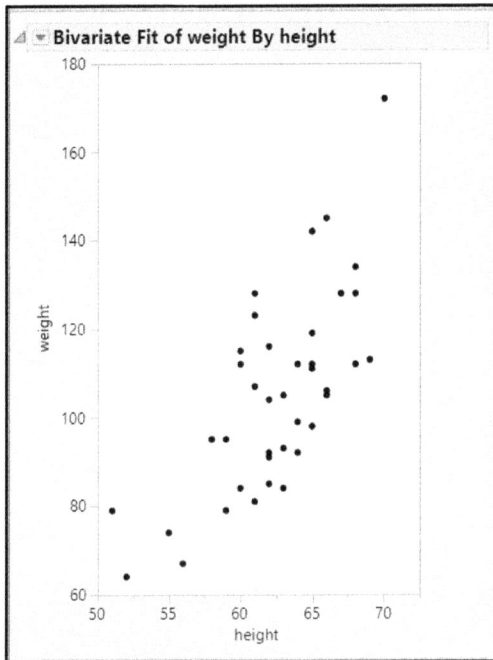

AxisBox

Perhaps you want to change the scale of the X axis of a graph. Interactively, you can right-mouse click the axis and select **Axis Settings**.

Figure 3.15 Accessing Axis Settings Interactively

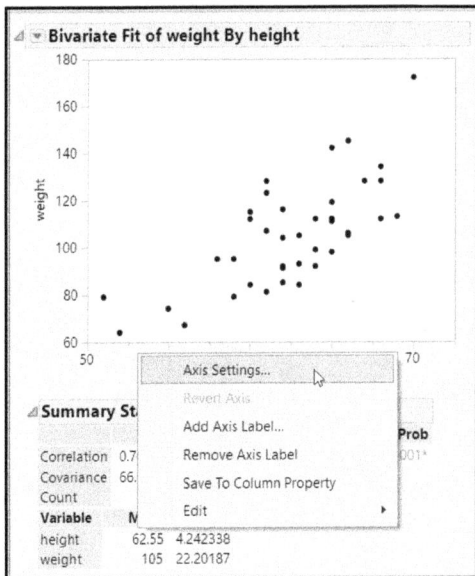

A window appears in which you can change the **Minimum**, **Maximum**, and **Increment** of the X-axis scale (see Figure 3.16), among other axis settings.

Figure 3.16 X Axis Specification Window

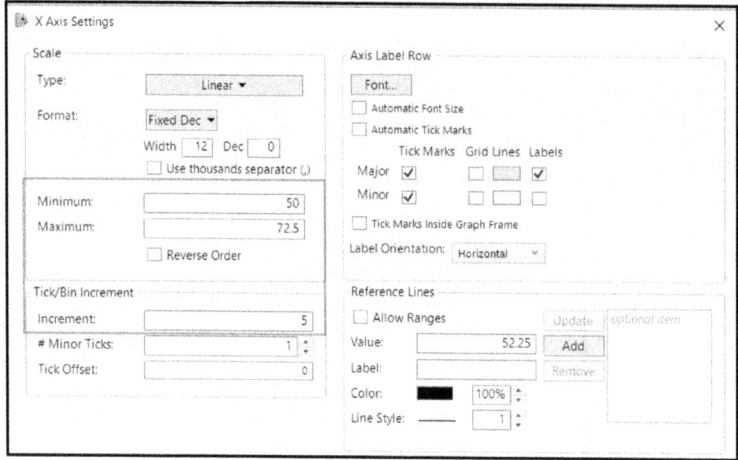

To send a message to an AxisBox, determine which AxisBox represents the X axis by looking again at the tree structure for this report. The X axis is represented by AxisBox(2).

Figure 3.17 X Axis Is AxisBox(2)

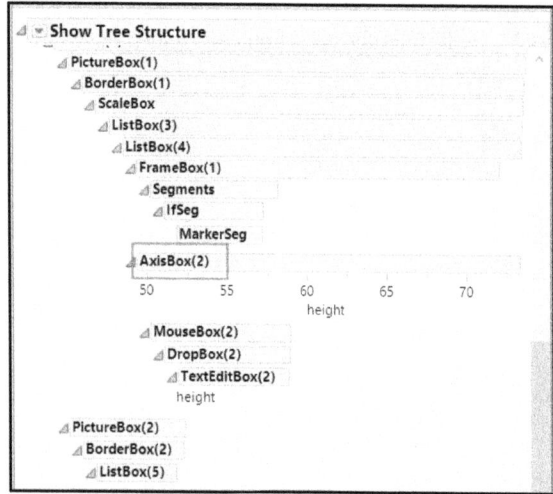

Go back to the Display Box Scripting Index and locate **AxisBox** in the left column.

Figure 3.18 AxisBox Messages

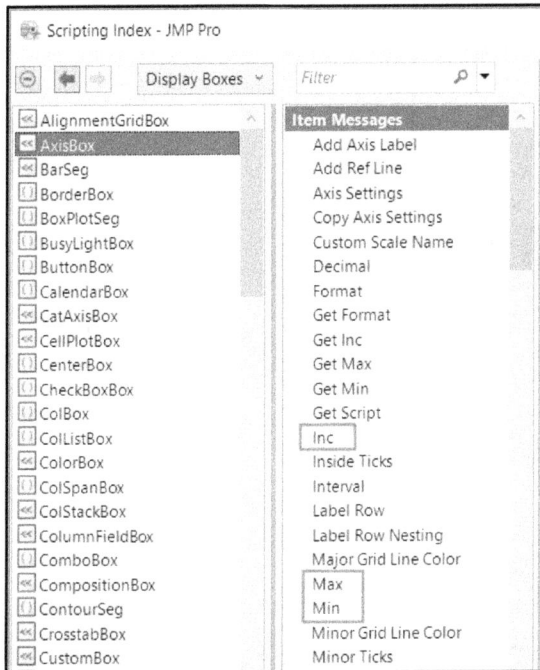

Look at the messages for AxisBox. Scrolling down the list, you will find the messages for **Min**, **Max**, and **Inc**. There are two ways to send these messages to the AxisBox. One way is to send the message as a combined **Axis Settings()** command:

```
repBiv[Axisbox( 2 )] << Axis Settings(
    Min( 45 ),
    Max( 70 ),
    Inc( 10 )
);
```

If you only wanted to change one of the settings, you could send the message as an individual command:

```
repBiv[Axisbox( 2 )] << Min( 45 );
repBiv[Axisbox( 2 )] << Max( 70 );
repBiv[Axisbox( 2 )] << Inc( 10 );
```

OutlineBox

Let's talk about a basic structure that is part of all JMP platform-generated reports: the OutlineBox. The OutlineBox represents a node, which is a single component of a JMP report. The typical JMP report has several of these nodes that are arranged vertically to form a hierarchy.

Figure 3.19 OutlineBox Hierarchy In a Oneway Report

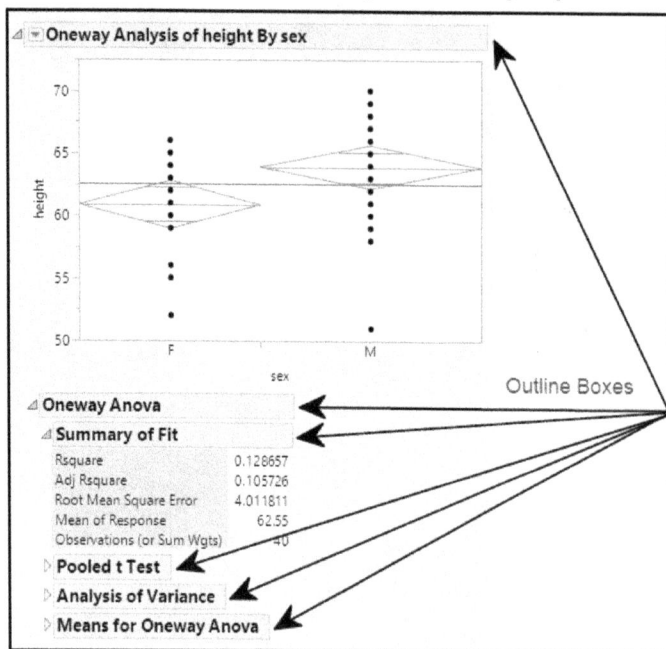

Note that in Figure 3.19, the contents of the **Summary of Fit** node are visible, while those of **Pooled t Test**, **Analysis of Variance**, and **Means for Oneway Anova** are not. To open those last three nodes interactively, you can click the gray disclosure icon on the left of each outline node. Clicking the gray disclosure icon toggles a node open or closed.

To perform the same action using JSL, you need to send a message to the OutlineBox of interest. For example, in Figure 3.20, when the report is created, all Outline Boxes are open.

```
ow = dt << Oneway(
    Y( :height ),
    X( :sex ),
    Means( 1 ),
    Box Plots( 0 ),
    Mean Diamonds( 1 )
);
```

Figure 3.20 Oneway with Open OutlineBox Nodes

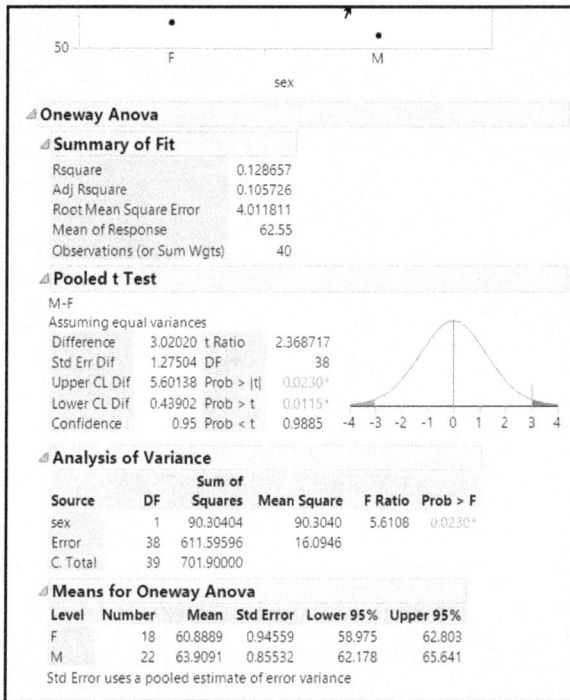

To close the **Pooled t Test** node, you need to find the right OutlineBox in the report. In addition to the report message to the Oneway reference, you can refer to the specific OutlineBox by its text string:

```
Report( ow )["Pooled t Test"]
```

> This method of referencing an OutlineBox by its title is preferred over specifying OutlineBox(n), which references the node by its number. This method eliminates the possibility of the incorrect node being referenced in the case of a user having a preference setting or even a different version of JMP where the box numbering is different. Please see chapter 7 for more information.

What message to the OutlineBox will close the node? Check the Display Boxes Scripting Index by selecting **Help ▶ Scripting Index.** In the **Scripting Index** window, click the **All Categories** button and select **Display Boxes** in the drop-down menu. In the left column, select **OutlineBox**, and then select **Close** in the middle column. In the column on the right, you will see the syntax needed to send the **Close** message to an **OutlineBox**:

```
obj << Close( bool );
```

The argument for **Close** is "bool". Remember that in scripting, the word Boolean means using "1" in an argument to indicate "true" and using "0" in an argument to indicate "false". In this case, to close the node, use "1":

```
Report( ow )["Pooled t Test"] << Close( 1 );
```

Figure 3.21 Oneway Report with Closed OutlineBox Node

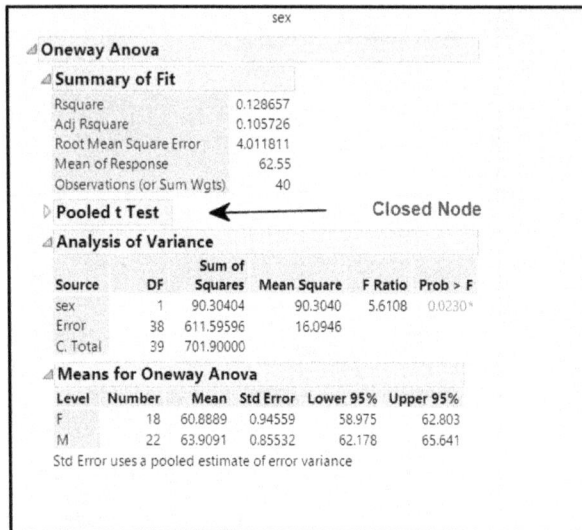

Accessing Items in a Report

How do you get a value out of a report and place it in a variable so that you can use it in another part of your script? We will show you an example where you extract the R-squared value from a Oneway report.

The following JSL code is used to generate the report shown in Figure 3.22:

```
dt = Open( "$SAMPLE_DATA/Big Class.jmp" );
ow = dt << Oneway( Y( :height ), X( :sex ),
                Means( 1 ), Mean Diamonds( 1 ) );
```

Figure 3.22 Oneway Report

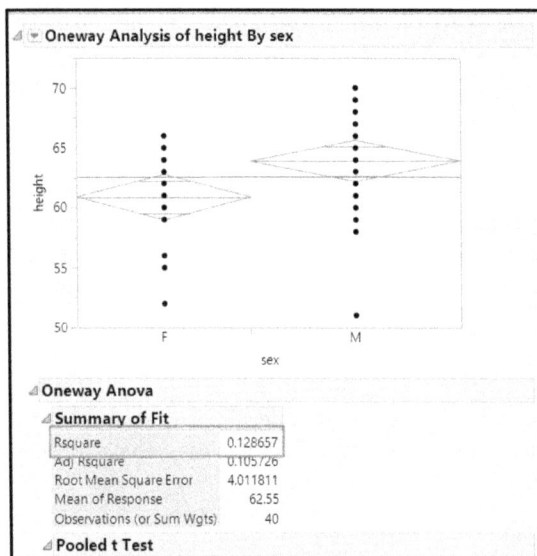

The R-squared value appears under the **Summary of Fit** outline node of the report.

To drill down to the value, you need to know more about the construction of the information in the **Summary of Fit** area. The best way to get started is to look at the tree structure. This time, right-click the gray triangle next to Summary of Fit and select **Edit ▶ Show Tree Structure**.

Selecting the tree structure from here shows only the Display Boxes that are included under this OutlineBox node.

Figure 3.23 Tree Structure for Summary of Fit Area

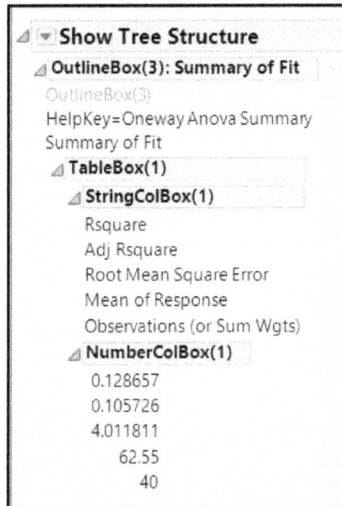

```
◢ ▼ Show Tree Structure
  ◢ OutlineBox(3): Summary of Fit
    OutlineBox(3)
    HelpKey=Oneway Anova Summary
    Summary of Fit
    ◢ TableBox(1)
      ◢ StringColBox(1)
        Rsquare
        Adj Rsquare
        Root Mean Square Error
        Mean of Response
        Observations (or Sum Wgts)
      ◢ NumberColBox(1)
        0.128657
        0.105726
        4.011811
           62.55
           40
```

In the tree structure in Figure 3.23, locate the TableBox. The TableBox is the container for the **Summary of Fit** table. Here it comprises a StringColBox and a NumberColBox. The value that we want to access is the first value in the NumberColBox. Use subscripts to drill down to that value as follows:

```
myRsquare = Report( ow )["Summary of Fit"][Number Col Box( 1 )][1];

Show( myRsquare );
```

The following output appears in the Log window:

```
/*:

myRsquare = 0.12865656133928;
```

You have successfully extracted the R-squared value from the **Summary of Fit** table.

Adding Items to a Report

Suppose you want to add a few notes to the report. For example, to add a note at the bottom of an OutlineBox node, use the **Append** message:

```
ow = dt << Oneway(
    Y( :height ),
    X( :sex ),
```

```
    Means( 1 ),
    Mean Diamonds( 1 )
);

Report( ow )["Summary of Fit"] << Append(
    Text Box( "Note the number of observations" )
);
```

Figure 3.24 Text Appended to an OutlineBox

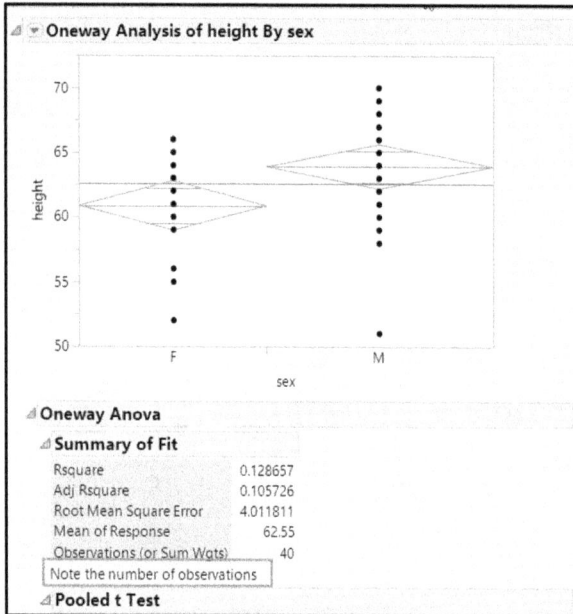

To place the text at the top of the node, use the **Prepend** message as follows:

```
Report( ow )["Summary of Fit"] << Prepend(
    Text Box( "Note the number of observations" )
);
```

Figure 3.25 Text Prepended to an OutlineBox

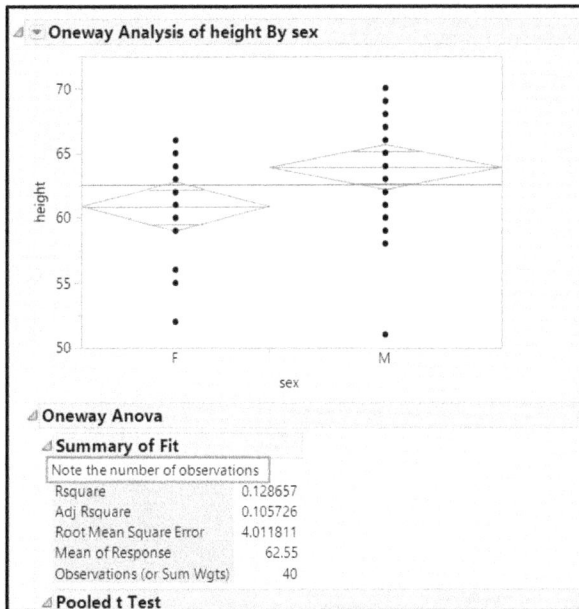

Removing Items from a Report

It is also possible to remove items from a report. Although it is possible to delete an entire Outline Box and its contents from a report created by a JMP platform, it is not recommended. If a section has been deleted that JMP attempts to reference later, stability is affected and unexpected behaviors might occur.

Suppose you wanted to remove the picture shown in the **Pooled t Test** node. Instead of deleting that section, let's search the tree structure to determine what type of Display Box it is and then what messages are available to help us.

1. Right-click the gray disclosure icon beside the **Pooled t Test** Outline node and select **Edit ▶ Show Tree Structure**.
2. Scroll down the tree structure and locate the image that you want to hide.
3. As you hold your mouse pointer over the FrameBox, notice that the corresponding area is highlighted in the report.
4. In this case, we want the entire area hidden. Hold your mouse pointer over the PictureBox and notice that it highlights all of the area that we want to hide.

Figure 3.26 Tree Structure with Report Highlighting

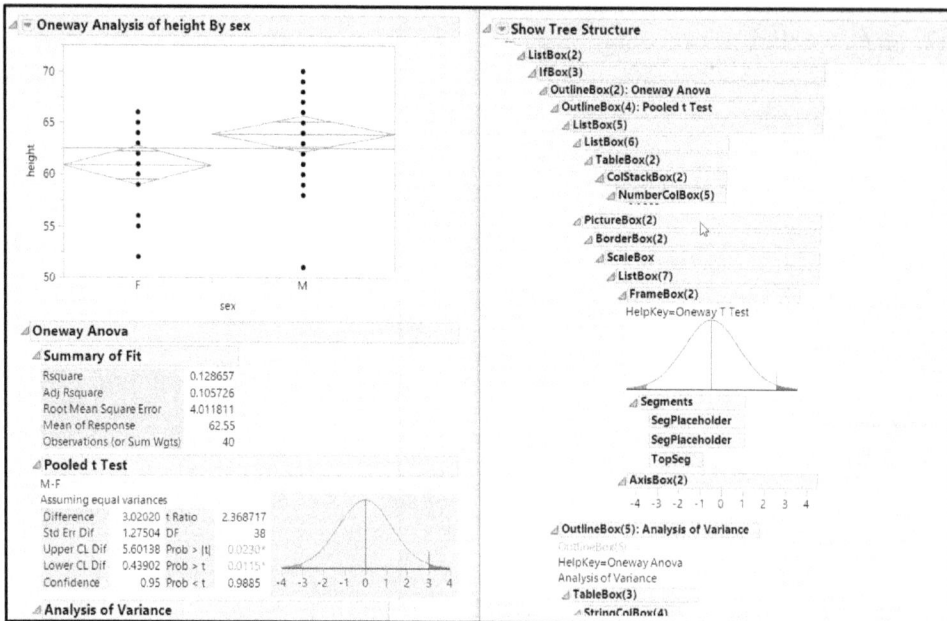

5. Open the Scripting Index (**Help ▶ Scripting Index**). In the Scripting Index window, click the **All Categories** button and select **Display Boxes** in the drop-down menu.

6. Scroll down to and select **PictureBox** in the left column.

7. Scroll down to and select **Visibility** in the messages list.

    Notice that the Visibility message enables you to make a Display Box hidden, collapsed, or visible again.

8. Try the following to collapse the PictureBox. Notice that PictureBox(1) is referenced because it is the first PictureBox under the **Pooled t Test** Outline node. For more information about relative referencing, please see the topic in chapter 7.

    ```
    Report( ow )["Pooled t Test"][PictureBox(1)] << Visibility( "Collapse" );
    ```

The image no longer appears on the report!

Saving Report Tables

JMP gives you the convenience of saving report tables as data tables interactively by right-clicking a section of the report and then selecting **Make into data table**.

Figure 3.27 Context Menu Selection for Making a Data Table

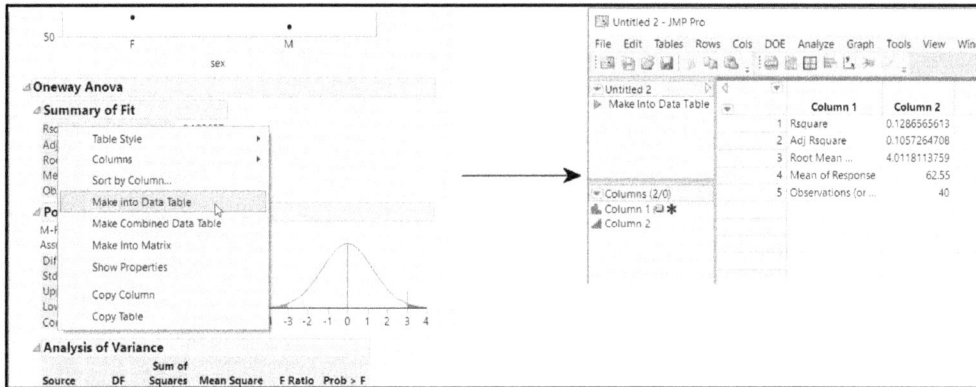

This action can be done in JSL, too:

```
ow = dt << Oneway(
    Y( :height ),
    X( :sex ),
    Means( 1 ),
    Mean Diamonds( 1 )
);

Report( ow )["Summary of Fit"][Table Box( 1 )] << Make Into Data Table;
```

Here a reference was made to the TableBox. The TableBox is the container for the table, as seen in the tree structure, and it typically includes StringColBoxes and NumberColBoxes. When sending the **Make Into Data Table** message to the TableBox, the contents of both StringColBoxes and NumberColBoxes are included in the new table.

Figure 3.28 Tree Structure Diagram for the Summary of Fit Node

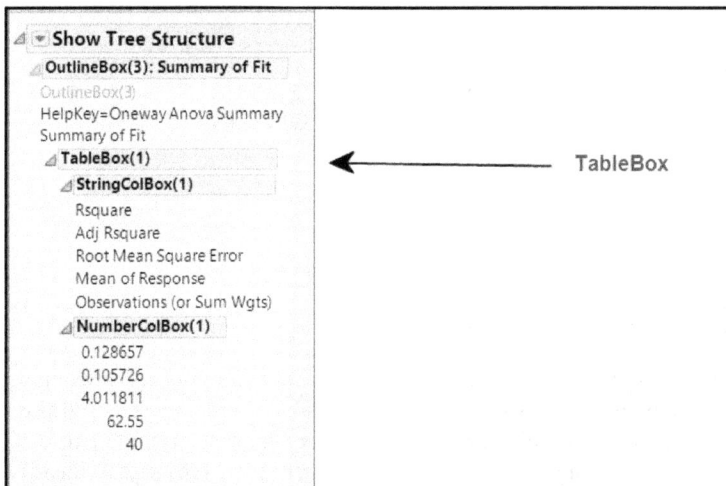

When using a By variable, a report object for each By member is packaged in the same report window:

```
ow = dt << Oneway(
    Y( :height ),
    X( :sex ),
    Means( 1 ),
    Mean Diamonds( 1 ),
    By( :age )
);
```

Figure 3.29 By Variable Report

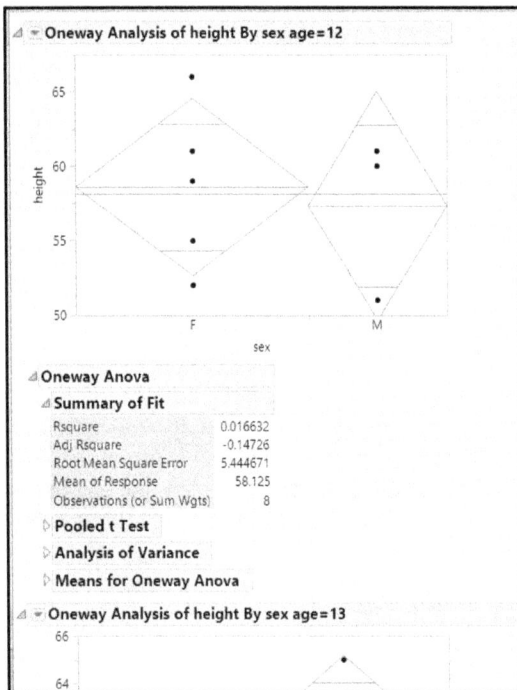

You can see how this works by using the **Show** command on the Oneway reference:

```
Show( ow );

/*:

ow = {Oneway[], Oneway[], Oneway[], Oneway[], Oneway[], Oneway[]};
```

Here you can see that **ow** represents a list of Oneway[] platform objects.

JMP provides a convenient method for making one table for all the related member nodes. For example, interactively, you would right-click in one of the **Summary of Fit** report tables, and then select **Make Combined Data Table** to create one data table for all the **Summary of Fit** data in the report. This can be done in JSL, also. Because **ow** represents a list of Oneway analyses, we must use a subscript to identify one of the Oneway analyses that we want to access. Note that the first Oneway object is referenced as **ow[1]**:

```
Report( ow[1] )["Summary of Fit"][Table Box( 1 )] << Make Combined Data Table;
```

The new data table contains the data from every report table that has columns of the same name and includes columns for each level of the By variable and the X and Y.

Figure 3.30 Table with Combined Summary of Fit Data from All By Members of the Report

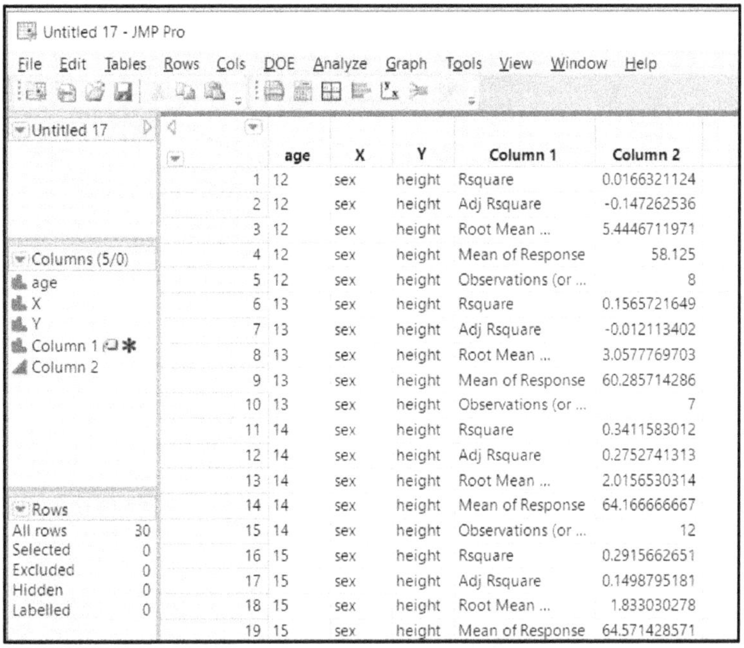

	age	X	Y	Column 1	Column 2
1	12	sex	height	Rsquare	0.0166321124
2	12	sex	height	Adj Rsquare	-0.147262536
3	12	sex	height	Root Mean ...	5.4446711971
4	12	sex	height	Mean of Response	58.125
5	12	sex	height	Observations (or ...	8
6	13	sex	height	Rsquare	0.1565721649
7	13	sex	height	Adj Rsquare	-0.012113402
8	13	sex	height	Root Mean ...	3.0577769703
9	13	sex	height	Mean of Response	60.285714286
10	13	sex	height	Observations (or ...	7
11	14	sex	height	Rsquare	0.3411583012
12	14	sex	height	Adj Rsquare	0.2752741313
13	14	sex	height	Root Mean ...	2.0156530314
14	14	sex	height	Mean of Response	64.166666667
15	14	sex	height	Observations (or ...	12
16	15	sex	height	Rsquare	0.2915662651
17	15	sex	height	Adj Rsquare	0.1498795181
18	15	sex	height	Root Mean ...	1.833030278
19	15	sex	height	Mean of Response	64.571428571

Summary

Now you have learned the basics of the JMP report and how the data and the display boxes for the data form the report. More importantly, you have observed how to modify the elements through scripting.

What's next?

Next, we will dive deeper into the fundamental concepts of the JSL language. Go get another cup of coffee!

Chapter 4: JSL Language Foundations

Overview

Now that your mind has started racing through all the possibilities, let's go over some of the foundational basics of the JMP scripting language. As we have said before, JSL is quite distinctive. In this section, we discuss JSL concepts from the perspective of someone who might not consider themselves a programmer.

Fundamental Concepts

JSL is a powerful language built upon the concepts of objects, operators, messages and arguments. Let's discuss each of these in detail.

JSL Statement Form

The basic premise of a JSL statement is that you send messages to JMP objects in order to tell them what to do.

The following is the basic form of a JSL statement:

```
object << Message( Argument );
```

Object

An object is the thing that you want to do something with. For now, let's think of objects as things that you can see, such as data tables, columns, or an analysis. But keep in mind that there are less visible objects that can accept messages, as well.

In the preceding statement form, the object can be specified by its name or a reference. For example, suppose the Big Class data table object reference was assigned to **dt** earlier in your script, such as when the table was opened. You could use either **dt** or **Data Table("Big Class")** to specify the desired data table as the object to receive the message.

Send Operator

The two less than signs (**<<**) together make up the **Send** operator. Essentially, these two symbols point to the object that will accept the message specified on the right. Keep in mind that there cannot be any space between these two symbols in order for JMP to correctly interpret them as the **Send** operator.

Message

A message is a command; it is the instruction that you want JMP to execute. In other words, it is what you want JMP to do to, or for, the specified object. Messages can also return a value. For example, you might want to add a new column to a data table. In this case, you would use the **Data Table()** function or reference as the object. Next would be the **Send** operator, followed by the **New Column()** message instructing JMP to add the new column to the specified data table. Because the **New Column()** message returns a reference to the column, you can also assign the reference when the column is created. Your JSL code might look something like the following, which instructs JMP to add a new column named "My New Col" to the Big Class data table:

```
col = Data Table( "Big Class" ) << New Column( "My New Col" );
```

Argument

An argument is supporting information for the message. Arguments provide any detail necessary for JMP to complete the task described by the message. In the preceding example, the name of the new column was provided as the argument. Sometimes the argument requires the use of a specific option name, known as a *named argument*, which can have arguments of its own. Expanding upon the **New Column()** code from the preceding example, the following includes a named argument called **Format()** to specify the format of the column:

```
col = Data Table( "Big Class" ) << New Column(
    "My New Col",   //argument
    "Numeric",   //argument
    "Continuous",   //argument
    Format( "Percent", 12, 1 ) //named argument
);
```

Messages can have multiple arguments. In some cases, all are required, or sometimes only some are required, while others are optional. Typically, options are separated by commas within the message and appear in a specific order. But there are also messages that do not require any argument at all. An example of a command that needs no argument is **Clear Select**.

```
    dt << Clear Select;
```

JMP does not need any additional information in order to deselect the currently selected rows.

Semicolon

Finally, we separate JSL statements with the all-important semicolon (;). Remember from chapter 1 that the semicolon is actually known as the **Glue** operator. This is a signal to JMP that indicates that the end of a JSL statement has been reached and that more might follow. Without an ending semicolon, you are likely to encounter interactive errors in JMP Error Alert windows, as well as in your log when JMP sees the next JSL statement. Plus, your script will come to an abrupt halt.

Fortunately, JMP does try to help you determine your problem. In the case of a missing semicolon, the error message might suggest there was a missing semicolon, as in the following example:

```
Data Table( "Big Class" ) << New Column( "My New Col" )
Data Table( "Big Class" ) << Add Rows( 1 );
```

When the preceding code is run, the following is returned in the log:

```
/*:

Unexpected "Data Table". Perhaps there is a missing ";" or ",".
Line 2 Column 1: ▶Data Table( "Big Class" ) << Add Rows( 1 );
The remaining text that was ignored was
Data Table"("Big Class)<<Add Rows(1);
```

But there is so much more to discover about JSL.

Functions

JSL functions are commands that perform a specific task. Like messages, they can accept arguments and return a result. However, they are not sent as a message to a specific object, but rather can be executed independently. There are both built-in JSL functions and functions that you can define yourself.

Built-In Functions

To see a list of built-in functions, click the **Help** menu and select **Scripting Index**. Change the drop-down selection to **Functions**, as shown in the following figure.

Figure 4.1 Scripting Index

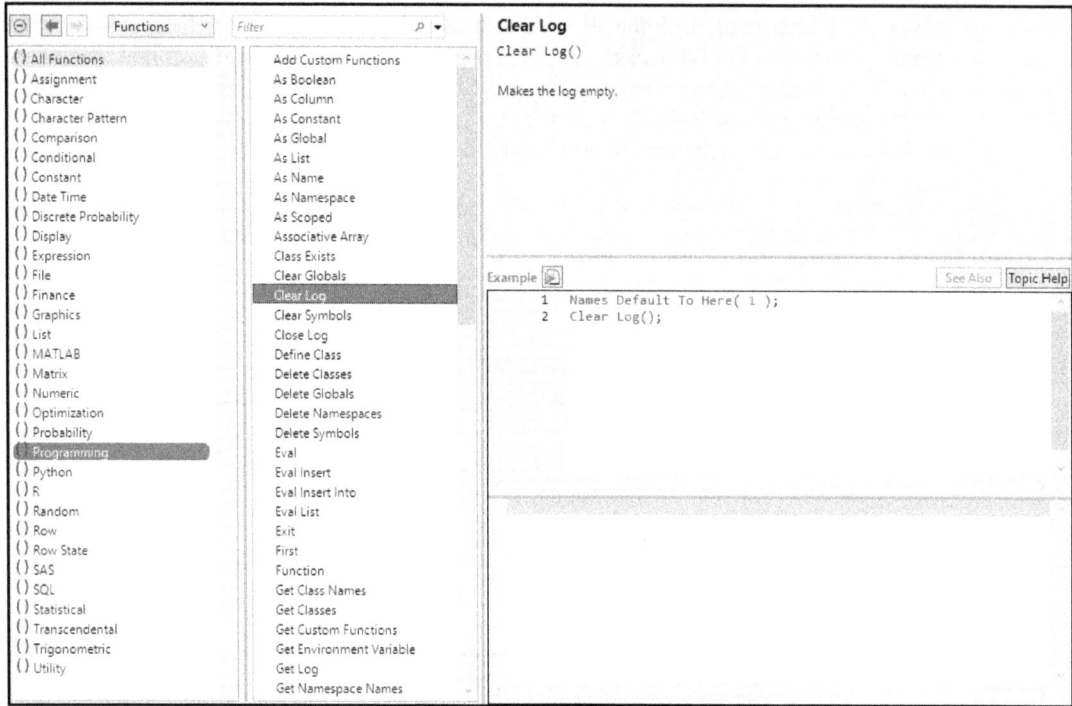

In the left column, select **Programming**. As you select function entries in the middle column, notice the syntax for each is listed at the top of the window, on the right. The symbols < > around an argument mean that it is an optional argument. Functions that return a value appear with a variable followed by an equal sign before the function name.

Select **All Functions** in the left column of the Scripting Index. Review each of the following functions and notice the types of arguments and return values.

Table 4.1 Examples of Built-In Functions

Function	Arguments	Return Value
Clear Log()	None	None
N Table()	None	The number of currently open data tables
Loc Max()	Matrix (Required)	The first position in the matrix of the maximum value found in the matrix
Concat Items()	List of Strings (Required) String Separator (Optional)	A single string made of all the list elements separated by a space or the specified separator

Function	Arguments	Return Value
Close()	Data Table Reference (Optional) NoSave | Save("path") (Optional)	None

Pay close attention to the return values from both messages and functions. Knowing what is returned is key to knowing how to proceed to the next step in your scripting project!

You can use functions within functions. The return value for the inner function is the argument to the outer function.

In the following code, we have altered the example from the Scripting Index entry for the **Abbrev Date()** function. Because the function returns a value, we can assign the result to a JSL variable. Notice that the argument for **Abbrev Date()** is another function called **Today()**. The **Today()** function returns the current date and time in a number of seconds since midnight, January 1, 1904. Since that is not an easily recognizable value, we use it with the **Abbrev Date()** function to ensure that the value returned is easily understood as a date.

```
todayDate = Abbrev Date( Today() );
Show( todayDate );
```

After executing this code, the **todayDate** JSL variable now represents a string representation of the date the function was executed, which was returned by the **Today()** function.

```
//:*/
todayDate = Abbrev Date( Today() );
Show( todayDate );

/*:

todayDate = "11/4/2017";
```

Custom Functions

You can also create your own custom functions by using the **Function()** function. This is very handy for a section of JSL script that you want to be able to reuse again and again. The basic syntax is as follows:

```
functionName = Function(
    {argument list},
    <{local variables}>,
    Script
);
```

Suppose you want to present informational or warning messages to the user during the script execution. The message displayed will change based upon specific conditions. For example, your small section of JSL code to create a window with specific settings might look like the following:

```
New Window( "Notice:",
    <<Modal,
    Lineup Box( N Col( 2 ), Spacing( 10 ),
        Icon Box( "Excluded" ),
        Text Box(
            "Selected column has all missing values.",
            <<Set Font Size( 12 )

        )
    )
);
```

Using a custom function enables you to define the function once, and then use it again and again simply by calling it by name and supplying any necessary arguments. You don't have to rewrite or copy and paste the same code in various places in your script. This helps keep your script more readable, as well.

In the following code, we have placed the preceding script into a custom function. The first argument indicates that there is one required argument, the message to be displayed. Notice that the text in the **TextBox()** function is replaced by the name of the custom function's argument, **message**.

```
alertMsg = Function( {message},
    New Window( "Notice:",
        <<Modal,
        Lineup Box( N Col( 2 ), Spacing( 10 ),
            Icon Box( "Excluded" ),
            Text Box( message, <<Set Font Size( 12 ) )
        )
    )
);
```

To call the function, simply use the function name and supply the text to be displayed.

```
//Call the function later in the script
alertMsg( "Selected column has all missing values." );
```

Figure 4.2 Warning Message

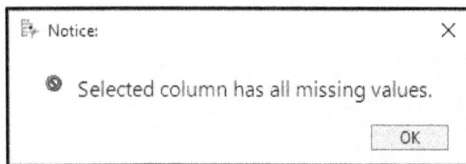

A JSL string variable could also be used as the function argument.

```
//Use a JSL string variable to call the function later in the script
msg = "Column must be numeric.";
alertMsg( msg );
```

Figure 4.3 Warning Message as JSL Variable

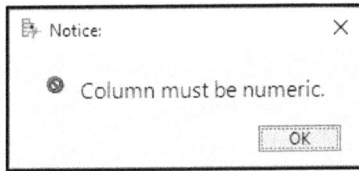

In the preceding example, the message argument is required. We could alter the function definition slightly to include a default value for message, which makes the argument optional.

```
alertMsg = Function( {message = "Operation cancelled."},
    New Window( "Notice:",
            <<Modal,
            Lineup Box( N Col( 2 ), Spacing( 10 ),
                    Icon Box( "Excluded" ),
                    Text Box( message, <<Set Font Size( 12 ) )
            )
        )
);
```

Now when the function is called, you can specify your desired text for the message argument or accept the default text.

```
alertMsg();
```

Figure 4.4 Default Warning Message

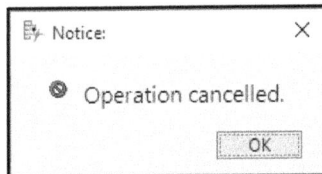

For the preceding example custom functions, in addition to the benefits already described, there is the added benefit of having a clean and consistent format for the messages that are presented to the user throughout your script.

Custom functions also enable you to specify that JSL variables should be local to the function. What does it mean to be *local to the function*? It means that the JSL variables and their values are not known to any other part of the script except for the function itself. Why would you want to keep a JSL variable local to the function? Well, you might not care—but you might. Variables that are local to the function are like temporary variables in other languages. The lifespan of the variable is limited to the execution of the function, as they do not persist after the function completes its script and returns. Using local variables is an easy way to keep your namespace cleared of any temporary JSL variable definitions.

Local variables can be specified in one of two ways:

- **{local variables}** – Specifies a list of variable names.
- **{Default Local}** – Using **{Default Local}** makes all unscoped JSL variables local to the function. See the Namespaces section in this chapter for further details about scoping and working with namespaces.

The default return value of a custom function is the value returned by the last evaluated expression in the function's script argument. However, you can specify the value to be returned by the function upon completion by using the **Return()** function in your script argument.

The **Return()** function is useful in a custom function for a couple of reasons:

- The **Return()** function can be used as a way to break out of a function. For example, suppose you needed to ensure that the argument supplied to the function was a number. You could use **Return()** to specify that a numeric missing value is returned instead of continuing with the script argument.

```
myFunction = Function( {x},
    If( !Is Number( x ),
            Return( . )
    );
    y = x * 5;
);
```

When the argument supplied to **myFunction** is a number, the value returned by the function is the value of y:

```
var1 = myFunction( 2 );
Show( var1 );
```

```
/*:

var1 = 10;
```

But when the argument supplied to **myFunction** is not a number, the value returned by the function is missing:

```
a = "abc";
var2 = myFunction( a );
Show( var2 );
```

```
/*:

var2 = .;
```

- The **Return()** function can be used to simply specify what is returned by the function. For example, if your function generates a data table, it would be a good idea to return a reference to that data table. In the following example, the function does the following:
  - accepts a data table reference
  - anonymizes the data
  - closes the original table
  - returns a data table reference

Notice that the function's argument is for a data table reference. By defining a default value, the function can be run with a specified data table reference, or the function will use the current data table, whatever table that might be at run time.

```
TestFn = Function( {dt = Current Data Table()},
    {Default Local},
    //If no table open, prompt to open
    If( N Table() == 0,
            dt = Open()
    );
    //Generate an anonymized data table
    anondt = dt << Anonymize();
    //Close the original table
    Close( dt, No Save );
    //Return a reference to the new table
    Return( anondt );
);

//Use default table reference to call the function
dtAnonymize = TestFn();

//OR

//Use a data table reference to call the function
fit_dt = Open( "$SAMPLE_DATA\Fitness.jmp" );
dtAnonymize = TestFn( fit_dt );
```

When you run a **Show()** function on the **dtAnonymize** JSL variable, you will see that it represents the new data table. Without using the **Return()** option, the value stored in **dtAnonymize** would be a missing value.

```
//:*/
Show( dtAnonymize );
/*:

dtAnonymize = DataTable("Fitness Anonymized");
```

Having trouble remembering when to use a comma versus a semicolon? A general rule of thumb is to use a comma to separate items, and to use a semicolon to glue JSL statements together. In the preceding examples, commas are used to separate arguments, and semicolons are used at the end of the JSL statements that make up the script argument within the function definition.

Operators

Earlier in this chapter we introduced the **Send** operator. In general, operators are the symbolic representation of built-in JSL functions. So just as the two less than signs (**<<**) make up the **Send** operator, there is also a corresponding **Send()** function that performs the same action.

```
// New column created using the Send operator
dt << New Column( "Test", Numeric, Continuous );

// Equivalent action using the Send() function
Send( dt, New Column( "Test", Numeric, Continuous ) );
```

You might also recall that the semicolon used at the end of JSL statements is known as the **Glue** operator. The following demonstrates the equivalent use of the Glue operator and the **Glue()** function:

```
// Assignment of values to the var1 and var2 variables
var1 = 1;
var2 = 2;

// Equivalent action using the Glue() function
Glue( var1 = 1, var2 = 2 );
```

Operators are quite useful for comparing values, performing arithmetic, defining lists and matrices, and scoping JSL names, among other actions. The following table organizes some of the more common operators by type with the corresponding built-in function.

Table 4.2 Common Operators by Type

Operator Type	Operator	Function	Syntax
Arithmetic	+	Add()	x + y Add(x, y)
	-	Subtract()	x - y Subtract(x, y)
	*	Multiply()	x * y Multiply(x, y)
	/	Divide()	x / y Divide(x, y)
Assignment	=	Assign()	x = 5 Assign(x, 5)
	+=	Add To()	x += 5 Add To(x, 5)
	++	Post Increment()	x++ Post Increment(x)
	--	Post Decrement()	x-- Post Decrement(x)
Character	||	Concat()	a || b Concat(a, b)
	||=	Concat To()	a ||= b Concat To(a, b)
Comparison	==	Equal()	a == b Equal(a, b)
	!=	Not Equal()	x != y Not Equal(x, y)

Operator Type	Operator	Function	Syntax
	>	Greater()	`x > y` `Greater( x, y )`
	>=	Greater or Equal()	`x >= y` `Greater or Equal( x, y )`
	<	Less()	`x < y` `Less( x, y )`
	<=	Less or Equal()	`x <= y` `Less or Equal( x, y )`
Logical	&	And()	`a & b` `And( a, b )`
	|	Or()	`a | b` `Or( a, b )`
	!	Not()	`!a` `Not( a )`
Programming	{}	List()	`{a, b}` `List( a, b )`
	[]	Matrix()	`[x, y]` `Matrix( {x, y} )`
	::	Index()	`x::y` `Index( x, y )`
Scoping	:	As Column()	`:columnName` `As Column( "columnName" )`
	::	As Global()	`::jslVariable` `As Global( "jslVariable" )`

Further details about each of these functions can be found in the Scripting Index.

Data Structures

Maybe you've heard the term "data structure" before. But if you haven't, it might seem confusing. Data structures are simply objects that organize and store data for easy retrieval. You use data structures of all types in your everyday life all the time.

Think about it. When you need items from the grocery store, you write a list. Some of you might even organize the list by the layout of the store so that you don't forget anything or have to retrace your steps when you get there. (You know who you are!) Or maybe you have several stores to go to. You probably organize your list by store. You wouldn't put items found in the grocery store in the same list as items found the hardware store, right?

In JMP, data structures refer to containers of data that are held in memory. According to the Scripting Guide, the basic data structures offered in JSL are lists, matrices, and associative arrays. But data tables can be considered data structures, too. Let's review each of these.

Data Tables

When you import data into JMP, you can see all of your data organized by rows and columns. In fact, tables are a common way to arrange, organize, and display data.

In JMP, you can easily reference your data by the column name and the row number. Here is an example of referencing a cell using the column name and row number:

```
/* Open the Big Class sample data table */
dt = Open( "$SAMPLE_DATA/Big Class.jmp" );

/* :columnName[row] */
student = :name[1];
```

Data tables make it easy to summarize, sort, subset, and transform the data, as well. Each of these actions can be performed by selecting the desired action from the **Tables** menu. After the desired table is generated, you can copy the JSL script from the **Source** table scripts, just as we have done in the early chapters.

Lists

Much like your shopping list, a JSL list is a container for storing items. A list is rather flexible in the items it can hold. Some common things stored in lists are strings, numbers, platform objects, and even other lists. The items stored do not have to be of a single type. Your list could contain any combination of these items.

Although a list is a JSL object, it does not have the same visual display that you see with a data table. You can define a list by using either the **List()** function or the corresponding list operator, **{}**.

```
mySchoolList = {"pencils", "paper", "notebook", "crayons"};
myWorkList = List( "travel mug", "coffee" );
```

But there are also times where JMP creates lists for you.

Suppose you wanted to extract the names of all the students in the Big Class sample data table. You can send the **Get Values** message to the column containing the names of the children.

```
/* Open the Big Class sample data table */
dt = Open( "$SAMPLE_DATA\Big Class.jmp" );

/* Store the children's names in a list */
classNames = :name << Get Values;
```

Because the **Get Values** message returns a list, the result is a list of every value in the column.

```
//:*/
Show( classNames );
/*:
classNames = {"KATIE", "LOUISE", "JANE", "JACLYN", "LILLIE", "TIM", "JAMES",
"ROBERT", "BARBARA", "ALICE", "SUSAN", "JOHN", "JOE", "MICHAEL", "DAVID", "JUDY",
"ELIZABETH", "LESLIE", "CAROL", "PATTY", "FREDERICK", "ALFRED", "HENRY", "LEWIS",
"EDWARD", "CHRIS", "JEFFREY", "MARY", "AMY", "ROBERT", "WILLIAM", "CLAY", "MARK",
"DANNY", "MARTHA", "MARION", "PHILLIP", "LINDA", "KIRK", "LAWRENCE"};
```

Functions can also return lists. An example of this is the **Files In Directory()** function.

```
fileList = Files In Directory( "$SAMPLE_DATA\Variability Data" );
```

Notice that the result is a list of all the file names in the directory.

```
//:*/
Show( fileList );
/*:
fileList = {"2 Factors Crossed.jmp", "2 Factors Nested.jmp", "3 Factors Crossed &
Nested.jmp", "3 Factors Crossed.jmp", "3 Factors Nested & Crossed.jmp", "3 Factors
Nested.jmp", "Gasket.jmp", "MSALinearity.jmp", "One Main Effect.jmp", "Wafer.jmp"};
```

If there were any folders in the Variability Data directory, the folder names would also be included in the returned list.

When you run a platform, such as **Bivariate**, what is returned is a reference to the platform object. When you use the **By()** option, the return value is a list of **Bivariate[]** objects.

```
/* Open a sample data table */
dt = Open( "$SAMPLE_DATA\Big Class.jmp" );

/* Run a Bivariate of height by weight */
biv1 = dt << Bivariate( Y( :height ), X( :weight ) );

/* Run the same Bivariate using age as the By variable */
biv2 = dt << Bivariate( Y( :height ), X( :weight ),
    By( :age )
);
```

When you compare the **biv1** and **biv2** variables, you will see that using the **By()** option returned one **Bivariate[]** object for each level of the By variable. In this case, that is one for each age represented in the data.

```
//:*/
Show( biv1, biv2 );
/*:
biv1 = Bivariate[];
biv2 = {Bivariate[], Bivariate[], Bivariate[], Bivariate[], Bivariate[],
Bivariate[]};
```

There are lots of useful things you can do with lists, such as accessing specific values. For example, suppose we wanted to fit a line on only the first **Bivariate[]** represented by **biv2**. We would send the **Fit Line** message as follows:

```
biv2[1] << Fit Line;
```

An important thing to keep in mind is that it is possible, and often desirable, to send a message to all the items in a list.

Continuing with the preceding example, suppose you wanted to add a horizontal line to show the mean of the Y for each Bivariate. The **Fit Mean** message can be sent to a **Bivariate[]** object to add the desired horizontal line. When you send that message to the list of **Bivariate[]** objects, the message is actually sent to every **Bivariate[]** object in the list. So all you have to do is send the **Fit Mean** message to **biv2**, as shown here.

```
biv2 << Fit Mean;
```

Matrices

A matrix is a data structure used for storing numbers in rows and columns. It is useful for performing calculations efficiently. Unlike lists, matrices are strictly made of numeric values. You can make a matrix from a list, but all the values must be numeric. A matrix containing only one row or only one column is also referred to as a vector.

```
m1 = [1, 2, 4, 8, 16];
m2 = Matrix( {2, 3, 5, 7, 11} );
```

JMP can create a matrix for you, as well. For example, you can extract a data table into a matrix. The **Get as Matrix** message can be sent to the data table to obtain a matrix of just the numeric values from the data table.

```
/* Open the Big Class sample data table */
dt = Open( "$SAMPLE_DATA/Big Class.jmp" );

/* Extract numeric values to a matrix */
m = dt << Get As Matrix;
```

Notice that the results contain the values for only the age, height, and weight columns.

```
/*:

[12 59 95,
 12 61 123,
 12 55 74,
 12 66 145,
 12 52 64,
 ...
```

The **Get All Columns As Matrix** message returns a matrix of all the data, including character columns.

```
/* Extract all data values to a matrix */
m = dt << Get All Columns As Matrix;
```

The character data are represented as numbers that are incremented according to the unique values in the column.

```
/*:

Matrix( 40, 5 ) assigned.
```

You can also use matrices as the argument for certain functions and to perform calculations.

```
Sqrt( m );
m3 = m1 + m2;
m4 = m*5;
```

There's an awful lot to know about using matrices in JMP. Therefore, if you are interested in learning more, we recommend that you carefully review the "Matrices" section of the "Data Structures" chapter in the *Scripting Guide* (**Help ▶ Books ▶ Scripting Guide**).

Associative Arrays

Associative arrays look a bit like lists but they are much more than that. An associative array consists of keys and their values. In a very general sense, you can think of the keys in an associative array as the column headings. The keys must all be unique, just as all column names in a data table must be unique.

A key's values are similar to the rows of data in a column. But with an associative array, the number of values for each key does not have to be the same. This means that each key and its values are not necessarily related to another key's values in the same way that a row of data is related.

Let's look at an example. Suppose we built an associative array containing data about a house.

```
homes = Associative Array();
homes["neighborhood"] = "Lakewood";
homes["city"] = "Riverside";
homes["type"] = "single family";
homes["bedrooms"] = {"master", "br2", "br3", "br4"};
homes["bathrooms"] = {"ba1", "ba2", "half"};
homes["sqft"] = 2250;
homes["garage"] = "Y";
homes["lotsize"] = 0.5;
homes["fireplace"] = "Y";
homes["basement"] = "N";

homes << Get Contents;
```

Notice that the keys are returned in alphabetic order, while the key values appear as assigned.

```
/*:
{
    {"basement", "N"},
    {"bathrooms", {"ba1", "ba2", "half"}},
    {"bedrooms", {"master", "br2", "br3", "br4"}},
    {"city", "Riverside"},
    {"fireplace", "Y"},
    {"garage", "Y"},
    {"lotsize", 0.5},
    {"neighborhood", "Lakewood"},
    {"sqft", 2250},
    {"type", "single family"}
}
```

Another way to visualize this would be as shown in Figure 4.5. The outer container is the associative array. Each key is represented with a darker background. And the values for each key are listed below the key name with a white background.

Figure 4.5 Visualization of Associative Array

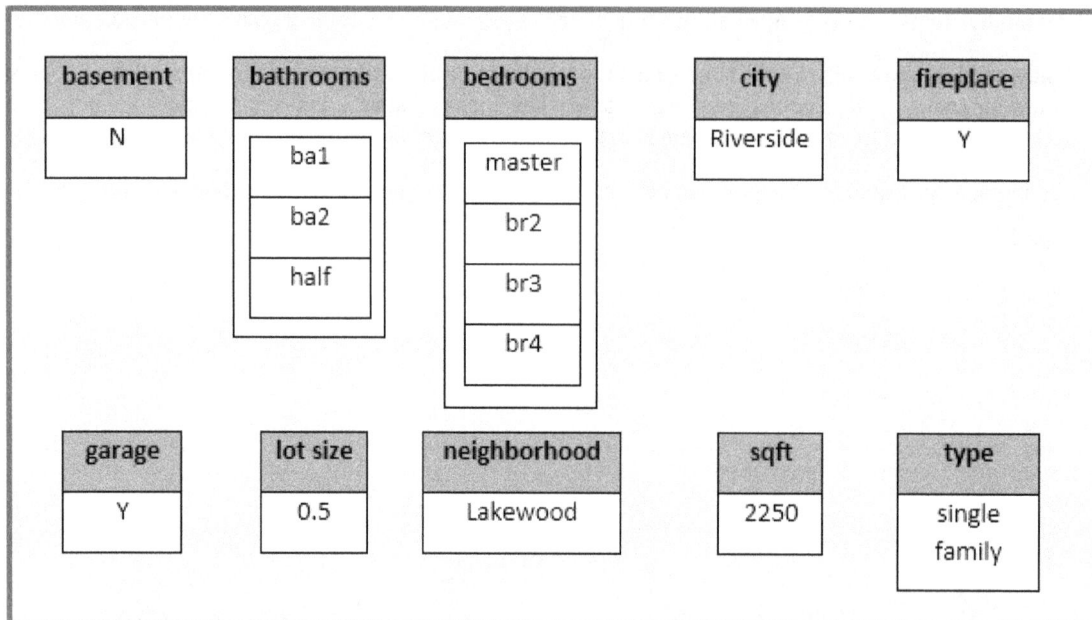

Namespaces

The concept of namespaces is somewhat abstract to those of us who weren't trained as programmers. A quick internet search returns lots of analogies to convey the concept of namespaces. For JMP, we think of namespaces in terms of a whiteboard. The whiteboard itself is representative of a single instance of JMP. Imagine that the whiteboard is divided into panes, like a window. Each pane is a namespace where all the JSL variables you have defined, along with their current values, are listed. When JMP is closed, all of the defined JSL variables are destroyed, regardless of the namespace where they are defined. The white board is wiped clean.

> What does scope mean? A scope gives context so that JMP knows where to find the definition of a name. You can specify that a JSL variable is defined in a specific namespace. You can also specify a data table as a scope so that JMP looks in the proper table for a column.

In JMP, there are a few types of namespaces. Here are the two most common:

- *Global* – Up to this point, our example scripts have created JSL variables in what's known as the global namespace. The global namespace is the default namespace and spans the current instance of JMP. This means that when you define variable x in one script, that variable and its value is known to any other script that you run in that instance of JMP. You know you are using the global namespace when you have done nothing to specify that the JSL variables are limited in scope, or you have used the **As Global()** function or double colon (**::**) scoping operator in front of your JSL variable names. JSL variables that are defined in the global namespace are referred to as global variables.

- *Here* – The Here namespace spans the current Script window. You turn on the Here namespace by placing **Names Default To Here(1);** at the beginning of your script. You've probably noticed this at the beginning of the examples in the Scripting Index. JSL variables defined in the Here namespace are not available to other Script windows in the same instance of JMP. This means that variable x in one Script window can have a value of 5, while the variable x defined in a different script with the Here namespace turned on can have a value of 10. The two variables do not affect one another. With the Here namespace, there is no special scoping required. When you turn on the option at the top of the script, JMP looks for the value in the Here namespace only—unless you have specified a different scope. For example, if you use double colons in front of a variable, JMP looks in the global namespace for that variable definition, even though you have the Here namespace specified at the top of the script. This means that you can use JSL variables defined in either namespace in the same script, as long as you properly scope the global variables.

Let's look at an example. In the following script, **var1** is defined in the global namespace. Even without looking at the results in the embedded log, you know this because no scoping operators are used and the Here namespace is not specified at the top of the script.

Figure 4.6 Global Namespace

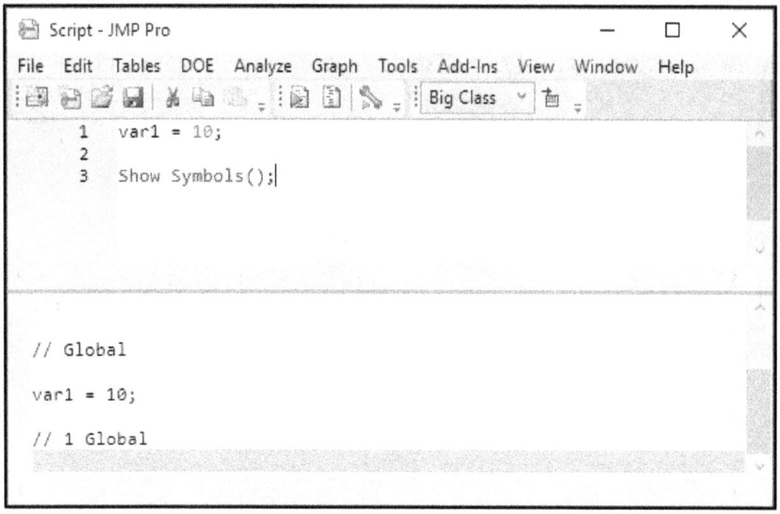

```
Script - JMP Pro                                —    □    ×
File  Edit  Tables  DOE  Analyze  Graph  Tools  Add-Ins  View  Window  Help

  1    var1 = 10;
  2
  3    Show Symbols();


// Global

var1 = 10;

// 1 Global
```

Show Symbols() presents the current value of all JSL variables known to the Script window in the log, separated by the namespace in which the variables are defined.

Now, in a second Script window, we specify to use the Here namespace and define a variable with the same name as our **var1** global variable, but with a different value.

On line 4, **var2** is defined in the global namespace using the double colon scoping operator with a string value.

Finally, the variable **var3** is defined by adding the values of the **var1** global variable to the **var1** variable defined in the Here namespace.

Figure 4.7 Here and Global Namespaces

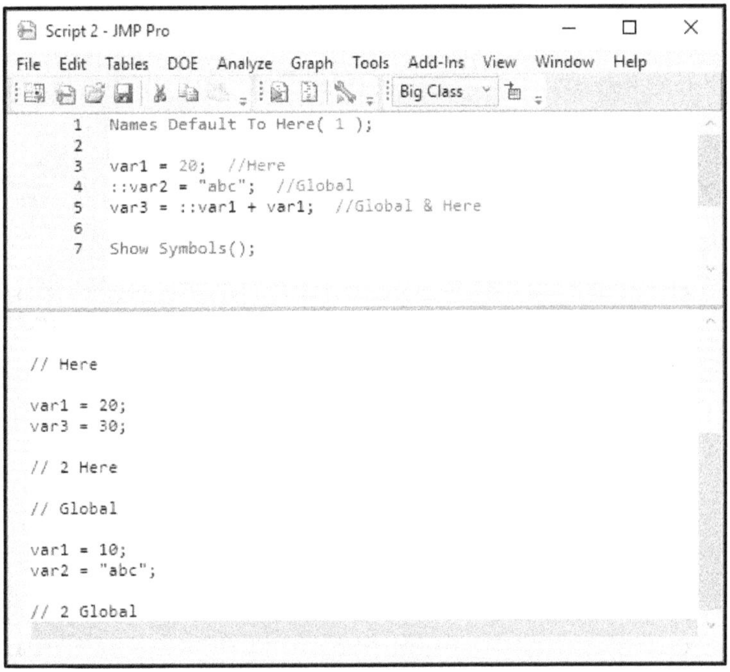

```
Script 2 - JMP Pro                          —    □    ×

File  Edit  Tables  DOE  Analyze  Graph  Tools  Add-Ins  View  Window  Help

    1    Names Default To Here( 1 );
    2
    3    var1 = 20;  //Here
    4    ::var2 = "abc";  //Global
    5    var3 = ::var1 + var1;  //Global & Here
    6
    7    Show Symbols();


// Here

var1 = 20;
var3 = 30;

// 2 Here

// Global

var1 = 10;
var2 = "abc";

// 2 Global
```

As you review the log, notice that there are now two variables defined in the Here namespace and two variables defined in the global namespace.

Now, let's run the **Show Symbols();** in the first script again. Notice that the new global variable is shown, but the variables that were defined in the Here namespace of the second script are not shown. This is because the variables defined in the Here namespace of the second script are known only by the second script.

Figure 4.8 Show Symbols() in the First Script Window

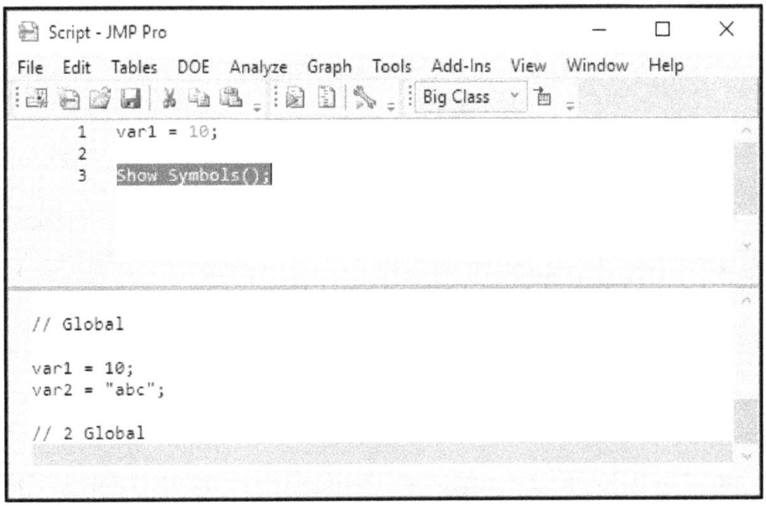

```
Script - JMP Pro                            —    □    ×

File  Edit  Tables  DOE  Analyze  Graph  Tools  Add-Ins  View  Window  Help

    1    var1 = 10;
    2
    3    Show Symbols();


// Global

var1 = 10;
var2 = "abc";

// 2 Global
```

Just to mix things up a bit, let's open a third Script window and use the Here namespace. Again, we define a variable named **var1**, which is the same name as a global variable and one that was defined in the second script's Here namespace.

As you review the results in the log, notice that the script only knows about the **var1** variable defined in the current Here namespace and the variables defined in the global namespace. None of the JSL variables defined in the Here namespace of the second script are known to any other Script window. The JSL variables defined in the global namespace are known by all of the Script windows.

Figure 4.9 Show Symbols() in a Third Script Window

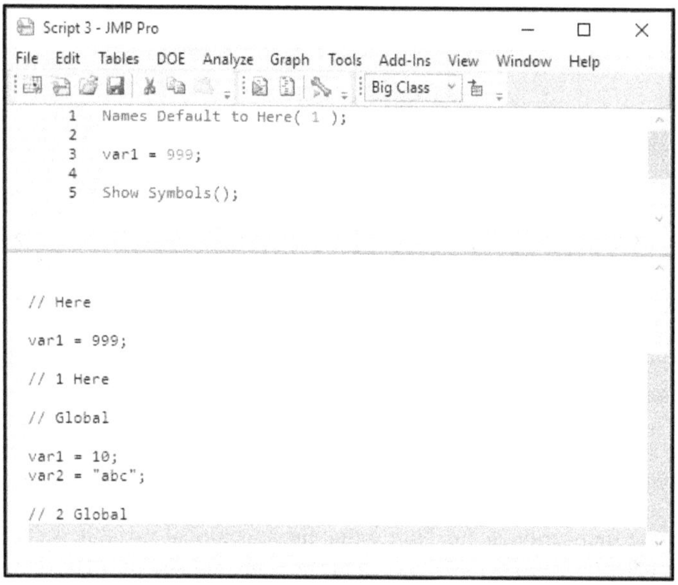

```
Script 3 - JMP Pro                                    —   □   ×

File  Edit  Tables  DOE  Analyze  Graph  Tools  Add-Ins  View  Window  Help

         Big Class

  1     Names Default to Here( 1 );
  2
  3     var1 = 999;
  4
  5     Show Symbols();



// Here

var1 = 999;

// 1 Here

// Global

var1 = 10;
var2 = "abc";

// 2 Global
```

Name Resolution

What is meant by the phrase *name resolution*? As you might guess, in the context of programming, it is the association or linking of a name to what it represents. What is a name? In JMP, a name is simply what you call something, whether it be a column, data table reference, report, string, number, function, expression, and so on.

There are some rules that must be followed when assigning a name. The complete list is included in the "Names" section of the "JSL Building Blocks" chapter in the *Scripting Guide*. However, the main thing to know is that names start with an alphabetic character or underscore. After the initial character, the name can include most characters that you would expect, such as alphabetic characters, numbers, spaces, and some special characters.

> Though you can use many different types of characters in a name, we recommend using only alphanumeric characters and underscores. Most importantly, names should make sense and work for your programming style.

After you have a name assigned, JMP needs to be able to resolve that name to what it represents. This is where proper scoping comes in. Scoping is simply a way to tell JMP where to find a name with its defined value. For example, you might want to tell JMP to look for the name in the global or Here namespace or as a data table column.

As we discussed previously, if the script has **Names Default To Here(1);** at the top, JMP tries to resolve any unscoped names in the Here namespace. If the script does not have **Names Default to Here()** turned on, or if the name is preceded by the double colon scoping operator, then JMP looks up the name in the global namespace. If the name is not found, then an error is returned.

There is a hierarchy that JMP uses to resolve names. We recommend that you review the "Rules for Resolving Names" section in the "JSL Building Blocks" chapter of the *Scripting Guide* for a full explanation.

Column Name Resolution

Proper scoping of column names is quite important so that JMP knows that the name is a column and also in which data table to find that column. We have found that this is one area that many scripters struggle with.

The following bullets identify two methods for ensuring that a name is resolved to the correct column. These methods have different return values, which is an important consideration when writing your script.

- **As Column():** A scoping function that returns a reference to a column in the specified data table on the current row. If the current row is not set, then a missing value is returned. This is because the current row in JMP is always zero unless specified otherwise.

  As noted in the JSL Syntax Reference, the following are equivalent syntax:

  ```
  dt:name
  As Column(dt, "name")
  ```

  Uses: As Column() and its operator equivalent are best used in messages and functions that control the current row. It is useful when a value from the column should be referenced and you have a string variable containing the column name. Some examples are **Select Where()**, formulas, and **For Each Row()**, because each evaluate on every row of the data table.

- **Column():** A function that returns a reference to a column in the specified data table as a whole unit, in its entirety. The **Column()** function is quite flexible because it can be used to reference the column as a unit or be subscripted to reference a value in a column. Because of this flexibility, you might find that this is your preferred function for referencing data table columns. The syntax for each is as follows:

  ```
  //Returns a reference to the entire column
  Column( dt, "name" )
  //Returns a reference to the value in the column on row i
  Column( dt, "name" )[i]
  ```

  Uses: The **Column()** function is commonly used where entire columns are referenced or consumed, such as when sending messages to the column or in platform calls. However, it is useful with a row subscript in order to return a single value from the specified row. For example, suppose you are using a **For()** loop to loop through all the rows of a data table. Because a **For()** loop does not control the current row, you could use the **Column()** function with the increment variable specified for the row number. If using it in **Select Where()**, formulas, or **For Each**

Row(), you can specify a row subscript using the **Row()** function, which references the current row, whatever that might be at that time.

```
//Returns a reference to the value in the column on the current row
Column( dt, "name" )[Row()]
```

More information about **For()** loops can be found in the "Looping" section of this chapter.

> The data table reference is technically optional for both the **As Column()** and **Column()** functions. However, it is recommended as a good scripting habit to prevent unexpected results.

Both the **As Column()** and **Column()** functions are flexible in the arguments that they accept:

- The actual column name as a string (in double quotation marks):
  ```
  As Column( dt, "age" );
  Column( dt, "age" );
  ```

- The column name stored as a string in a JSL variable:
  ```
  var = "age";
  As Column( dt, var );
  Column( dt, var );
  ```

- The column by index:
  ```
  As Column( dt, 2 );
  Column( dt, 2 );
  ```

- The column by index stored as a JSL numeric variable:
  ```
  n = 2;
  As Column( dt, n );
  Column( dt, n );
  ```

Consider the example in Figure 4.9. As described earlier in this section, notice that the **As Column()** scoping methods return missing values because JMP is looking for the value in the Age column on the current row, which is zero. Also notice that the **Column()** function returns a reference to the column as a whole, except when it is subscripted.

Figure 4.10 Result of As Column() and Column()

Now let's look at what happens when we change the context by sending column messages. Either method for referencing columns can be used for sending messages to the column. For example, suppose you wanted to change the modeling type of a column or add a column property.

```
/* Change the modeling type to ordinal using a scoping operator */
dt:age << Set Modeling Type( "Ordinal" );

/* Add a column property using the Column() function to reference the column */
Column(dt, "age") << Set Property( "Row Order Levels", 1 );
```

Figure 4.11 Before

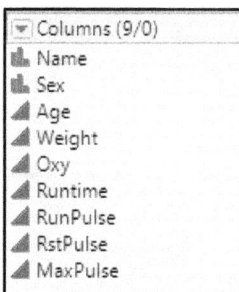

Figure 4.12 After

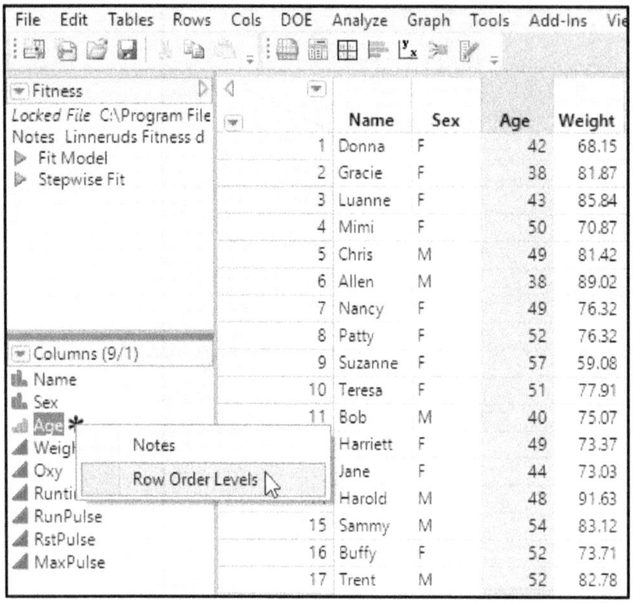

Notice in Figure 4.12 that the modeling type of the Age column is changed to Ordinal, and the Row Order Levels column property has been added. In this context, JMP is able to accept either method for referencing the column, because the message is valid for the column.

Name()

When saving a script from JMP, you might have seen a column name wrapped in a **Name()** function, also known as the Name parser. This happens when the column name contains characters that do not follow JMP rules for column names. For example, a column name that has a forward slash in the name would be **Name("Height/Weight")**. See the **Name()** function in the Scripting Index for details about valid characters for use in column names.

The **Name()** function is quite inflexible because the only acceptable argument is a string containing the actual column name. For this reason, we recommend that you use either **As Column()** or **Column()** for referencing columns.

Conditional Logic

The ability to control your script based upon specific conditions is powerful. You might want certain steps to happen based upon an expected value, but different steps to happen if a different value is encountered.

JMP offers several built-in functions to help you write a script that conditionally directs the next action. Here we discuss the **If()**, **Match()**, and **Choose()** functions, which we think you will find quite useful.

If()

The **If()** function is probably the most commonly used conditional function. It is easy to understand and read in a script. In addition, it enables you to make a variety of comparisons.

The generic syntax is as follows. Notice that each argument is separated by a comma.

```
If( condition, then, else );
```

Here is a simple equality example:

```
If(
    //Condition
    :Response == "Y"
,
    //Then - executes if the condition is true
    string = "Customer wants dessert."
,
    //Else - executes if the condition is false
    string = "Customer does not want dessert."
);
```

The preceding example specified only one condition: Response is equal to "Y". But you can specify multiple conditions, each with its own individual actions. In addition, the **If()** function's flexibility enables you to specify expressions that make any comparison that would return a zero or nonzero result. In this case, zero is considered not true and any nonzero result would be considered true. This means that you can do things such as check for a value in a list, make numeric comparisons, and even specify multiple criteria. The following example checks multiple conditions and uses multiple comparisons:

```
If(
    //Condition 1
    :Response == "Y" & :Age < 5
,
    //Then 1
    :Promo = "Free"
,
    //Condition 2
    :Response == "Y" & (5 <= :Age <= 12 | :Age >= 60)
,
    //Then 2
    :Promo = "$1 off"
);
```

But what if you want more than one thing to happen when a condition is met? No problem! Simply use semicolons between the *then* statements. To make the example more clear, we have placed the commas separating each of the arguments for the **If()** function on their own lines.

```
If(
    Is Missing( :Topping ), //Condition 1
        :Order = "Customer does not want ice cream." //Then
,
    :Topping == 0, //Condition 2
        :Order = "Plain ice cream."; //Then Stmt 1
        :Allergen = "M"; //Then Stmt 2
,
    :Topping == 1, //Condition 3
        :Order = "Ice cream with hot fudge sauce."; //Then Stmt 1
        :Allergen = "M"; //Stmt 2
,
    :Topping == 2, //Condition 4
        :Order = "Ice cream with caramel sauce."; //Then Stmt 1
        :Allergen = "M/S"; //Then Stmt 2
```

```
    '
        :Topping == 3, //Condition 5
            :Order = "Ice cream with fresh strawberries."; //Then Stmt 1
            :Allergen = "M"; //Then Stmt 2
    '
        //Else
        :Order = "Ice cream with EVERYTHING!"; //Else Stmt 1
        :Allergen = "M/S/P"; //Else Stmt 2
);
```

Match()

You might be familiar with **Match()** as a handy interactive function used in a formula to capture all the unique values in the column automatically. An example of how to do this can be found in the "Examples and Tutorials" section of the "Formula Editor" chapter in the *Using JMP* book.

But **Match()** can also be used in a script. Though **Match()** is only useful for equality comparisons, a benefit is that the condition is not written for each comparison. This means that the code is a little more succinct than for an **If()** when used outside the context of a formula.

The following is a simple example that demonstrates recoding values in a column using **Match()**.

```
/* Open a sample data table */
dt = Open( "$SAMPLE_DATA\Popcorn Trials.jmp" );

/* Recode oil amt values */
For Each Row(
    Match( :oil amt,
        "little" //Value 1
    '
            :oil amt = "1 tsp" //Then 1
    '
        "lots" //Value 2
    '
            :oil amt = "4 Tbsp" //Then 2
    )
);
```

The following example is an adaptation of the last **If()** example from the previous section using **Match()** instead. When you only have equality comparisons, you might find that you prefer using **Match()** because you only have to enter the value being compared instead of the entire equality condition.

```
Match( :Topping,
    ., //Value 1
        :Order = "Customer does not want ice cream." //Then
    '
    0, //Value 2
        :Order = "Plain ice cream."; //Then Stmt 1
        :Allergen = "M"; //Then Stmt 2
    '
    1, //Value 3
        :Order = "Ice cream with hot fudge sauce."; //Then Stmt 1
        :Allergen = "M"; //Stmt 2
    '
    2, //Value 4
        :Order = "Ice cream with caramel sauce."; //Then Stmt 1
        :Allergen = "M/S"; //Then Stmt 2
```

```
        3, //Value 5
            :Order = "Ice cream with fresh strawberries."; //Then Stmt 1
            :Allergen = "M"; //Then Stmt 2

        //Else
        :Order = "Ice cream with EVERYTHING!"; //Else Stmt 1
        :Allergen = "M/S/P"; //Else Stmt 2
    );
```

Choose()

The **Choose()** function might be a little less commonly used, but it is particularly convenient when you are unloading values from a dialog. With **Choose()**, the first expression should evaluate to an index. It is this index that is used to determine which supplied result value is returned.

To see what we mean, let's go through an example. Suppose you wanted to query your users to select their preferred size of vehicles. You could build a dialog that presents a question, as shown in the following code:

```
nw = New Window( "Car Preferences",
    <<Modal,
    <<Return Result,
    Outline Box( "What size vehicle do you prefer?",
        cat = Radio Box( {"Small", "Midsize", "SUV", "Sporty"} )
    )
);
```

When users make their selections, the result returned to **nw** will be something like the following:

```
nw = {cat = 4, Button(1)};
```

In this case, the value selected in the **Radio Box** was **"Sporty"**. Now you can use the return value, which represents an index, in your **Choose()** function.

```
Print(
    "The customer might like a " ||
    Choose( nw["cat"], //Resolves to 4
        "Honda Civic",       //1st result
        "Toyota Camry",      //2nd result
        "Chevrolet Tahoe",   //3rd result
        "Ford Mustang"       //4th result
    )
);
```

That means that the value provided to the **Choose()** function by **nw["cat"]** was a 4, which indicates that the fourth result value was returned by **Choose()**. Thus, the following was printed in the log:

```
"The customer might like a Ford Mustang"
```

Further details and examples of **If()**, **Match()**, and **Choose()** can be found in the "Conditional Functions" section of the "JSL Building Blocks" chapter in the *Scripting Guide*.

Looping

Looping in JMP refers to repeatedly executing a sequence of JSL code until some condition is met. There are several types of loops, but each share this same overall purpose. You can use loops in JMP to loop through lists, columns, and rows; to repeat processing a specific number of times; or to repeat processing until a condition is encountered.

> A bit of warning at the start: Before you run any type of loop, we suggest that you save your work. It is pretty easy to make a mistake and find that JMP is in an infinite loop. Trust us. Save your work first.

For()

The **For()** loop is flexible and probably the easier to understand of the methods in JMP for looping. **For()** loops enable you to continually process a set of JSL code until a specified condition is met. The generic syntax for a **For()** loop is as follows:

```
For( start, whileExpr, increment, script );
```

start – The starting value of the increment variable. This is evaluated only at the time the **For()** loop begins.

whileExpr – The condition that specifies how long to continue the processing. This condition is checked at the beginning (top) of each loop (iteration).

increment – The amount to increase or decrease the increment variable for each iteration of the loop. This occurs at the bottom of each iteration of the loop after the script has been executed.

script – The JSL code that should be processed repeatedly.

There are any number of reasons why you might need to use a **For()** loop. The following is an example that demonstrates how to loop through a list of continuous columns to analyze.

```
/* Open a sample data table */
dt = Open( "$SAMPLE_DATA\Big Class.jmp" );

/* Extract a list of the continuous columns in the table */
colList = dt << Get Column Names( Continuous, String );

/* Loop through the list and create a Oneway analysis of each */
For( i = 1, i <= N Items( colList ), i++,
    dt << Oneway(
            Y( Column( dt, colList[i] ) ),
            X( :age ),
            Means( 1 ),
            Mean Diamonds( 1 )
    )
);
```

There are many more examples of looping in Section 2 of this book.

For Each Row()

For Each Row() loops through every row of a data table. The current data table is used, unless the optional data table reference is specified, which we do recommend doing. And as we mentioned earlier, **For Each Row()** controls the current row during execution. So there is no need for row subscripting.

The following example demonstrates how to use **For Each Row()** to assign a value to a column without using a formula.

```
/* Open a sample data table */
dt = Open( "$SAMPLE_DATA\Travel Costs.jmp" );

/* Create a new column to store the Month */
dt << New Column( "Month", Numeric, Nominal );

/* Loop though each row and set the value to the month
   of the Departure Date */
For Each Row( dt,
    dt:Month = Month( :Departure Date )
);
```

While()

The **While()** loop allows the loop to continue until the condition returns 0, or false. Especially for the new scripter, we find that **While()** loops can be a little more challenging to grasp because you can easily end up in an infinite loop.

Suppose you wanted to know the corresponding degrees in Fahrenheit for every degree Celsius from 0 to 100. The following example uses the **While()** loop to calculate the degrees in Fahrenheit and print the values to the log.

```
/* Initial value in Celsius */
c = 0;

/* Continue until c equals 100 */
While( c <= 100,
    f = c * 9 / 5 + 32;
    Print(
        Char( c ) || " degrees Celsius = " ||
        Char( f ) || " degrees Fahrenheit" );
    c++;
);
```

Always save everything you've worked on before trying your loop the first time. This will save you from some really bad headaches! Wait... did we say that before? Yes, but we feel that strongly about it!

Break() and Continue()

At times, you might need to escape a loop iteration or get out of the loop entirely. The **Break()** and **Continue()** functions are just for these situations.

Break() – Breaks out of the loop and continues with the next JSL statement after the closing parenthesis of the current loop.

Continue() – Breaks out of the current iteration of the loop and returns control back to the top of the loop for the next iteration.

Both **Break()** and **Continue()** work in **For()**, **For Each Row()** and **While()** loops.

Summary

This chapter provides basic programming fundamentals. Familiarizing yourself with these concepts will help you to better understand the solutions demonstrated in Section 2 of this book.

Next, let's look at some helpful resources and how to handle unexpected situations.

Chapter 5: Close Your Eyes and Jump!

Overview

You are almost ready to begin your journey of scripting on your own. You have learned how to give your scripting project a kick-start by letting JMP generate the initial script for you. You have learned how to put together various scripts that are generated by JMP. You have learned how to access the layers of a report. And you have learned some fundamentals of the JMP scripting language.

So what's left?

In this chapter, you will learn about the following:

- useful features of the Script Editor
- resources available at your fingertips
- what to do in times of trouble
- the JSL Debugger

The Script Editor

As mentioned in chapter 1, the Script window is the workhorse of scripting. This window is also known as the *Script Editor* or *JSL Editor*, and it is where you will primarily develop your scripting projects.

Essentially, the Script Editor is a simple text editor, but with some really cool features.   There are several ways to access the Script Editor:

- Click the **New Script** button on the toolbar.
- From the **File** menu, select **New ▶ Script**.
- Press the Ctrl+T keys.

In this section, we go over a few handy features, but a complete list of features can be found in the *Scripting Guide*. We also encourage you to review the preference settings available by going to **File ▶ Preferences ▶ Script Editor**. Here is an image of the Script Editor preferences with some of our favorite options already set.

Figure 5.1 Script Editor Preferences

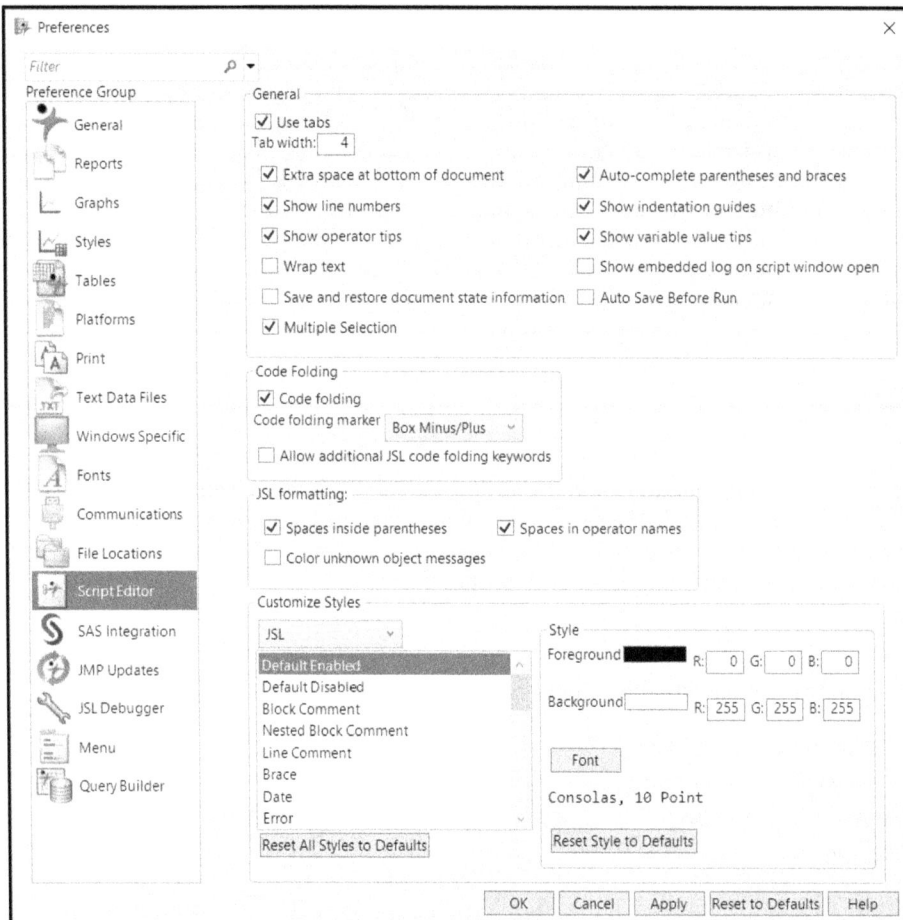

You can develop your script code in any text editor. But once you learn all the features of the JMP Script Editor, we doubt you will want to use anything else!

Useful Features of the Script Editor

So what's so special about the Script Editor? Over time, the Script Editor has become a very user-friendly and helpful tool. Some of its helpful features include the following:

- matching fences
- automatic formatting
- color coding
- line numbers
- tooltips

- embedded log
- code folding
- comment/uncomment block
- selective execution

Matching Fences

Because each opening parenthesis, curly brace, or square bracket needs a closing parenthesis, curly brace, or square bracket, the Script Editor offers highlighting so that you can quickly find their matches. This feature is very helpful when debugging your code.

Figure 5.2 Matching Parentheses

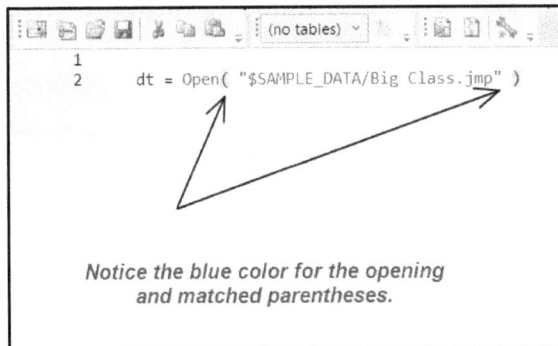

Notice the blue color for the opening
and matched parentheses.

Also, when you enter an opening parenthesis, curly brace, or square bracket, the Script Editor automatically enters the closing parenthesis, curly brace, or square bracket for you. If you enter the closing parenthesis, it overwrites the one JMP added for you.

> If you find this feature to be an annoyance, it can easily be disabled in the Script Editor Preference group. To access this setting, select **Preferences** from the **File** menu. Scroll down and click the **Script Editor** icon. Finally, deselect the **Auto-complete parentheses and braces** option.

Automatic Formatting

The Script Editor's automatic formatting makes your scripts more readable because it uses consistent spacing and indentions throughout the script.

You can instruct JMP to format your script for you by simply right-clicking anywhere in the Script Editor window and selecting **Reformat Script**. In addition, there is a **Reformat Script** toolbar button.

Figure 5.3 Before Reformatting

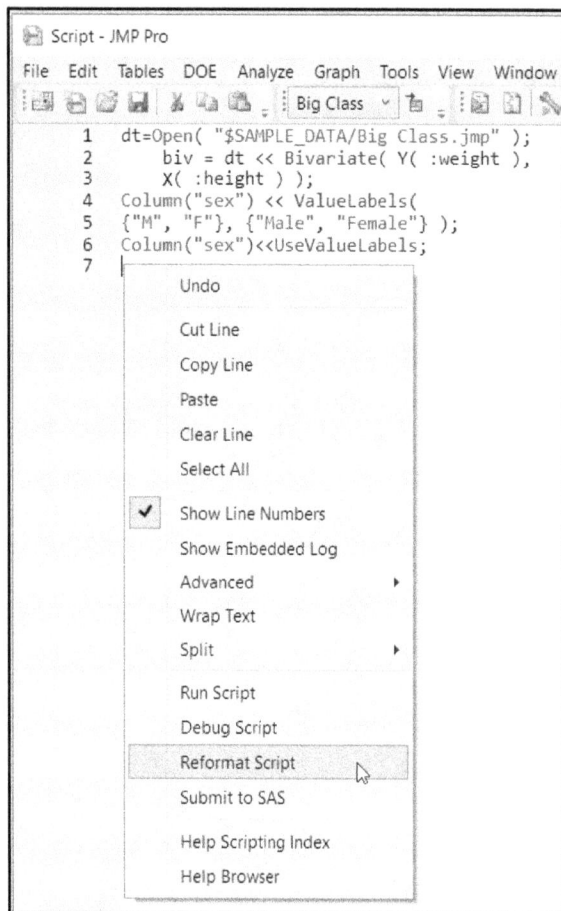

The reformatted script is shown in Figure 5.4.

Figure 5.4 After Reformatting

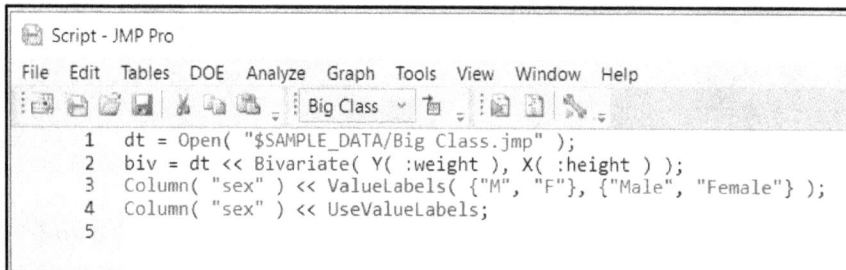

Color Coding

Color coding, also known as syntax highlighting, makes it easy to recognize comments (green), strings (dark magenta), numerics (teal), dates in ddMonyyyy format (green), JSL messages (dark blue), and JSL functions (medium blue) in the Script window. These are the default JSL colors, which can be changed along with the fonts used in the **Customize Styles** section of the Script Editor Preference group.

In addition to JSL styles, you can customize colors and fonts used for other languages that you might be coding with in the Script Editor, such as SAS Code, R, Matlab, Python, SQL and others.

Line Numbers

As mentioned briefly in chapter 2, we recommend that you turn on the **Show line numbers** option in the Script Editor preferences. Having the line numbers present is very helpful when debugging your script, because the line number where the error was encountered is often included in the messages printed in the log.

Tooltips

Tooltips are what you see when you hold your mouse pointer over a JSL function, message, or variable in the Script Editor. For JSL functions, the tooltip contains the syntax and a brief description. For messages, only a description of the message appears in the tooltip.

After you run your script, holding your mouse pointer over a JSL variable shows you the variable name and its current value. If you see only a JSL variable name in the tooltip, then the variable does not yet have a value.

Embedded Log

The Log window provides important details about executed scripts. Instead of a separate window, you can turn on an embedded log in your Script window. To do so, right-click inside the Script Editor and select **Show Embedded Log**. The Script window will be split into two sections. The top portion is your normal Script Editor. The bottom portion is the log where your return values and other messages will appear.

> If you like this feature, you can turn on the **Show embedded log on script window open** option in the Script Editor preferences. This preference is selected in Figure 5.1, where we show our favorite Script Editor preference settings.

Code Folding

If you are working on a long script that seems a bit unwieldy, use code folding markers to collapse and expand sections of code.

First, go to the Script Editor preferences (**File ▶ Preferences ▶ Script Editor**) and select the box beside **Code folding**, as shown in Figure 5.5.

Figure 5.5 Code Folding Preference

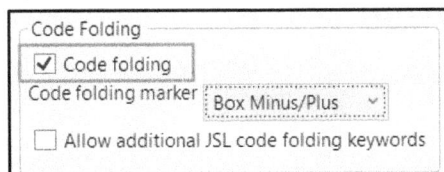

Code folding markers are added to the beginning and end of the functions and expressions, as shown in Figure 5.6. You can click the buttons to expand or collapse.

Figure 5.6 Script with Code Folding Markers Added

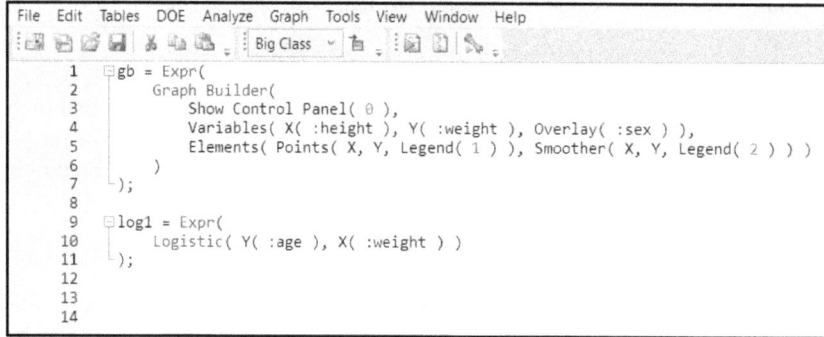

```
File  Edit  Tables  DOE  Analyze  Graph  Tools  View  Window  Help

 1   gb = Expr(
 2       Graph Builder(
 3           Show Control Panel( 0 ),
 4           Variables( X( :height ), Y( :weight ), Overlay( :sex ) ),
 5           Elements( Points( X, Y, Legend( 1 ) ), Smoother( X, Y, Legend( 2 ) ) )
 6       )
 7   );
 8
 9   log1 = Expr(
10       Logistic( Y( :age ), X( :weight ) )
11   );
12
13
14
```

Comment/Uncomment Block

To comment out a block of code, you would place the characters /* at the beginning of the section and */ at the end of the section to be commented out. An easy way to do this is to simply select the code, right-click inside the script, and select **Advanced ▶ Comment Block**. To uncomment the selected code, right-click inside the script, and select **Advanced ▶ Uncomment Block**. Please note that if you select a single line of code by clicking in the margin with the line numbers and then select **Advanced ▶ Comment Block,** you might generate the // symbol, which is used for commenting out single lines of code.

Selective Execution

There are a few ways to run only a portion of the code in your script. Here are some examples:

- Pressing the Enter key on a numeric keypad with no code selected executes only the code on the line where the cursor appears in the Script Editor. The line must contain a complete JSL statement. Otherwise, an error results.
- Selecting a section of code executes only the section of the script that is highlighted when you run the script.
  - To select multiple sections of code that are not connected, press the Ctrl key while selecting the desired sections of script code.
  - Pressing the Enter key on the numeric keypad also executes any selected sections of code.
- Selecting a single JSL variable prints the value to the log when the script is run.

Resources Available at Your Fingertips

As you begin your scripting projects, you might hit a roadblock or two. You know what you want JMP to do, but where do you go to find available message names or correct syntax if JMP didn't generate it for you?

There are several resources available to you that are filled with helpful information if you know how to access them.

Scripting Index

The Scripting Index is probably *the most useful tool* for scripters of all experience levels. Here you can find syntax, messages for objects, links to JMP Help, and script examples that you can run directly from the Scripting Index interface.

From within JMP, click the **Help** menu and select **Scripting Index**. The Scripting Index includes a composite index, **All Categories**, as well as a filter to access three category indexes to help you find available functions and lists of messages that are appropriate for the object you are working with. You can use the search option to filter results for **All Categories**, or for a narrower range by selecting **Functions**, **Objects**, or **Display Boxes**.

Figure 5.7 Scripting Indexes

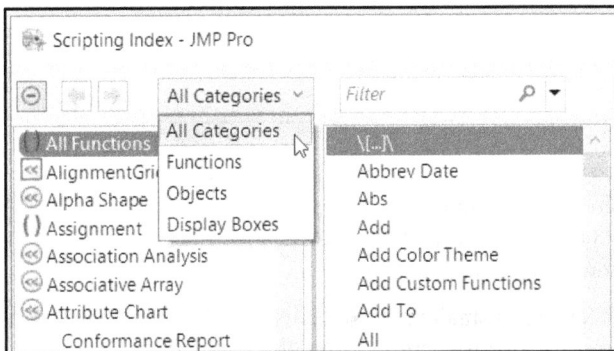

> If you have a question about a specific function while in a Script window, you can open the Scripting Index to the entry for the corresponding function. In the Script Editor window, do one of the following:
>
> - Right-click a function name and select **Help Scripting Index**.
> - Press the Alt key and double-click a function name.

- The **Functions** index contains a list of JSL commands and functions with the proper syntax, including arguments. This is a great place to look, because most items include sample scripts, which can be run independently so that you can see the results immediately.
- The **Objects** index contains a list of objects and the messages that are available for each object. For example, suppose you wanted to add a column to a data table. From this index, you can click **Data Table Cols** under **Data Table** on the left and then scroll through the list of possibilities on the right. Approximately halfway through the list, you will find **New Column**. Selecting **New Column** shows the syntax, as well as an example script in the right panel. Clicking the down arrow beside Example 1 shows that a second example script is available. In addition, the **See Also** button directs you to similar topics in the Scripting Index, and the **Topic Help** button opens a window into **JMP Help** for more information for the **New Column** message.

Figure 5.8 Objects Scripting Index Example

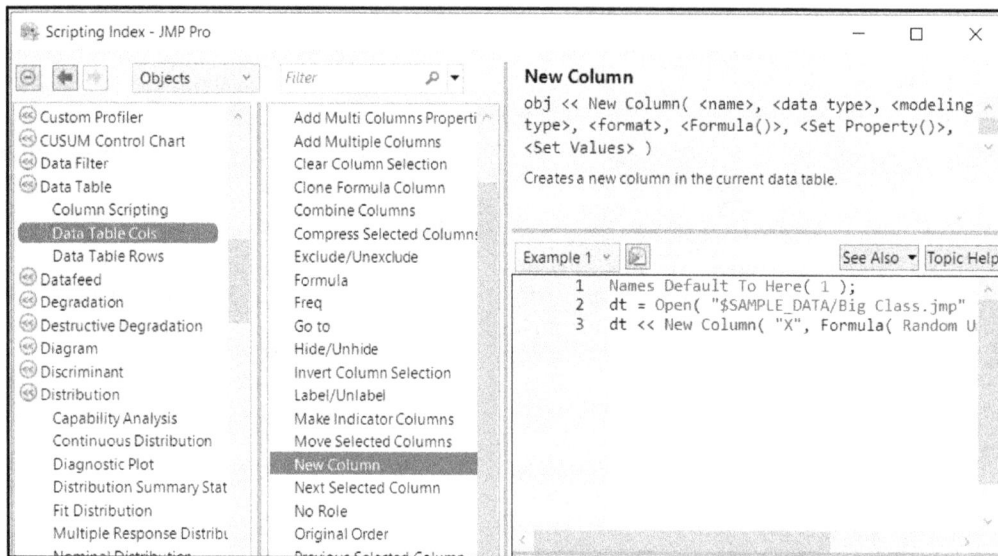

- The **Display Boxes** index is similar to the **Objects** index. As you read in chapter 3, this index contains a list of display boxes and the corresponding messages that are available for each. Of course, the syntax, description, and example scripts are also shown on the right.

- The Scripting Index also has the following built-in features:

  ○ a toggle button for large mode (default) and small mode ❶ : Large mode is the typical wide screen view of the Scripting Index. For a narrow presentation of the window, toggle the button to small mode.

  ○ back and forward buttons ❷: These buttons enable you to go back and forth to the previous window contents of the Scripting Index.

  ○ a **See Also** button ❸: Clicking this button shows a drop-down menu listing related topics you can explore by selecting.

  ○ a **Topic Help** button ❹: Selecting this button opens a window in the JMP Syntax Reference and provides more information about the topic.

Figure 5.9 Scripting Index Buttons

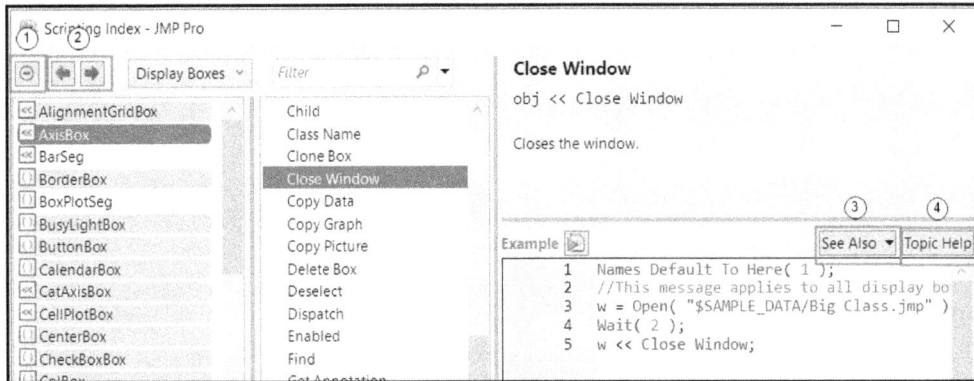

Show Properties

As we discussed in chapter 3, you can run a **Show Properties** command with the object you are working with. This command prints to the log a list of all messages that are appropriate for that particular object. Below is the basic syntax. Notice that the object (or a reference to the object) you are working with is used as the argument:

```
Show Properties( object );
```

Documentation

Included with your JMP installation are PDF books that provide in-depth information about using JMP for statistical analyses, as well as, for programmatic purposes. These books are accessed from the main menu by selecting **Help ▶ Books**. Of interest to the JMP scripter are the following book guides in the menu:

- *Scripting Guide* – The *Scripting Guide* is full of information and is a good resource for various topics regarding JMP scripting. We think that it is a great reference manual for scripters who have a little prior experience. And, as a PDF document, it can be searched very easily for topics of interest.
- *JSL Syntax Reference* – The *JSL Syntax Reference* provides important details about syntax, arguments, and return values for JSL functions and messages.

JMP User Community

The JMP website hosts a User Community at https://community.jmp.com/ where you can find a discussion forum, file exchange, and blogs on all subjects related to JMP.

Discussions

In this online forum, JMP users help each other by answering questions, offering guidance, and sharing a wealth of knowledge about the software. And yes, you will find many scripting topics in this forum. You can search through past questions and answers to find possible solutions to your issue. If you do not find a solution, you can join the forum and post your question.

File Exchange

The File Exchange offers a wealth of add-ins, scripts, and sample data that other JMP users have shared. If there is a particular problem that you are trying to address, or if you have written a script that you want to share, you might want to check out this site.

JSL Cookbook

A new addition to the JMP User Community is the JSL Cookbook. Here you will find a knowledge base of JSL code snippets written by JSL experts that demonstrate how to accomplish specific tasks. The content of the JSL Cookbook is growing, so be sure to check it out often!

JMP Blogs

The blog section of the JMP User Community contains group blogs and individual blogs by the JMP thought leaders on a variety of topics, including scripting.

- *JMP Blog* – A blog of various broad topics such as statistics, data visualization, design of experiments, and so on.
- *JMPer Cable* – A blog that is more technical in nature and is full of how-tos and tips on using JMP.

Webcasts

On the JMP website, under the **Events** topic, are live and on-demand webcasts from various series. Here you can find topics designed to enhance your JMP skills. Of special interest to scripters is the **Automating Analyses and Reporting Using JMP Scripts** on-demand webcast from the **Mastering JMP** series.

Training and Mentoring Services

A team of JMP technical experts offer help on all topics related to JMP, including JSL. If you need assistance creating a script for a project or need help with revising or troubleshooting a complex application, JMP Software Mentoring Services can provide technical expertise for a fee.

Publications

A number of SAS Press books authored by JMP users are available on a variety of topics, including scripting. Please visit the SAS Press website, https://support.sas.com/en/books.html, to find the latest books by JMP users available as ebooks and hard copy.

What to Do in Times of Trouble

We have all experienced it: After executing a script, you might find yourself facing unexpected results or error messages in the log. What went wrong and, more importantly, how do you fix it?

Although it is impossible to give you a list of all the possible error messages and what to do about each, we can offer some advice based upon years of helping people with their scripting questions.

Common Issues

First, let's go over some common issues. These are issues that seem to stand out as being common among scripters, regardless of experience level.

- common error messages
- problems with identifying the current data table
- timing issues with uncompleted tasks

Common Error Messages

Below we address some of the more common error messages and things to check in your code to address the issue. Many of these can be resolved by ensuring that proper scoping is used. For that reason, we again recommend that you review the "Rules for Name Resolution" section of the "JSL Building Blocks" chapter in the *Scripting Guide*.

Name Unresolved

You might see the "Name Unresolved" error in your log. This error means that JMP could not find the reference or resolve the name. Here are three cases that might generate this message:

- A message is being sent to a JSL variable before it is defined. Sometimes this happens when you are writing code but forget to execute the line that defined the JSL variable. In this case, make sure the definition of the variable is established before sending messages to the variable.

This example program creates a window that queries the user about his favorite flower:

```
New Window( "Favorite Flower",
      <<Modal,
      V List Box(
            Text Box( "Select your favorite flower and click OK:" ),
            cb = Check Box( flowerList ),
            Button Box( "OK", flrSel = cb << get selected )
      )
);

flowerList = {"rose", "sunflower", "hydrangea", "daisy"};
```

However, executing the code generates this error:

```
Name Unresolved: flowerList in access or evaluation of 'flowerList' ,
flowerList/*###*/

In the following script, error marked by /*###*/
New Window( "Favorite Flower",
      <<Modal,
      V List Box(
            Text Box( "Select your favorite flower and click OK:" ),
            cb = Check Box( flowerList/*###*/ ),
            Button Box( "OK", flrSel = cb << get selected )
      )
);
flowerList = {"rose", "sunflower", "hydrangea", "daisy"};
```

> The location of the error in the code is marked by the placement of /*####*/ in the log. In a long script, it is easy to find the point of error by searching for these symbols.

The problem is that the variable, flowerList, needs to be defined *before* it is used by the **New Window()** function. Moving the variable definition prior to the **New Window()** function solves the problem.

```
flowerList = {"rose", "sunflower", "hydrangea", "daisy"};

New Window( "Favorite Flower",
        <<Modal,
        V List Box(
                Text Box( "Select your favorite flower and click OK:" ),
                cb = Check Box( flowerList ),
                Button Box( "OK", flrSel = cb << get selected )
        )
);
```

- The correct data table is not being accessed. If you have more than one data table open during the script execution, check to determine whether your script is acting on the current data table instead of the one you intended. See the next section, "Problems with Identifying the Current Data Table," for further details about ensuring that your script uses the intended data table.
- A custom function call is misspelled. Good coding practice dictates that functions are defined in the beginning of a program. Because of this, it is easy to accidentally misspell the function name when it is used later in the script.

The following example uses a custom function to count words in a string:

```
myString = "The weather today in Colorado is cold, dry, windy, and sunny";

CountWords = Function( {s},
        N Items( Words( s, " " ) )
);

CountWord( myString );
```

But if you run this code, the "Name Unresolved" error is written to the log:

```
/*:

Name Unresolved: CountWord in access or evaluation of 'CountWord' , CountWord(
myString ) /*###*/

In the following script, error marked by /*###*/
myString = "The weather today in Colorado is cold, dry, windy, and sunny";
CountWords = Function( {s},
      N Items( Words( s, " " ) )
);
CountWord( myString ) /*###*/;
```

Calling the custom function by the proper name allows the script to execute properly.

```
CountWords( myString );
```

> See the "Using JSL Variables in Formulas" section of this chapter for another example of the "Name Unresolved" error.

Send Expects Scriptable Object

This error indicates that JMP cannot find your reference. Make sure you have defined the object and that the name matches the reference.

If the object was closed and then referenced again later, the error will appear. For example, suppose you close a data table that had a Distribution open. When the table is closed, the report will also be closed. Any references to that Distribution after that point will return this error.

```
dt = Open( "$SAMPLE_DATA/big class.jmp" );

dist = dt << Distribution(
        Continuous Distribution( Column( :weight ) ),
        Nominal Distribution( Column( :age ) )
);

Close( dt, no save );

Report( dist )["Summary Statistics"] << Make into data table;
```

Executing the script, as is, creates this error in the log window:

```
Send Expects Scriptable Object in access or evaluation of 'Send' , Report(
dist )["Summary Statistics"] <<  /*###*/Make into data table/*###*/

In the following script, error marked by /*###*/
dt = Open( "$SAMPLE_DATA/big class.jmp" );
dist = dt << Distribution(
        Continuous Distribution( Column( :weight ) ),
        Nominal Distribution( Column( :age ) )
);
Close( dt, no save );
Report( dist )["Summary Statistics"] <<  /*###*/Make into data table/*###*/;
{}
```

When the data table closed, so did its dependent Distribution report. The solution is to close the data table after you are finished with any tasks involving the distribution report:

```
dt = Open( "$SAMPLE_DATA/big class.jmp" );

dist = dt << Distribution(
   Continuous Distribution( Column( :weight ) ),
   Nominal Distribution( Column( :age ) )
);

Report( dist )["Summary Statistics"] << Make into data table;

Close( dt, no save );
```

Unexpected End of Input

This error is common, especially in longer and more complicated scripts with nested **For()** loops and complicated functions. Use the Script Editor feature to match fences as described earlier in this chapter. If using If-Then-Else functions, check the clauses to determine that each is appropriately delimited by a comma.

This code example uses nested **For()** loops to traverse a data table, and it uses a conditional If-Then statement to find missing values and replace each with a zero:

```
Current Data Table( dt );

For( i = 1, i <= N Col( dt ), i++,
    For( j = 1, j <= N Row( dt ), j++,
        If( Is Missing( Column( i )[j] , Column( i )[j] = 0 )

);
```

However, the processing that occurs before the execution step does not parse correctly and generates an error:

```
Unexpected end of input. Perhaps there is a missing "," or ")".
Trying to parse arguments of function "For".
Line 22 Column 3: );▶
```

The issue is that there are two unmatched parentheses. Matching fences helps to locate the missing parentheses. Here is the corrected script:

```
Current Data Table( dt );

For( i = 1, i <= N Col( dt ), i++,
    For( j = 1, j <= N Row( dt ), j++,
        If( Is Missing( Column( i )[j] ), Column( i )[j] = 0 )
    )
);
```

Deleted Object Reference

The deleted object reference error in the log is observed when running a script where an object has been created earlier but is no longer available when attempting to send messages to it.

An example is where a table is opened, a window with a platform analysis is created, and then the data table is closed, as shown in the following code. The problem is that the window containing the distribution analysis closes also when the table is closed. Therefore, attempting to send the **Append** message to the **New Window** reference, **nw**, results in the deleted object reference error.

```
dt = Open( "$SAMPLE_DATA\Big Class.jmp" );

nw = New Window( "My Graphs", dt << Run Script( "Distribution" ) );

Close( dt, No Save );

nw << Append( Outline Box( "Final Results:" ) );
```

```
/*:

deleted object reference: nw << Append(Outline Box("Final Results:")) in access or
evaluation of 'Glue' , dt = Open( "$SAMPLE_DATA\Big Class.jmp" ); /*###*/nw =
New Window( "My Graphs", dt << Run Script( "Distribution" ) ); /*###*/
Close( dt, No Save ); /*###*/nw << Append( Outline Box( "Final Results:" ) )
/*###*/;

In the following script, error marked by /*###*/
dt = Open( "$SAMPLE_DATA\Big Class.jmp" ); /*###*/nw =
New Window( "My Graphs", dt << Run Script( "Distribution" ) ); /*###*/
Close( dt, No Save ); /*###*/nw << Append( Outline Box( "Final Results:" ) )
/*###*/;
```

A simple fix for this issue would be to wait until you are finished with all operations involving the "My Graphs" window before closing the data table.

Subscript Range Error

This is a common error when issuing a subscript for a list member, a column value, or an associative array element. Check the subscript range for the object receiving the message, especially if the range is dynamically changing at run time. If the error is occurring in a **For()** loop, make sure that the **For()** loop while expression is not causing the loop to exceed the actual number of items in the list, column, or associative array.

This JSL code generates the error in the log. The while expression argument, **i <= 5**, expects a list of 5 members, but the list s is only defined to have 3 members:

```
Names Default To Here( 1 );
s = {"a", "b", "c"};
For( i = 1, i <= 5, i++,
    Print( s[i] )
);
```

```
/*:

"a"
"b"
"c"
Subscript Range in access or evaluation of 's[i]' , s[/*###*/i]

In the following script, error marked by /*###*/
Names Default To Here( 1 );
s = {"a", "b", "c"};
For( i = 1, i <= 5, i++,
    Print( s[/*###*/i] )
);
```

Correct the while expression argument count to 3, and the problem is resolved:

```
Names Default To Here( 1 );
s = {"a", "b", "c"};
For( i = 1, i <= 3, i++,
    Print( s[i] )
);
```

A more robust solution is to use the **N Items()** function so that the loop stops when it reaches the number of items in the list. This is useful when you do not know in advance how many items are in the list.

```
s = {"a", "b", "c"};

For( i = 1, i <= N Items(s), i++,
    Print( s[i] )
);
```

Specified Column Not Found in Data Table

If you have more than one data table open while the script executes, make sure the script is accessing the correct table when it is referencing the column. During script development, scripters typically have in mind the data table that is expected to be current at various stages in the script. However, because of background processes, the table that is actually current can be a different table. See the next section, "Problems with Identifying the Current Data Table" for further details about ensuring that your script uses the intended data table.

Invalid Row Number

This error typically occurs when you have a column name and JSL variable name that are the same. If this is the case, change the global name to something else or properly scope the JSL variable and column names each time they are used.

This code snippet illustrates the problem with using a global name that is the same as a column name:

```
dt = Open( "$SAMPLE_DATA/Big Class.jmp" );

/* Initialize the variable 'name' with the first value of the column, name */
name = :name[1];
```

And here is the error it shows in the log:

```
/*:

Cannot set value for the column 'name' because the row number (0) is not valid.
```

The solution is to either change the name of the variable or scope it using the double colons, as shown here:

```
::name = :name[1];
```

Problems with Identifying the Current Data Table

When multiple data tables are opened and closed during the processing of a script, how do you know which data table is the current data table? Though you might think JMP is looking at one table, sometimes JMP is looking at another table. Therefore, it is best for your script to be data table-specific everywhere possible. This is even more important when you have multiple tables that have the same column names.

So how can we deal with this?

You might have seen code that specifies the current data table with a **Current Data Table()** function. The reference to the data table is used as its argument. For example, suppose that **dt** is the name (or reference) you have assigned to a specific data table:

```
dt = Data Table( "Big Class" );
```

Then you would use **dt** as the argument for the **Current Data Table()** command:

```
Current Data Table( dt );
```

This makes it clear to JMP which data table should be the current, or active, data table—*at that moment*. However, this is not foolproof! When data tables are opened or generated in some way, the new table becomes the current, or active, table. But as noted in the next section, there are background processes that can cause the current data table to change.

> We recommend that you save yourself some trouble and never assign a data table reference using the **Current Data Table()** function in a production script. For example, to avoid potential headaches, do *not* do this:
>
> ```
> dt = Current Data Table();  //Unreliable
> ```

Here are some more reliable ways to ensure that your script uses the table that you expect:

- Specify the data table that should be used for an analysis by sending the analysis platform as a message to a specific data table:

  ```
  dt << Distribution( Nominal Distribution( Column( :age ) ) );
  ```

  By doing this, you let JMP know that it will find the **age** column in the data table referenced by **dt**.
- Use the optional data table reference when performing a **For Each Row()** loop. Including the data table reference eliminates the possibility of the loop performing on the incorrect data table due to a different data table being current at run time. The optional data table reference was added to **For Each Row()** in JMP 12.

  ```
  For Each Row( dt,
      If( :Age > 55 & :Gender == "M", Print( :Name ) )
  );
  ```

- Send the **New Column()** function as a message to the data table where the new column should be added. This ensures that JMP will add the column to the desired table instead of the current data table.

  ```
  dt << New Column( "New Height", Numeric, Continuous );
  ```

- Use the optional data table reference when using the **Summarize()** function. The optional data table reference was added to **Summarize()** in JMP 12.

  ```
  Summarize( dt, a = By( :age ) );
  ```

- When you have multiple data tables open that contain some of the same column names, you can use JSL functions that provide the necessary scoping. For example, the **As Column()** and **Column()** functions with the optional data table reference tells JMP exactly which table to look in for a column by the name specified in the second argument. See the "Column Name Resolution" section of chapter 4 for further details about resolving column names to the correct data table.

Timing Issues with Uncompleted Tasks

JMP considers certain tasks as system-related and performs them in the background. These tasks include the following:

- formula evaluation
- closing data tables
- screen updates

Although updating the contents of a screen would not be likely to cause you trouble, incomplete formula evaluation or delayed data table closing can most definitely cause you issues.

The **Run Formulas** command forces all pending formulas in a data table to evaluate completely before the next JSL statement can be executed. The syntax for **Run Formulas** is as follows:

```
dt << Run Formulas;
```

All analysis platforms and tables menu items automatically send a **Run Formulas** command to the data table before performing the analysis. This is to ensure that the analysis will not be performed on any columns that have incomplete data.

> Confusion Alert: The **Rerun Formulas** command forces all formulas to evaluate again.

Another way to address timing issues is to include **Wait()** statements. Adding a **Wait()** statement allows time so that pending system-related tasks have an opportunity to complete.

When data tables are opened and closed within a **For()** loop, it is possible for the actual closing of a data table to occur later than you expect. This is because closing data tables is one of those tasks JMP performs in the background.

In instances such as this, adding a **Wait(n)** statement with a short period of time (in number of seconds) as the argument might give just enough time to complete the closing of the data table before moving on to the next task.

A special case is using the zero argument for **Wait()**. Using it will cause the script execution to pause until the task is completed.

```
Wait( 0 );
```

> Significant improvements have been made to eliminate the need for **Wait()** statements. Ideally, you should not need them for your projects, but the function is available if you do.

Using JSL Variables in Formulas

There are times when you want to use variables when constructing a column formula. For example, you might query the user for a value that is to be used in the formula. However, errors can occur when using JSL variables directly in a formula.

The following example illustrates the problem. Executing the script adds a formula to the data table where a list of values is used to describe categories.

```
dt = Open( "$SAMPLE_DATA/Big Class.jmp" );
phases = {"early", "mid", "late"};

dt << New Column( "Adolescent Phase",
    "Character",
    Formula( If( :age <= 12, phases[1], 12 < :age >= 15, phases[2], phases[3] ) ) )
);
```

After the script executes, the new column in the data table is populated as expected. But if the table is opened in a new session of JMP and the formulas are rerun, errors are generated.

Figure 5.10 Errors generated when rerunning formulas

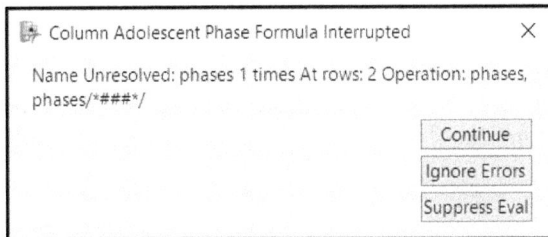

The new session of JMP cannot find the list variable, **phases**. The values referenced in the variable were lost when the original JMP session was closed.

The best way to resolve this issue is to substitute the **phases** values into the formula at run time when the new column or formula is created using the **Eval(), Expr(),** and **Eval Expr()** functions. It might look at bit complicated, but it is really just a simple two-step process.

Let's walk through an example of adding a new formula column using a JSL variable:

1. Place the entire **New Column()** statement inside the **Eval Expr()** function, and then wrap each variable instance with an **Expr()** function. The **Eval Expr()** instructs JMP to evaluate the variables inside the **Expr()** functions at execution time For example, it will replace **phases[1]** with "early*"*, **phases[2]** with "mid", and **phases[3]** with "late".

```
dt = Open("$SAMPLE_DATA/Big Class.jmp");
phases = {"early", "mid", "late"};
Eval Expr(
    dt << New Column( "Adolescent Phase",
        "Character",
        Formula(
            If(
                :age <= 12, Expr( phases[1] ),
                12 < :age >= 15, Expr( phases[2] ),
                Expr( phases[3] )
            )
        )
    )
)
```

2. Step 1 creates the correct expression, but for JMP to take action and generate the new column, you need to wrap the entire expression that you built in step 1 with the **Eval()** function.

```
dt = Open( "$SAMPLE_DATA/Big Class.jmp" );
phases = {"early", "mid", "late"};
Eval(
    Eval Expr(
            dt << New Column( "Adolescent Phase",
                "Character",
                Formula(
                        If(
                                :age <= 12, Expr( phases[1] ),
                                12 < :age >= 15, Expr( phases[2] ),
                                Expr( phases[3] )
                        )
                )
            )
    )
);
```

The result shown in the formula editor of the new column (Figure 5.11) indicates that the list values were substituted correctly. This means that the formula is no longer dependent on a JSL variable to be resolved in order to use the value.

Figure 5.11 Formula Editor View

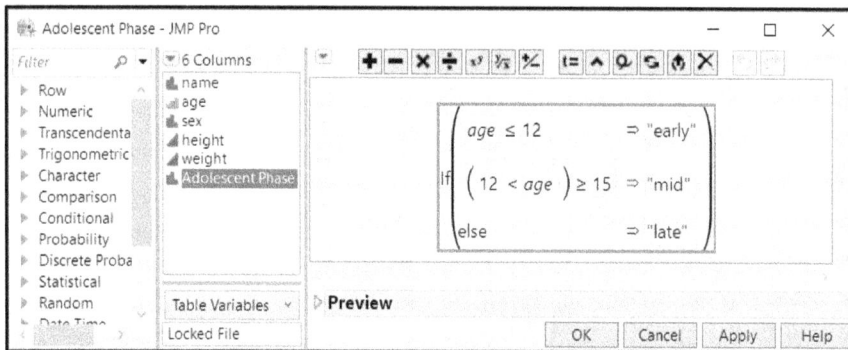

Debugging Tips

It happens to all of us, beginning and advanced scripters alike: There are problems or bugs in our code. We will show you some good general tips for preventing and remedying these issues.

Script with Style!

If you choose not to use the Script Editor's automatic formatting feature, adopt a method of formatting your code for readability. Here are some things to consider:

- Use consistent naming conventions.
- Include comments.
- Use indentions.
- Increase readability by adding blank lines.

Commenting and formatting your script is not only helpful for debugging, but also for quickly identifying sections of code that you might want to copy and use in a future scripting project.

> To easily recognize variable names, begin each variable name with a lowercase letter, using mixed case (CamelCase) for multiple words. Conversely, begin each JSL command with an uppercase letter. These are suggestions only and are not required by JMP.

Keep It Simple!

Build the script in small sections, running each section of code independently to verify its success before moving on to the next section.

If **For()** loops are included, be sure to run the code within the loop to ensure it will run successfully for each iteration of the loop.

> You can run an entire script at once. Don't forget that you can see results of an individual section of your script. Just highlight the desired section, or sections, of code and use one of the methods mentioned previously to run it. Another way to run the highlighted code is to press the **Enter** key on the numeric keypad.

Check the Log

Was there an error message or were the results not what you expected?

First, check the log for messages, paying close attention to any specific line numbers where an error was encountered. To go directly to the line in your script where the error occurred, from the **Edit** menu, select **Go to Line**. You are then prompted to enter a line number. This moves your cursor to the line number that you specify.

If no line numbers are included in the log message, the message itself should give you some clue about what JMP did not understand or know how to process. Some common mistakes that people make are to have unequal fences or to forget a semicolon. The error messages generated for these items are generally very specific. However, if you include an extraneous comma, the problem can be quite a bit harder to find, even for an experienced scripter.

Isolate the Problem

Attempt to narrow down where the problem originated. Here are some suggestions:

- Run the script line by line or in small sections until it produces the erroneous results.
- Run the code within any **For()** loops to verify that the entire loop can be executed successfully.
- Check the values for any variables that are mentioned in and around error messages.
- Use a **Show()** command at various points in your script to display variable values as your script runs. Here is the syntax for the **Show()** command:
  ```
  Show( dt );
  ```

○ Use **Show Symbols()** to display the names and values of all JSL variables that have been defined in the current instance of JMP.

○ Use **Delete Symbols()** at the top of the script to clear out all the names and values used previously in the JMP session before executing the script.

> After the script has been executed, hold your mouse pointer over a global variable in the Script window. JMP displays the current value of that variable. This is another helpful feature of the Script Editor!

Is There a Better Way?

Ask yourself if there is a simpler way to accomplish the same goal. For example, if you just need to know how many levels there are in a column, don't create a whole Summary table that only groups by the desired column. Instead, use the **Summarize()** function to get a list of the levels and use the **N Items()** function to find out how many levels there are. Using the **Summarize()** function prevents the creation of a data table that must be managed, uses less memory, and is faster, while providing the same information.

> A sample script that uses the **Summarize()** function is included in Section 2: Jump On!

Or suppose you need to know how many rows were selected as the result of a **Select Where** command. What would you do? You could loop through each row, check the row state of each row, and keep a count of those rows that had a selected row state. But a better solution would be to capture a matrix of the row numbers that are selected using the **Get Selected Rows** message and then find out the number of rows in the matrix.

So instead of code like this:

```
c = 0;
For Each Row( If( Selected( Row State() ), c++ ) );
```

Your code would look much more concise and be much faster:

```
selRows = N Row( dt << Get Selected Rows );
```

JSL Debugger

The JMP application comes with a debugger tool that can help you pinpoint exactly where your script fails or generates an error. The debugger interface window makes it easy for you to view your variable values while stopping and starting your script at specified breakpoints without using extra statements to debug or looking at the log window constantly. The basic functions of the debugger are covered here, but for a comprehensive review of its features with examples, please look for the topic in the *Scripting Guide* at **Help ▶ Books**.

First, it is important to know that the JSL Debugger opens a new, separate instance of JMP when it is invoked, and the original Script window cannot be accessed while the debugger window is open.

> If your script prompts for user input, you will need to click on the original instance to switch focus and respond to the prompt. You can then switch back to the debugger to continue debugging your script.

To use the JMP Debugger for one of your scripts, perform one of these actions:

- Click the wrench icon in the Script window toolbar:
- Select **Edit ▶ Debug Script** from the main menu.
- Use this keyboard sequence on Windows: Ctrl + Shift + R

The JSL Debugger Window

The JSL Debugger window functions as a console with these components:

- icons at the top to provide options for execution ❶
- breakpoint icons (red dot) and execution line icons (green arrow) that are displayed between the row numbers and code ❷
- a code panel where the script is displayed ❸
- panels at the bottom of the window where information about variables and values is displayed (left) ❹ as well as names and locations of breakpoints that you set (right) ❺

Figure 5.12 JSL Debugger Window

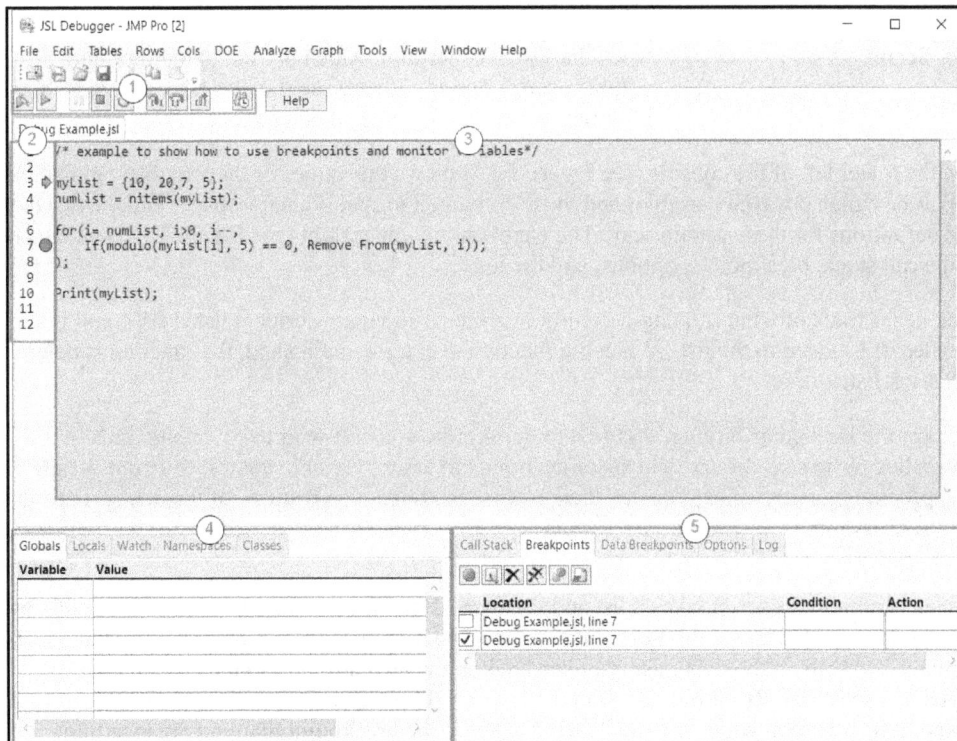

Debugger Buttons

The buttons at the top of the debugger console give you control on how the script is executed.

Run		Execute the script, and halt the script at breakpoints or when reaching the end of script.
Run without breakpoints		Execute the entire script without stopping at any breakpoints.
Break All		Click this button to halt execution and return to the debugger. This feature is useful when you are debugging a very large or complex script, and you need to stop the execution.
Stop		Halt the debugger session and return to the Script window.
Restart		Close the current debugger session and initiate a new one for your script.
Step Into		Enter and execute a function, expression, or included script file.
Step Over		Execute an expression without stepping into.
Step Out		Execute to a breakpoint or to the end of the script, returning to the calling point.
Profile JSL Script		Open the JSL Profiler tool, which is used to monitor and optimize script timing. Please see the *Scripting Guide* for more information about using this advanced tool.

The panel on the lower left of the console (see Figure 5.12) shows the values of the variables: global and local, as well as designated **watch** variables and those contained in specific namespaces and classes (see chapter 4 for definitions for these categories). The panel on the lower right (see Figure 5.12) has tabs for monitoring the call stack, breakpoints, options, and the log.

The call stack keeps track of what is being currently executed. The main script is listed first, and if a function is called, it is added to the list. When the function execution is finished, the function is deleted from the call stack list.

> For the beginning scripter, it is best to familiarize yourself with using breakpoints in the debugger to stop the script at specified points to assess variable values. As your scripts become more complex, you can then explore the other rich features of the debugger to troubleshoot your script issues.

In the following example, the script takes a list and removes all numbers in that list that are divisible by 5. A breakpoint has been added inside the **For()** loop on line 7 to monitor the variables as they change. To add a breakpoint to a script in the debugger, you can click in the area adjacent to the row number of interest, or you can select the **Breakpoints** tab in the lower right panel and click the red circle icon to bring up the Breakpoint Information window to add specifics about the breakpoint that you are inserting.

To execute the script to the breakpoint, click the **Run** icon.

Figure 5.13 Click Run Button to Start Execution to Breakpoint

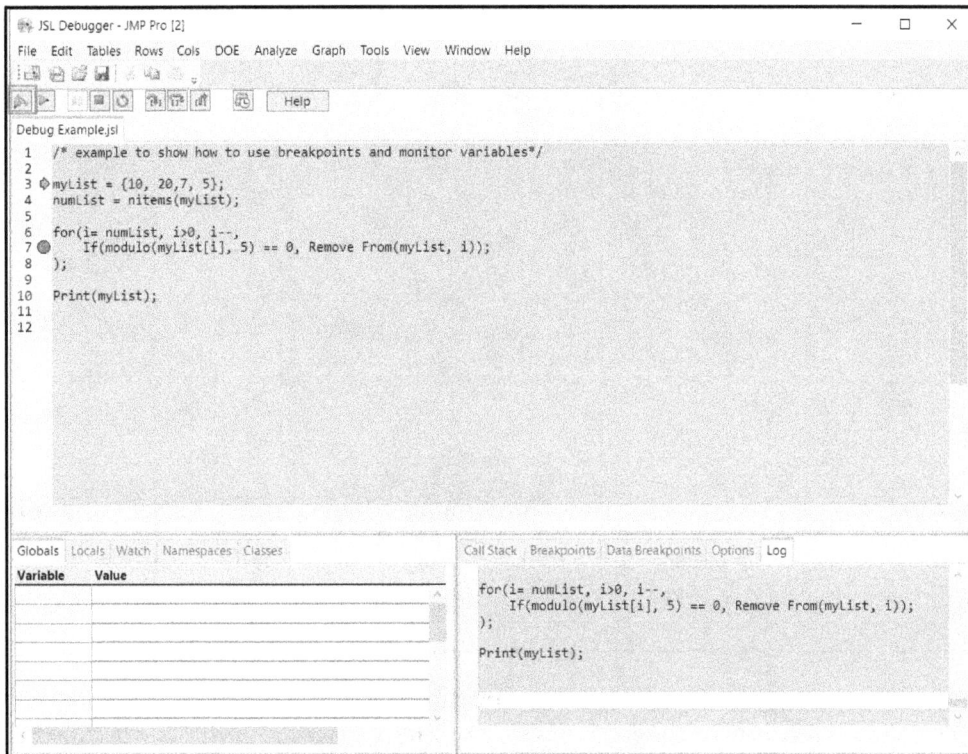

The Variable area in the lower left panel will be populated with values for myList, numList, and i.

Figure 5.14 First Iteration to Breakpoint

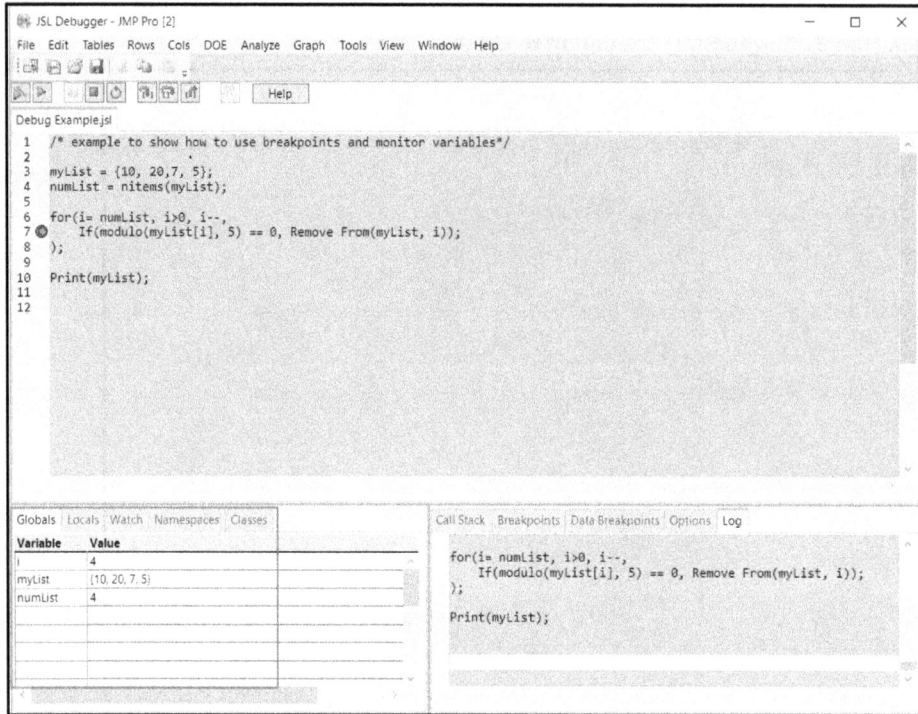

Click the **Run** icon again to iterate another time inside the **For()** loop.

Figure 5.15 Second Iteration to Breakpoint

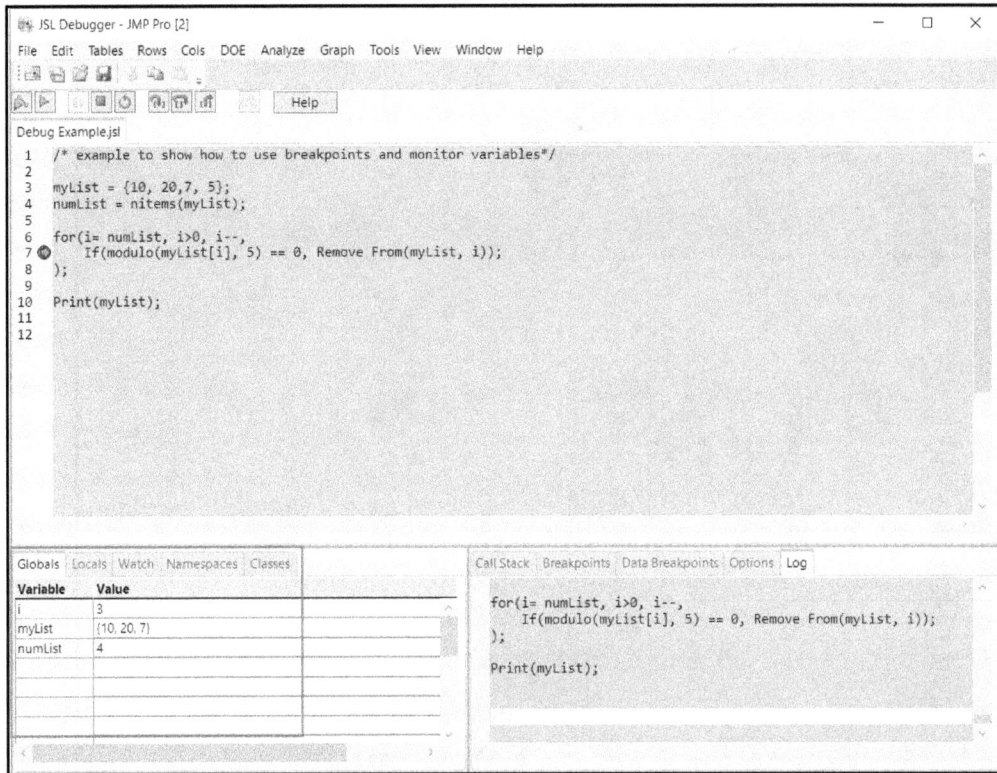

Click the **Run** button three more times, noting the change in variable values between each execution. Figure 5.16 shows the debugger when the script execution is finished.

Figure 5.16 Execution Finished

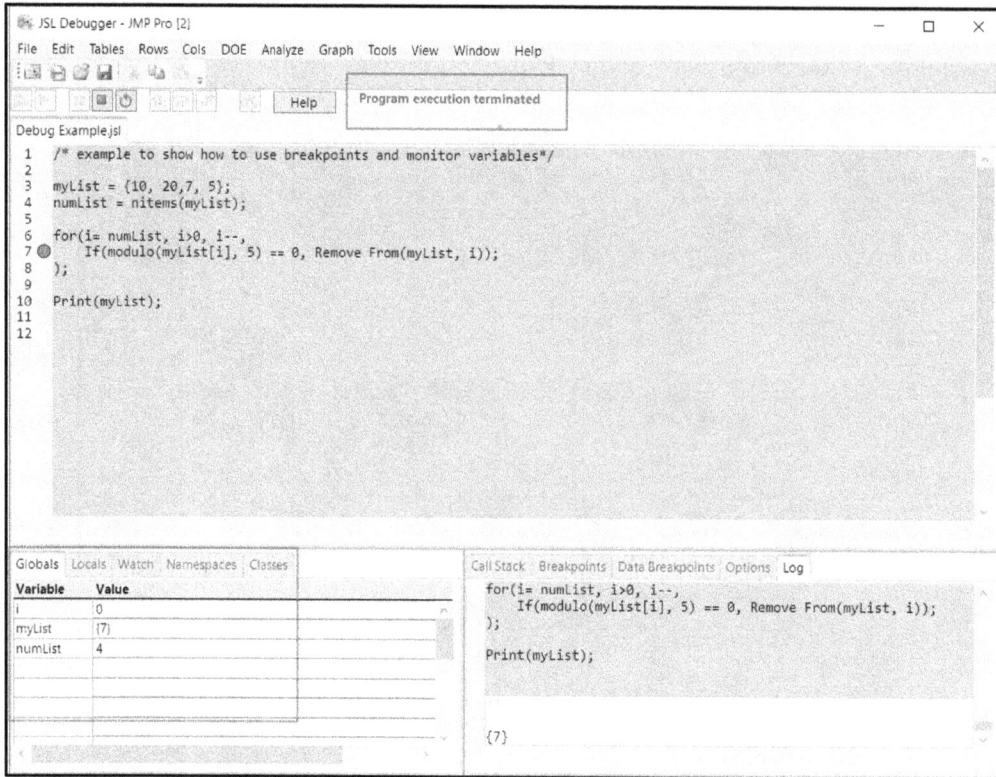

To close the debugger session and return to the original Script window, click the **Stop** icon.

Another handy feature of the debugger tool is the **Run to Cursor** option. To execute the script to a certain line in the script, right-click the line, and select **Run to Cursor** from the context menu. JMP immediately runs the script, stopping execution where the cursor was placed.

Figure 5.17 Run to Cursor

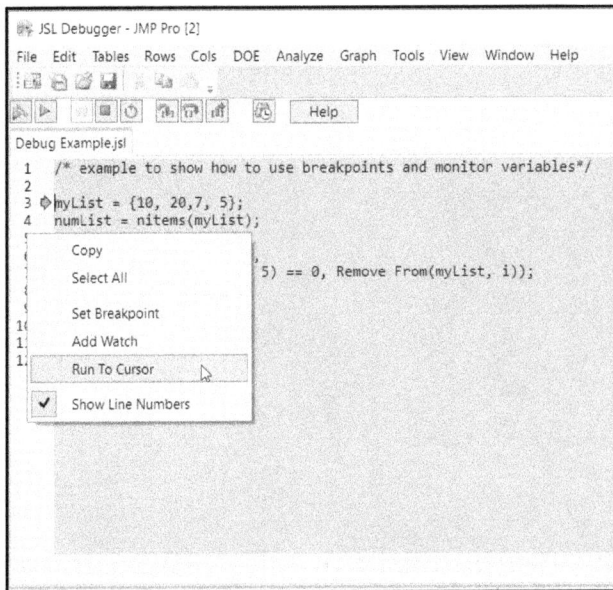

The JSL Debugger has many options to help you debug your scripts. We have just shown you some basics here to help get you started. As you advance on your scripting journey, you can read more in the *Scripting Guide* about how this tool can assist you.

Summary

Now you are ready to get your scripting projects started. You know how to make JMP do a lot of the work for you. You know where to get help. And you know what steps to take to debug a problem. There's no stopping you now!

Next, we will introduce you to building custom windows. We will also explore the Application Builder and related tools as easy ways to create dashboards and build custom applications.

Chapter 6: The Dashboard and Application Builders

Overview

There are tools built into JMP software that can accelerate your progress when creating reports, dashboards, and applications. In this chapter, we discuss the following:

- building reports and dashboards using the interactive method, Combine Windows
- creating custom dashboards using the Dashboard Builder
- using the features of the Application Builder for application development

Combine Windows, the Dashboard Builder, and the Application Builder

If you love building complicated custom windows and reports from scratch, that's fine. However, JMP provides you with some much easier options through the Application Builder and its related platforms.

There are three major features of the Application Builder suite of tools:

- Combine Windows is a feature that enables the user to combine reports and tables seen on the screen into one report, which can then be used as a combination report or dashboard as is, or edited in the Application Builder with the click of a button. The report generated is sometimes called an instant application because it is so easy to create. The Combine Windows feature is a great way to build a simple report or dashboard, or to initiate the report building and customization process using the Dashboard Builder or Application Builder later.
- The Dashboard Builder is a specialized form of the Application Builder with which you create your own dashboard by combining windows and reports from the JMP desktop or using a series of templates. The Dashboard Builder requires no scripting.
- The Application Builder is a platform in JMP that provides an interface to easily combine reports and windows by clicking, dragging, and dropping reports and dependent data tables within a console. This feature was initially conceived and developed to ease the complexity of building custom JSL applications from scratch.

All these software features enable you to develop a report, dashboard, or application with an underlying script that can be used to re-create it. Scripting the display boxes in a custom window can be a very tedious and iterative process. In contrast, using Combine Windows, the Dashboard Builder, or the Application Builder makes the task so much easier. The following sections provide more details about each of the three time-saving features.

Combine Windows

Using the Combine Windows feature is the easiest way to combine reports and data table windows generated by JMP.

Keep in mind that JMP will attempt to combine the windows in exactly the same configuration as you see on the screen. So to save yourself trouble later, be sure to align the windows as you want to see them in the final combined report.

In this example, we show how to combine two reports into one window:

1. Arrange the reports in the configuration that you want to show in the report (see Figure 6.1). JMP will do its best to keep the configuration as shown on the desktop.

Figure 6.1 Arrange Windows

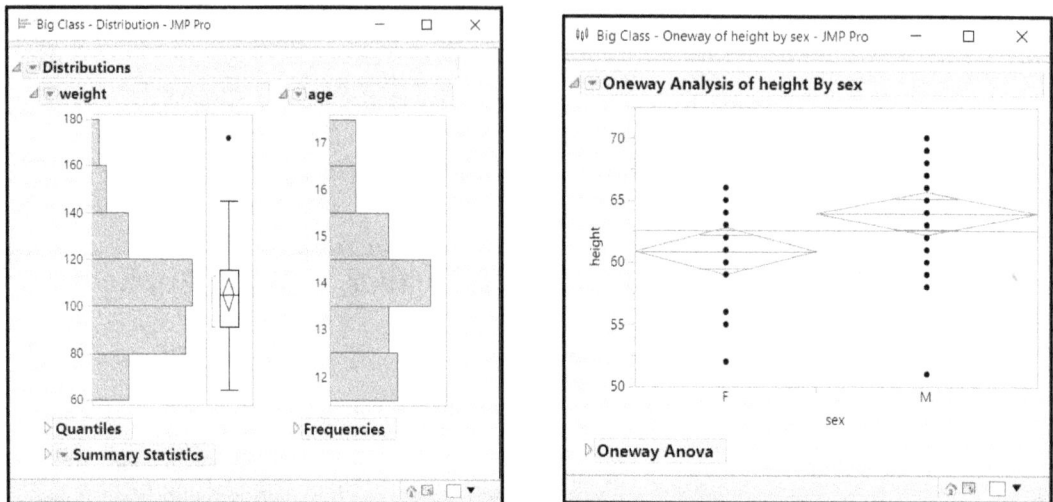

2. Place a check in each window box for those selected for the combined report.

Figure 6.2 Check Boxes for Windows

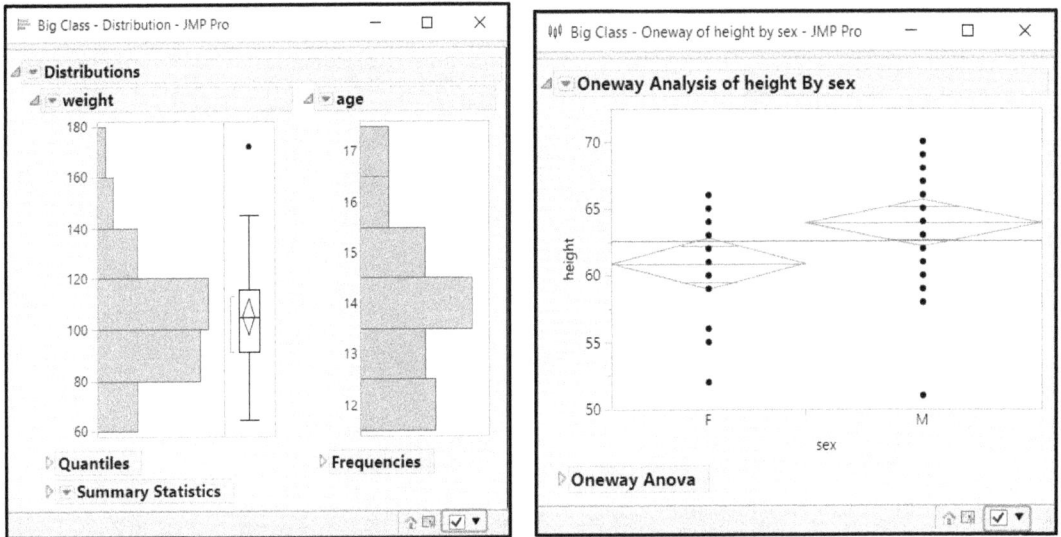

3. Click the black arrow of one of the windows and select **Combine Windows** from the drop-down menu.

Figure 6.3 Select Combine Windows Option

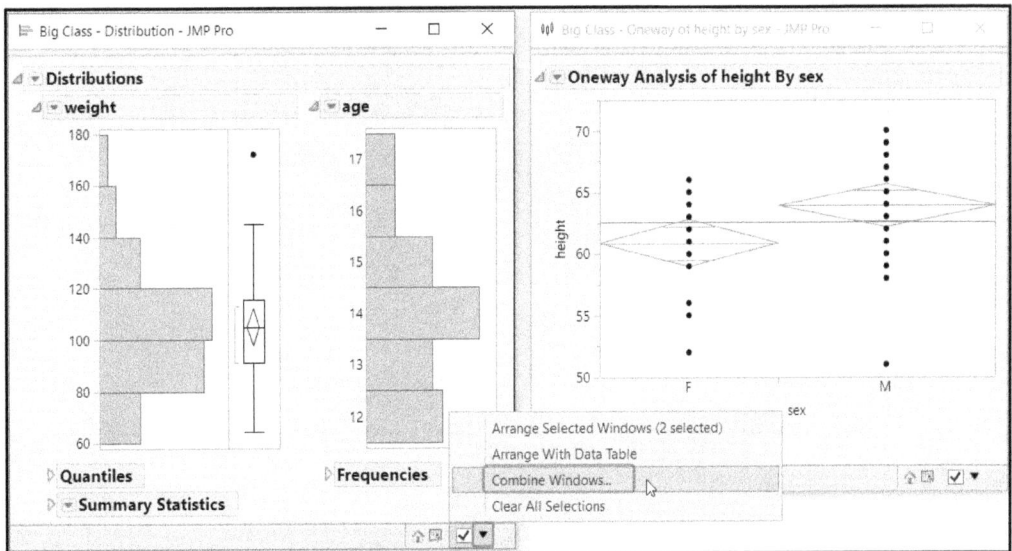

4. In the resulting dialog, enter a title for your combined report, and then click OK.

Figure 6.4 Combine Windows Dialog

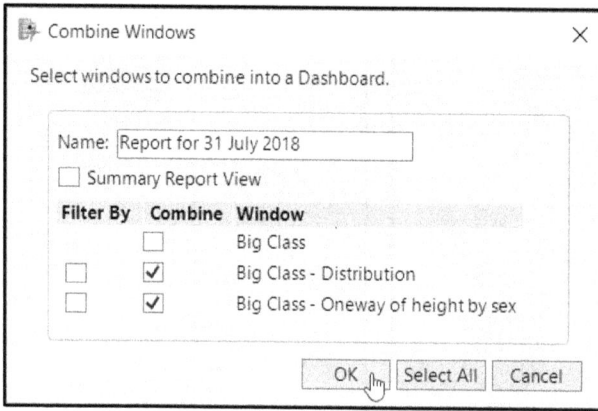

5. The combined report is created.

Figure 6.5 Report from Combining Windows

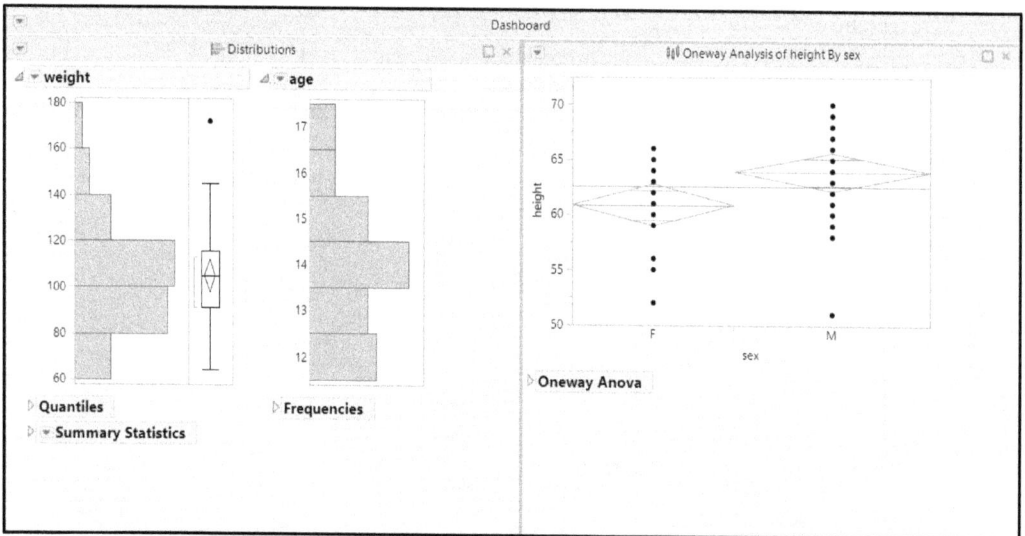

6. If you want to save a script of the report or edit the report in the Dashboard Builder or Application Builder, click the red triangle in the upper left corner of the report to display the menu with options.

Figure 6.6 Option for Editing

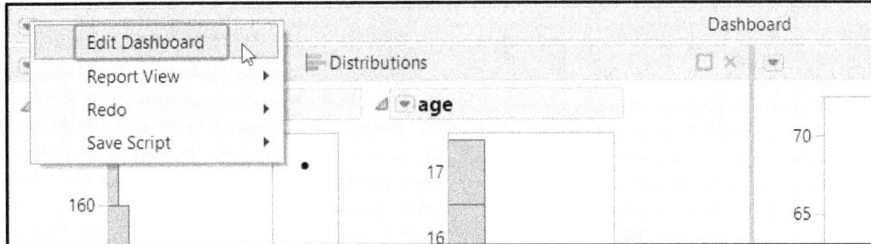

Using Combine Windows is one way to create a dashboard or instant application. Keep in mind that the dashboard or application is dependent on the columns in the data table used for its construction. Using a different table when invoking the dashboard or script will likely result in errors.

Next, we will show you another way to build a dashboard.

Dashboard Builder

The Dashboard Builder makes it easy to build a dashboard from your open reports and tables. The interface offers several templates to choose from, and all you have to do is drag and drop into the configuration that you selected. No scripting is needed.

Open the Dashboard Builder by selecting **File ▶ New ▶ Dashboard**. The interface that opens offers **Custom Templates** where you can save templates that you create, **Templates** in multiple configurations that JMP provides, and **Samples** where you can explore ready-built dashboards.

Figure 6.7 The Dashboard Builder Template Gallery

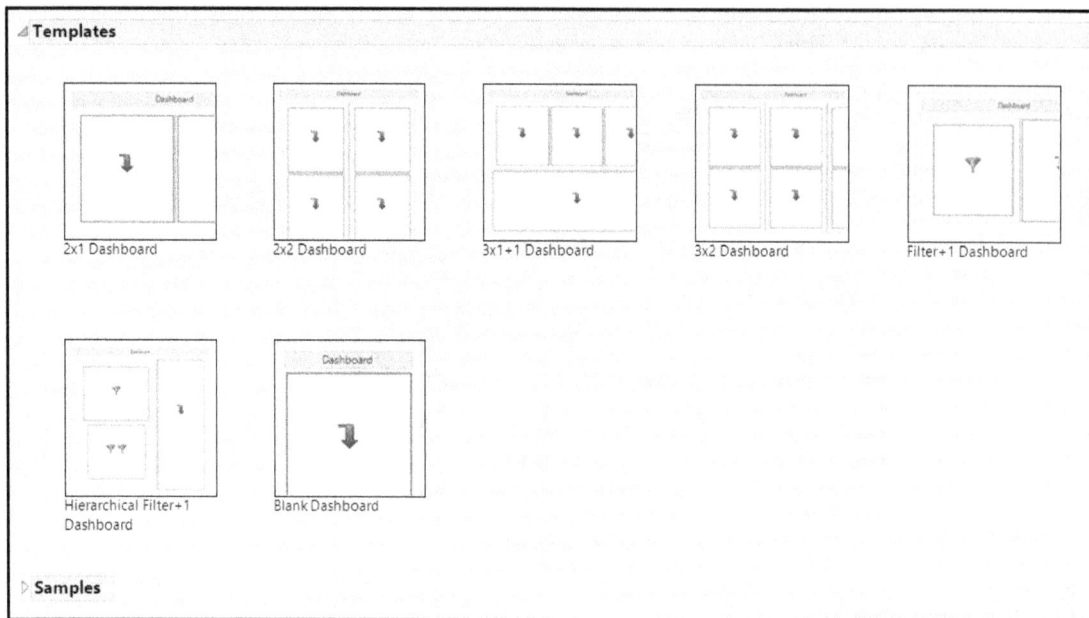

An example is the best way to show how it works. Using weather data from various stations around the US, we will we create a graph of the stations to use as a filter on another graph that shows temperature highs, lows, and means over time for the stations. The Filter + 1 Dashboard template is the best option for our purposes.

1. Open the sample data table, Weekly Weather Data.jmp, from the sample data directory.
2. Execute the script named Weather Station Locations, which is embedded in the data table.

Figure 6.8 Run Weather Station Locations Script

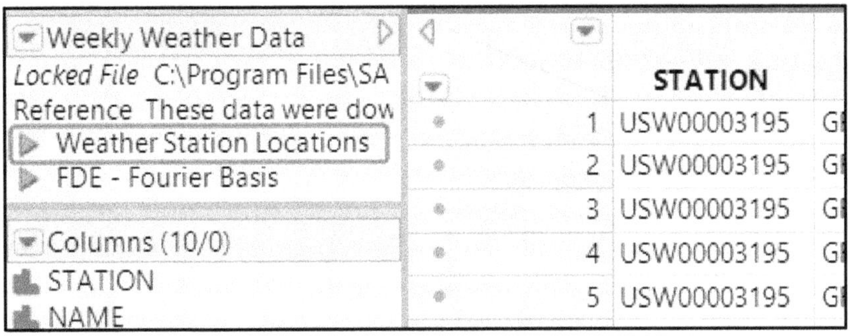

Figure 6.9 Weather Station Locations Graph

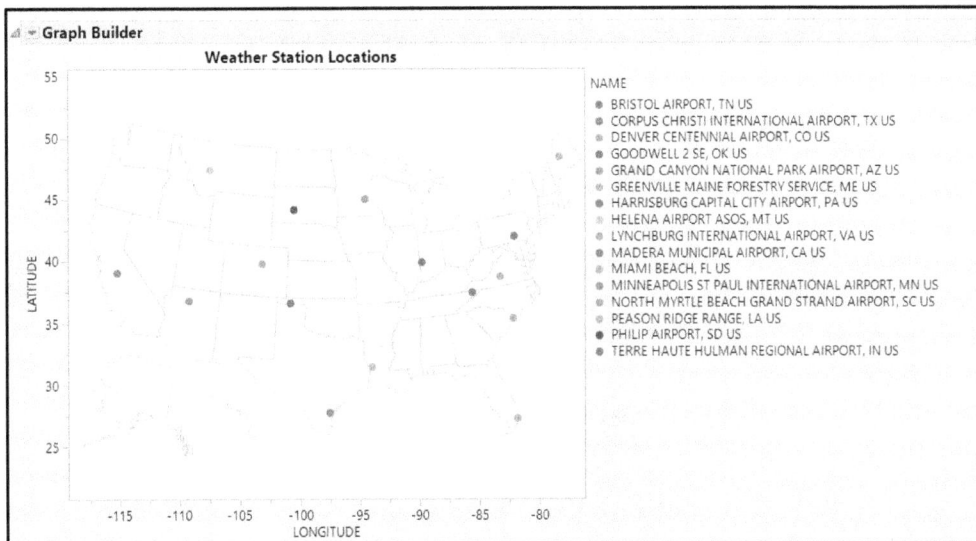

3. Create a graph showing the temperature highs, lows, and averages using Graph Builder:

   a. Open Graph Builder by selecting **Graph ▶ Graph Builder**.

   b. Drag and drop the **DATE** variable onto the X axis.

   c. Select **TMIN**, **TMAX**, and **TAVG**, and then drag them all and drop onto the Y axis.

   d. Click the **Done** button.

Figure 6.10 Temperature Graph

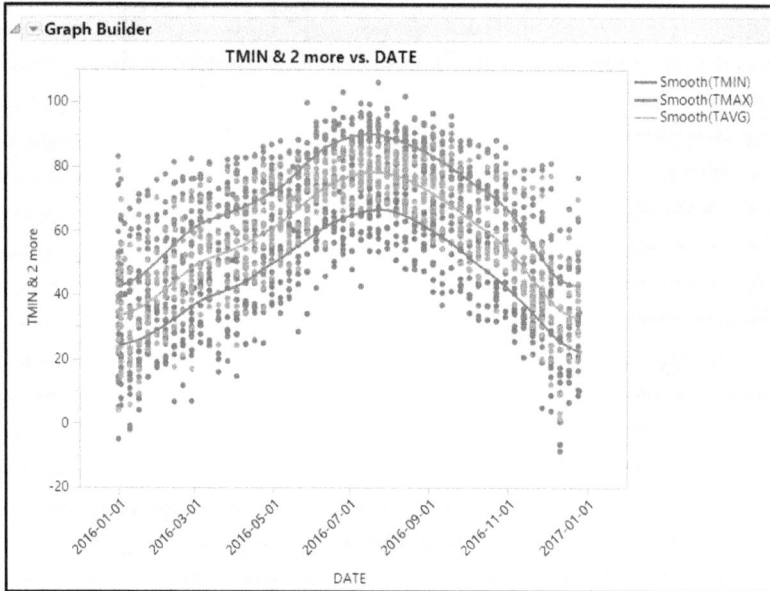

4. Open the Dashboard Builder (**File ▶ New ▶ Dashboard**), and then click the **Filter + 1 Dashboard** template.

5. On the left, under Sources, are the two graphs created earlier. On the right is the grid that holds the chosen template.

Figure 6.11 Dashboard Builder Main Window

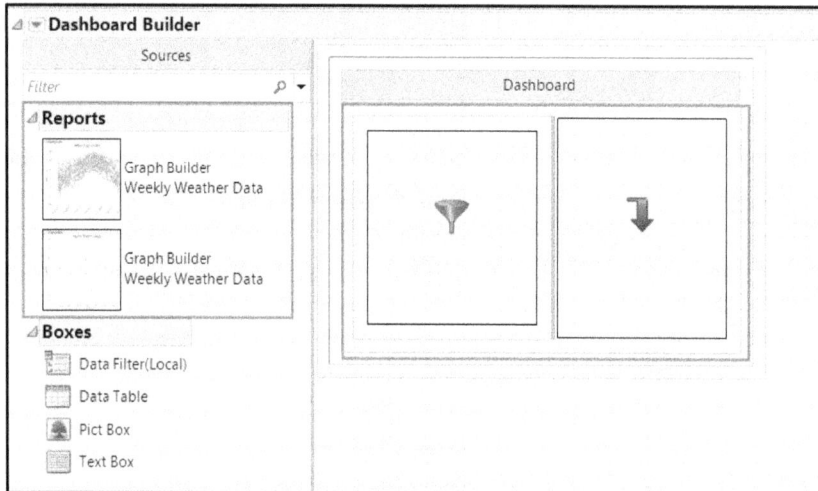

6. Drag and drop the graph with the US map with the weather station locations into the left box of the template, which contains the filter symbol. Then drag and drop the temperature graph into the box on the right side of the template. The plots should snap into place.

Figure 6.12 Dashboard Builder with Graphs in Place

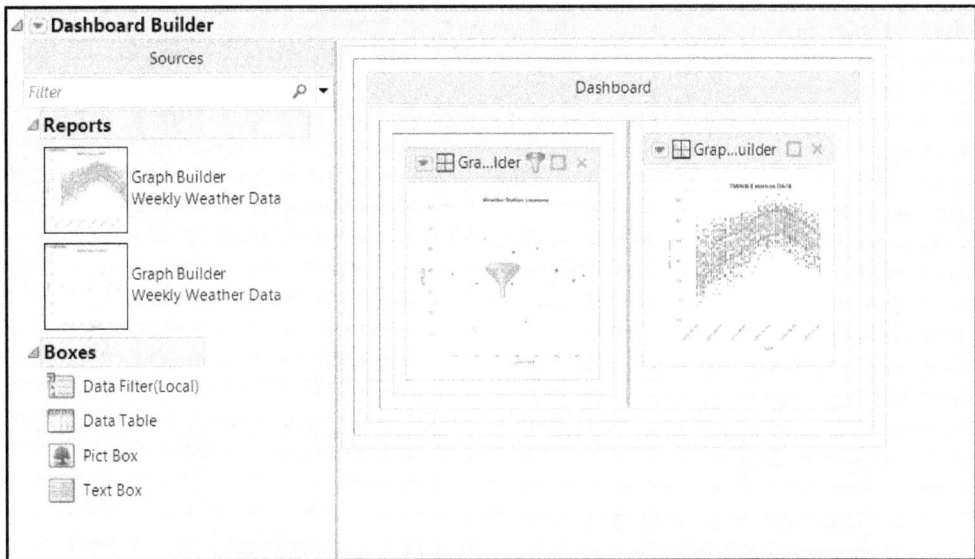

7. Launch the dashboard by clicking the red triangle icon and selecting **Run Dashboard** (for more information about the red triangle menu items, see the topic in the Application Builder section that follows). Another option is to click the **Run Script** button in the toolbar menu to launch the dashboard (see Figure 6.34).

Figure 6.13 Run Dashboard

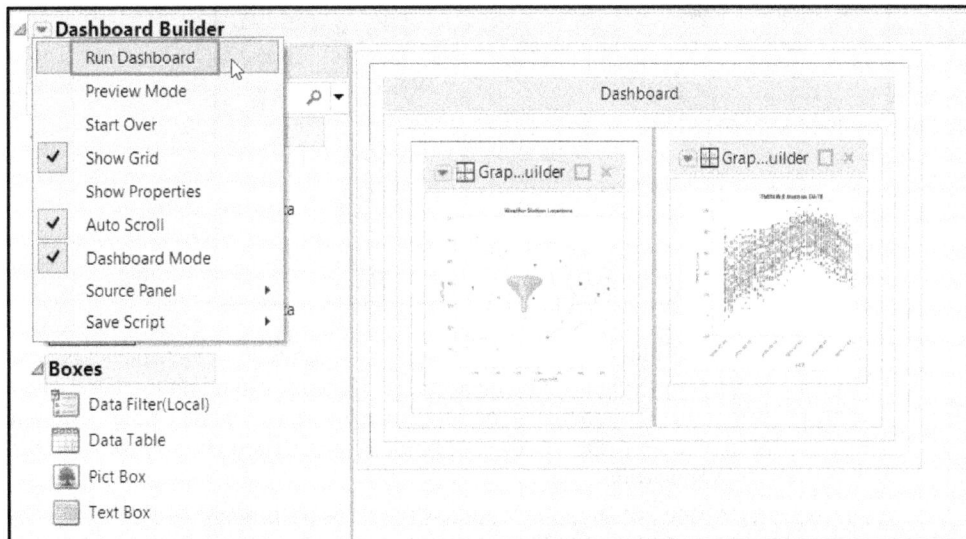

The dashboard appears in a new window. Click any of the station dots in the US Map graph to filter the temperature graph.

Figure 6.14 Weather Dashboard

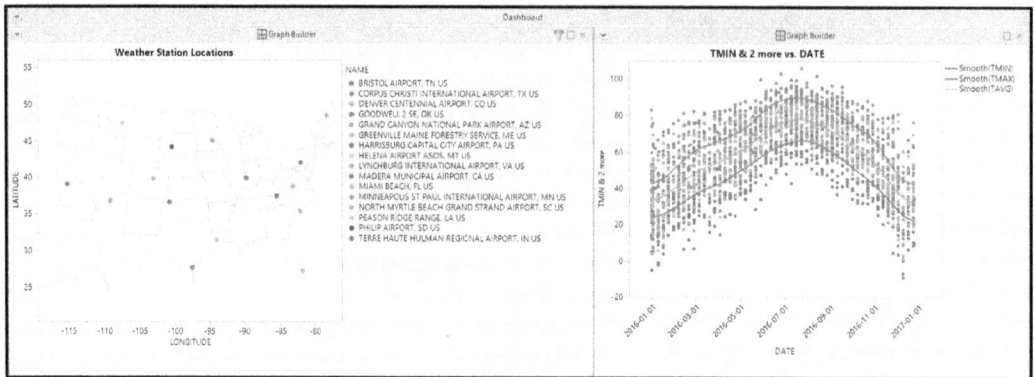

8. To create a copy of the dashboard script, click the upper left red triangle and select **Save Script** from the menu.

Figure 6.15 Save the Dashboard Script

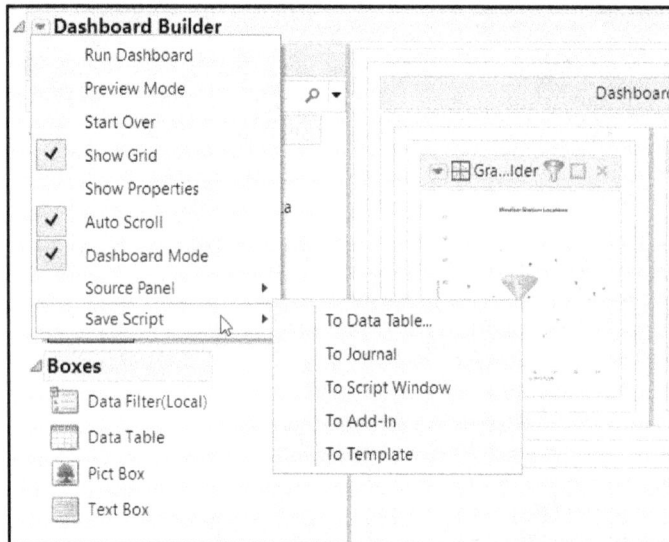

There are multiple options for saving a script of your dashboard. A script can be saved to the data table, a journal, a script window, or an add-in. If you think you might use the dashboard as the starting point for other dashboards in the future, save it as a template. Your custom template scripts are listed when you open a new dashboard or application (**File ▶ New ▶ Dashboard**, or **File ▶ New ▶ Application**).

9. You have three options when saving your dashboard as a file from the **File ▶ Save As** menu:

   a. A **JMP Source File (.jmpappsource)**: When you have your application saved as this file type and then open it, the dashboard opens in the Dashboard Builder, where you can continue to build your dashboard.

b. A **JMP Application File (.jmpapp)**: When you have your application saved as this file type and then open it, the dashboard opens as the dashboard application. Consider this file for the finished product.

c. A **JMP Script**: This last option saves your dashboard as a script. After opening the script file, you can execute the script to bring up the dashboard in the Dashboard Builder.

Figure 6.16 File Type Options When Saving a Dashboard

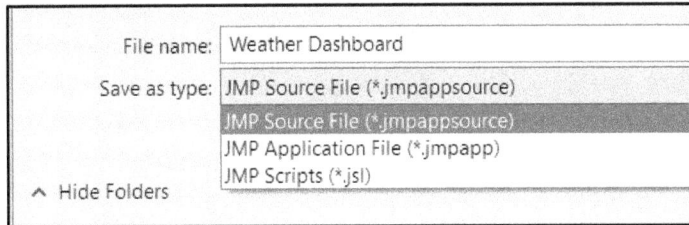

For more information about using the Dashboard Builder, please see the "Display Trees" chapter in the *Scripting Guide* (**Help ▶ Books ▶ Scripting Guide**).

Application Builder

If you are looking to build an application that is more complex than a dashboard or instant application, use the feature-rich Application Builder. Scripting an application from scratch can be very tedious, especially when trying to arrange and space display boxes to look good. The Application Builder makes the task a snap.

The interface for the Application Builder is much like the Dashboard Builder, but there are many more options. Whereas the Dashboard Builder shows a few display boxes or containers for dragging and dropping into the workspace, the Application Builder offers more than a dozen. Also, a couple of important features of the Application Builder are the modules and the script windows for each. You will not see these in the Dashboard Builder interface.

Application Builder Interface

A good place to start is to open the platform and take a tour of the features.

First, open the sample data table, Big Class.jmp, and then run the table scripts for Distribution and Bivariate. These two reports will be used in the example.

To create a new instance of the Application Builder, select **File ▶ New ▶ Application**:

Figure 6.17 Open the Application Builder

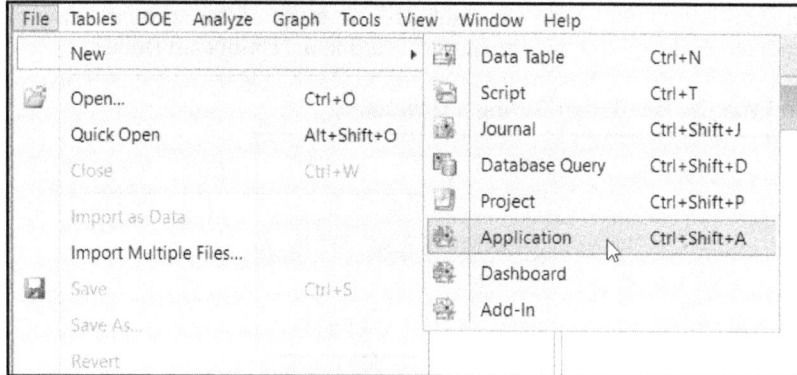

The first window that opens offers a gallery of options:

1. **Custom templates** (optional): If you save your application as a template after you build it, an icon is saved to this area. You will not see this heading unless you have purposefully saved your dashboard or application as a template previously.

2. **Templates**: These are the built-in templates that come with JMP. All of these templates, except one, open in the Dashboard Builder, which is a streamlined version of the Application Builder. The Blank Application template opens in the Application Builder.

3. **Samples**: JMP offers several sample applications. Choose one to see how a particular application was built or scripted, and execute it to observe how it works. If you learn best by looking at examples, be sure to open these sample applications and explore how they were implemented.

Figure 6.18 The Template Gallery

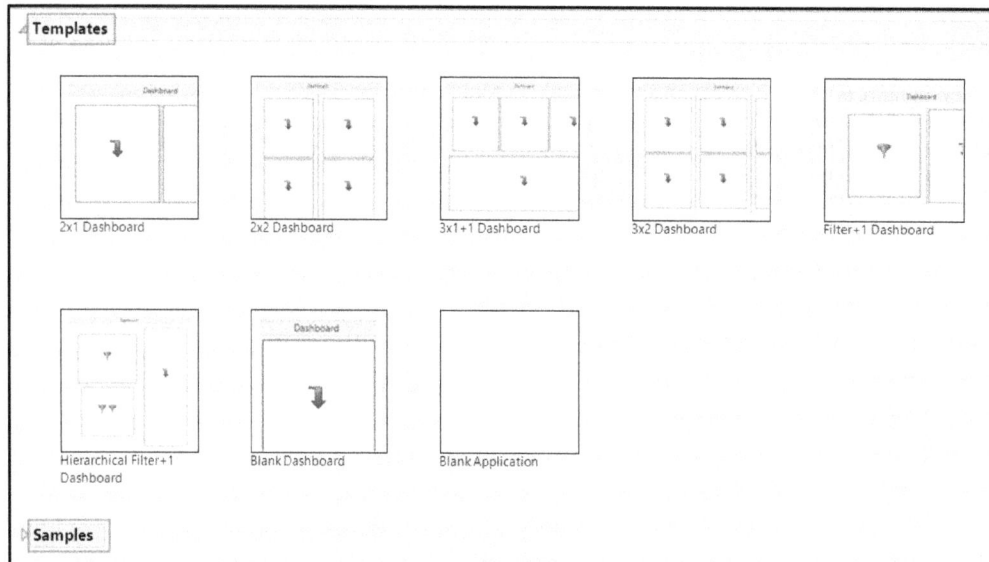

Click the icon for the **Blank Application** to view the Application Builder interface.

Figure 6.19 Blank Application

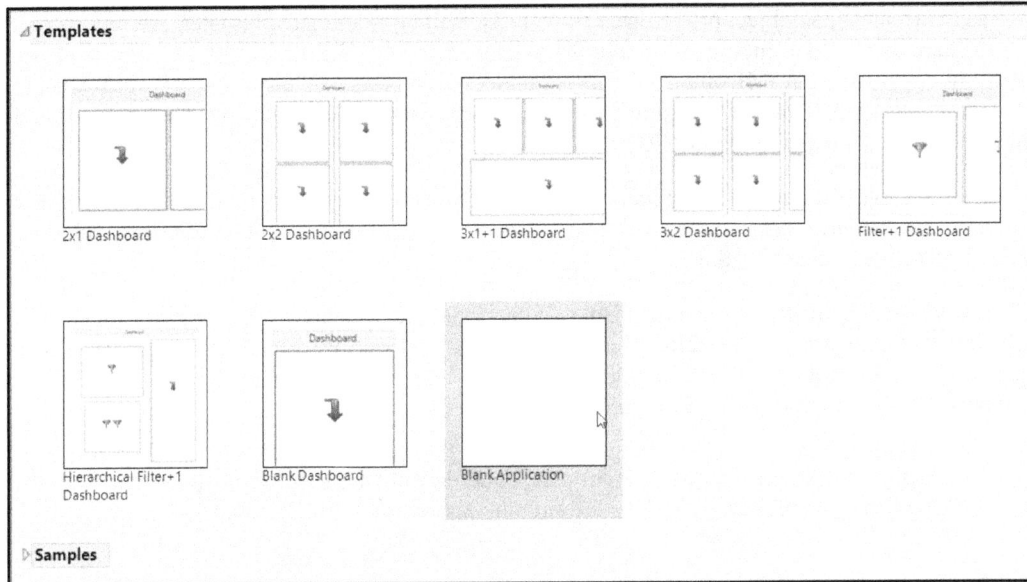

After you click the **Blank Application** icon, the builder opens. Here is where all your tools are laid out to create your application. Notice how the window is divided into three main panels: Sources, the workspace, and Objects/Properties.

Figure 6.20 The Three Panels of the Application Builder Window

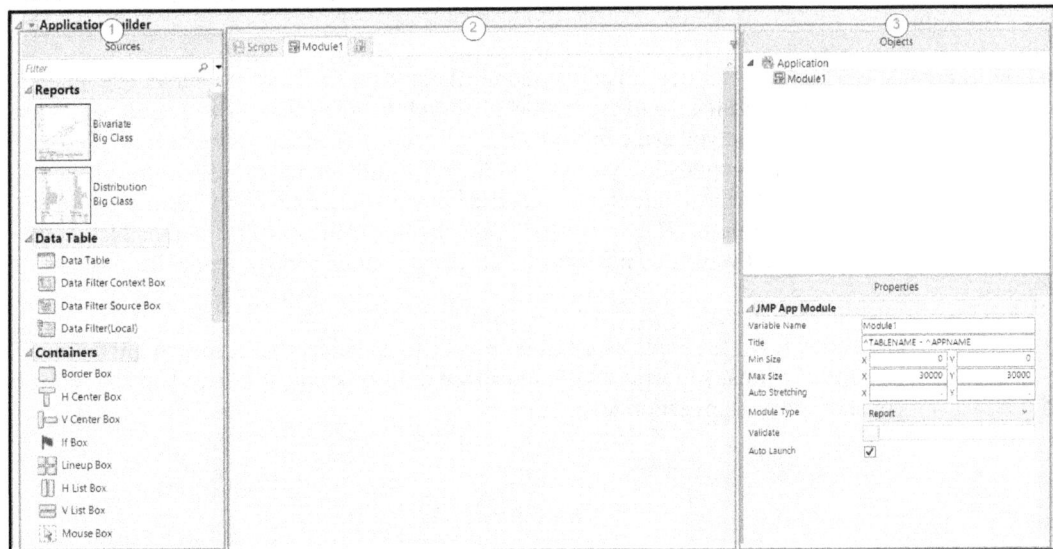

Sources Panel

The Sources panel ❶ displays the potential building blocks of your application. It shows what you can drag and drop into the workspace ❷. The Objects and Properties panels ❸, which provide information about object placement and object properties, respectively, will be examined a bit later. All reports that are open in JMP are displayed as thumbnails under the heading Reports. In Figure 6.20, two reports, Bivariate and Distribution, are open in JMP and are displayed under the Reports heading. Any report shown can be used in your application. However, keep in mind that custom windows cannot be used in the Application Builder and are not shown in the report list.

Under the Data Table heading, there are four boxes related to data tables. Use the first one to drag and drop a copy of the current data table into the workspace. The other three boxes facilitate filtering, including hierarchical filtering in an application.

The Containers section displays choices of display boxes that hold or contain other objects, which are essential in establishing the configuration of elements in your application. The other categories of sources are Spacers, Display, Tables, Buttons, and Input. The list is long, so be sure to scroll down the entire Sources panel to view all the choices available.

> Right-click any box in the Sources panel, and then click **Scripting Help** to open the Scripting Index, which displays information about that particular object.

Workspace Panel

The workspace panel is where you can get creative and design your application. Roll up your sleeves and start dragging and dropping containers, reports, data tables, and more into the workspace to build your application.

But first, look at the tabs at the top of the workspace. You will see the first tab is named **Scripts** and the second is **Module1**.

Module: A module is a container for objects in your application. You can have more than one module. To add modules, click the **Add Module** icon to the right of the **Module** tab or tabs. The default names are Module1, Module2, and so on, but you can edit the names to specify something more meaningful, depending on the purpose of the application you are building. Clicking on the different **Module** tabs exposes the workspace for each. Each module can represent a window for your application, and each module creates a separate namespace. The variables in each module namespace are not visible to other module namespaces. It is a great way to compartmentalize an application and prevent collisions of variables.

Scripts: If your application is not as simple as a dashboard, scripting behind the scenes might be required. If you click the tab named **Scripts**, you will see a **Namespace** drop-down menu where you can select the script for each module or for the application level.

Figure 6.21 Namespace Drop-down Menu

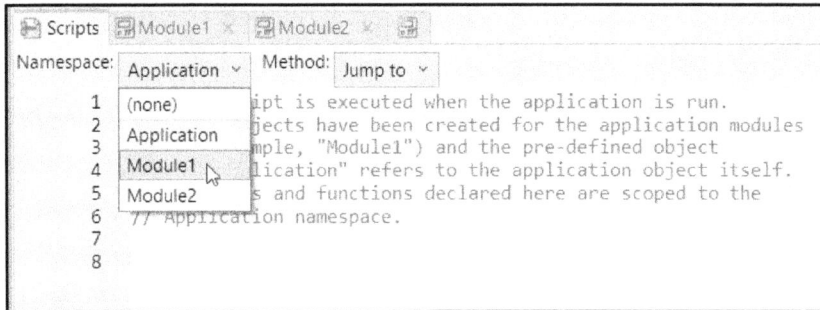

Select each and notice how each **Script** tab window contains helpful comments to get you started.

Figure 6.22 Script Tab Window

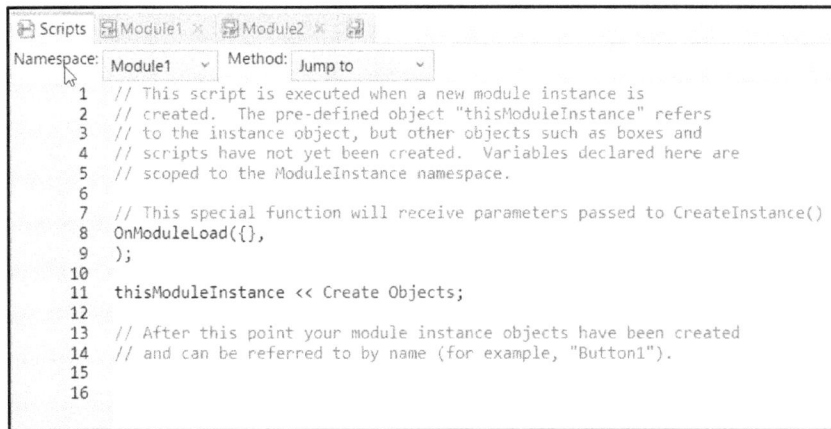

Each module script displays a rudimentary **OnModuleLoad** function and also a command to create an instance of the module.

Figure 6.23 Built-In OnModuleLoad Function

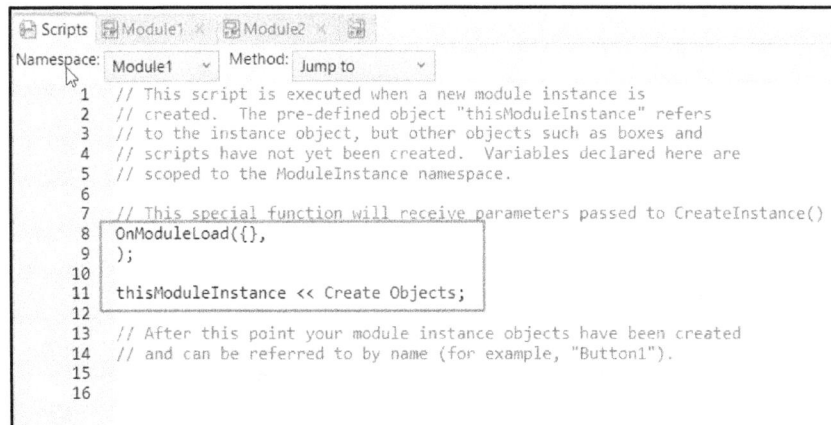

To view a good example showing passing parameters using the **OnModuleLoad** function, open the **Graph Launcher** application from the Sample Applications Directory, select the **Scripts** tab, and examine the LaunchModule and Graph Module scripts.

Click **Application** in the **Namespace** drop-down menu.

Figure 6.24 Application Script

```
Scripts    Module1  ×    Module2  ×

Namespace:  Application  ∨    Method:  Jump to  ∨

   1   // This script is executed when the application is run.
   2   // Named objects have been created for the application modules
   3   // (for example, "Module1") and the pre-defined object
   4   // "thisApplication" refers to the application object itself.
   5   // Variables and functions declared here are scoped to the
   6   // Application namespace.
   7
   8
```

It is helpful to understand the hierarchy of the application and module scripts. Each module has its own namespace, and the application namespace encompasses all the modules. If you declare a variable at the application level, it is global or visible to all module namespaces. In the Figure 6.25 schematic, the variable x is declared and initialized at the application level. Therefore, x is global to all three modules.

Figure 6.25 The Application Namespace

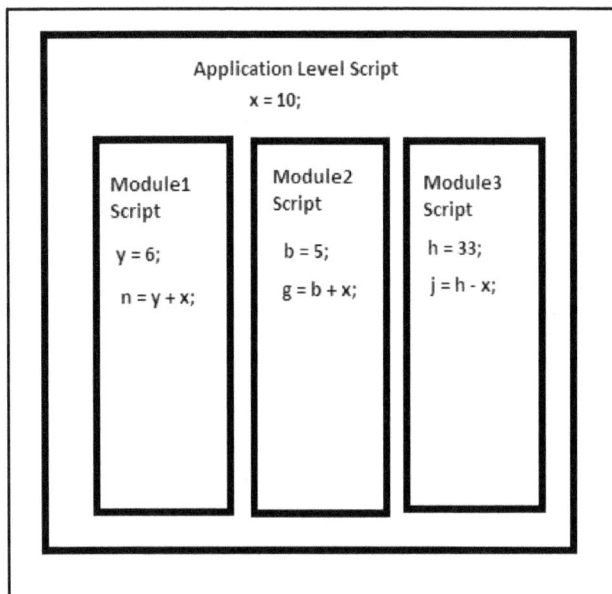

Application Level Script
$x = 10;$

Module1
Script

$y = 6;$

$n = y + x;$

Module2
Script

$b = 5;$

$g = b + x;$

Module3
Script

$h = 33;$

$j = h - x;$

The **Method** menu offers a way to skip down to a variable declaration, function, or expression. This is especially useful if the module script is long. In Figure 6.26, the module named LaunchModule shows five declarations, and by using the **Method** drop-down menu, you can easily get to the script area of one of the listed declarations by selecting the name.

Figure 6.26 Method Menu

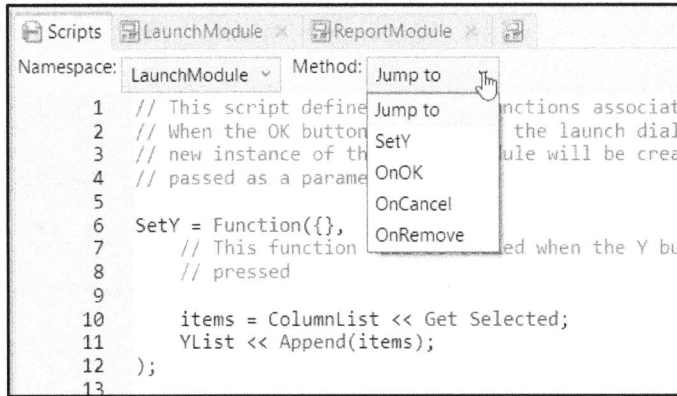

Objects and Properties Panels

The third area of the Application Builder window, on the far right, consists of two sections: the Objects panel and the Properties panel. The Objects panel displays the contents of the application, including the objects of each module that you have placed into the workspace. What you see is a hierarchy or tree structure. This gives you a visual representation of the relationships of the objects to each other. By clicking on the gray disclosure triangles, you can fully expand the tree, as Figure 6.27 shows.

Figure 6.27 Objects Tree

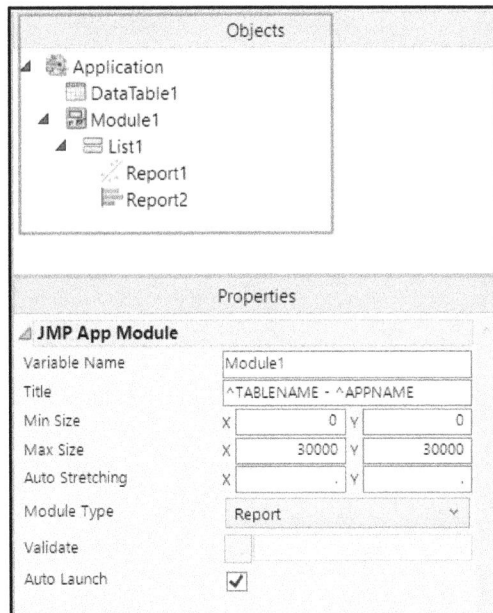

You can right-click any object in the tree structure to bring up a context menu where you can choose an action:

Menu Item	Action
Move to Corner	Moves the selected item to upper left corner of the workspace.
Align	Provides options to move the item left, center, right, top, middle, and bottom.
Change Container	Swaps out the selected item for a container of your choosing.
Add Container	Wraps the selected item in container of your choosing.
Use as Selection Filter	Specifies to use the selected report as a filter for other reports in the window.
Scripting Help	Brings up explanatory information about the selected item.
Module	Shows options for adding and deleting modules.
Edit Platform Script	Opens a script window where you can edit the selected platform script.
Copy	Copies the selected item to the clipboard.
Cut	Copies the selected item to the clipboard and deletes it.
Paste	Pastes the selection from the clipboard.
Delete	Deletes the selected item.

Figure 6.28 Objects Tree Context Menu

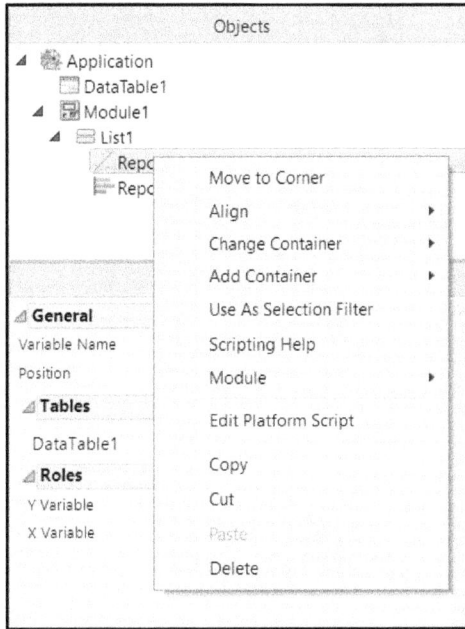

This context menu is also available when you right-click a selected item in the workspace.

If you select an object in the Objects panel or workspace, the properties of the object are shown in the Properties panel.

Figure 6.29 Properties Panel

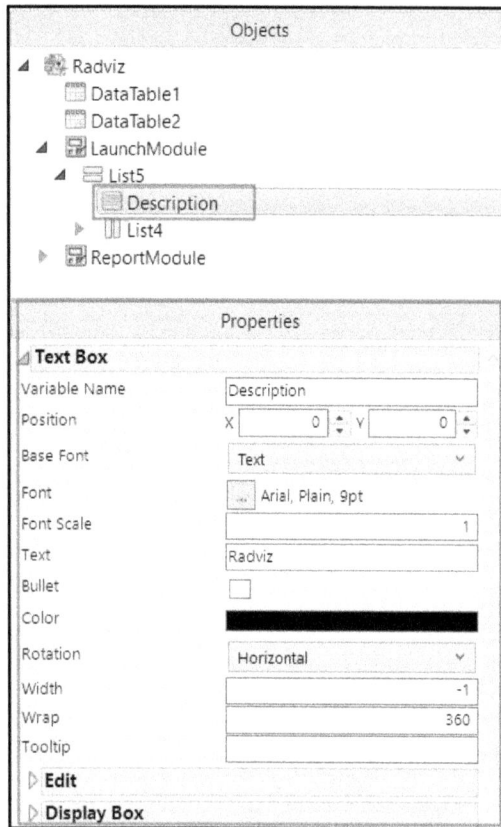

The Properties panel is where you can change the variable name for the object from the given default, view and edit positioning information regarding the object, specify properties or characteristics for the object in the Edit area, and change box limitations in the Display Box area.

If you click a module in the Objects tree, you can see in its Properties panel several properties, including those for name, title, and windows resizing.

Figure 6.30 Select Module to Show Properties

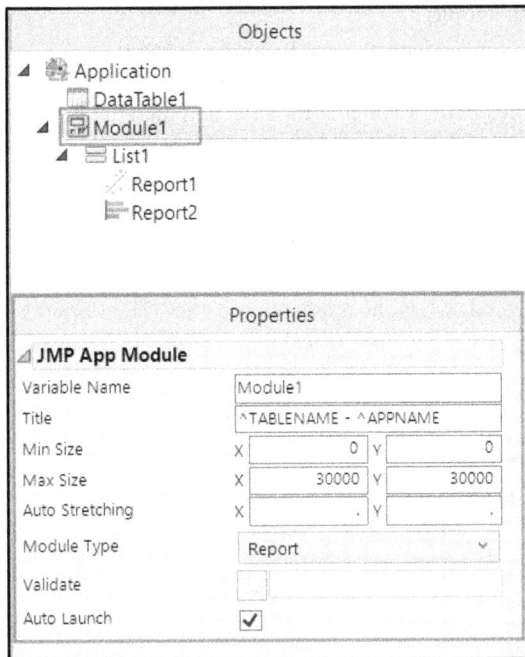

Here are two important properties to note:

1. **Module Type**: Here is where you can choose from one of six types of displays for this module, as shown in Figure 6.31:

Figure 6.31 Module Type

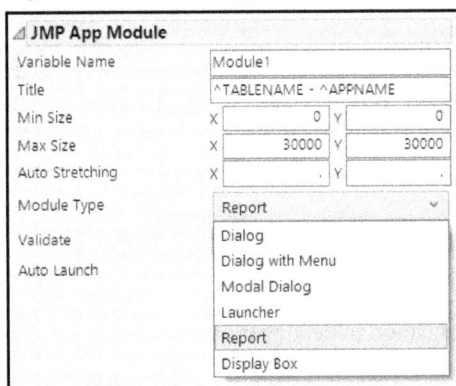

For example, if your module's function is to query the user, consider specifying the module type as **Dialog.** The sample application Data Table Application.jmpappsource shows an example of a **Dialog** module type. If a window menu is needed, specify **Dialog with Menu**.

Another option is **Modal Dialog,** which is much like the modal **New Window** function. However, there are differences, as the **Modal Dialog** module type has some special characteristics in the context of the Application Builder. Consult the "Creating Applications" chapter in the *Scripting Guide* for more information about this topic.

If you need a platform-type launcher that generates a report, use a **Launcher** module type, paired with a **Report** module type. The sample application Launcher Report.jmpappsource provides an example of casting data table columns into roles in the Launcher module, and then the Report module creates the graph.

2. **Auto Launch**: This setting determines whether the module instance is automatically executed when the application is invoked (selected), or if the module instance is conditionally executed by scripting action (unselected).

   For example, if you have a Launcher and Report module combo, the Launcher module will be set to automatically launch (**Auto Launch** is selected) when the application is run. The Report module will not be selected to automatically launch, because its instance should not occur until the Launcher module conditionally calls it.

Figure 6.32 Auto Launch

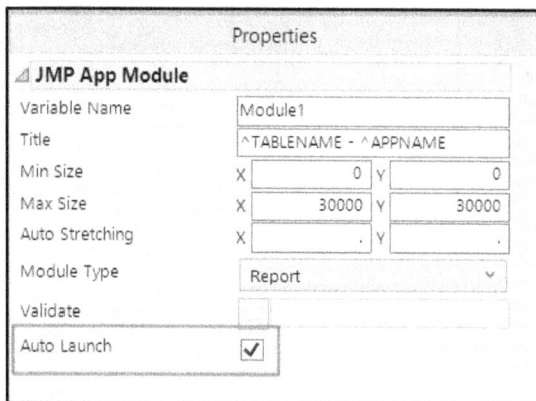

The Application Red Triangle Menu

The red triangle menu for the Application Builder offers the option to run the application so that you can see whether it works as you wish, or to use the debugger to investigate issues. You can also modify the design area grid and panels from this menu. The following table itemizes and briefly explains the menu items:

Menu Item	Action
Run Application	Executes the application program.
Debug Application	Executes the application in debugger mode.
Start Over	Closes the current window and returns to the template window for the selection.
Snap to Grid	Restricts the design area grid to 10 x 10. *
Show Grid	Shows a grid in the design area. *

Menu Item	Action
Show Properties	Exposes the Objects and Properties panels. *
Auto Scroll	Scrolls the workspace design area if a box is dragged to the bottom of the screen. *
Dashboard Mode	Arranges a report within the window and decreases the options shown. **
Source Panel	Offers options to Show Sources and Group by Category.
Save Script	Saves the application script to a specified destination.

*On by default but can be toggled off from the menu.

**Off by default when using the Application Builder.

The options for saving a script of your application are the same as with the dashboard. A script can be saved to the data table, a journal, a script window, or an add-in. If you think you might use the application as the starting point for future applications, save it as a template to decrease your development work. Your custom template scripts are listed when you open a new dashboard or application (**File ▶ New ▶ Dashboard**, or **File ▶ New ▶ Application**).

Figure 6.33 Red Triangle Menu and Save Script Options

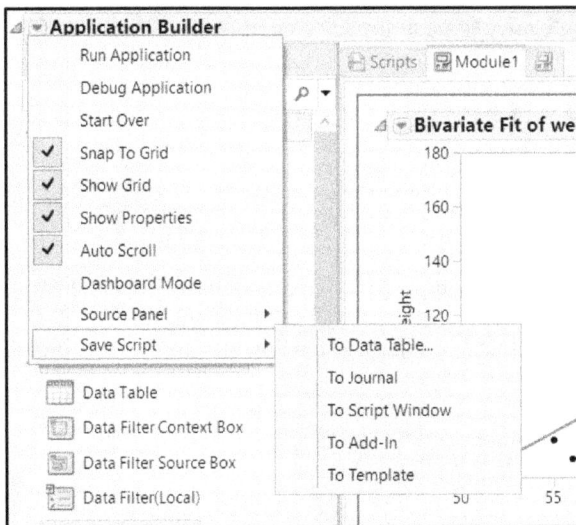

Using the Toolbar, Saving Applications, and Accessing Sample Applications

The toolbar at the top of the Application Builder has many features to make building your application easier with the click of a button. You can hold your mouse pointer over each icon to display its role. Keep in mind that one or more objects must be selected in the workspace for most of the buttons to be active. Clicking in the Objects or Properties panel dims all buttons except **Open** and **Save**.

Figure 6.34 The Application Builder Toolbar

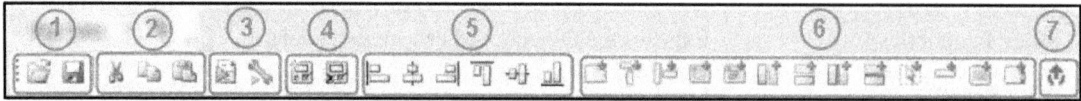

On the far left are the **Open** and **Save** icons ❶, for opening and saving other applications or saving the current application.

Just to the right are the **Cut**, **Copy**, and **Paste** icons ❷, which are used to perform these actions on components of your workspaces.

Next are the script-related buttons ❸. Use the **Run Script** button to execute your application script or a portion thereof. Use the other button, **Debug Script**, to start the JMP Debugger if you have encountered issues and need a little help determining where the problem lies.

Although you can add or delete modules from the workspace tabs, another option is to use the toolbar buttons for those actions ❹.

When you are working with lots of display boxes, it is nice to have an easy method for aligning them, and here are the buttons that will take the guesswork out of that task. You can align left, right, center, horizontal, and vertical ❺.

The toolbar also offers buttons for adding thirteen different containers ❻. Hold your mouse pointer over any container if you are unsure which container it might be. Select an object or objects in your workspace to highlight, and then click the container button of choice to wrap the selected object or objects in that chosen container.

The last button in the toolbar is the **Peel** button ❼, which is so handy if you have added a container and then have second thoughts about it. If you need to remove a container, select it in the workspace or Objects tree, and then click the **Peel** button to delete it.

Saving Your Application as a File

You have the same three options when saving your application as a file from the **File ▶ Save As** menu as you do when saving a dashboard. You can save the file as a JMP Source File (.jmpappsource), a JMP Application File (.jmpapp), or a JMP Script (.jsl). For more details, see step 9 in the "Dashboard Builder" topic in this chapter.

Figure 6.35 File Type Options When Saving an Application

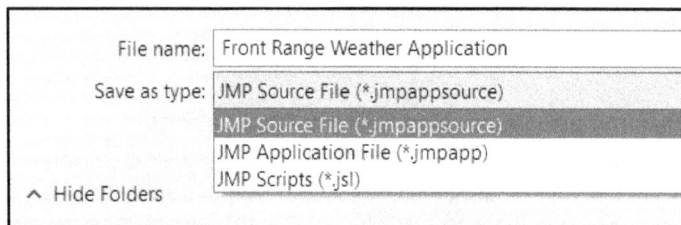

This is just a brief introduction and exploration of the Application Builder. For more comprehensive information, please visit the "Creating Applications" section of the *Scripting Guide* (**Help ▶ Books ▶ Scripting Guide**).

As mentioned earlier, you can access example applications when opening a new blank application, but these examples can also be found in the Sample Applications Directory. To access the examples, select **Help ▶ Sample Data**, and then click **Open the Sample Applications Directory**.

Figure 6.36 Opening the Sample Applications Directory

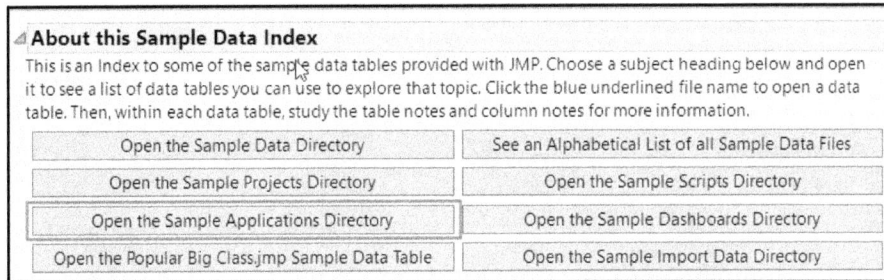

◢ **About this Sample Data Index**

This is an Index to some of the sample data tables provided with JMP. Choose a subject heading below and open it to see a list of data tables you can use to explore that topic. Click the blue underlined file name to open a data table. Then, within each data table, study the table notes and column notes for more information.

Open the Sample Data Directory	See an Alphabetical List of all Sample Data Files
Open the Sample Projects Directory	Open the Sample Scripts Directory
Open the Sample Applications Directory	Open the Sample Dashboards Directory
Open the Popular Big Class.jmp Sample Data Table	Open the Sample Import Data Directory

Summary

This brief exploration of the Application Builder suite of tools has shown you how these platforms can be used when creating reports, dashboards, and applications. By clicking, dragging, and dropping, sometimes with little or no scripting, you can save time and effort.

Next, we will discuss some advanced scripting concepts to help you understand the scripting language.

Chapter 7: Advanced Topics

Overview

As you become more proficient in JSL, there are some tools and concepts that will help you along the way. In this chapter, we discuss the following:

- building user dialogs that wait for user input, or not
- using programmatic methods for navigating your reports
- understanding the mysterious ways of expression functions
- making your scripts more robust

Building Custom Dialogs

When you need to create a script to ask the user for a response or choice, use a dialog window. There are a couple of options available in JMP scripting to do the work. We explain the basics here.

Modal and Non-modal Dialogs: What Is the Difference?

The two main types of dialog windows are modal and non-modal. A modal window halts the script and waits until the user gives a response before the script execution continues. In contrast, for a non-modal window, the script does not wait for a response from the user. The window remains open until requested to close. Responses made by the user might initiate another section of script execution or other actions. Examples of non-modal windows include the built-in analysis windows in JMP.

The **New Window()** function offers both modal and non-modal options, which are explored in the following sections, as well as another modal option, **Column Dialog()**.

New Window(): Modal

Use the modal option for the **New Window()** function when you need to force the script to stop and wait for a response from the script user.

For example, suppose you are developing a JMP script that surveys users about the types of pets they own. Start the script with a **New Window()** command. The basic syntax looks like this with the modal message added:

```
nw = New Window( title, <<Modal, displaybox );
```

We set up our display to ask the user a question with a text box and show the choices for answers in a list box. A horizontal list box is used to align the **Text Box** and **List Box**.

```
nw = New Window( "Pet Survey",
    <<Modal,
    H List Box(
        Text Box(
            "What type pets do you currently own?  Select all that apply."
        ),
        lb1 = List Box(
            {"Horse", "Dog", "Cat", "Rodent", "Pig", "Goat",
             "Llama or Alpaca", "Other Exotic"}
        )
    )
);
```

This script looks pretty good so far, but how do you retrieve the results and use them? You have a couple of options.

1. Add the **Return Result** message, and then subscript the new window reference:
   ```
   nw = New Window( "Pet Survey",
       <<Modal,
       <<Return Result,
          H List Box(
           Text Box(
               "What type pets do you currently own?  Select all that apply."
           ),
           lb1 = List Box(
               {"Horse", "Dog", "Cat", "Rodent", "Pig", "Goat",
                "Llama or Alpaca", "Other Exotic"}
           )
       )
   );

   Show( nw["lb1"] );
   ```

2. Use a **Button Box** script to get the selected results. When the user clicks the **OK** button, the results are placed in the variable named **results**:
   ```
   nw = New Window( "Pet Survey",
       <<Modal,
           H List Box(
            Text Box(
                "What type pets do you currently own?  Select all that apply."
            ),
            lb1 = List Box(
   ```

```
                    {"Horse", "Dog", "Cat", "Rodent", "Pig", "Goat",
                      "Llama or Alpaca", "Other Exotic"}
                ),
                Button Box( "OK", results = lb1 << Get Selected ),
                Button Box( "Cancel" )
            )
    );

    Show( results );
```

You might have noticed that we did not script an **OK** button in the first example. That is because JMP automatically adds a simple **OK** button to a modal dialog window if you do not.

When using the modal option with **New Window()**, there are other special options available. Please see the *JSL Syntax Reference* or the *Scripting Guide* for more information about these features.

New Window: Non-modal

The non-modal window does not halt the script action waiting for a response. Any code after the **New Window()** script is executed immediately.

Using the pet survey example again, we ask the survey respondent the same question as before regarding what type pets the user owns. Instead of an **OK** button, we will use a **Submit** button that, when clicked, gets the selected items as in the modal dialog. We also add a script to create yet another non-modal window that queries the user for any additional comments about the survey. Notice that all commands to print to the log are within **Button Box** scripts. If you place these commands after the main **New Window()** statement, they will be executed prior to getting the results of your survey.

As with the modal example, horizontal and vertical list boxes strategically wrap the display boxes to provide a more pleasing arrangement for the user interface.

Notice that both the **Submit** and **Cancel** buttons use << **Close Window** messages in this non-modal window example. The modal dialog window buttons perform this action automatically.

```
nw = New Window( "Pet Survey",
    H List Box(
        Text Box(
            "What type pets do you currently own?  Select all that apply."
        ),
        lb1 = List Box(
            {"Horse", "Dog", "Cat", "Rodent", "Pig", "Goat",
             "Llama/alpaca", "Reptile"} ),
        V List Box(
            Button Box( "Submit Survey",
                results = lb1 << Get Selected;
                Print( results );
                nw << Close Window;
                AddComment = New Window( "Comments",
                    H List Box(
                        Text Box(
                            "Comments about this survey? Please add: "
                        ),
                        teb = Text Edit Box( "  <comments>  " ),
                        V List Box(
                            Button Box( "Submit",
                                userComment = teb << get text;
```

```
                                  Print( userComment );
                                  addComment << Close Window;
                              ),
                              Button Box( "Cancel",
                                  Add Comment << Close Window
                              )
                          )
                      )
                  );
              ),
              Button Box( "Cancel", nw << Close Window )
          )
      )
  );
```

The **New Window()** function offers many more options than are shown here. Please see the *JSL Syntax Reference* or the *Scripting Guide* for more information about these features. Additional examples of using **New Window()** are in chapter 8 of this book, "Dialog Windows."

Column Dialog()

Column Dialog() is a specialized modal dialog function that presents the user with a dialog window with the columns of the current data table. If you need a launch window to prompt users to cast columns in roles, this function is for you.

The main display component of **Column Dialog()** is the **ColList()** element, but this window also accommodates container boxes for display, such as list boxes, check boxes, and radio buttons. You can specify the minimum and maximum columns to be cast in for each variable, as well as the data types and modeling types. There is no need to script buttons, as this is a modal dialog with the buttons already built in.

```
colDlg = Column Dialog(
    gb_y = ColList( "Temperature Variables",
           Min Col( 1 ),
           Max Col( 3 ),
           Data Type( "Numeric" )
    ),
    gb_x = ColList( "Date", Max Col( 1 ), Data Type( "Numeric" ), )
);

Show(colDlg);
```

What is returned after running the dialog script might look like this, if the **:TMIN, :TMAX, :TAVG**, and **:Date** columns were selected and the **OK** button was clicked:

```
colDlg = {gb_y = {:TMIN, :TMAX, :TAVG}, gb_x = {:DATE}, Button(1)};
```

Note: If the **Cancel** button was clicked instead, **Button(-1)** would be returned, and the variables **gb_y** and **gb_x** would be empty lists.

To use the results from a modal dialog window, you must reference the values by subscripting the list result to use elsewhere in the script. But first, remove the last item in the list, **Button(1)**, and then evaluate the list:

```
Remove From( coldlg, N Items( coldlg ) ););

    Show( colDlg );
```

```
colDlg = {gb_y = {:TMIN, :TMAX, :TAVG}, gb_x = {:DATE}};
```

```
Eval List( coldlg );
Show( gb_y, gb_x );
```

```
gb_y = {:TMIN, :TMAX, :TAVG};
gb_x = {:DATE};
```

Now you are ready to use your variable in your scripted platform.

Keep in mind you can also script your own column dialog from scratch using the **New Window()** function, which offers more options. However, the **Column Dialog()** function is quick and easy.

For more information about syntax and options, reference the Scripting Index. See chapter 8 for another example of a column dialog window.

Navigating Reports Programmatically

In chapter 3, we discussed platform objects and how they are constructed. Specifically, we showed that the resulting reports consist of two layers: the analysis layer and the report layer. In each of the examples discussed, we used a subscripting method to retrieve values, change axis settings, and add or remove items from a report. Let's dive a little deeper into navigating reports using subscripting and explore XPath as an alternative for locating items in the XML representation of a report.

Subscripting

In JSL, subscripting is useful for accessing values in various objects, such as columns, lists, matrices, and display boxes. Since the report layer consists of display boxes, subscripting is an easy way to reference items in a report.

When you look at the Tree Structure window, you will notice that most items have a number in parentheses after the display box name. Using these numbers is not a reliable method for referencing specific display boxes, because the numbers can be affected by a variety of things, such as preference settings and the version of JMP being used.

A more robust approach is to subscript the report by the title of the Outline Box that is the container for the desired value. This method is known as relative referencing. The desired value can be accessed in relation to that Outline Box as a subscript.

In chapter 3, we discussed extracting the R-squared value from a Oneway report. In that example, we referenced the Number Col Box that contained the R-squared value as a subscript of the **Summary of Fit** Outline Box title. However, the number shown in the tree structure for the Number Col Box happened to be the same as we used in our script. That will not always be the case. So let's look at a different example that exposes the problem with using the display box number shown in the tree structure.

Suppose you wanted to extract the height estimate from the Parameter Estimates table in a Bivariate report. We will begin by looking at the tree structure. Since we are specifically interested in Parameter Estimates, we can right-click the gray disclosure icon beside Parameter Estimates, and select **Edit ▶ Show Tree Structure** to see only the part of the tree structure that pertains to the Parameter Estimates Outline Box .

Figure 7.1 Parameter Estimates and Tree Structure

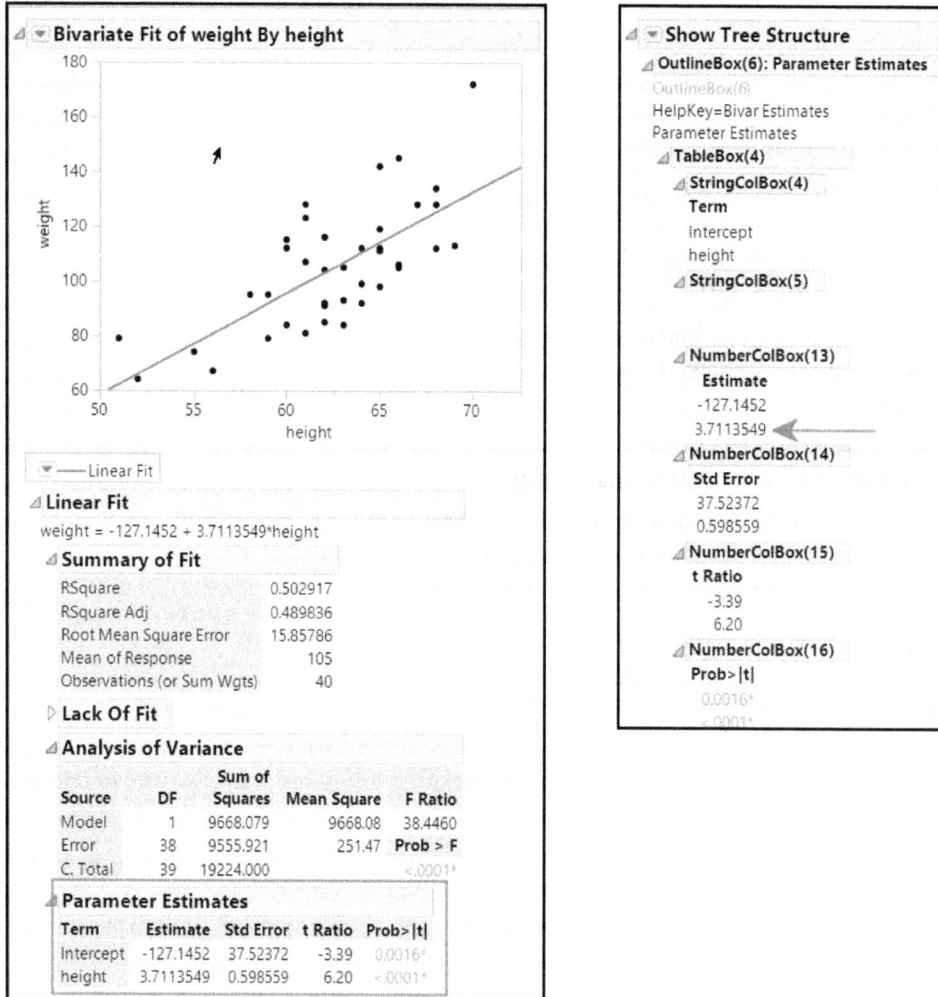

Based on what we learned in chapter 3, the proper way to access the height estimate would be to first access the report layer. To use relative referencing, we then subscript using the title of the Parameter Estimates Outline Box, followed by the Number Col Box in relation to the Outline Box, and the location of the value in that Number Col Box.

That script would look like this:

```
dt = Open( "$SAMPLE_DATA\Big Class.jmp" );

biv = dt << Bivariate(
    Y( :weight ),
    X( :height ),
    Fit Line
);

heightEstimate =                    //Assign a variable to the result
  Report( biv )                     //Report Layer
      ["Parameter Estimates"]       //"Parameter Estimates" Outline Box
          [Number Col Box( 1 )]     //First NumberColBox
              [2];                  //Second item

Show( heightEstimate );
```

```
/*:

heightEstimate = 3.71135489385953;
```

By using the string **"Parameter Estimates"** as the first subscript, we directed JMP to that Outline Box, regardless of what number is shown for **Outline Box(n)** in the tree structure.

Though the tree structure shows **NumberColBox(13)** in Figure 7.1, the Number Col Box is the first Number Col Box under the Parameter Estimates Outline Box. Therefore, **Number Col Box(1)** is the next subscript.

The last subscript, **[2]**, refers to the second item in that Number Col Box, which is the actual value that we wanted.

> Look at the GIF file named Chapter7_SubscriptDemo.gif, included in the files that accompany this book, to see a visual demonstration of the items subscripted.

Now, what would happen if another user ran this same script but had different preference settings? Suppose the user has turned on the Summary Statistics preference.

Figure 7.2 Bivariate Preferences

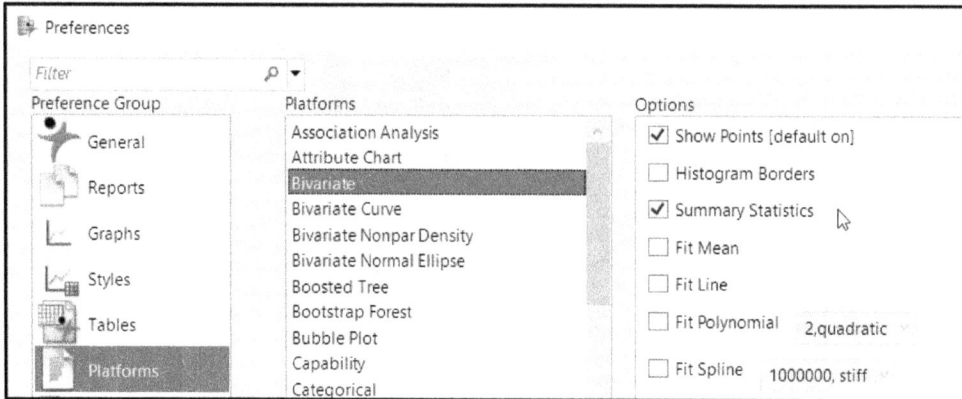

Because we subscripted by the Parameter Estimates Outline Box title, the script will produce the report and extract the correct value, as shown in Figure 7.3.

Figure 7.3 Report and Log

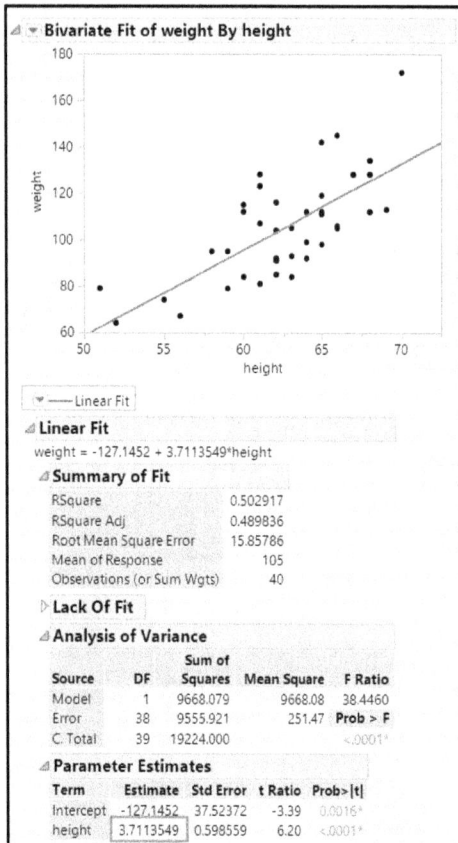

```
dt = Open( "$SAMPLE_DATA\Big Class.jmp"
);

biv = dt << Bivariate(
    Y( :weight ),
    X( :height ),
    Fit Line
);

//Assign a variable to the result
heightEstimate =
    //Report Layer
    Report( biv )
        //Outline Box  Title
        ["Parameter Estimates"]
            //First NumberColBox
            [Number Col Box( 1 )]
                //Second item
                [2];

Show( heightEstimate );
```

```
/*:

heightEstimate = 3.71135489385953;
```

If we had not used relative referencing and instead used **NumberColBox(13)** as shown in the tree structure, JMP would have attempted to extract a value from a Number Col Box in the Lack Of Fit report table instead of the Parameter Estimates report table.

Figure 7.4 Report and Tree Structure with Summary Statistics

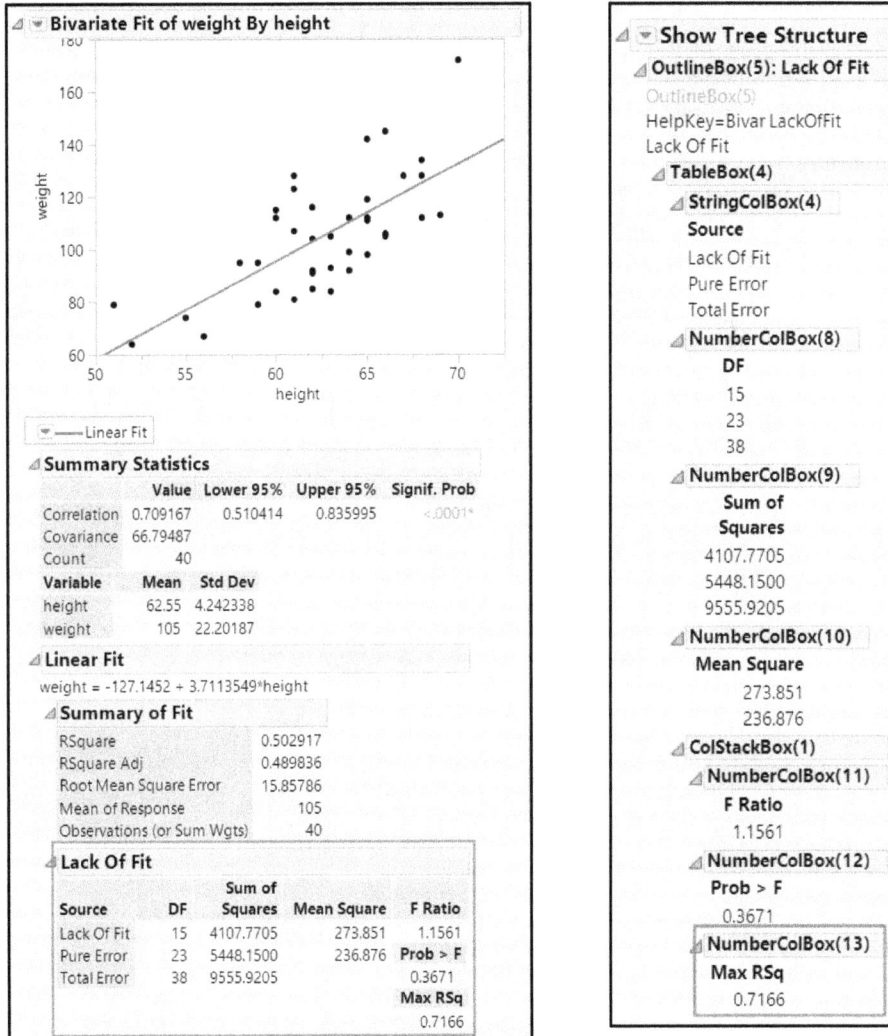

Notice that there is only one item in this **NumberColBox(13)**. Therefore, an error is generated in the log when we attempt to subscript to an item that does not exist.

```
dt = Open( "$SAMPLE_DATA\Big Class.jmp" );

biv = dt << Bivariate(
    Y( :weight ),
    X( :height ),
    Fit Line
);
```

```
heightEstimate = Report( biv )[Number Col Box( 13 )][2];
```

```
/*:

index in access or evaluation of 'Get' , Get( 2 ) /*###*/
```

As this example demonstrates, relative referencing ensures that your script runs correctly even when another JMP user has different preference settings. This is one reason relative referencing is considered a best practice and overall good scripting habit.

Another way to prevent preferences from affecting how your script behaves is to add the **Ignore Platform Preferences(1)** option to your platform call. Although you can probably think of instances where this option would be useful, it might be undesirable. For any options that the user prefers to appear in the report (or not, as the case may be), the user would have to make those changes either to the script or interactively.

As stated earlier, preferences are only one reason the display box numbering could be different from what you expect at the time you create your script. Because JMP is always improving and listening to customer requests and feedback, report structure might also differ between releases of JMP. By using relative referencing, you are guarding your script against the effects of those types of changes.

XPath

Many of us are familiar with XML documents. For those who are not, XML stands for Extensible Markup Language. It is a markup language that establishes a set of rules for documents that are readable and understood by machines. XPath is a query language that enables you to navigate your XML documents.

Though XML looks quite a bit like HTML, their purposes are different. The purpose of HTML is to display content, whereas the purpose of XML is more about data storage and conveying content.

Let's discuss a few of the primary components of an XML document:

- **Tags** – Tags are what makes XML look a bit like HTML. Tags generally start with an opening less than sign (<) and end with a closing greater than sign (>). The tag name is specified between the < and > signs, and it is not a predefined value. Instead, the author of the document must establish the tag names. As in HTML, tags must be closed with a forward slash to represent an ending tag (for example, <tagname> content </tagname>).
- **Elements** – An element consists of an entire tag statement, if you will. An element begins with the < of the opening tag all the way to and including the > of the closing tag. Elements can contain other elements, as well.
- **Attributes** – Attributes are metadata or additional details about an element. An attribute is specified in the opening tag and can only have one value, specified in double quotation marks. A tag can have multiple attributes, but only one of each type.
- **Content** – Content is the data. It is the text, numbers, and other characters between the opening and closing tags that make up an element.

Consider the following example XML file. The **openTables** element is the root element in which all other elements appear. The table element has an attribute called **current**, which has a value of 0 or 1. Inside each table element are three additional elements: **name**, **numCols**, and **numRows**. The data appears between the tags.

```
<openTables>

    <table current="1">
        <name>Big Class</name>
        <numCols>5</numCols>
        <numRows>40</numRows>
    </table>

    <table current="0">
        <name>Fitness</name>
        <numCols>9</numCols>
        <numRows>31<numRows>
    </table>

</openTables>
```

Now that we understand the structure of an XML document, we can apply that knowledge to the structure of a JMP report as an XML document. To see the XML representation of a JMP report, send the **Get XML** message to the report layer. The XML will appear in the log (**View ▶ Log**).

> A bit of warning: Do not be alarmed by the magnitude of the XML that appears in the log. It still has the same format of the preceding simple example, just with more elements, attributes, and content.

Let's look at an example. Suppose you wanted to programmatically determine how many Outline Boxes appeared in a Distribution report.

```
dt = Open( "$SAMPLE_DATA\Big Class.jmp" );

dist = dt << Distribution(
    Stack( 1 ),
    Continuous Distribution(
        Column( :height ),
        Horizontal Layout( 1 ),
        Vertical( 0 )
    )
);
```

You could use JSL to step through the display boxes and check their type, but it would be a rather tedious task. Instead, let's look at the XML representation.

```
Write( Report( dist ) << Get XML );
```

The result shown in the log is a string that is nearly 180 lines long. Don't be overwhelmed! Scroll to the top of the log and look at just the first tag:

```
/*:
<OutlineBox width="717" height="277" helpKey="Distrib" isOpen="true">
```

The tag is named **OutlineBox** and it has four attributes: **width**, **height**, **helpKey**, and **isOpen**. Everything that comes next is the content of the element, which is the title of the Outline Box and other elements. As you look at the other elements, notice that the element names are the same as the display box names in the tree structure but in an XML format.

Figure 7.5 XML Elements Compared to Tree Structure

```
<OutlineBox attributes>Title
  <ListBox attributes>
    <DropBox attributes>
      <SpacerBox attributes>
    </DropBox>
    <OutlineBox attributes>Title
    etc...
```

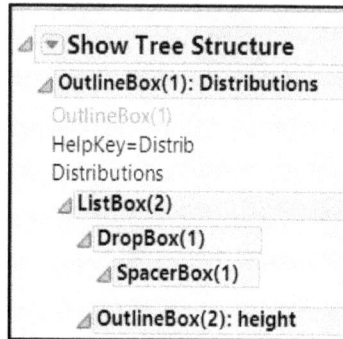

Now that we know the tag name of the element that we are searching for, let's explore how we can use XPath to find out how many Outline Boxes there are.

> As mentioned, XPath is a query language. It is not specific to JMP or JSL. Rather, there are many resources on the internet to help you understand all the details of XPath. In this book, we demonstrate some of the options available in XPath.

In JMP, the **XPath()** message is sent to either the platform object or the report object. Its argument is an XPath expression used to retrieve information from the XML representation of the report. You do not have to use **Get XML** before you can use the **XPath()** message. But you might find it helpful to review the structure and available attributes.

The following will search the report for any Outline Boxes and return a list of references to each Outline Box.

```
obList = Report( dist ) << XPath( "//OutlineBox" );
Show( obList );
```

```
/*:

obList = {DisplayBox[OutlineBox], DisplayBox[OutlineBox], DisplayBox[OutlineBox],
DisplayBox[OutlineBox]};
```

We could simply use the **NItems()** function on **obList** to obtain the number of Outline Box references are stored in the list. Or as you learn more about the XPath language, you can use the **XPath Count()** function to return the count instead of a reference to each Outline Box.

```
obCount = N Items( Report( dist ) << XPath( "//OutlineBox" ) );
//OR
obCount = Report( dist ) << XPath( "count(//OutlineBox)" );
```

Now let's look at a more interesting example. Suppose we wanted to display only the Mean and Std Dev columns in a Means and Std Deviations table of a Oneway report.

Figure 7.6 Oneway with Means and Std Deviations

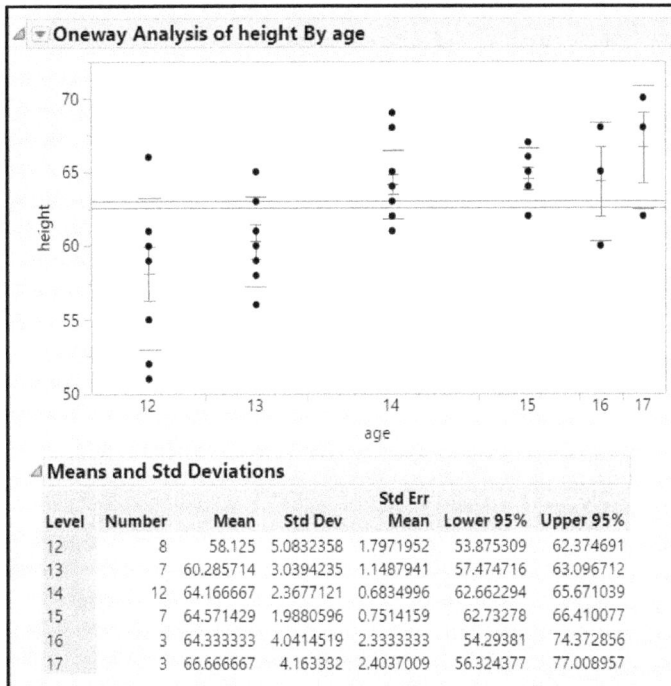

```
dt = Open(
  "$SAMPLE_DATA\Big
Class.jmp"
);

ow = dt << Oneway(
    Y( :height ),
    X( :age ),
    Means and Std Dev( 1
),
    Mean Error Bars( 1 ),
    Std Dev Lines( 1 ),
    Mean of Means( 1 )
);
```

⊿ **Means and Std Deviations**

Level	Number	Mean	Std Dev	Std Err Mean	Lower 95%	Upper 95%
12	8	58.125	5.0832358	1.7971952	53.875309	62.374691
13	7	60.285714	3.0394235	1.1487941	57.474716	63.096712
14	12	64.166667	2.3677121	0.6834996	62.662294	65.671039
15	7	64.571429	1.9880596	0.7514159	62.73278	66.410077
16	3	64.333333	4.0414519	2.3333333	54.29381	74.372856
17	3	66.666667	4.163332	2.4037009	56.324377	77.008957

We can return a list of just the Number Col Box references under the Means and Std Deviations table using a combination of subscripting and XPath:

```
/* Return a list of NumberColBox references */
ncbList = Report( ow )["Means and Std Deviations"] << XPath( "//NumberColBox" );
```

Using a JSL **For()** loop, we can check the heading of the column and change the visibility property to collapsed if the heading is anything other than Mean or Std Dev.

```
/* Loop through each item to show only the Mean, Std Dev columns */
For( i = 1, i <= N Items( ncbList ), i++,
    rptColName = ncbList[i] << Get Heading;
    If( !Contains( {"Mean", "Std Dev"}, rptColName ),
        ncbList[i] << Visibility( "Collapse" )
    )
);
```

But again, there is a way in XPath to accomplish the same result without the need for the **For()** loop. Look at an excerpt of the XML representation of a Number Col Box from the report:

```
<NumberColBox leftOffset=\!"40\!" topOffset=\!"0\!" isVisible=\!"false\!">
<NumberColBoxHeader>Number</NumberColBoxHeader>
```

Notice that there is an element within the **NumberColBox** element called **NumberColBoxHeader**. This element contains the report column heading. XPath enables us to capture that text and perform comparisons. Only references to Number Col Boxes that have a heading that are anything other than Mean or Std Dev are returned in a list.

```
colsToHide = Report( ow )["Means and Std Deviations"] << XPath(
    "//NumberColBox[NumberColBoxHeader[not(text() = 'Mean')
        and not(text() = 'Std Dev')]]"
);
```

This XPath query looks at **NumberColBoxHeader** elements that appear within a **NumberColBox** element. The Text function extracts the text from the **NumberColBoxHeader** element. In this example, if the text meets the criteria, meaning that the text is not mean and not Std Dev, then the reference is returned in a list.

Sending the **Visibility()** message to that list applies the setting to every item in the list.

```
    colsToHide << Visibility( "Collapse" );
```

Figure 7.7 Oneway After Columns Are Hidden

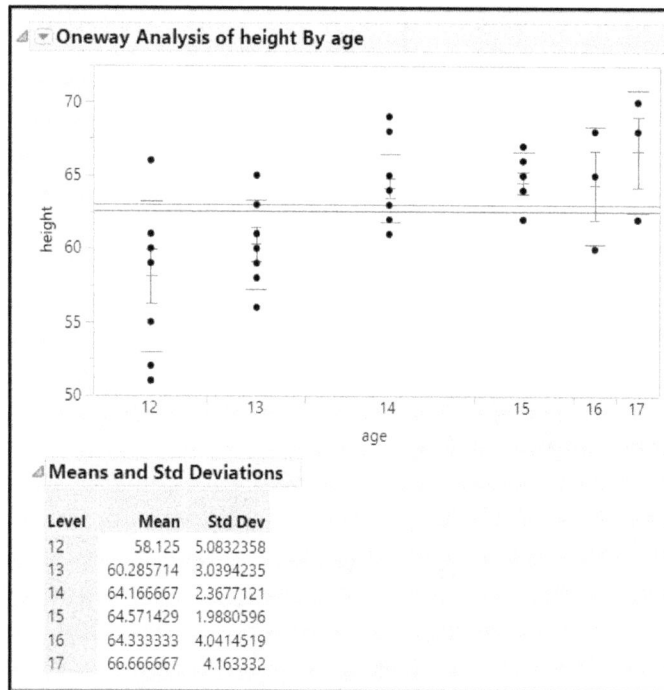

Expression Handling

What is an expression? In JMP, it is something that can be evaluated. It can be a combination of variables, constants, or even a collection of scripting commands linked by operators. Why is it important to a scripter? Because there are times when you want to wait to evaluate, or simply control when to evaluate, such as when a user must be prompted for a response that will be used to initialize a variable.

JSL provides expression-handling functions to facilitate this control. **Eval()** is used to evaluate arguments, whereas others, such as **Expr()** and **Eval Expr()**, are containers that control how their expression arguments are evaluated.

Expr()

Everything within the argument of the **Expr()** function is considered an expression. The argument contents can be numeric or string literals, variables, arithmetic expressions, or a combination of any or all. These examples are all expressions:

```
Expr( 5 + 1 );
Expr( y = m * x + b );
Expr( "The weather is sunny " || "in Aspen." );
Expr( For (i = 1, i <= 5, i++, Print(i) ) );
```

If you execute these in a script window, the results show the arguments for each **Expr()** function. No attempts were made to simplify the expressions or evaluate any variable.

Eval()

The **Eval()** function evaluates the expression and returns the result. If we wrap all the preceding expressions in **Eval()**, we see these simplified results:

```
Eval( Expr( 5 + 1 ) );
m = 0.5; x = 2; b = 5; Eval( Expr( y = m * x + b ) );
Eval( Expr( "The weather is sunny " || "in Aspen." ) );
Eval( Expr( For( i = 1, i <= 5, i++, Print( i ) ) ) );
```

```
//:*/
Eval( Expr( 5 + 1 ) );
/*:

6
//:*/
m = 0.5; x = 2; b = 5; Eval( Expr( y = m * x + b ) );
/*:

6
//:*/
Eval( Expr( "The weather is sunny " || "in Aspen." ) );
/*:

"The weather is sunny in Aspen."
//:*/
Eval( Expr( For( i = 1, i <= 5, i++, Print( i ) ) ) );
/*:

1
2
3
4
5
```

Eval Expr()

A good method to evaluate an expression within any expression is to use the **Eval Expr()** function. This function replaces each **Expr()** argument with its evaluated value.

The syntax is very simple. The given argument must be an expression:

```
Eval Expr( expr )
```

In this example, we want to create a bivariate plot using a Where statement, and the value to be used for the Where statement is stored in the **selVar** variable.

```
dt = Open( "$SAMPLE_DATA/Fitness.jmp" );
selVar = "M";
biv = dt << Bivariate( X( :MaxPulse ), Y( :RstPulse ), Where( :sex == selVar ) );
```

If we simply use **Where (:sex == selVar)**, the graph appears to be correct, but the Where statement above the graph shows the variable name, not the variable value:

Figure 7.8 Bivariate Report without Using Expressions

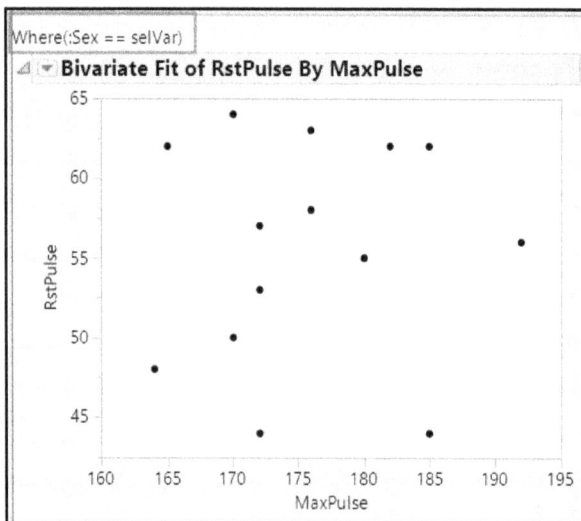

Put the **Bivariate** command in an expression, and wrap the variable, **selVar**, in an **Expr()** function:

```
bivExpr = Expr(
    dt << Bivariate( X( :MaxPulse ), Y( :RstPulse ), Where( :sex == Expr( selVar
) ) )
);
```

Place the **bivExpr** as argument to **Eval Expr()**:

```
EvalExpr( bivExpr )
```

If you execute this code, you will see in the log that the value of **selVar** has been inserted into the expression **bivExpr**:

```
Bivariate( X( :MaxPulse ), Y( :RstPulse ), Where( :sex == "M" ) )
```

In order to execute the expression, the **Eval()** function should encompass the **Eval Expr()** function:

```
biv = Eval( Eval Expr( bivExpr ) );
```

The complete code is as follows:

```
dt = Open( "$SAMPLE_DATA/Fitness.jmp" );

selVar = "M";

bivExpr = Expr(
    dt << Bivariate( X( :MaxPulse ), Y( :RstPulse ), Where( :sex == Expr( selVar ) )
)
);

biv = Eval( Eval Expr( bivExpr ) );
```

The desired results are achieved, as Figure 7.9 shows.

Figure 7.9 Bivariate Where Statement When Using Eval Expr()

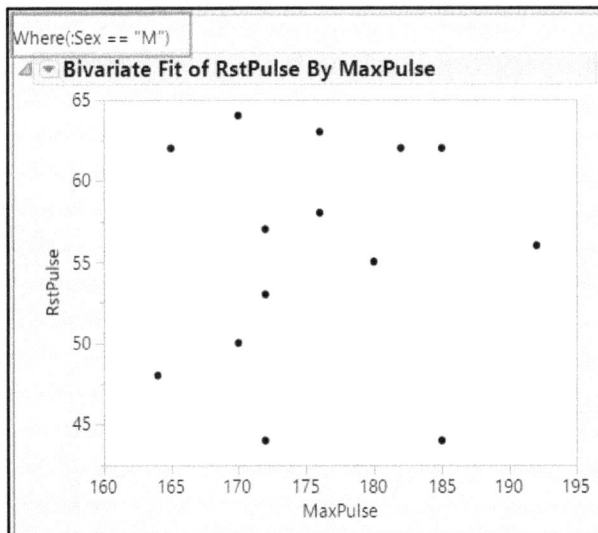

Using **Eval Expr()** is also a favorite method when replacing variable values in a column formula. This example shows how to use it in a column formula, replacing a value at run time.

We have a table on wine data, including a ranking of each wine. A column with a formula is added to the table to show that if a wine has a rank above the threshold, then "YES" is assigned, and when the rank is below the threshold, then "NO" is assigned. The threshold, determined by the user, is initialized in the variable **thresholdRank**.

The problem is that if the following script is executed, the formula in the new column retains the variable **ratingThreshold**, which is not initialized and produces an error when the table is opened in a subsequent new session of JMP:

```
dt = Open( "$SAMPLE_DATA/Design Experiment/Wine Data.jmp" );

ratingThreshold = 10;

thresCol = dt << New Column( "Above Rating Threshold",
    "Character",
    "Nominal",
    Formula( If( :Rating >= ratingThreshold, "YES", "NO" ) )
);
```

Figure 7.10 Formula Editor

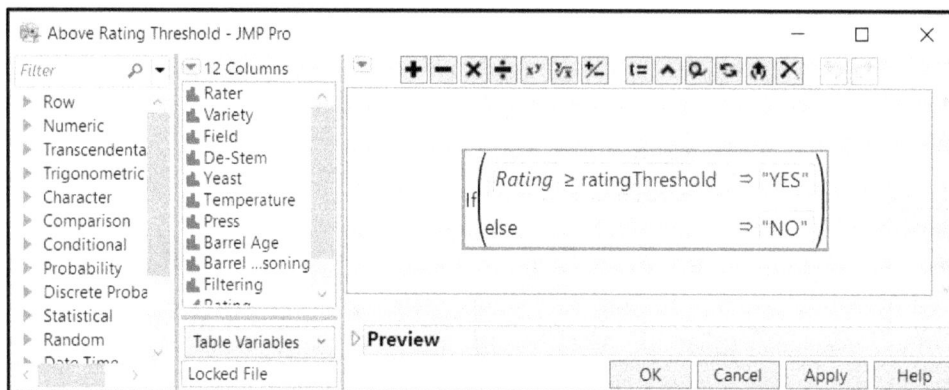

A better way to handle this is to use **Eval Expr()** to replace the variable with its evaluated value in the formula:

```
dt = Open( "$SAMPLE_DATA/Design Experiment/Wine Data.jmp" );

ratingThreshold = 10;

thresCol = Eval(
    Eval Expr(
        dt << New Column( "Above Rating Threshold",
            "character",
            "nominal",
            Formula( If( :Rating >= Expr( ratingThreshold ), "YES", "NO" ) )
        )
    )
);
```

Figure 7.11 Formula after Using Eval Expr()

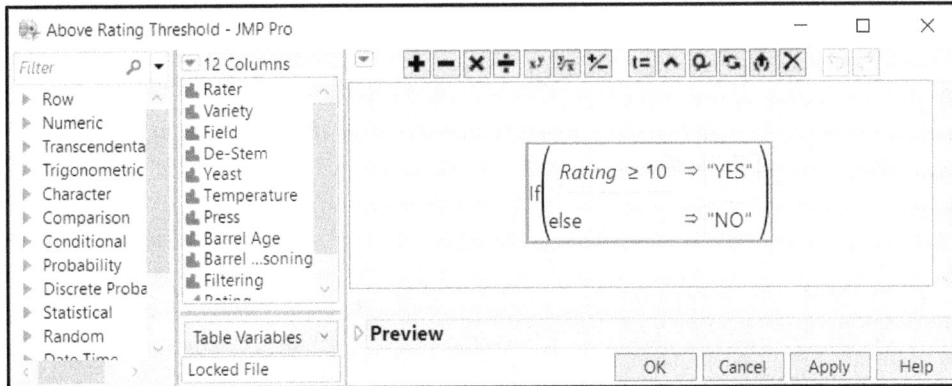

Substitute()

Sometimes you need to replace a value in an expression before it is evaluated. This happens frequently when you are creating the expression dynamically at run time. The **Substitute()** expression-handling function can replace parts of your expression with the stored argument.

Here is the syntax for this function:

```
Substitute( x, patternExpr1, replacementExpr1, …)
```

In the **Eval Expr()** example shown previously in this chapter (see Figure 7.8), we can instead use **Substitute()** to place the value of **selVar** into an expression containing the **Bivariate** command.

Here is the original script:

```
dt = Open( "$SAMPLE_DATA/Fitness.jmp" );
selVar = "M";
biv = dt << Bivariate( X( :MaxPulse ), Y( :RstPulse ), Where( :sex == selVar ) );
```

Create the **Bivariate** expression:

```
Expr(
    Bivariate( X( :MaxPulse ), Y( :RstPulse ), Where( :sex == choice ) )
)
```

The variable **choice** was inserted as a placeholder. Notice that the entire command is wrapped with the **Expr()** function.

Next, use the **Bivariate** expression as the first argument for the **Substitute()** function, and then add the second argument as the expression that will be replaced. The third argument is the variable value to be used as the replacement:

```
Substitute(
    Expr(
        Bivariate( X( :MaxPulse ), Y( :RstPulse ), Where( :sex == choice ) )
    ),
    Expr( choice ), selVar
)
```

If you execute the **Substitute()** function as is, you will see in the resulting log that the replacement has been made:

```
Bivariate( X( :MaxPulse ), Y( :RstPulse ), Where( :sex == "M" ) )
```

Substitute() has made the replacement in the expression, but to execute the expression, the **Substitute()** function must be wrapped in an **Eval()** function:

```
Eval(
    Substitute(
        Expr(
            Bivariate( X( :MaxPulse ), Y( :RstPulse ), where( :sex == choice ) )
        ),
        Expr( choice ), selVar
    )
)
```

The finished code looks like this, and produces the results shown in Figure 7.12.

```
dt = Open( "$SAMPLE_DATA/Fitness.jmp" );

selVar = "M";

biv = Eval(
    Substitute(
        Expr(
            Bivariate( X( :MaxPulse ), Y( :RstPulse ), Where( :sex == choice ) )
        ),
        Expr( choice ), selVar
    )
);
```

Figure 7.12 Bivariate Report Using Expressions and the Substitute() Function

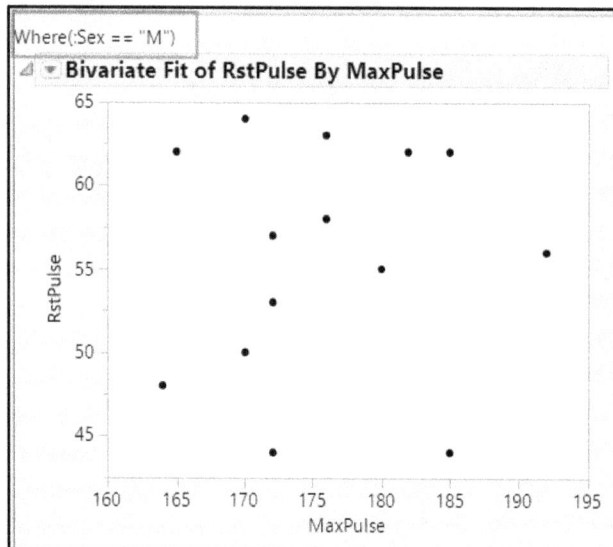

The **Substitute()** function is very handy. It can also be used if you need to replace multiple occurrences of the same variable within an expression. Please see its entry the Scripting Index for additional examples.

Finally, there are other helpful functions to investigate, such as **Eval Insert()**, **Name Expr(), Parse()**, and **Eval List()**. Search for these in the Scripting Index to learn how these functions can help you in your scripts.

Defensive Programming Strategies

You might have heard the saying that 80% of the work is done in 20% of the time. That is definitely true when it comes to writing a complex script. For many of us, it is fun to write a script that builds a neat interface and accomplishes an important task. That's where creativity is most fulfilled, right? It is that last 20% of the work that ensures that all the details are taken care of that will prevent your script from breaking.

In the context of JMP scripts, the concept of defensive programming encompasses various types of condition handling to prevent exceptions. These strategies are used to make your script durable. Remember, not all errors are unexpected.

Condition Handling

At the start of your script development, it is important to spend time considering possible situations and how they should be handled. For example, suppose your script prompts the user to open a data file. What if a text file was selected but you were expecting an Excel file? Or what if the user supplies fewer columns to your custom launch window than is necessary for the remainder of your script to run successfully? What if they just click **Cancel**? These are examples of conditions that you can easily handle in your script. The following are some things you can do to handle such situations:

- **Wrong File Type** – The **Pick File()** function offers a filter list option, which limits the files shown in the dialog to those that are specified. If your script's **Open()** function has options that are specific to a particular file type, such as Excel, you can specify only Excel file types in the filter list option. Here is an example that demonstrates the filter list:

```
excelFile = Pick File(
    "Select Excel File",       //Prompt message
    "$SAMPLE_IMPORT_DATA",      //Initial directory
    {"Excel Files|xlsx;xls"},   //Filter list (with Excel file types only)
    1,                          //Filter to show (if more than one filter)
    0,                          //File action: Open = 0, Save = 1
    "",                         //No file initially selected
    //"Multiple"                //Option to allow selection of >1 file
);
```

Figure 7.13 Pick File() Dialog

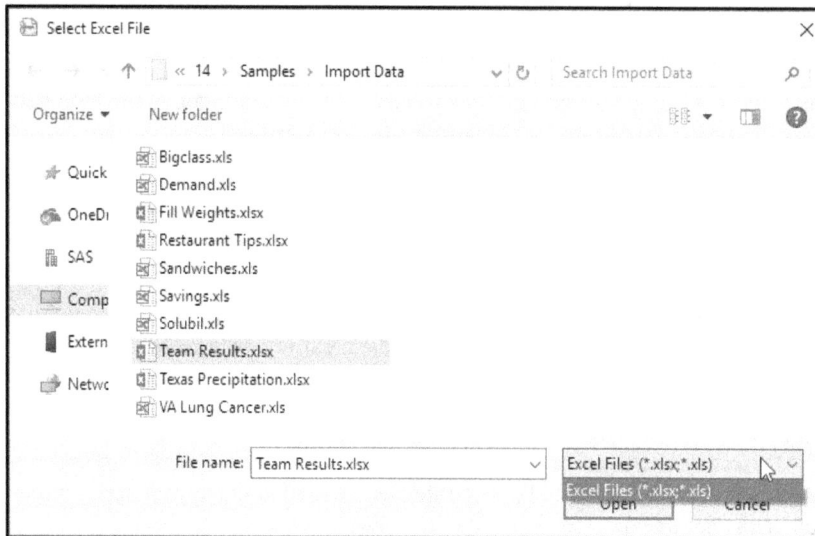

- **Incorrect User Input** – When you are building a script with custom dialogs, it is easy to focus on getting your code to work for the expected inputs. But you should also take care that the expected inputs are the only inputs allowed. Familiarizing yourself with the options available for the display boxes that make up your custom dialog helps you do just that.

In the following example script, we use a Col List Box to prompt the user to select a column:

```
nw = New Window( "Launch",
    <<Modal,
    V List Box( Align( "Right" ),
        Panel Box( "Select columns to analyze",
            Lineup Box( N Col( 3 ), Spacing( 5 ),
                clbAll = Col List Box( Data Table( dt ), "All" ),
                Button Box( ">>",
                    clbGet = clbAll << Get Selected;
                    clbSelect << Append( clbGet );
                ),
                clbSelect = Col List Box( )
            )
        ),
        H List Box(
            Button Box( "OK",
                analyzeCols = clbSelect << Get Items;
            ),
            Button Box( "Cancel" )
        )
    )
);
```

Figure 7.14 Custom Launch Dialog

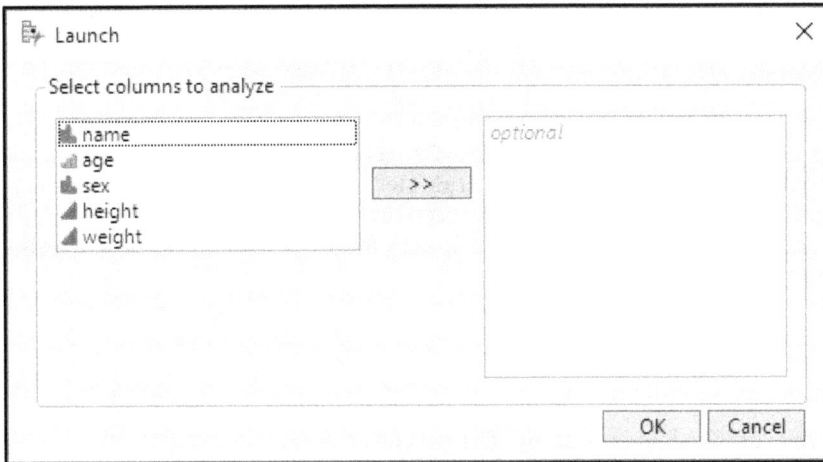

This dialog, though simple, looks okay. Little is done to ensure that the expected columns are selected. Notice the word *optional* in the box on the right? This means that columns of any data type can be selected, but no columns have to be selected, which is not likely what you want. So although your script would work perfectly for the expected inputs, you need to prevent any unexpected inputs.

By reviewing the Col List Box entries in the Scripting Index and the *JSL Syntax Reference*, you will find optional arguments that enable you to control the number of columns that can be added, as well as the data type and modeling type, if desired. By adjusting the options in the Col List Box referenced by **clbSelect**, we can ensure that only one numeric column is selected.

```
clbSelect = Col List Box(
     Data Table( dt ),    //Optional data table reference
     "Numeric",           //Numeric columns only
     MinItems( 1 ),       //At least one column required
     MaxItems( 1 ),       //No more than one column accepted
     Nlines( 5 )          //Number of lines to show
)
```

Now the box on the right shows the text *required numeric*, which provides a clear indication for the user that a numeric column should be selected.

Figure 7.15 Updated Custom Dialog

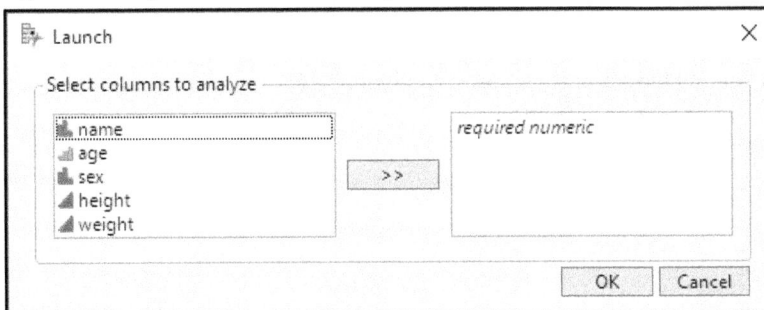

> There are many more options to discover that would enable you to specify both data and modeling types, and more. So we definitely recommend that you review the options in the documentation. Also, be sure to check out chapter 9 for more examples of custom dialogs!

- **User Clicks Cancel** – If the user were to click **Cancel** in the **Pick File()** dialog, the value in **excelFile** would be an empty string. If the **"Multiple"** option were used (commented out in the preceding example), then the value stored in **excelFile** would be an empty list. To ensure your script exits gracefully, you can add a check that stops the script when the value in **excelFile** is either an empty string or an empty list.

```
If( excelFile == "" | excelFile == {},        //Check for either
    Throw( "User clicked Cancel." )
);
```

In this case, if either condition is true, the **Throw()** function is used to stop the script execution and to print a message in the log.

If the user were to click **Cancel** in the modal New Window, you would need to check the value of the **nw** reference. In this case, the value of **nw** would be **{Button(-1)}**.

```
If( nw["Button"] == -1,
    Throw( "User clicked Cancel." )
);
```

This script checks for the **-1** value returned by the button. If the condition is true, the **Throw()** function is used again to stop the script execution and to print a message in the log.

- **Differences in User Results** – When you are scripting an analysis, it's easy to assume that the results you see are exactly what another user will see when they run your script. Neglecting to consider that others might have different preference settings that could affect the results of your script is certainly an easy thing to do.

Consider the following example. The script opens a sample table and runs a Distribution on two columns.

```
dt = Open( "$SAMPLE_DATA\SATByYear.jmp" );

dist = dt << Distribution(
    Continuous Distribution( Column( :SAT Verbal ) ),
    Continuous Distribution( Column( :SAT Math ) )
);
```

The output when you run the script is as shown in Figure 7.16.

Figure 7.16 Expected Output

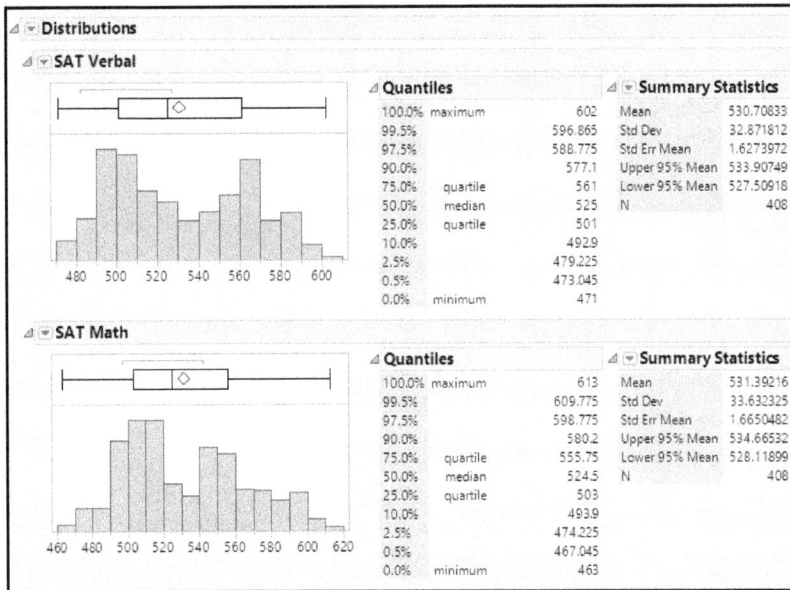

Figure 7.16 Expected Output

But when your colleague runs the same script, the result is as shown in Figure 7.17.

Figure 7.17 Output for Another User

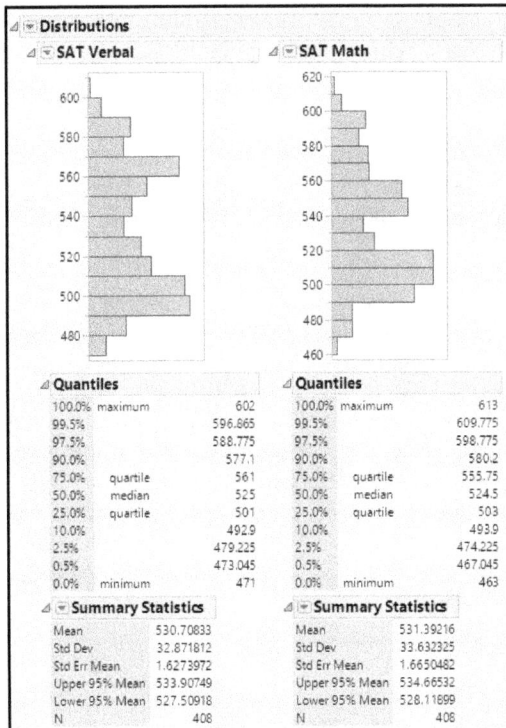

So what happened? Because your script does not explicitly stack the output, the results for this colleague do not have the eye-pleasing layout that you intended. And it appears that your colleague has the Outlier Box Plots turned off in their preferences.

If the layout and options that you see are important to what you are trying to convey, then those options need to be explicitly accounted for in your script. For this example, you can ensure the output is stacked and the Outlier Box Plots are turned on by making the following hightlighted adjustments:

```
dist = dt << Distribution(
    Stack( 1 ),
    Continuous Distribution(
        Column( :SAT Verbal ), Outlier Box Plot( 1 ) ),
    Continuous Distribution(
        Column( :SAT Math ), Outlier Box Plot( 1 ) )
);
```

Now the script will generate the desired output regardless of the user's preference settings. As we said, it is an easy mistake. It might have been that you turned on the Stack option in your Distribution platform preferences so long ago that you have forgotten that it is not the default. Or maybe it just never occurred to you that someone would turn off a default setting. The point here is that if it is important to your result, be sure it is included in your script.

Exception Handling

With plenty of condition handling in the script, we hope you won't have to deal with any exceptions. But sometimes there are problems with the logic in the script, or there is a situation that you just did not think of that causes an error. Shocking, right? But it does happen. So what are some other things you can do to limit the chances that your script will fail or otherwise behave inappropriately when something unexpected happens?

Catch and Escape Exceptions

The **Try()** function evaluates an expression supplied as the first argument. If that expression causes an error, an optional second argument is evaluated and then the remainder of the script is executed. Sounds a bit like a get out of jail free card, doesn't it?

Sometimes, you might want the script to stop executing when an error is encountered. In that case, you would include a **Throw()** function in the second argument. Although **Try()** and **Throw()** are often used together, they can each be used alone. Let's consider a situation where a **Try()** might be useful.

Suppose your script is designed to import data that might or might not contain a specific column. If you tried to reference a column that was not found in the data table, then your script would stop executing and in the log you would find an error. Depending on how you referenced the column, you might see errors such as **Name Unresolved** or **Scoped data table access requires a data table column or variable** or something similar.

So before your script continues, how can you find out if the column exists? In the following example, we just try a simple action to test if an error will be produced. If the evaluation returns an error, then we print a message to the log and add the desired column. After the **Try()** is complete, the script will continue to execute:

```
Try(
    dt:Calories from Fat << Get Name,
    Print( "Adding Calories from Fat column" );
    dt << New Column( "Calories from Fat" );
);

Print( "Script continues..." );
```

Some of you might be thinking that there are other ways to check the existence of a column. And you are right. As with most things in JSL, there's more than one way to accomplish this task. In the following example, we demonstrate that you can capture a list of column names and then check to see whether the name is included in the list.

```
colNames = dt << Get Column Names( "String" );

If( !Contains( colNames, "Calories from Fat" ),
    Print( "Adding Calories from Fat column" );
    dt << New Column( "Calories from Fat" );
);

Print( "Script continues..." );
```

As you can see, it took a little bit more script to write, but it accomplishes the same task.

Test Your Script Thoroughly

Another saying you might have heard is that no software is fully tested until it gets into the hands of the users. That is so true. When you know what the script is supposed to do, it can be hard to think of ways to make it fail. We suggest that you have a second set of eyes to try out your script. Even ask them to try to break it. Very often, this will unveil conditions that you have not accounted for in your script.

As an added bonus, you will probably get some feedback. Whether that results in new requirements and ideas for a future version, or causes you to reconsider certain aspects of your approach, feedback is a good thing.

Summary

The key to being a good scripter is knowing how to put together all the concepts and methods discussed to this point. In the next section, we will show you how to accomplish various tasks using the concepts described in the first section of this book.

Section 2

Jump On!

After learning the basics discussed in the first section of this book, you are ready to think about specific tasks you want to accomplish using JMP scripting. Typically, when users contact JMP Technical Support with scripting questions, the questions are in the form of, "How do I do *this* or *that* in a script?" Or, "I need an example that shows me the syntax to get *this* done."

Therefore, we have dedicated this section of the book to those of you who want to find a good example of how to do something in JSL. Here, you will find over fifty examples on a variety of topics that are divided into five categories:

- Rows, Columns, and Tables
- Dialog Windows
- Analyses
- Graph Components
- Reports and Journals

Each example answers a question with a script sample, including embedded explanatory comments. In addition, the examples include discussion to explain functions in detail or give helpful references when necessary. Finally, there are plenty of images, so you can see what should happen before you try yourself. These script samples can be copied and pasted into a script window and executed immediately using sample data tables to show you exactly how the solution works.

As you look through the examples, you might notice that there are multiple ways to accomplish the same task. The methods we use assume that you are a beginning scripter, and thus few advanced methods are demonstrated. As you become more proficient in your scripting, we encourage you to experiment with your code.

Enjoy!

Chapter 8: Rows, Columns, and Tables

Question 8.1: I can manipulate a data table interactively, such as by selecting and deleting rows, by adding new columns, and so on. How can I get JMP to produce the script for these actions?

Solution 8.1:

As we mentioned in chapter 1, JMP does not record your steps. It can, however, reproduce the data table or column in its current state using the **Get Script** command:

```
Current Data Table() << Get Script;

:colName << Get Script;
```

Note: The result of running the previous code is pasted in the log. You can copy the **New Table()** or **New Column()** commands from the log and paste into your main script.

If you have only a few manipulations, it might be easier to write the code yourself for the desired manipulation. The following code demonstrates how to do a few of the table manipulations mentioned previously. Further details can be found in the "Data Tables" chapter of the *Scripting Guide*.

```
/* Open the sample data table, Big Class.  */
dt = Open( "$SAMPLE_DATA/Big Class.jmp" );

/* Select rows where the age is 15 or greater. */
dt << Select Where( :age >= 15 );

/* Delete the selected rows. */
dt << Delete Rows;

/* Add a new column containing a formula to calculate
   the weight/height ratio. */
dt << New Column( " Weight Height Ratio", Numeric, "Continuous", Formula( :weight /
:height ) );
```

Result 8.1:

The resulting data table should have 27 rows and 6 columns, as shown in Figure 8.1.

Figure 8.1 Data Table After After Deleting Rows and Adding a Formula Column

		name	age	sex	height	weight	Weight Height Ratio
▼ Big Class							
Locked File C:\Program Files\SAS\J	1	KATIE	12	F	59	95	1.61016949
▷ Distribution	2	LOUISE	12	F	61	123	2.01639344
▷ Bivariate	3	JANE	12	F	55	74	1.34545455
▷ Oneway	4	JACLYN	12	F	66	145	2.1969697
▷ Logistic	5	LILLIE	12	F	52	64	1.23076923
▷ Contingency	6	TIM	12	M	60	84	1.4
▷ Fit Model	7	JAMES	12	M	61	128	2.09836066
▷ Set Sex Value Labels	8	ROBERT	12	M	51	79	1.54901961
▷ Set Age Value Labels	9	BARBARA	13	F	60	112	1.86666667
▷ Graph Builder Smoother Line	10	ALICE	13	F	61	107	1.75409836
▷ Graph Builder ...and Bar Charts	11	SUSAN	13	F	56	67	1.19642857
▷ Graph Builder Line Chart	12	JOHN	13	M	65	98	1.50769231
▷ Graph Builder Heat Map	13	JOE	13	M	63	105	1.66666667
▷ JMP Applicati... Quality Graphs	14	MICHAEL	13	M	58	95	1.63793103
	15	DAVID	13	M	59	79	1.33898305
▼ Columns (6/0)	16	JUDY	14	F	61	81	1.32786885
name	17	ELIZABETH	14	F	62	91	1.46774194
age	18	LESLIE	14	F	65	142	2.18461538
sex							
height							
weight							
Weight Height Ratio ✚							

Question 8.2: How can I select rows where more than one condition is true? How can I select rows where at least one of the specified conditions is true?

Solution 8.2:

Use the logical operator AND or '&' to select within a selection, as shown in the following code:

```
/* Open the sample data table, Big Class.jmp. */
dt = Open( "$SAMPLE_DATA/Big Class.jmp" );

/* Select rows where age is greater than 14
   AND height is less than 65. */
dt << Select Where( :age > 14 & :height < 65 );
```

Use the logical operator OR or '|' to extend a selection:

```
/* Select rows where age is greater than 14
   OR height is less than 65. */
dt << Select Where( :age > 14 | :height < 65 );
```

Result 8.2:

The following images show the results of using the '&' and '|' operators for selecting rows.

Figure 8.2 Row Selection Where Age > 14 and Height < 65

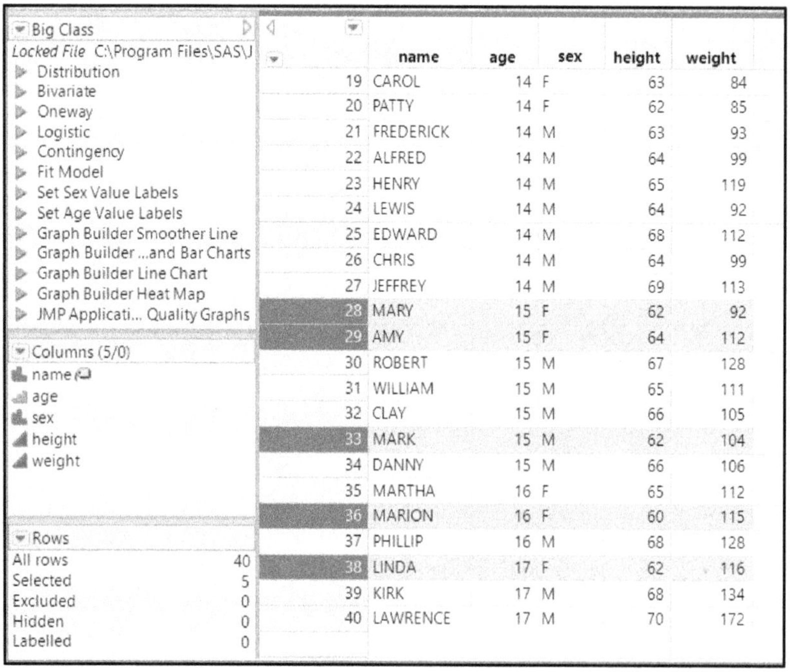

Figure 8.3 Row Selection Where Age > 14 or Height < 65

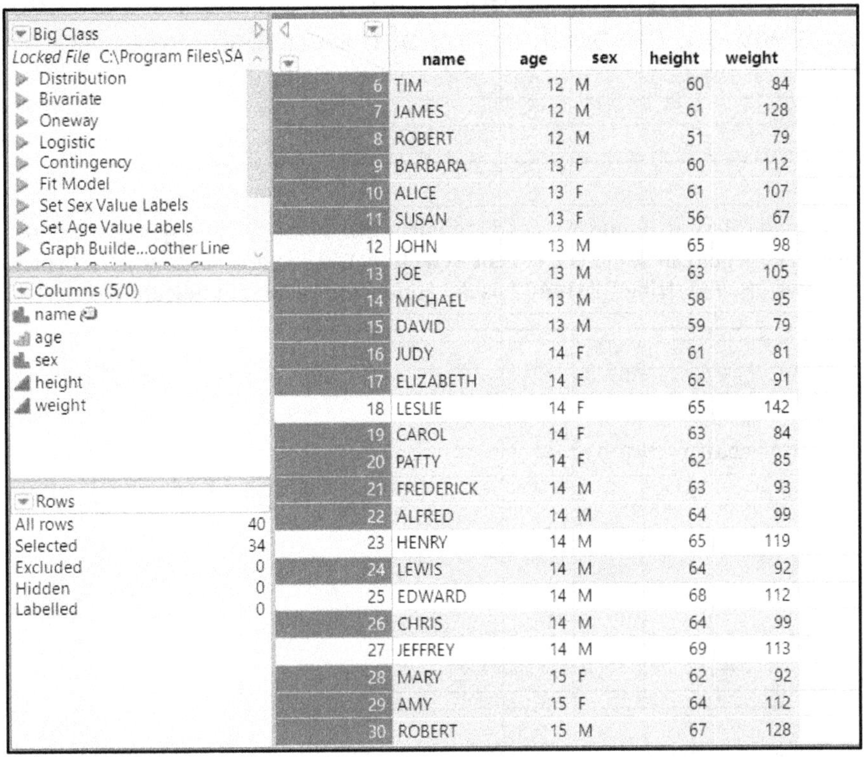

	name	age	sex	height	weight
6	TIM	12	M	60	84
7	JAMES	12	M	61	128
8	ROBERT	12	M	51	79
9	BARBARA	13	F	60	112
10	ALICE	13	F	61	107
11	SUSAN	13	F	56	67
12	JOHN	13	M	65	98
13	JOE	13	M	63	105
14	MICHAEL	13	M	58	95
15	DAVID	13	M	59	79
16	JUDY	14	F	61	81
17	ELIZABETH	14	F	62	91
18	LESLIE	14	F	65	142
19	CAROL	14	F	63	84
20	PATTY	14	F	62	85
21	FREDERICK	14	M	63	93
22	ALFRED	14	M	64	99
23	HENRY	14	M	65	119
24	LEWIS	14	M	64	92
25	EDWARD	14	M	68	112
26	CHRIS	14	M	64	99
27	JEFFREY	14	M	69	113
28	MARY	15	F	62	92
29	AMY	15	F	64	112
30	ROBERT	15	M	67	128

Big Class
Locked File C:\Program Files\SA

- Distribution
- Bivariate
- Oneway
- Logistic
- Contingency
- Fit Model
- Set Sex Value Labels
- Set Age Value Labels
- Graph Builde...oother Line

Columns (5/0)
- name
- age
- sex
- height
- weight

Rows

All rows	40
Selected	34
Excluded	0
Hidden	0
Labelled	0

Question 8.3: There are already rows selected in my data table. How can I select additional rows without deselecting any of the currently selected rows?

Solution 8.3:

The **Select Where()** command offers an optional second argument that enables you to specify the type of selection to be performed. The argument name is **Current Selection()**. To instruct JMP to select rows without deselecting any rows, use the string **"Extend"** as the argument to **Current Selection()**.

```
/* Open the sample data table, SATbyYear.jmp. */
dt = Open( "$SAMPLE_DATA/SATbyYear.jmp" );

/* Select the data where the SAT Verbal score is 580 or greater. */
dt << Select Where( :SAT Verbal >= 580 );

Wait( 1 );  //For demonstration purposes.

/* Select rows where the SAT Math score is 600 or greater,
   without deselecting any of the previously selected rows. */
dt << Select Where(
    :SAT Math >= 600,
    Current Selection( "Extend" )
);
```

Note: If these two selection criteria were being applied at the same time, the conditions would be specified with the logical operator OR or '|' to extend a selection. See Solution 8.2 for an example using the OR operator.

The "Select Rows" section of the "Rows" chapter in the *Scripting Guide* (**Help ▶ Books ▶ Scripting Guide**) provides many additional examples of using **Select Where()**.

Result 8.3:

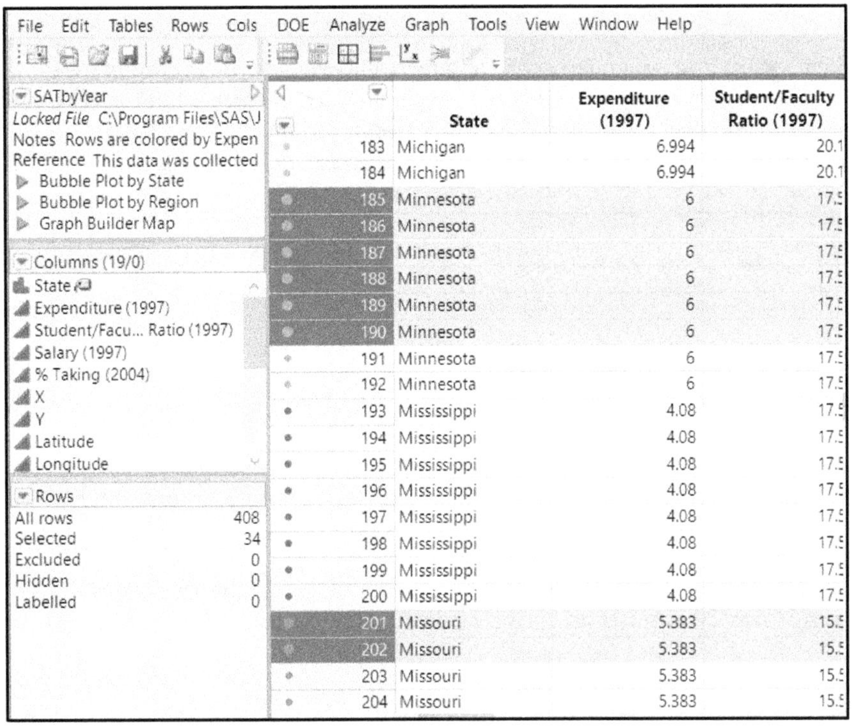

Figure 8.4 Extended Row Selection

Question 8.4: How can I select from the currently selected rows?

Solution 8.4:

The **Select Where()** command offers an optional second argument that enables you to specify the type of selection to be performed. The argument name is **Current Selection().** To instruct JMP to select from only the currently selected rows, use the string **"Restrict"** as the argument to **Current Selection().**

```
/* Open the sample data table, SATbyYear.jmp. */
dt = Open( "$SAMPLE_DATA/SATbyYear.jmp" );

/*  Select the data from the Northeast region.  */
dt << Select Where( :Region == "Northeast" );

Wait( 1 );  //For demonstration purposes.

/* Select rows in the current selection where
   the 2004 ACT score was greater than 21. */
dt << Select Where(
    As Column( "ACT Score (2004)" ) > 21,
    Current Selection( "Restrict" )
);
```

Note: If these two selection criteria were being applied at the same time, the conditions would be specified with the logical operator AND or '&' to select within a selection. See Solution 8.2 for an example using the AND operator.

The "Select Rows" section of the "Rows" chapter in the *Scripting Guide* (**Help ▶ Books ▶ Scripting Guide**) provides many additional examples of using **Select Where().**

Result 8.4:

Figure 8.5 Restricted Row Selection

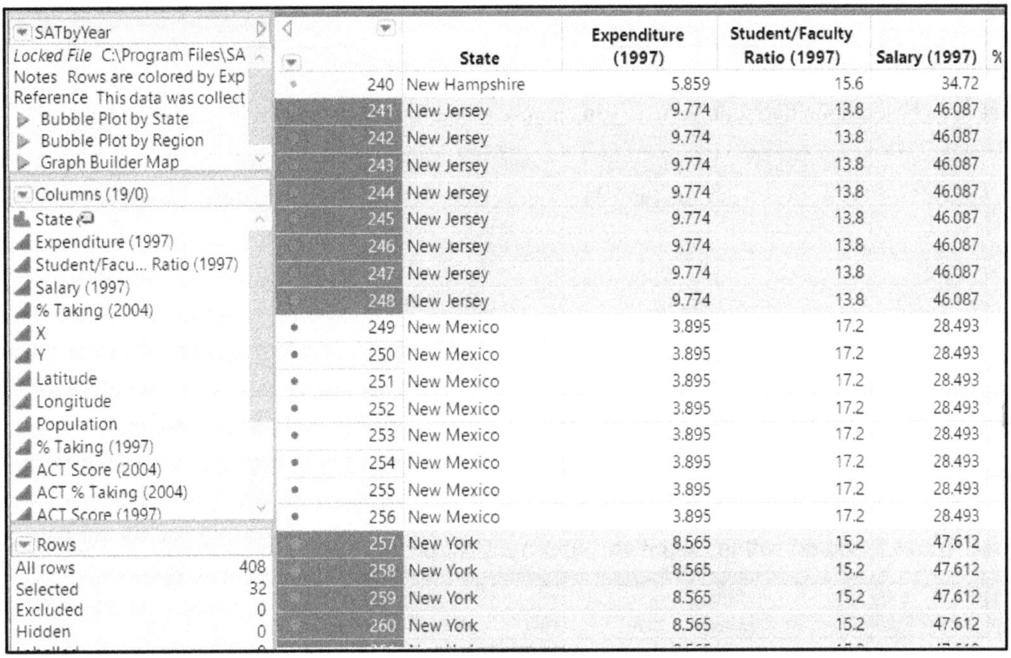

Question 8.5: How can I perform a Select Where on numeric datetime values?

Solution 8.5:

To select rows based upon datetime values, you can use a date literal, as shown in the following code.

```
/* Open the sample data table, Abrasion.jmp. */
dt = Open( "$SAMPLE_DATA/Abrasion.jmp" );

/* Select rows where the date and time are between
   noon, April 30, 1995 and noon, May 1, 1995. */
dt << Select Where( 30Apr1995:12:00:00 <= As Column( "Date/Time" ) <= 01May1995:12:00:00
);
```

Notice that a date literal does not need to be placed within double quotation marks. For more information about date literals, visit the "Date-Time Functions and Formats" section in the *Scripting Guide*.

Result 8.5:

Figure 8.6 Rows Selected within Specified Datetime Criteria

		Abrasion	Date	Time	Shift	Date/Time	time2
	1	133	04/29/1995	12:07:00 AM	A	04/29/1995 7:00:00 AM	:0:07:00
	2	138	04/29/1995	12:09:00 AM	A	04/29/1995 9:00:00 AM	:0:09:00
	3	143	04/29/1995	12:11:00 AM	A	04/29/1995 11:00:00 AM	:0:11:00
	4	138	04/29/1995	12:01:00 PM	A	04/29/1995 1:00:00 PM	:0:13:00
	5	140	04/29/1995	12:03:00 PM	B	04/29/1995 3:00:00 PM	:0:15:00
	6	137	04/29/1995	12:05:00 PM	B	04/29/1995 5:00:00 PM	:0:17:00
	7	143	04/29/1995	12:07:00 PM	B	04/29/1995 7:00:00 PM	:0:19:00
	8	135	04/29/1995	12:09:00 PM	B	04/29/1995 9:00:00 PM	:0:21:00
	9	136	04/30/1995	12:07:00 AM	A	04/30/1995 7:00:00 AM	:0:07:00
	10	139	04/30/1995	12:09:00 AM	A	04/30/1995 9:00:00 AM	:0:09:00
	11	140	04/30/1995	12:11:00 AM	A	04/30/1995 11:00:00 AM	:0:11:00
	12	140	04/30/1995	12:01:00 PM	A	04/30/1995 1:00:00 PM	:0:13:00
	13	146	04/30/1995	12:03:00 PM	B	04/30/1995 3:00:00 PM	:0:15:00
	14	144	04/30/1995	12:05:00 PM	B	04/30/1995 5:00:00 PM	:0:17:00
	15	149	04/30/1995	12:07:00 PM	B	04/30/1995 7:00:00 PM	:0:19:00
	16	144	04/30/1995	12:09:00 PM	B	04/30/1995 9:00:00 PM	:0:21:00
	17	141	05/01/1995	12:07:00 AM	A	05/01/1995 7:00:00 AM	:0:07:00
	18	138	05/01/1995	12:09:00 AM	A	05/01/1995 9:00:00 AM	:0:09:00
	19	139	05/01/1995	12:11:00 AM	A	05/01/1995 11:00:00 AM	:0:11:00
	20	135	05/01/1995	12:01:00 PM	A	05/01/1995 1:00:00 PM	:0:13:00
	21	135	05/01/1995	12:03:00 PM	B	05/01/1995 3:00:00 PM	:0:15:00

Abrasion
Locked File C:\Progra

Columns (6/0)
Abrasion
Date
Time
Shift
Date/Time
time2

Rows
All rows   40
Selected   8
Excluded   0
Hidden   0

Question 8.6: How can I determine the number of selected, excluded, or hidden rows in a data table?

Solution 8.6:

Use the **Get Selected Rows**, **Get Excluded Rows**, and **Get Hidden Rows** functions to obtain a matrix of corresponding row numbers. Then use the **N Row()** function to obtain the number of rows in the matrix, as shown in the following code:

```
/* Open the sample data table, Fitness.jmp. */
dt = Open( "$SAMPLE_DATA/Fitness.jmp" );

/*  Select, exclude, and hide some rows for demonstration
    purposes  */
dt << Select Where( :age <= 40 ) << Exclude( 1 ) << Hide( 1 );

selRows = N Row( dt << Get Selected Rows );

exclRows = N Row( dt << Get Excluded Rows );

hidnRows = N Row( dt << Get Hidden Rows );

/* Print variable values in the log. */
Show( selRows, exclRows, hidnRows );
```

Result 8.6:

Figure 8.7 Log After Script Was Executed

```
/* Open the sample data table, Fitness.jmp. */
dt = Open( "$SAMPLE_DATA/Fitness.jmp" );

/*  Select, exclude, and hide some rows for demonstration
    purposes  */
dt << Select Where( :age <= 40 ) << Exclude( 1 ) << Hide( 1 );

selRows = N Row( dt << Get Selected Rows );

exclRows = N Row( dt << Get Excluded Rows );

hidnRows = N Row( dt << Get Hidden Rows );

/* Print variable values in the log. */
Show( selRows, exclRows, hidnRows );


selRows = 4;
exclRows = 4;
hidnRows = 4;
```

Question 8.7: I am attempting to select some rows, and then create a subset data table. When no rows are selected, all the rows are included in the subset data table. How can I create a subset only if there were rows selected?

Solution 8.7:

Get the number of rows selected using the **Get Selected Rows** command, and then verify that the result is greater than 0 before creating the subset, as shown in the following code:

```
/* Open the Big Class sample data table. */
dt = Open( "$SAMPLE_DATA/Fitness.jmp" );

/* Attempt to select rows based on the desired conditions. */
dt << Select Where( :sex == "F" & :age < 35 );

/* Perform a subset if rows were selected. Otherwise, print
   a message in the log. */
If( N Row( dt << Get Selected Rows ) > 0,
    dt << Subset( Output Table Name( "Females, Under 35" ) ),
    Print( "No rows selected." )
);
```

Result 8.7:

Because the Fitness sample data table does not contain any rows that meet the criteria specified in the **Select Where** statement, the statement "No rows selected." is printed in the log upon running the script.

Figure 8.8 Log After Script Was Executed

```
/* Open the Big Class sample data table. */
dt = Open( "$SAMPLE_DATA/Fitness.jmp" );

/* Attempt to select rows based on the desired conditions. */
dt << Select Where( :sex == "F" & :age < 35 );

/* Perform a subset if rows were selected. Otherwise, print
   a message in the log. */
If( N Row( dt << Get Selected Rows ) > 0,
    dt << Subset( Output Table Name( "Females, Under 35" ) ),
    Print( "No rows selected." )
);


"No rows selected."
```

Question 8.8: How can I determine the number of selected columns in a table? How can I get a list of the selected columns?

Solution 8.8:

Use the **Get Selected Columns** command to obtain a list of column names, and then use the **N Items()** function to obtain the number of selected columns in the list, as shown in the following code:

```
/* Open a sample data table for demonstration purposes. */
dt = Open( "$SAMPLE_DATA/Big Class.JMP" );

/* Select the first two columns for demonstration purposes. */
Column( "name" ) << Set Selected( 1 );
Column( "age" ) << Set Selected( 1 );

/* Store the list of selected columns in a variable. */
selColList = dt << Get Selected Columns;

/* Store the number of items in the list in a variable. */
numSelCols = N Items( selColList );

/* Show variable values in the log. */
Show( selColList, numSelCols );
```

Result 8.8:

Figure 8.9 Log After Script Was Executed

```
//:*/
/* Open a sample data table for demonstration purposes. */
dt = Open( "$SAMPLE_DATA/Big Class.JMP" );

/* Select the first two columns for demonstration purposes. */
Column( "name" ) << Set Selected( 1 );
Column( "age" ) << Set Selected( 1 );

/* Store the list of selected columns in a variable. */
selColList = dt << Get Selected Columns;

/* Store the number of items in the list in a variable. */
numSelCols = N Items( selColList );

/* Show variable values in the log. */
Show( selColList, numSelCols );


selColList = {:name, :age};
numSelCols = 2;
```

Question 8.9: I want to delete all the character columns in a data table. How can I do this?

Solution 8.9:

The data table message **Get Column Names** returns a list of all column names in the data table. By specifying the optional **Character** argument, a list of only the character columns in the table is returned. Use **Delete Columns** to delete all columns named in the list.

```
/* Open the sample data table, Big Class.jmp. */
dt = Open( "$SAMPLE_DATA/Big Class.jmp" );

/* Store all the character column names in a list. */
cols = dt << Get Column Names( "Character" );

/* Delete the columns. */
dt << Delete Columns( cols );
```

Result 8.9:

Figure 8.10 Data Table After All Character Columns Were Deleted

	age	height	weight
1	12	59	95
2	12	61	123
3	12	55	74
4	12	66	145
5	12	52	64
6	12	60	84
7	12	61	128
8	12	51	79
9	13	60	112
10	13	61	107
11	13	56	67
12	13	65	98
13	13	63	105
14	13	58	95
15	13	59	79

Question 8.10: Are there any JSL commands for recoding data, as in **Cols▶ Recode**?

Solution 8.10:

You can select the desired column(s) and then use the **Recode** command to bring up the Recode launch dialog for the user to make their desired changes.

```
/* Open a sample data table for demonstration purposes. */
dt = Open( "$SAMPLE_DATA/Cities.jmp" );

/* Select the State column. */
:State << Set Selected( 1 );

/* Bring up the Recode launch dialog. */
dt << Recode;
```

Currently, there are no JSL commands specifically for Recode from the **Cols** menu. Instead, there are a variety of functions available that you can use to perform the same actions. For example, when you interactively select **Formula Column** as the destination for the new values, JMP creates a new column and uses the **Match()** function in the formula to recode the values. You can easily write a **Match()** function and choose to place the results in a new column (no formula), a formula column, or in place. The following code samples demonstrate each of these options.

New Column

```
/* Open a sample data table */
dt = Open( "$SAMPLE_DATA\Big Class.jmp" );

/* Create a new formula column for the recoded values */
dt << New Column( "New Column", Character );

/* Assign new values to the New Column in loop */
For Each Row( dt,
    /* Use Match() to assign the new values
    To the new column */
    :New Column = Match( :sex,
        "F", "FEMALE",
        "M", "MALE",
        :sex
    )
);
```

Formula Column

```
/* Open a sample data table */
dt = Open( "$SAMPLE_DATA\Big Class.jmp" );

/* Create a new formula column for the recoded values */
dt << New Column( "Formula Column",
    Character,
```

```
    Formula(
    /* Use Match() to assign the new values */
    Match( :sex,
        "F", "FEMALE",
        "M", "MALE",
        :sex )
    )
);
```

In Place

```
/* Open a sample data table */
dt = Open( "$SAMPLE_DATA\Big Class.jmp" );

/* Assign new values in loop */
For Each Row( dt,
    /* Use Match() to assign the new values
    to the same column */
    :sex = Match( :sex,
        "F", "FEMALE",
        "M", "MALE",
         :sex
    )
);
```

Result 8.10:

Figure 8.11 Big Class after Each Recode Method

	name	age	sex	height	weight	New Column	Formula Column
1	KATIE	12	FEMALE	59	95	FEMALE	FEMALE
2	LOUISE	12	FEMALE	61	123	FEMALE	FEMALE
3	JANE	12	FEMALE	55	74	FEMALE	FEMALE
4	JACLYN	12	FEMALE	66	145	FEMALE	FEMALE
5	LILLIE	12	FEMALE	52	64	FEMALE	FEMALE
6	TIM	12	MALE	60	84	MALE	MALE
7	JAMES	12	MALE	61	128	MALE	MALE
8	ROBERT	12	MALE	51	79	MALE	MALE
9	BARBARA	13	FEMALE	60	112	FEMALE	FEMALE
10	ALICE	13	FEMALE	61	107	FEMALE	FEMALE
11	SUSAN	13	FEMALE	56	67	FEMALE	FEMALE
12	JOHN	13	MALE	65	98	MALE	MALE
13	JOE	13	MALE	63	105	MALE	MALE
14	MICHAEL	13	MALE	58	95	MALE	MALE

File Edit Tables Rows Cols DOE Analyze Graph Tools View Window Help

▼ Big Class
Locked File C:\Program Files\SAS\J
▷ Distribution
▷ Bivariate
▷ Oneway
▷ Logistic
▷ Contingency
▷ Fit Model
▷ Set Sex Value Labels
▷ Set Age Value Labels
▷ Graph Builder Smoother Line
▷ Graph Builder ...and Bar Charts
▷ Graph Builder Line Chart
▷ Graph Builder Heat Map
▷ JMP Applicati... Quality Graphs

▼ Columns (7/0)
🔒 name ⇌
◁ age
🔒 sex

The following are JSL functions that map to some of the red triangle options. Examples of each of these can be found in the Scripting Index (**Help ▶ Scripting Index**).

Table 8.1 Functions for Red Triangle Options

Red Triangle Option	JSL Function	Description
Convert to Titlecase	Titlecase()	Changes to uppercase any a-z character encountered after a character that is not a-z, except apostrophe
Convert to Uppercase	Uppercase()	Changes any lowercase letters to uppercase letters
Convert to Lowercase	Lowercase()	Changes any uppercase letters to lowercase letters
Trim Whitespace	Trim Whitespace() Trim()	Removes leading, trailing, or both leading and trailing spaces
Collapse Whitespace	Collapse Whitespace()	Removes leading, trailing, and duplicate interior spaces

Note: To script the remaining options accessible from the red triangle menu would require additional knowledge not discussed in this book or access to internal functions, which are not currently available.

Question 8.11: I have a set of values that I want to use as the control limits for a data table column. How can I use these values to create the Control Limits column property?

Solution 8.11:

When working with column properties, we recommend adding the property interactively first. Then right-click on the column to bring up the context menu, where you can select the option to **Copy Column Properties** in order to retrieve the proper syntax for the column property. Once you have the correct syntax, you can then modify it to fit your needs.

When using a variable in the assignment of a column property, you must do something to replace the variable with its value before it can be assigned. In the following example, we have demonstrated the use of **Eval()**, **Eval Expr()**, and **Expr()** for this purpose.

As noted in the comments, the variable is wrapped in the **Expr()** function. This identifies the variable is something to be evaluated. The **Eval Expr()** function searches the expression for the **Expr()** function. It evaluates the variable and returns the expression with the variable replaced with its value. Finally, the outer **Eval()** function evaluates the entire expression after the replacement has occurred.

```
/* Open a sample data table for demonstration purposes. */
dt = Open( "$SAMPLE_DATA/Quality Control/Pickles.jmp" );

/* Create the list of values to be used in the Control Limits property. */
newAvg = 8.25;
newLCL = 7.5;
newUCL = 13;
newSubgroup = 4;

/* Replace the limits and subgroup variables with the listed values. */
Eval(//Evaluates the expression after replacement has occurred.
    Eval Expr(//Evaluates anything inside of the Expr() function.
            :acid << Set Property(
                    "Control Limits",
                    {XBar(
                            Avg( Expr( newAvg ) ),
                            LCL( Expr( newLCL ) ),
                            UCL( Expr( newUCL ) ),
                            Subgroup Size( Expr( newSubgroup ) )
                    )}
            )
    )
);
```

Result 8.11:

Figure 8.12 Control Limits Assigned with Actual Values

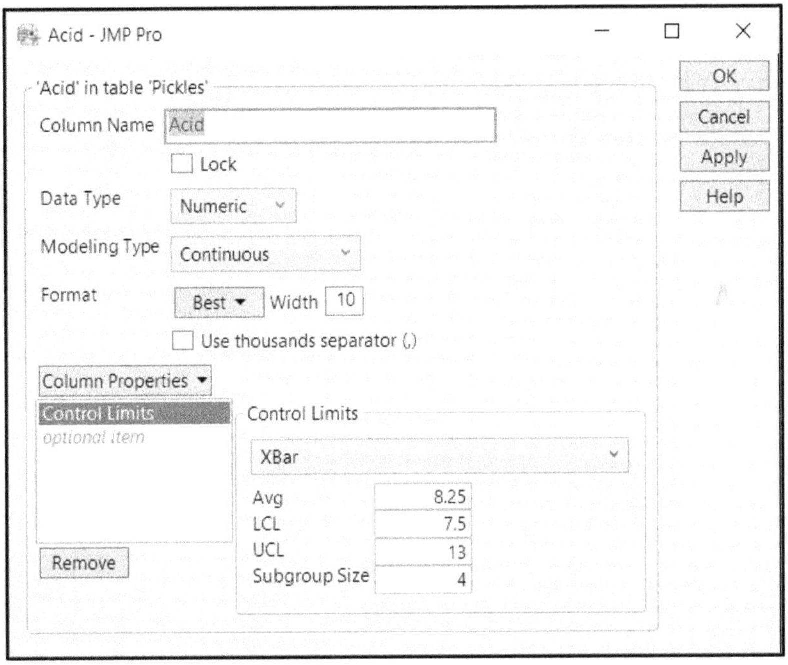

Question 8.12: How can a character column containing datetime values be converted to a numeric column of JMP date values using a script?

Solution 8.12:

In order to change a character column of datetime values to a numeric column of JMP datetime values, the format must be specified in the **Data Type()** message for the column. Otherwise, the data will be converted to missing.

In the following example, we first demonstrate concatenating a character date column with a character time column into a new character column called DateTime. The new column is then converted to numeric with the proper datetime format. Afterward, we also demonstrate converting the Date and Time columns to numeric separately.

```
/* Open a sample data table that contains date and time columns */
dt = Open( "$SAMPLE_DATA\Quality Control\Pickles.jmp" );

/* Create a new column that concatenates the Date and Time columns */
dt << New Column( "DateTime", "Character", Formula( :Date || " " || :Time ) );
/* Remove the formula */
:DateTime << Delete Formula;

/* Convert the new column to numeric with the proper date time format */
:DateTime << Data Type( "Numeric", Format( "m/d/y h:m:s" ) )
    << Modeling Type( "Continuous" );

/* Alternately, convert the Date and Time columns to numeric columns with the proper
formats */
:Date << Data Type( "Numeric", Format( "m/d/y" ) )
    << Modeling Type( "Continuous" );
:Time << Data Type( "Numeric", Format( "h:m:s" ) )
    << Modeling Type( "Continuous" );
```

Result 8.12:

Figure 8.13 Conversion of Dates from Character to Numeric

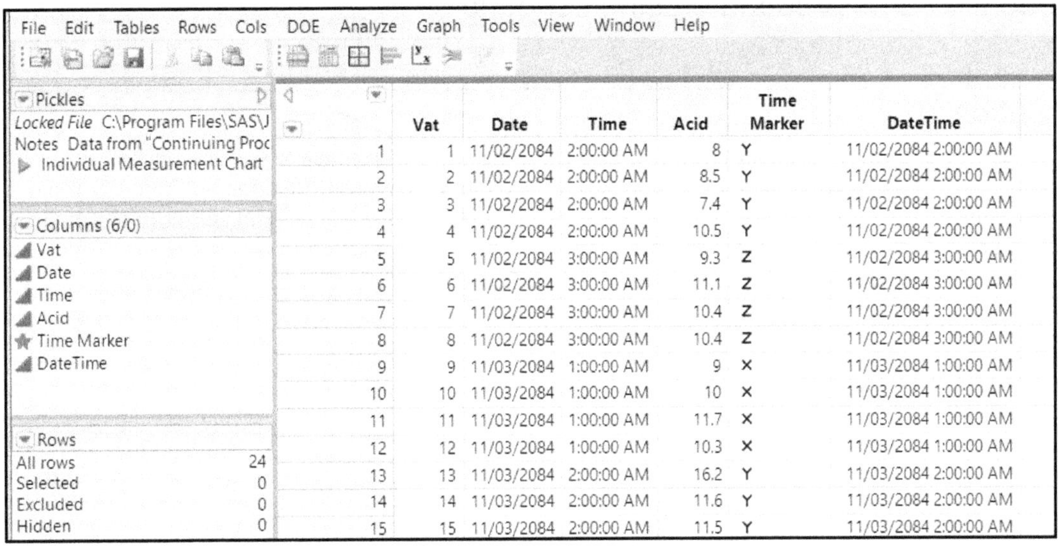

	Vat	Date	Time	Acid	Time Marker	DateTime
1	1	11/02/2084	2:00:00 AM	8	Y	11/02/2084 2:00:00 AM
2	2	11/02/2084	2:00:00 AM	8.5	Y	11/02/2084 2:00:00 AM
3	3	11/02/2084	2:00:00 AM	7.4	Y	11/02/2084 2:00:00 AM
4	4	11/02/2084	2:00:00 AM	10.5	Y	11/02/2084 2:00:00 AM
5	5	11/02/2084	3:00:00 AM	9.3	Z	11/02/2084 3:00:00 AM
6	6	11/02/2084	3:00:00 AM	11.1	Z	11/02/2084 3:00:00 AM
7	7	11/02/2084	3:00:00 AM	10.4	Z	11/02/2084 3:00:00 AM
8	8	11/02/2084	3:00:00 AM	10.4	Z	11/02/2084 3:00:00 AM
9	9	11/03/2084	1:00:00 AM	9	X	11/03/2084 1:00:00 AM
10	10	11/03/2084	1:00:00 AM	10	X	11/03/2084 1:00:00 AM
11	11	11/03/2084	1:00:00 AM	11.7	X	11/03/2084 1:00:00 AM
12	12	11/03/2084	1:00:00 AM	10.3	X	11/03/2084 1:00:00 AM
13	13	11/03/2084	2:00:00 AM	16.2	Y	11/03/2084 2:00:00 AM
14	14	11/03/2084	2:00:00 AM	11.6	Y	11/03/2084 2:00:00 AM
15	15	11/03/2084	2:00:00 AM	11.5	Y	11/03/2084 2:00:00 AM

Question 8.13: I can replace all the missing numeric values in a table with zeros interactively by performing **Edit▸Search▸Find and Replace**. How can I do the same procedure using scripting?

Solution 8.13:

After getting a list of all the numeric columns in the table, use a **For()** loop to traverse each of the numeric columns. The **Get Rows Where()** function nested with the **Is Missing()** function will return a vector with the missing values for the named column. This vector can be used as the column subscript to set all missing rows to zero with a single statement.

```
dt = Open( "$SAMPLE_DATA/Cities.jmp" );

/* Obtain a list of all numeric column names as strings. */
numCols = dt << Get Column Names( Numeric, String );

/* Loop through each numeric column. */
For( i = 1, i <= N Items( numCols ), i++,
    missingRows = dt << Get Rows Where( Is Missing( As Column( numCols[i] ) ) );
    Column( numCols[i] )[missingRows] = 0;
);
```

Result 8.13:

Figure 8.14 Find and Replace Missing Values with Zeros

	Longitude	State	Region	pop- m	POP	Max deg. F Jan	OZONE	CO	SO2	NO	PM10	Lead
1	73°48' W	NY	N	0.85	846	30	0.13	6	0.061	0.00	30	0.050
2	106°37' W	NM	W	0.49	486	47	0.11	11	0.000	0.02	43	0.040
3	84°25' W	GA	S	2.66	2657	51	0.17	8	0.052	0.03	46	0.050
4	74°27' W	NJ	N	0.30	303	41	0.15	0	0.025	0.00	0	0.040
5	76°37' W	MD	N	2.30	2303	41	0.19	10	0.043	0.03	43	0.110
6	71°01' W	MA	N	2.84	2842	36	0.17	7	0.057	0.03	38	0.070
7	73°14' W	VT	N	0.13	127	25	0.1	4	0.027	0.02	23	0.000
8	80°00' W	SC	S	0.50	502	59	0.11	8	0.063	0.02	34	0.030
9	80°50' W	NC	S	1.09	1091	50	0.16	8	0.020	0.00	36	0.070
10	104°48' W	WY	W	0.08	76	37	0	0	0.000	0.00	19	0.000
11	87°41' W	IL	MW	6.20	6199	29	0.22	7	0.044	0.03	47	0.140
12	84°30' W	OH	MW	1.44	1438	37	0.17	5	0.061	0.03	45	0.180
13	81°41' W	OH	MW	1.85	1851	33	0.14	7	0.069	0.03	57	1.090
14	104°52' W	CO	W	1.65	1645	43	0.12	16	0.025	0.04	45	0.080
15	93°37' W	IA	MW	0.39	385	27	0.06	5	0.000	0.00	40	0.000
16	83°06' W	MI	MW	4.36	4362	31	0.16	8	0.056	0.02	52	0.240
17	90°41' W	IA	MW	0.09	91	24	0	7	0.052	0.00	35	0.000
18	94°54' W	TX	TX	0.21	211	59	0	0	0.000	0.00	25	0.040

Question 8.14: How can I delete the formula from every column in my data table?

Solution 8.14:

In the previous version of this book, we demonstrated using the **Get Property** command to capture the formula, if any, and then conditionally delete the formula property, as shown in the following code:

```
/* Open the IRLS Example sample data table. */
dt = Open( "$SAMPLE_DATA/Nonlinear Examples/IRLS Example.jmp" );

/* Loop through each column in the data table. */
For( i = 1, i <= N Col( dt ), i++,
    /* Obtain the formula column property. */
    fmla = Column( dt, i ) << Get Property( "Formula" );
    /* Delete the formula, if one exists. */
    If( !Is Empty( fmla ),
        Column( dt, i ) << Delete Formula
    );
);
```

As we've mentioned before, there are multiple ways to accomplish this task. In the following example, we demonstrate how you could just wrap the **Delete Formula** expression in a **Try()** function. The **Try()** will escape any error generated when attempting to delete a formula from a column that has no formula.

```
/* Loop through each column in the data table. */
For( i = 1, i <= N Col( dt ), i++,
    /* Attempt to delete the formula from each column. */
    Try( Column( dt, i ) << Delete Formula )
);
```

Result 8.14:

Figure 8.15 Before Deleting the Formulas

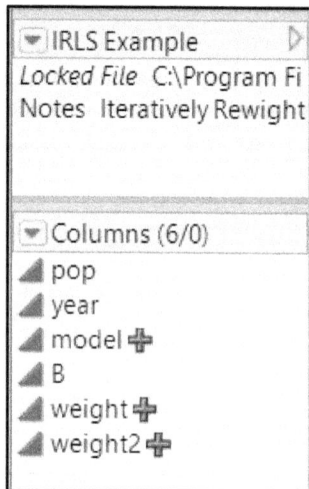

Figure 8.16 After Deleting the Formulas

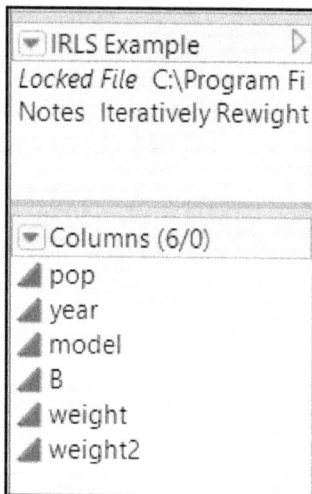

Question 8.15: How can I use a variable in a new column with a formula?

Solution 8.15:

When using JSL variables in column formulas, the variable should be replaced with its value before it is assigned to the formula. If you do not replace the variable with its value in the formula, the result of the formula can change each time the value of the variable changes, such as when formulas are added in a **For()** loop.

As explained in chapter 7, **Eval Expr()** searches its expression argument for **Expr()** functions. For every **Expr()** function found, JMP evaluates and replaces the variable with its evaluated value. So in the following example, JMP will replace **Expr(colList)** with **{:SAT Verbal, :SAT Math}**. The outer **Eval()** function will cause JMP to evaluate the entire **New Column** statement after the replacement has occurred.

```
/* Open a sample data table */
dt = Open("$SAMPLE_DATA\SATByYear.jmp");

/* Establish a list of columns */
colList = {:SAT Verbal, :SAT Math};

Eval( //Evaluate New Column expression after replacement
    Eval Expr( //Return expression with the evaluated value
        dt << New Column( "SAT Total",
            Numeric,
            Continuous,
            Formula( Sum( Expr( colList ) ) )
        )
    )
);
```

Result 8.15:

Figure 8.17 Column Formula Showing Variable Replaced with List Values

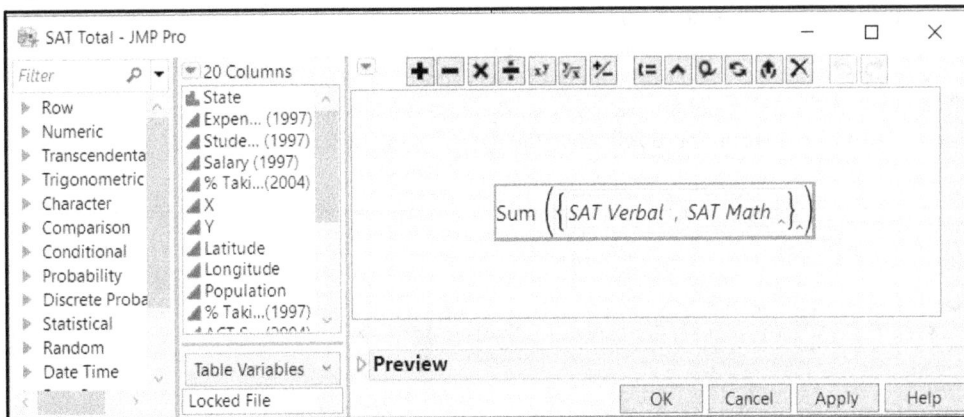

Question 8.16: How can I add multiple columns with formulas in a loop? I want one new column for each continuous column that calculates the mean by a grouping column.

Solution 8.16:

In this example, the user does not know how many columns they will need to create because it will depend upon how many numeric, continuous columns there are in the table. Using the **Get Column Names()** function, we can obtain a list of the column names of all the numeric, continuous columns in the table. We can create the loop based upon the number of items in that list.

Just as in Question 8.15, we use the **Eval()**, **Eval Expr()**, and **Expr()** functions to replace any JSL variable(s) with the evaluated value.

```
/* Open a sample data table */
dt = Open( "$SAMPLE_DATA\Big Class.jmp" );

/* Obtain a list of all the numeric, continuous column names as strings */
colList = dt << Get Column Names( Continuous, String );

/* Loop through each string in the list */
For( i = 1, i <= N Items( colList ), i++,
    Eval( //Evaluate New Column expression after replacement
        Eval Expr( //Return expression with the evaluated value
            dt << New Column( "Mean of " || colList[i] || " by Age",
                Numeric,
                Continuous,
                Formula( Col Mean( As Column( Expr( colList[i] ) ), :age ) )
            )
        )
    )
);
```

In chapter 4, we discussed two functions for column name resolution: **As Column()** and **Column()**. In the preceding code, we used **As Column()**. The following script will accomplish the same goal but demonstrates using the **Column()** function with the **Row()** subscript. Remember that the **Column()** function returns a reference to the column as a whole. Because the formula evaluates on each row, the **Row()** function is added as a subscript to reference the current row, which is controlled by the formula evaluation.

```
/* Open a sample data table */
dt = Open( "$SAMPLE_DATA\Big Class.jmp" );

/* Obtain a list of all the numeric, continuous column names as strings */
colList = dt << Get Column Names( Continuous, String );

/* Loop through each string in the list */
For( i = 1, i <= N Items( colList ), i++,
    Eval( //Evaluate New Column expression after replacement
        Eval Expr( //Return expression with the evaluated value
            dt << New Column( "Mean " || colList[i] || " by Age",
```

```
                                Numeric,
                                Continuous,
                                Formula( Col Mean( Column( Expr( colList[i] ) ) )[Row()], :age )
)
                        )
                )
        )
);
```

Result 8.16:

Figure 8.18 Formula for Mean Height by Age Using As Column()

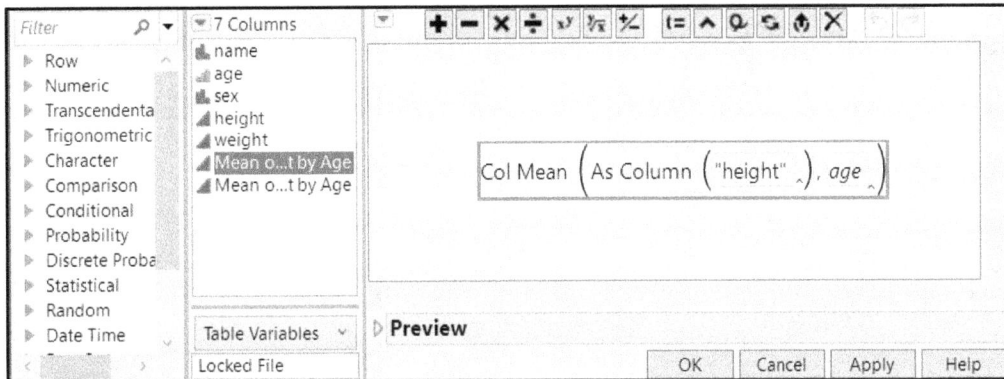

Figure 8.19 Formula for Mean Weight by Age Using As Column()

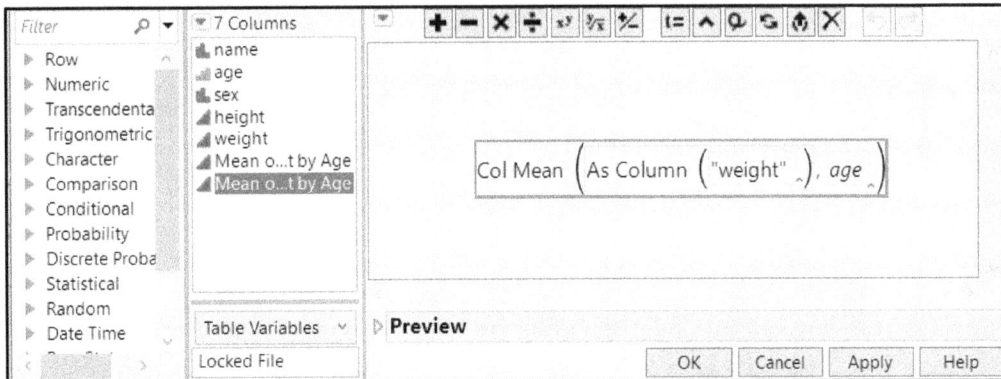

Figure 8.20 Formula for Mean Height by Age Using Column() with Row() Subscript

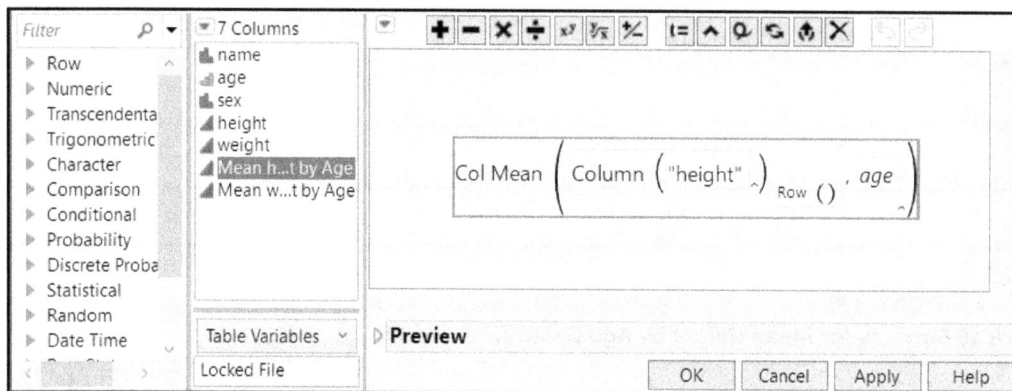

Figure 8.21 Formula for Mean Weight by Age Using Column() with Row() Subscript

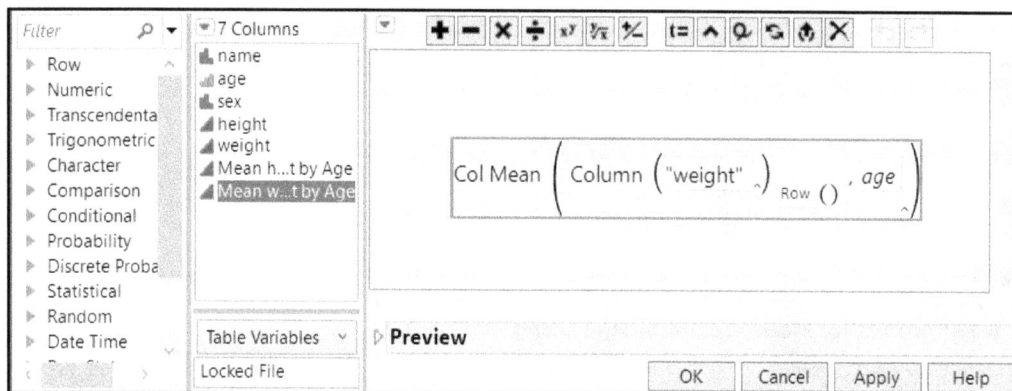

Question 8.17: How can I get a list of all open data tables?

Solution 8.17:

New in JMP 14, the **Get Data Table List()** function returns a list of references to the open data tables. Although invisible tables are included, private tables are not included in the list that is returned.

```
/* Open some sample tables */
Open("$SAMPLE_DATA\Air Traffic.jmp");
Open("$SAMPLE_DATA\Aircraft Incidents.jmp");
Open("$SAMPLE_DATA\Airline Delays.jmp");

/* Obtain a list of visible and invisible data tables */
dtList = Get Data Table List();
```

Figure 8.22 Log After the Preceding Script Is Run

```
/* Open some sample tables */
Open("$SAMPLE_DATA\Air Traffic.jmp");
Open("$SAMPLE_DATA\Aircraft Incidents.jmp");
Open("$SAMPLE_DATA\Airline Delays.jmp");

/* Obtain a list of visible and invisible data tables */
dtList = Get Data Table List();


{Data Table( "Airline Delays" ), Data Table( "Aircraft Incidents" ),
Data Table( "Air Traffic" )}
```

Prior to JMP 14, a **For()** loop was needed to access each table name and then insert the name into a list. The **N Table()** function returns the number of tables open. The **Get Name** command returns the name of the data table. **Insert Into()** inserts the value in the second argument (the data table name, in this example) into the list specified in the first argument.

```
/* Initialize an empty list where the table names will be stored. */
dtNames = {};

/* Loop through each open data table and insert its name into the list. */
For( i = 1, i <= N Table(), i++,
    Insert Into( dtNames, Data Table( Data Table( i ) ) )
);

/* Print names in the log. */
Print( dtNames );
```

Figure 8.23 Log After the Preceding Script Is Run

```
/* Initialize an empty list where the table names will be stored. */
dtNames = {};

/* Loop through each open data table and insert its name into the list. */
For( i = 1, i <= N Table(), i++,
    Insert Into( dtNames, Data Table( Data Table( i ) ) )
);

/* Print names in the log. */
Print( dtNames );


{DataTable("Air Traffic"), DataTable("Airline Delays"), DataTable("Aircraft Incidents")}
```

Question 8.18: How can I open and concatenate multiple files that have the same format?

Solution 8.18:

In JMP 14, there is a new feature called **Multiple File Import**. As we discussed in chapter 1, you can perform the import and stacking of the data interactively and then extract the Source table script to re-create the same action.

If you don't have JMP 14 yet, you can still import and concatenate multiple files. It will just take a little more scripting.

This example uses the **Pick File()** function to prompt the user to select the four UN Malaria CSV files in the sample data. The list returned includes the full path for each file. Then the script loops through the list of the files to open and concatenate each file into a main table.

```
/* Create a list of all the files to be concatenated. */
fileList = Pick File(
    "Select the 4 UN Malaria CSV Files:",
    "$SAMPLE_IMPORT_DATA\",
    {"CSV Files|csv"},
    1,
    0,
    "",
    "multiple"
);

/* Loop through each file */
For( i = 1, i <= N Items( fileList ), i++,
    /* Import each file. */
    dt = Open( fileList[i] );
    /* Add a column containing the table name. */
    dt << New Column( "File Name", Character, Set Each Value( dt << Get Name ) );
    /* If this is the first file, assign it to mainDt and give it a name. */
    If( i == 1,
            mainDt = dt;
            mainDT << Set Name( "Concatenated Files" );
    ,
            /* Else, concatenate the data to the main table. */
            mainDt = mainDt << Concatenate( dt, "Append to First Table" );
            /* Close the most recently opened table. */
            Close( dt, NoSave );
            Wait( 0 );
    );
);
```

At the end of each loop, the data table is closed. Because JMP considers the closing of a data table a system-related task, it is possible that the table is actually closed at a later time than you expect. Because we are reassigning the global variable that represents a different data table in each iteration of the loop, it is necessary for JMP to close the data table before starting the next iteration. To ensure that JMP has time to complete any system-related task, a **Wait()** statement was added with an argument of zero. This tells JMP to pause until pending system-related tasks are completed. Further information about the **Wait()** function can be found in the Scripting Index (**Help ▶ Scripting Index**).

Result 8.18:

Figure 8.24 Table Result from Concatenation

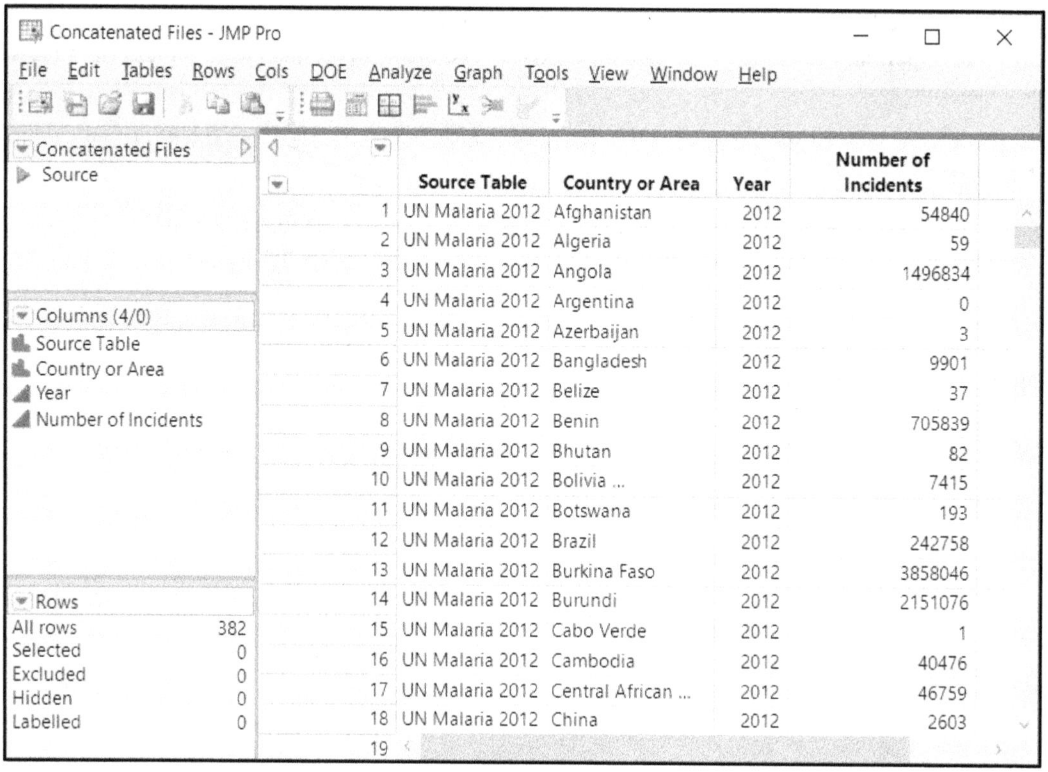

	Source Table	Country or Area	Year	Number of Incidents
1	UN Malaria 2012	Afghanistan	2012	54840
2	UN Malaria 2012	Algeria	2012	59
3	UN Malaria 2012	Angola	2012	1496834
4	UN Malaria 2012	Argentina	2012	0
5	UN Malaria 2012	Azerbaijan	2012	3
6	UN Malaria 2012	Bangladesh	2012	9901
7	UN Malaria 2012	Belize	2012	37
8	UN Malaria 2012	Benin	2012	705839
9	UN Malaria 2012	Bhutan	2012	82
10	UN Malaria 2012	Bolivia ...	2012	7415
11	UN Malaria 2012	Botswana	2012	193
12	UN Malaria 2012	Brazil	2012	242758
13	UN Malaria 2012	Burkina Faso	2012	3858046
14	UN Malaria 2012	Burundi	2012	2151076
15	UN Malaria 2012	Cabo Verde	2012	1
16	UN Malaria 2012	Cambodia	2012	40476
17	UN Malaria 2012	Central African ...	2012	46759
18	UN Malaria 2012	China	2012	2603
19				

Question 8.19: I have imported several files and performed some data cleanup. How can I concatenate all the open tables without knowing exactly how many tables are open?

Solution 8.19:

If you have JMP 14, you can use the new **Get Data Table List()** to return a list of references to all the open visible and invisible tables. This list can then be used to concatenate all the files at once.

```
/* Open some sample data tables and make invisible */
Open( "$SAMPLE_Import_DATA/UN Malaria 2009.csv", Invisible );
Open( "$SAMPLE_Import_DATA/UN Malaria 2010.csv", Invisible );
Open( "$SAMPLE_Import_DATA/UN Malaria 2011.csv", Invisible );
Open( "$SAMPLE_Import_DATA/UN Malaria 2012.csv", Invisible );

/* Obtain a list of open data tables. */
dtList = Get Data Table List();

/* Assign one table to be primary. */
main = dtList[1];
/* Remove the main table from the list. */
Remove From( dtList, 1 );

/* Concatenate the remaining tables to main. */
main << Concatenate( dtList,
    "Create Source Column",
    Output Table Name( "Concatenated Files" )
);
```

If you do not yet have JMP 14, you can create a list of open data tables using the **NTables()** function.

```
/* Open some sample data tables and make invisible*/
Open( "$SAMPLE_Import_DATA/UN Malaria 2009.csv", Invisible );
Open( "$SAMPLE_Import_DATA/UN Malaria 2010.csv", Invisible );
Open( "$SAMPLE_Import_DATA/UN Malaria 2011.csv", Invisible );
Open( "$SAMPLE_Import_DATA/UN Malaria 2012.csv", Invisible );

/* Assign one table to be primary. */
main = Data Table( 1 );

/* Establish a list variable to hold the data table references */
dtList = {};

/* Loop through the remaining open tables */
For( i = 2, i <= N Table(), i++,
    /* Insert a table reference into the list */
    Insert Into( dtList, Data Table( Data Table( i ) << Get Name ) )
);

/* Concatenate the tables to main */
main << Concatenate( dtList,
    "Create Source Column",
    Output Table Name( "Concatenated Files" )
);
```

Result 8.19:

Figure 8.25 Table Result from Concatenation

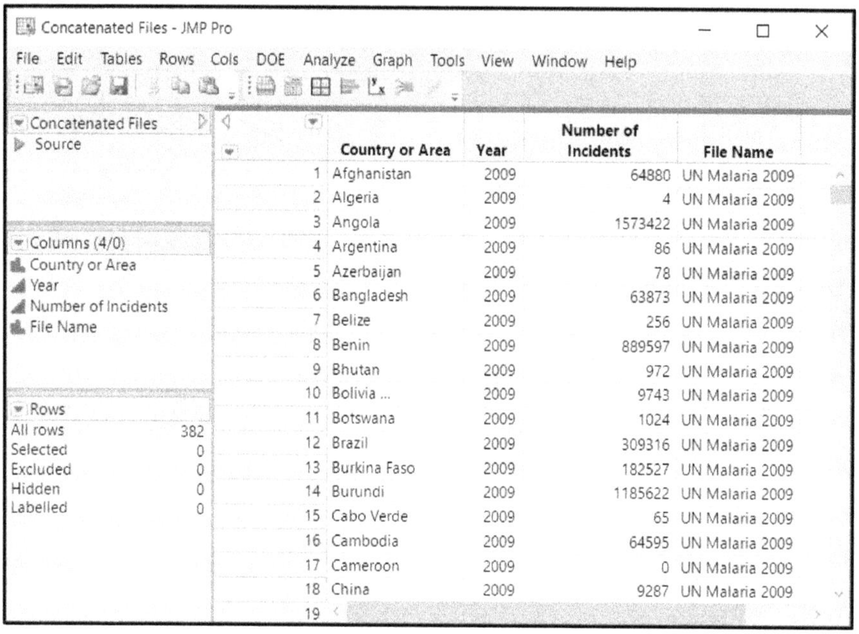

Chapter 9: Dialog Windows

Question 9.1: How can I prompt the user to select columns to be used in an analysis?

Solution 9.1:

A quick way to build a dialog that will allow a user to select columns from a data table is to use the **Column Dialog()** function. The design and formatting of the window is built into **Column Dialog()**. The result is a modal window that includes all the columns in the data table.

```
/* Open the sample data table, Big Class */
dt = Open( "$SAMPLE_DATA/Big Class.jmp" );

/* Query the user for a single column */
cdlg = Column Dialog(
    yCol = ColList( "Y, Response", MinCol( 1 ), MaxCol( 1 ) ),
    xCol = ColList( "X, Factor", MinCol( 1 ), MaxCol( 1 ) )
);

/* Unload the values from the Column Dialog */
my_Y = cdlg["yCol"][1];
my_X = cdlg["xCol"][1];

/* Use the column selections in an analysis */
fit = Fit Y By X( Y( my_Y ), X( my_X ) );
```

Remember from chapter 7 that the value returned by **Column Dialog()** must be unloaded before it can be used in the analysis. Also, there are multiple ways to unload the values from **Column Dialog()**. See the "Column Dialog()" section in chapter 7 for an alternate method.

More information regarding constructors that are specific to **Column Dialog()** can be found in the "Modal Dialogs" section of the "Display Trees" chapter in the *Scripting Guide*.

Result 9.1:

Figure 9.1 Column Dialog Window with One Column Selected

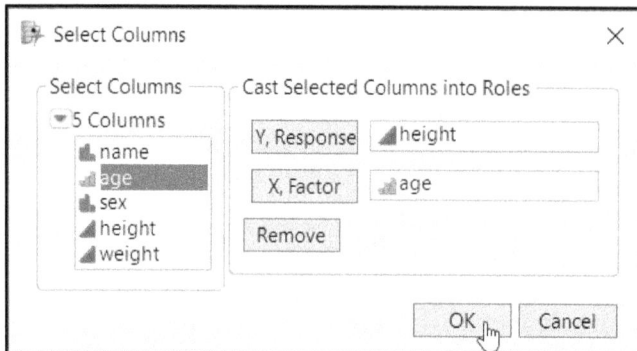

Figure 9.2 Oneway of Selected Column

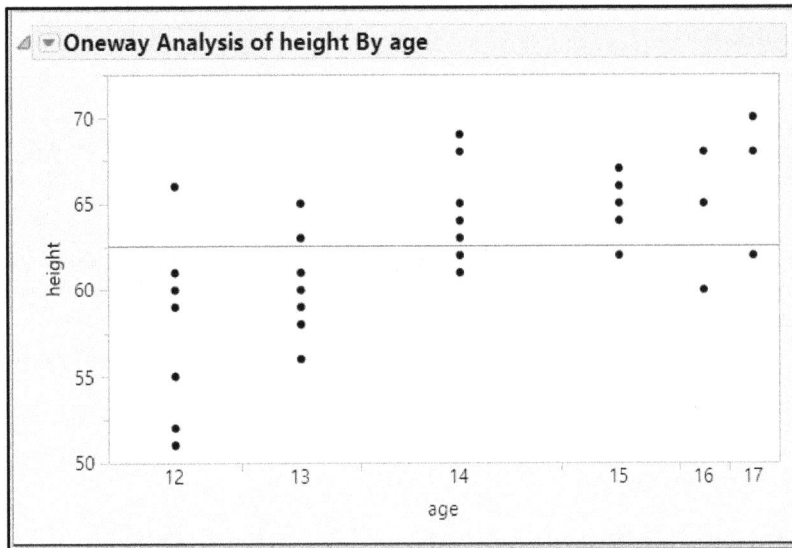

Question 9.2: How can I stop a script if a user clicks the Cancel button in a dialog window?

Solution 9.2:

Prompting the user for information is a fairly common scripting objective. In order to prevent your script from generating errors, the script should stop executing if the user clicks the **Cancel** button or closes the window.

The following example demonstrates a modal **New Window()** to prompt the user for information. If the **OK** button is clicked, the value of **ageVar** is shown in the log. If the **Cancel** button is clicked or if the user closes the window, `Cancelled!` is printed in the log, and the script stops.

```
/* Create a modal New Window to query the user */
ageDlg = New Window( "How old are you?",
    <<Modal,
    <<Return Result,
    LineupBox( NCol( 1 ), Spacing( 5 ),
            Text Box( "How old are you?" ),
            ageVar = Number Edit Box( 29 )
    ),
    H List Box( Button Box( "OK" ), Button Box( "Cancel" ) )
);

/* Test the result: If button = -1, the Cancel button was clicked */
If( ageDlg["button"] == -1,
    Throw( "Cancelled!" );
);

/* Show variable result in log if OK was clicked */
Show( ageDlg["ageVar"] );
```

If the user clicks the **Cancel** button or closes the window, the **Throw()** function stops further execution of the script. The last line of the example script is only executed if the user clicks the **OK** button in the modal **New Window()**.

Result 9.2:

Figure 9.3 Dialog Window Where Cancel Is Clicked

Figure 9.4 Log After Cancel Was Clicked

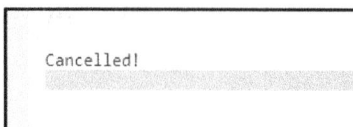

Question 9.3: How can I prompt the user to select a file in a specific directory? I want to display only those files of a specific type, such as text.

Solution 9.3:

As we discussed in chapter 7, you can use the **Pick File()** function to allow the user to navigate to and select a file. In addition, you can limit the files shown by specifying the file types in the third argument of the **Pick File()** function.

```
/* Prompt the user to select a TXT or CSV file */
textFile = Pick File(
    "Select a Text File",
    "$SAMPLE_IMPORT_DATA",
    {"TXT Files|txt", "CSV Files|csv"},
    1,
    0
);

/* Open the file the user selected and give it a reference */
dt = Open( textFile );
```

More information about **Pick File()** and its arguments can be found in the "File and Directory Operations" section of the "Programming Methods" chapter in the *Scripting Guide*.

Result 9.3:

Figure 9.5 File Selection

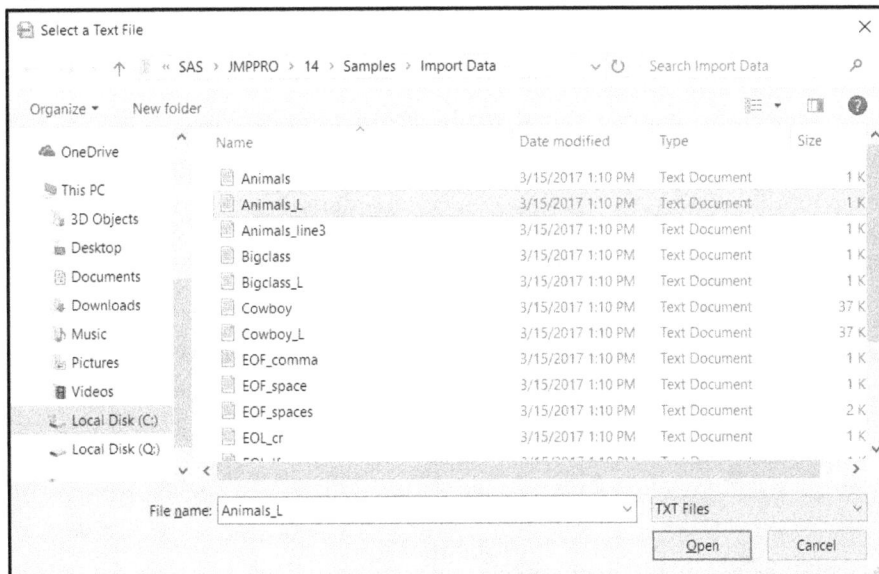

Question 9.4: Can a wildcard character be used to open several data tables that contain specific characters in the filename?

Solution 9.4:

On Windows operating systems, you can use wildcards in an Open dialog to filter the list of files to select from.

Figure 9.6 File Dialog Using Wildcards

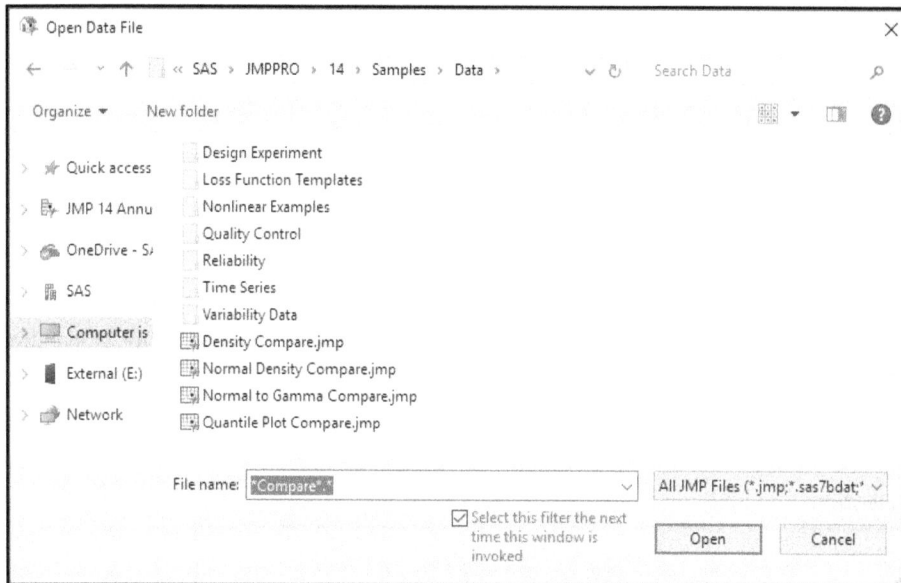

However, that is not a programmatic approach. Unfortunately, there are no available wildcard characters that can be used for limiting files by a portion of the name using a script.

Instead, you can use the **Pick Directory()** function to prompt the user for a directory and extract the files using the **Files In Directory()** function. Finally, you can loop through each file name and keep only the files with the specified character string in the name.

In the following example, we want to open any file that contains the characters COMPARE in the file name. The **Uppercase()** function is used to ensure that the case of the actual filename is not a differentiating factor in the comparison of the search term, COMPARE.

```
/*  Prompt the user to select a directory */
path = Pick Directory(
    "Select the Samples > Data Directory ", "$SAMPLE_DATA"
);

/* Obtain a list of all the files in the directory */
listOfFiles = Files In Directory( path );
```

```
/* Loop through each item in the list */
For( i = N Items( listOfFiles ), i >= 1, i--,
    /* If the filename contains the desired string, open the file */
    If( Contains( Uppercase( listOfFiles[i] ), "COMPARE" ),
            Open( path || listOfFiles[i] ),
            /* Else, remove the file name from the list */
            Remove From( listOfFiles, i )
    )
);
```

In the **For()** loop used in the example, notice that the loop starts at the end of the list and is incremented by subtracting 1 from the increment variable. Why did we do this instead of starting with the first item in the list? Because we are removing items from the list, the number of items in the list is expected to change. By starting at the end of the list, our index is unaffected by removing an item from the list.

Result 9.4:

Figure 9.7 Pick Directory

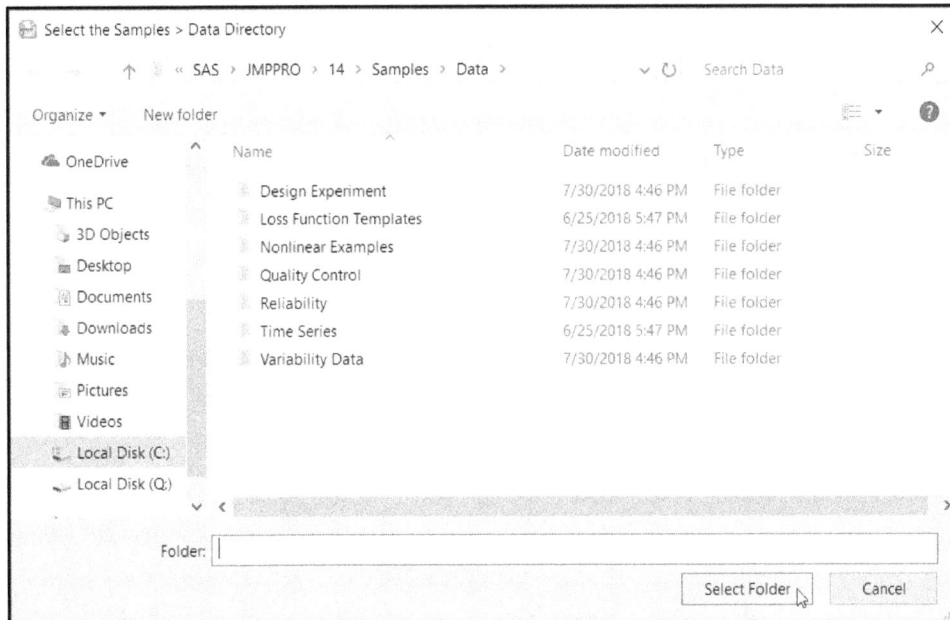

Figure 9.8 Tables Opened That Contain "COMPARE" in the Filename

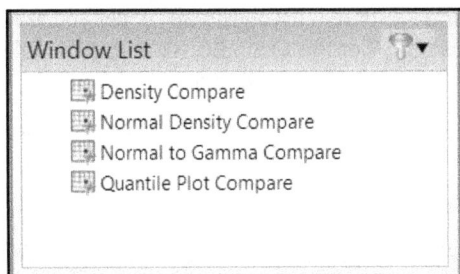

Question 9.5: How can I can prompt the user for information, and then use that value in the SQL string for extracting data from a database?

Solution 9.5:

When connecting to a database, the SQL query is passed as a string to the data source. There are multiple ways to insert the value from a JSL variable into a string.

In the following example, we prompt the user for information with a modal **New Window()**. That value is then concatenated into the SQL query stored in **sqlStr**. You can also use **Eval Insert()** to evaluate the variable within carets (^). This method is shown in the commented section marked /** **Alternate method** **/**. The **sqlStr** string variable is later used as the SQL query specified in second argument for the **Open Database()** command.

```
/* Prompt user for a name to be used in the SQL query */
nw = New Window("Enter Name",
    <<Modal,
    Lineup Box( Ncol( 2 ), Spacing( 5 ),
            Text Box("Enter your first name: "),
            teb = TextEdit Box( "Robert" )
    ),
    Button Box("OK", fname = teb << Get Text )
);

/* Stop if user closed the window */
If(nw["Button"]==-1, Throw());

/* Create a string that contains the SQL concatenated
with the user-specified value from the dialog */
sqlStr = "SELECT * FROM [dbitest].[Big_Class] WHERE dbitest.Big_Class.name = '" ||
Uppercase(fname) || "'";

/** Alternate method **/
/* Use Eval Insert() with carets (^) around the user
specified value from the dialog */
//sqlStr = Eval Insert( "SELECT * FROM [dbitest].[Big_Class] WHERE
//dbitest.Big_Class.name = '^Uppercase(fname)^'");

/* Use the variable as the second argument */
dt = Open Database( "Connect Dialog", sqlStr );
```

Notice, the first argument in the **Open Database()** function is listed as **"Connect Dialog"**. You might choose to include the actual connection information for your data source. If you run this code, you are prompted to select a data source that is available on your machine. For this example, we opened a table that has the same layout and data as the Big Class sample data table stored in an SQL Server database.

Detailed information about the **Open Database()** function can be found in the "Database access" section of the "Extending JMP" chapter in the *Scripting Guide*.

Result 9.5:

Figure 9.9 Dialog Window

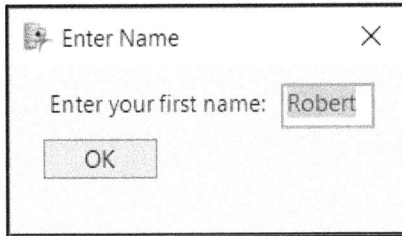

Figure 9.10 Select SQL Server Data Source

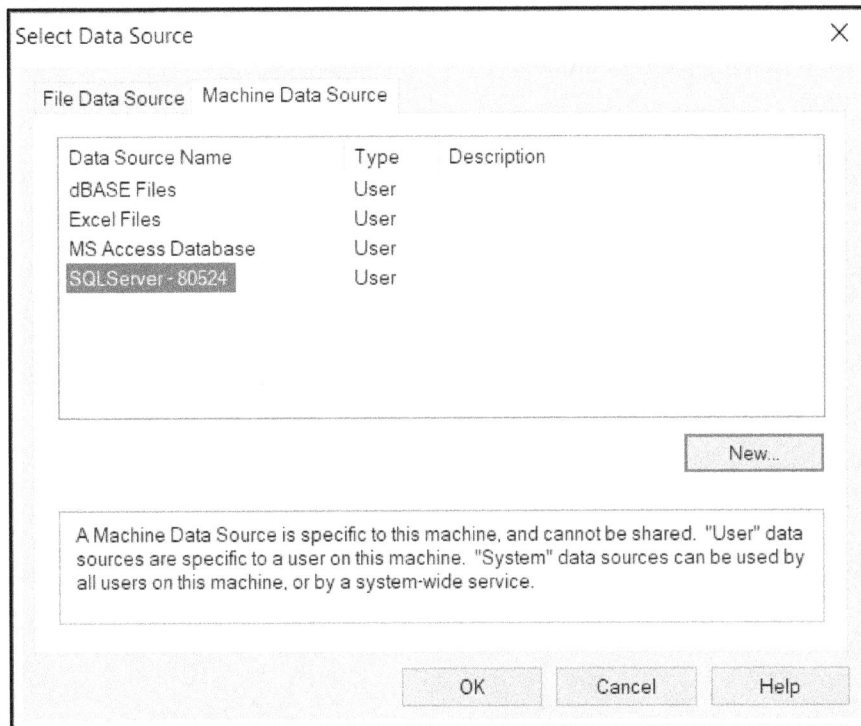

Figure 9.11 Imported Data That Honored the User Selection

Question 9.6: How can I prompt the user to select starting and ending dates, as well as a title to be used in a report?

Solution 9.6:

When you provide a datetime format for a Number Edit Box, you get a little calendar icon that appears inside the left edge of the Number Edit Box. When the user clicks the icon, a neat pop-up calendar appears in which they can easily select a date and time value. The value stored in the Number Edit Box is a JMP datetime value.

An alternative is to use the **Calendar Box()** instead of the **Number Edit Box()** to collect the dates, as **Option #2** shows.

In the following example, we demonstrate using a Lineup Box to arrange the text and input display boxes in two columns. The button script captures all the user's input in variables for later use.

Option #1:

```
/* Create a modal user dialog */
New Window( "Select Date Range:",
    <<Modal,
    /* Arrange display boxes in two columns */
    Lineup Box( N Col( 2 ), Spacing( 10 ),
        /* Prompt for a report title */
            Text Box( "Report Title:" ),
            teb = Text Edit Box( "Weekly Report" ),
            /* Prompt for start and end dates */
            Text Box( "Start Date:" ),
            Text Box( "End Date:" ),
            /* Number Edit Box with a calendar pop-up */
            neb1 = Number Edit Box(
                    Today() - In Weeks( 1 ),
                    12,
                    <<Set Format( Format( "m/d/y", 12 ) )
            ),
            /* Number Edit Box with a calendar pop-up */
            neb2 = Number Edit Box(
                    Today(),
                    23,
                    <<Set Format( Format( "m/d/y", 12 ) )
            ),
            /* Placeholder so OK button is on right */
            Text Box( "" ),
            /* OK button captures the values */
            Button Box( "OK",
                    rtitle = teb << Get Text;
                    sdate = neb1 << Get;
                    edate = neb2 << Get;
            )
    )
);
```

Option #2:

```
/* Create a modal user dialog */
New Window( "Select Date Range:",
    <<Modal,
    /* Arrange DisplayBoxes in two columns */
    Lineup Box( N Col( 2 ), Spacing( 10 ),
        /* Prompt for a report title */
        Text Box( "Report Title:" ),
        teb = Text Edit Box( "Weekly Report" ),
        /* Prompt for start and end dates */
        Text Box( "Start Date:" ),
        Text Box( "End Date:" ),
        /* Calendar Box with a calendar pop-up for Start Date */
        cal1 = Calendar Box(),
        /* Calendar Box with a calendar pop-up for End Date */
        cal2 = Calendar Box(),
        /* Placeholder so OK button is on right */
        Text Box( "" ),
        /* OK button captures the values */
        Button Box( "OK",
                rtitle = teb << Get Text;
                sdate = cal1 << Get Date;
                edate = cal2 << Get Date;
        )
    )
);
```

Result 9.6:

Figure 9.12 Modal User Dialog for Option 1

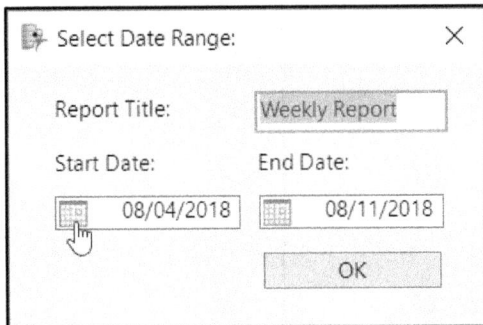

Figure 9.13 Modal User Dialog with Calendar Pop-Up Displayed with Option 1

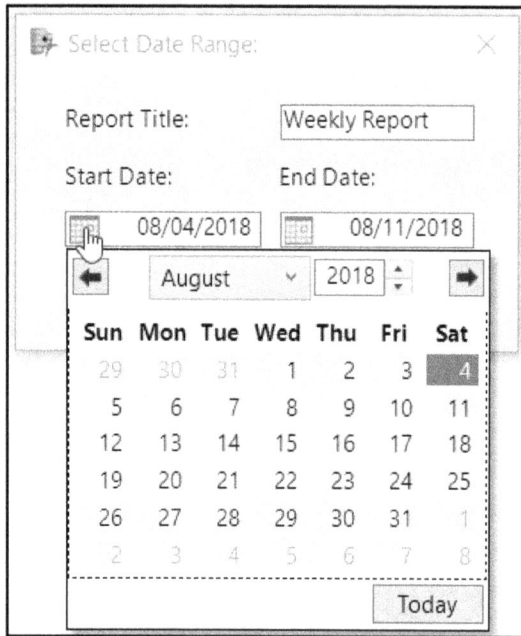

Figure 9.14 Modal User Dialog for Option 2

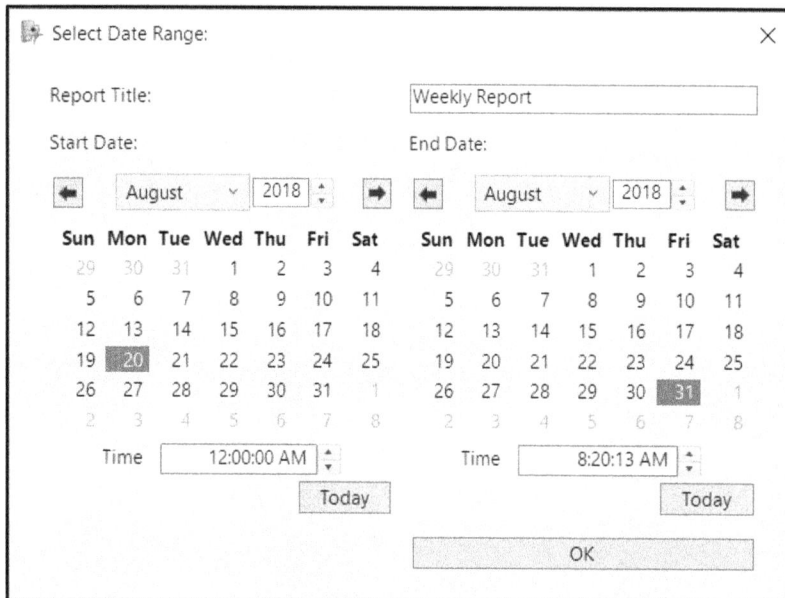

Question 9.7: How can I populate a Combo Box based upon what a user selects in another Combo Box, and then generate a subset table that meets the selection criteria?

Solution 9.7:

This example prompts the user to select a make of cars. Based on the selection, another Combo Box is populated with the available models by the selected auto manufacturer. When the **OK** button is clicked, a subset table is generated that contains the data that meets the selection criteria with all columns included.

We've included the **Set Function()** option in the first **Combo Box()** section to demonstrate how it can be used to self-reference the display box. See the embedded comments for details about what each section is doing.

```
/* Open the sample data table invisibly */
dt = Open( "$SAMPLE_DATA/Cars 1993.jmp", invisible );

/* Obtain a list of the unique values in the Manufacturer column */
Summarize( dt, autoMaker = By( :Manufacturer ) );

/* Insert an empty value at the beginning of the list */
Insert Into( autoMaker, "<Select>", 1 );

/* Use New Window() to create a non-modal dialog to display
   manufacturer and model for user to choose */
nw = New Window( "Choose Models by Manufacturer",
    V List Box(
        Align( "right" ), //Align button to the right side
        hb = H List Box( //Arrange Panel Boxes side by side
            Panel Box( "Select a Manufacturer",
                select1 = Combo Box(
                    autoMaker,
                    /* Function runs when a change in selection is made */
                    <<Set Function(
                        //Allows self referencing using 'this'
                        Function( {this},
                            /* Find corresponding rows in the table */
                            selManufacturer = this << Get Selected;
                            r = dt << Get Rows Where( :Manufacturer == selManufacturer );
                            /* Update second ComboBox with models
                            for the selected manufacturer */
                            cbModel << Set Items( dt:Model[r] );
                        )
                    )
                )
            ),
            /* Initial PanelBox for selecting a model */
            pb = Panel Box( "Choose a Model", cbModel = Combo Box( " " ) )
        ),
        /* When the user clicks OK, a subset table is generated based
        upon the user selections and the window is closed */
        Button Box( "OK",
```

```
                /* Find corresponding rows for selected model */
                rs = dt << Get Rows Where( :Model == (cbModel << Get Selected) );
                /* Create subset with only the desired manufacturer/model */
                subdt = dt << Subset(
                    Rows( rs ),
                    Selected Columns Only( 0 ),
                    Output Table Name( "Vehicle Details" )
                );
                nw << Close Window;
        )
    )
);
```

In this sample script, the user is being prompted to select a vehicle manufacturer. After that selection is made, JMP populates another Combo Box with the models produced by the selected manufacturer. Further, when the user clicks the **OK** button to dismiss the window, JMP produces a subset data table that contains the data for the selected manufacturer and model.

Result 9.7:

Figure 9.15 New Window Showing Only the Cadillac Models

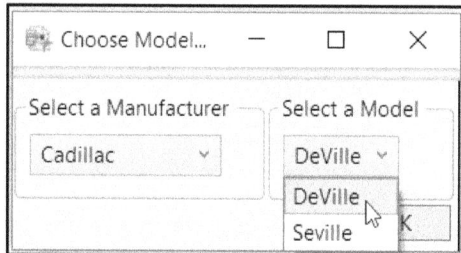

Figure 9.16 Data Table Subset of Only Cadillac DeVille

		Manufacturer	Model	Vehicle Category	Minimum Price ($1000)	Midrange Price ($1000)
▼ Vehicle Details						
Notes Robin H. Lock, "1993						
▼ Columns (26/0)	1	Cadillac	DeVille	Large	33	34.7

Question 9.8: How can I use Column Switcher to affect multiple graphs in the same window?

Solution 9.8:

Column Switcher is a nice feature that enables you to change analysis columns without having to re-create the analysis for each column. At this time, Column Switcher is limited to changing one analysis column in one graph. With a little bit of scripting, you can still get the desired effect but without using Column Switcher.

The following example demonstrates a custom New Window with a list of selectable columns and two analyses that are updated based upon the column selected by the user. The Distribution and Graph Builder will remain live, so histogram bars can be clicked to select rows in the data table.

```
/* Open the sample data table, Candy Bars */
dt = Open( "$SAMPLE_DATA\Candy Bars.jmp", Invisible );

/* Create a function for actions to occur when a column is selected */
multipleColSwitch = Function( {col},
    vb << Delete;   //Delete previous VlistBox
    hb << Append(   //Append new VListBox
        vb = V List Box(  //Container for two analyses
            dist = dt << Distribution(
                Continuous Distribution( Column( col[1] ) ),
                Horizontal Layout( 1 )
            ),
            gb = dt << Graph Builder(
                Size( 537, 464 ),
                Show Control Panel( 0 ),
                Variables( X( :Brand ), Y( Column( col[1] ) ) ),
                Elements( Points( X, Y, Legend( 11 ),
                    Summary Statistic( "Median" ), Error Bars( "Range" ) ) ),
                SendToReport(
                    Dispatch(
                        {},
                        "Brand",
                        ScaleBox,
                        {Label Row( {Lower Frame( 1 ),
                            Tick Mark Style( "Long Divider" )} )}
                    )
                )
            )
        )
    );
);

/* Create a New Window containing columns and analyses */
nw = New Window( "Test",
    hb = H List Box(  //Container to place column list beside analyses
        Outline Box( "Select a column:",
            /* Insert a ColListBox containing the continuous columns */
            clb = Col List Box(dt,
                All,
```

```
                MaxSelected( 1 ),
                /* Nlines calculation = number of continuous columns +1 */
                Nlines( N Items( dt << Get Column Names( "Continuous" ) ) + 1 ),
                <<Set Analysis Type( "Continuous" ),
                /* Actions to be taken when a column is selected */
                colSelected = clb << Get Selected;
                If( N Items( colSelected ) == 1,
                    multipleColSwitch( colSelected )
                );
            )
        ),
        vb = V List Box() //Initial VlistBox
    )
);
```

Note: Included in the Jump into JMP Scripting Add-In is an extra script that includes all of the preceding code, plus an animation feature.

Result 9.8:

Figure 9.17 Initial Window of Column Names

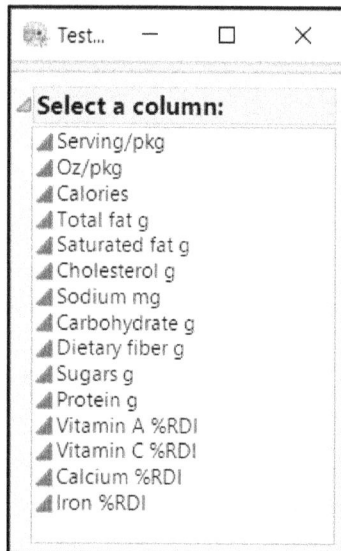

Figure 9.18 Live Analyses of Selected Column

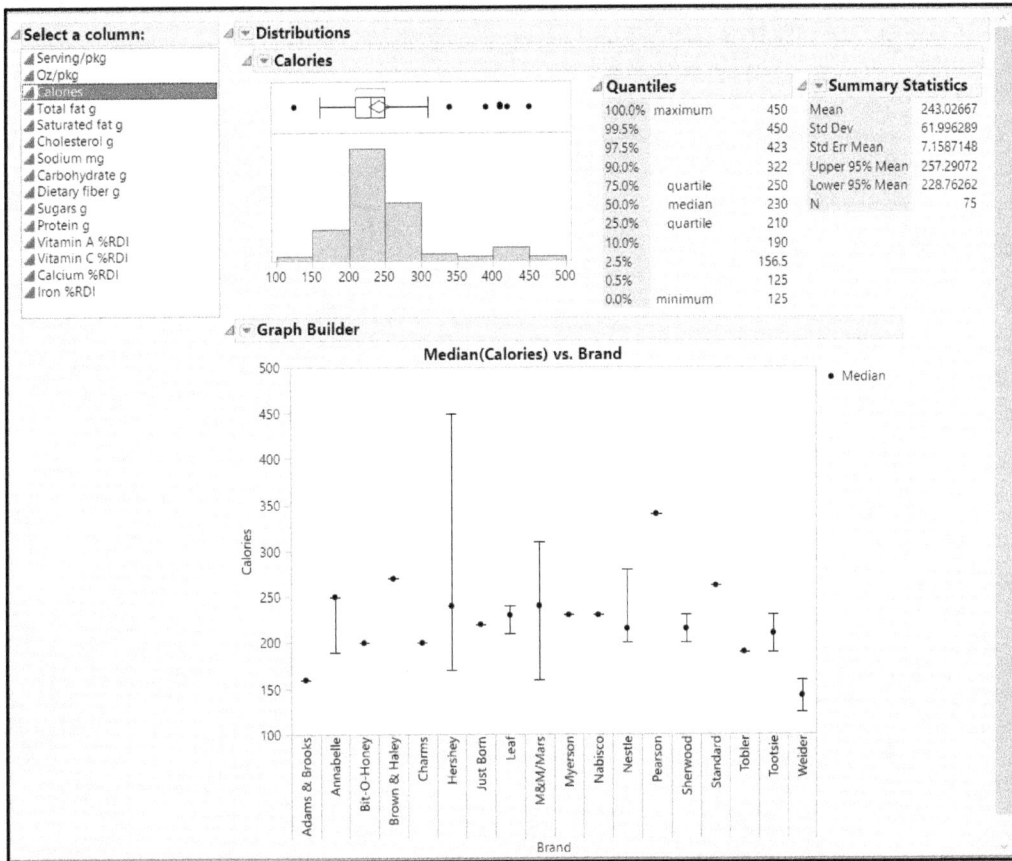

Question 9.9: Is it possible to show or hide a display box based upon a user's prior selection in the same window?

Solution 9.9:

In this example, we demonstrate showing a ListBox of ice cream flavors only if the ice cream Check Box item is selected. When the item is deselected, the ListBox becomes hidden.

```
/* Establish a list of ice cream flavors */
iceCreamFlavors = {"Butter Pecan", "Chocolate", "Coffee", "Cookie Dough", "Cookies 'N
Cream", "Mint Chocolate Chip", "Maple Walnut", "Neopolitan", "Rocky Road", "Strawberry",
"Vanilla"};

/* Create a function to handle the conditional visibility of the ListBox containing the
ice cream flavor choices */
selectFxn = Function( {cb, item},
    If(
        /* If ice cream is checked, show the flavor choices */
        item == 1 & cb << Get( item ) == 1, lbIC << Visibility( "Visible" ),
        /* If ice cream is NOT checked, hide the flavor choices */
        item == 1 & cb << Get( item ) == 0, lbIC << Visibility( "Hidden" )
    )
);

/* Create a user interface to prompt the user */
nw = New Window( "Summer Treats",
    /* Visual enhancement: Adds a border around the contents */
    Border Box( Left( 10 ), Right( 10 ), Top( 10 ), Bottom( 10 ), Sides( 15 ),
        V List Box(   //Arranges the Text Box and Lineup Box vertically
            Text Box(
                "Please Select Your Favorite \!nSummertime Treat:",
                <<Set Font Size( 14 ),
                <<Font Color( "Blue" )
            ),
            /* Arrange the CheckBox and ListBox side by side with some padding */
            Lineup Box( N Col( 2 ), Spacing( 10 ),
                Check Box(
                    {"Ice Cream", "Fruit"}, //CheckBox options
                    /* Function call runs each time an item is clicked and
                    allows access to itself (this) and the index (icheck) */
                    <<SetFunction(
                        Function( {this, icheck}, selectFxn( this, icheck ) )
                    )
                ),
                /* Visual enhancement: Adds text and a border */
                lbIC = Panel Box( "Ice Cream Flavors",
                    /* Allow selection of one flavor */
                    List Box( iceCreamFlavors, Max Selected( 1 ) ),
                    /* Hides the Panel Box */
                    <<Visibility( "Hidden" )
                )
            )
        )
    )
);
```

You could change the **Visibility** setting to **"Collapse"**, as well. We selected **"Hidden"** so that the size of the window is not adjusted for the appearance or disappearance of the ListBox.

Result 9.9

Figure 9.19 Treat Selection Dialog

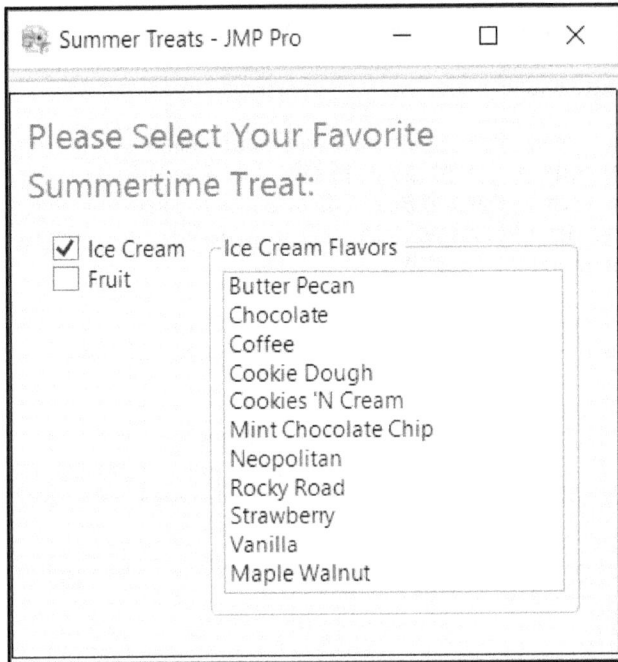

Question 9.10: Why does the Excel Wizard open when I import data from my New Window?

Solution 9.10:

On the General preference group (**File** ▶ **Preferences**), the default setting for the *Excel Open Method* is *Use Excel Wizard*. Although the Excel Wizard is a very nice addition to JMP, you might want to just open the Excel file when running a script from a custom dialog window.

When running a script, JMP is in batch mode. For example, if you have an **Open()** function with the path to an Excel file as the argument, JMP opens the file. Any messaging appears in the log. However, when the script is associated with an interactive feature, such as a Button Box, JMP switches to interactive mode where all messaging is presented interactively. The user must click the button in order for the script to be executed. Therefore, JMP is in interactive mode and the Excel Wizard appears.

The **Batch Interactive()** function can be used in your custom dialog's Button Box script to ensure that JMP just opens the Excel file rather than presenting the user with the Excel Wizard, assuming default preference settings.

Note: This solution uses an experimental function called **Batch Interactive()**. Since the function is considered experimental, it is not included in the JMP documentation or Scripting Index. Although usage of this function is not supported, we are not aware of any issues that are attributed to the usage of **Batch Interactive()**.

```
/* Opens the Excel worksheet */
New Window( "My Custom Dialog",
    Lineup Box( N Col( 1 ), Spacing( 5 ),
            Text Box( "When you are ready, please click: " ),
            Button Box( "Open Grouped Team Results",
                    Batch Interactive( 1 );  //Batch
                    Open(
                            "$SAMPLE_IMPORT_DATA\Team Results.xlsx",
                            Worksheets( "Grouped Team Results" ),
                            Worksheet Settings(
                                    1,
                                    Has Column Headers( 1 ),
                                    Number of Rows in Headers( 1 ),
                                    Headers Start on Row( 3 ),
                                    Data Starts on Row( 4 ),
                                    Data Starts on Column( 1 )
                            )
                    );
                    Batch Interactive( 0 );  //Interactive
            )
    )
);
```

Result 9.10:

Figure 9.20 Custom Dialog with Button

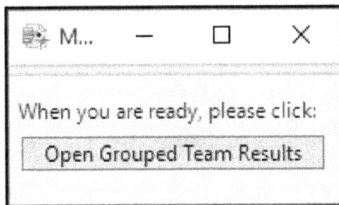

Figure 9.21 Imported Excel File

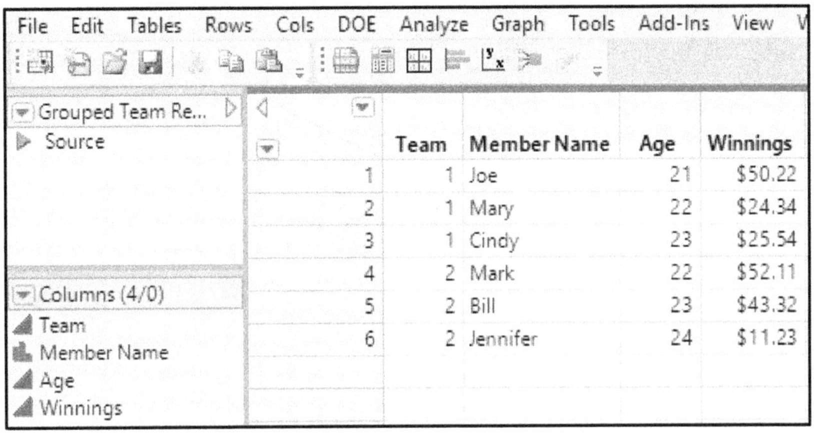

Question 9.11: When I try to limit the columns shown in a Col List Box to numeric, no columns appear. Why?

Solution 9.11:

The Col List Box can either show columns from a data table or be a receiver of selected columns. The first argument for Col List Box is a data table reference. It is the second argument that determines whether the Col List Box will show columns or receive columns. The options are as follows:

- **"All"** – Using this argument causes all columns from the data table to be available to appear.
- **"Numeric"** – Using this argument causes the Col List Box to be a receiver of only numeric columns.
- **"Character"** – Using this argument causes the Col List Box to be a receiver of only character columns.

To limit the columns that appear from the data table, you can use the <<**Set Data Type** and << **Set Analysis Type** options.

```
/* Open a sample data table */
dt = Open( "$SAMPLE_DATA\Fitness.jmp" );

/* Create a window to prompt the user to select columns */
nw = New Window( "Launch Dialog",
    <<Modal,
    V List Box(
        Align( "right" ),
        H List Box(
            Panel Box( "Select Columns",
                /* Show only numeric columns from the table */
                clb = ColListBox( dt, all, <<Set Data Type( "Numeric" ) )
            ),
            Panel Box( "Cast Selected Columns into Roles",
                Lineup Box( N Col( 2 ), Spacing( 5 ),
                    Button Box( "X, Treatment", clbX << Append( clb << Get Selected ) ),
                    /* Receive at least 1 numeric column */
                    clbX = Col List Box( "Numeric", MinItems( 1 ), MaxItems( 2 ), nlines( 2 )),
                    Button Box( "Y, Response", clbY << Append( clb << Get Selected ) ),
                    /* Receive at least 1 numeric column */
                    clbY = Col List Box( "Numeric", MinItems( 1 ), MaxItems( 2 ), nlines( 2 )),
                    Button Box( "Remove",
                        clbX << Remove Selected;
                        clbY << Remove Selected;
                    )
                )
            )
        ),
        H List Box(
            Button Box( "OK",
                /* Retrieve the selected items as column references */
                xVars = clbX << Get Items( "Column Reference" );
                yVars = clbY << Get Items( "Column Reference" );
            ),
```

```
        Button Box( "Cancel" )
    )
  )
);
```

TIP: When you use the optional **"Column Reference"** argument for the **Get Items** message, the result is a list of column references instead of a list of column names as strings.

Result 9.11:

Figure 9.22 New Window Showing Numeric Columns

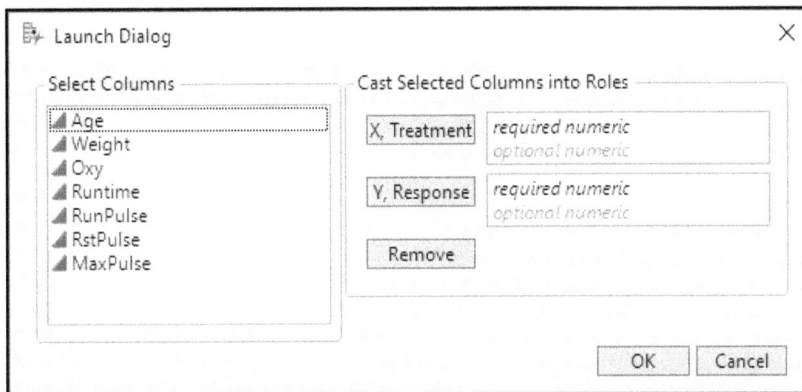

Chapter 10: Analyses

Question 10.1: How can I save the Parameter Estimates table from my Bivariate analysis into a new data table?

Solution 10.1:

In order to create a data table from a report table, send the **Make into Data Table** message to the Table Box located within the outline box of choice. In this case, the message is sent to the table box in the Parameter Estimates outline box.

```
/* Open the Big Class sample data table */
dt = Open( "$SAMPLE_DATA/Big Class.jmp" );

/* Generate the Bivariate using Age as the By variable */
biv = dt << Bivariate( Y( :height ), X( :weight ), Fit Line );

/* Create the combined data table of Parameter Estimates */
Report( biv )["Parameter Estimates"][Table Box( 1 )] << Make into Data Table;
```

The solution uses relative referencing of the Table Box. After the report object is referenced, **Report(biv)**, the quoted outline box name is used, followed by the Table Box number, **["Parameter Estimates"][Table Box(1)]**. Notice that when examining the report, you can see that the Parameter Estimates outline box holds only one Table Box.

For more information about using relative referencing to access elements in a report, please see the "Display Boxes" topic in chapter 3 and the "Subscripting" topic in chapter 7.

Result 10.1:

Figure 10.1 Report Showing Parameter Estimates

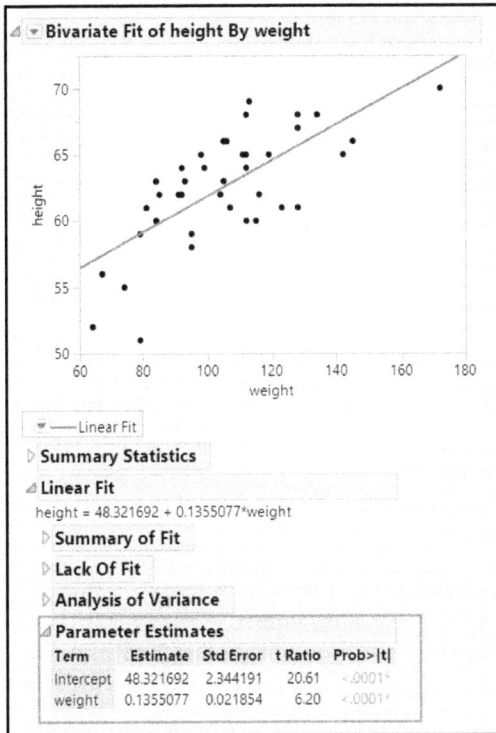

Bivariate Fit of height By weight

— Linear Fit

Summary Statistics

Linear Fit

height = 48.321692 + 0.1355077*weight

Summary of Fit

Lack Of Fit

Analysis of Variance

Parameter Estimates

Term	Estimate	Std Error	t Ratio	Prob>|t|
Intercept	48.321692	2.344191	20.61	<.0001*
weight	0.1355077	0.021854	6.20	<.0001*

Figure 10.2 The Data Table Result from Make Into Data Table

	Term	Estimate	Std Error	t Ratio	Prob>|t|
1	Intercept	48.321691635	2.3441908413	20.61	<.0001
2	weight	0.1355076987	0.0218543719	6.20	<.0001

Untitled 15
Make Into Data Table

Question 10.2: How can I save the Parameter Estimates table from my Bivariate analysis into a new data table when I am using a By variable?

Solution 10.2:

Send the **Make Combined Data Table** message to one of the Bivariate reports to create one data table with parameter estimate values from each By group report:

```
/* Open the Big Class sample data table */
dt = Open( "$SAMPLE_DATA/Big Class.jmp" );

/* Generate the Bivariate using Age as the By variable */
biv = Bivariate( Y( :height ), X( :weight ), Fit Line, By( :age ) );

/* Create the combined data table of Parameter Estimates */
Report( biv[1] )["Parameter Estimates"][Table Box( 1 )] << Make Combined Data Table;
```

The report generated in this example contains a Bivariate report for each of the six members of the By group **age**. You need only send the **Make Combined Data Table** message to one of these reports to make a combined data table for all. In this case, the message was sent to the **biv[1]** report. The results would be the same if you sent the message to **biv[2]** or **biv[3]** reports.

The solution uses relative referencing of the Table Box. After the report object is referenced, **Report(biv[1])**, the quoted outline box name is used, followed by the Table Box number, **["Parameter Estimates"][Table Box(1)]**. Notice that when examining the report, you can see that the Parameter Estimates outline box holds only one Table Box.

For more information on relative referencing, please see the "Display Boxes" topic in chapter 3 and the "Subscripting" topic in chapter 7.

Result 10.2:

Figure 10.3 Bivariate Report Showing Parameter Estimates

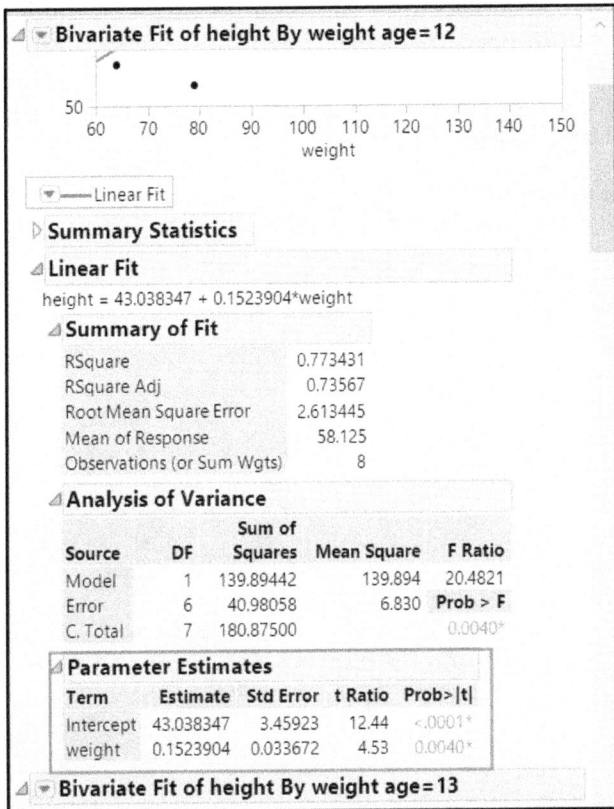

◢ ▾ **Bivariate Fit of height By weight age=12**

▾——Linear Fit

▷ **Summary Statistics**

◢ **Linear Fit**

height = 43.038347 + 0.1523904*weight

◢ **Summary of Fit**

RSquare	0.773431
RSquare Adj	0.73567
Root Mean Square Error	2.613445
Mean of Response	58.125
Observations (or Sum Wgts)	8

◢ **Analysis of Variance**

Source	DF	Sum of Squares	Mean Square	F Ratio
Model	1	139.89442	139.894	20.4821
Error	6	40.98058	6.830	**Prob > F**
C. Total	7	180.87500		0.0040*

◢ **Parameter Estimates**

Term	Estimate	Std Error	t Ratio	Prob>|t|
Intercept	43.038347	3.45923	12.44	<.0001*
weight	0.1523904	0.033672	4.53	0.0040*

◢ ▾ **Bivariate Fit of height By weight age=13**

Figure 10.4 The Data Table Result from Make Combined Data Table

▾Untitled 13				X	Y	age	Term	~Bias	Estimate	Std Error	t Ratio	Prob>|t|
			1	weight	height	12	Intercept		43.038346614	3.4592302991	12.44	<.0001
▾Columns (9/0)			2	weight	height	12	weight		0.1523904382	0.0336721565	4.53	0.0040
X			3	weight	height	13	Intercept		49.171544715	6.2562983428	7.86	0.0005
Y			4	weight	height	13	weight		0.1173441734	0.0652380699	1.80	0.1320
age			5	weight	height	14	Intercept		55.43352879	3.2789190378	16.91	<.0001
Term ▱✱			6	weight	height	14	weight		0.0866096318	0.0320657191	2.70	0.0223
~Bias			7	weight	height	15	Intercept		50.550543697	6.2779806643	8.05	0.0005
Estimate			8	weight	height	15	weight		0.1294804672	0.0577271414	2.24	0.0749
Std Error			9	weight	height	16	Intercept		26.979262673	42.103143412	0.64	0.6372
t Ratio			10	weight	height	16	weight		0.3156682028	0.3551901426	0.89	0.5375
▾Rows			11	weight	height	17	Intercept		48.538336052	9.6694427201	5.02	0.1252
All rows	12		12	weight	height	17	weight		0.1288743883	0.0678127559	1.90	0.3084
Selected	0											
Excluded	0											

Question 10.3: I am using the Neural platform and need to add the Prediction Profiler to the Neural report. How can I do this?

Solution 10.3:

In the case of the Neural platform, there are options you can add that belong to a fit rather than the entire report. This is a special case requiring special consideration .

To add the Prediction Profiler to the report, send the **Profiler(1)** message to **Fit**, subscripting it, as there can be more than one model in the platform report. Then send the reference that results to the Neural platform reference:

```
/* Open the sample data table, Boston Housing.jmp */
dt = Open( "$SAMPLE_DATA/Boston Housing.jmp" );
/* Create the Neural Report */
neu = dt << Neural(
    Y( :mvalue ),
    X( :crim, :zn, :indus, :chas, :nox, :rooms, :age, :distance, :radial, :tax, :pt, :b,
:lstat ),
    Informative Missing( 0 ),
    Transform Covariates( 1 ),
    Validation Method( "Holdback", 0.2 ),
    Set Random Seed( 1234 ),
    Fit( NTanH( 3 ), Transform Covariates( 1 ) )
);
/* Add Profiler option to the Model Report */
neu << (Fit[1] << Profiler( 1 ));
```

Figure 10.5 Neural Report with Prediction Profiler Added

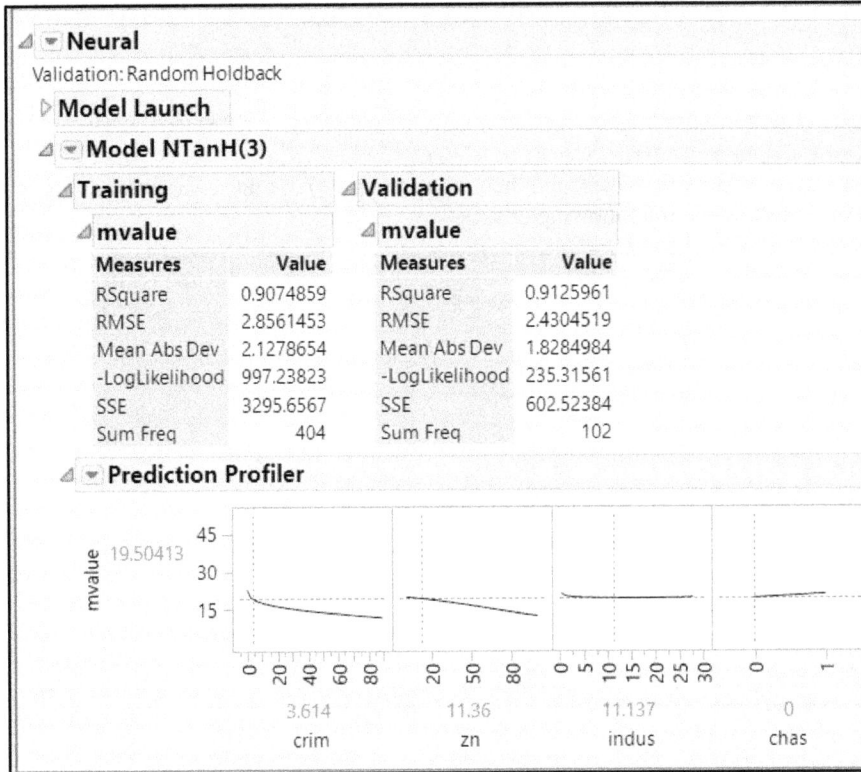

Question 10.4: How do I use global variables for limit values in a Control Chart script?

Solution 10.4

Initialize your global variables with limit values, and then (as appropriate) use these variables as arguments to **LCL, UCL**, and **AVG**, as shown in the following code:

```
/* Open the sample data table, Pickles.jmp */
dt = Open( "$SAMPLE_DATA/Quality Control/Pickles.jmp" );

/* Assign values to the limits global variables */
upper = 14;
lower = 7;
average = 11;

/* Create Control Chart using the variable values */
cc = dt << Control Chart(
    Sample Label( :Date ),
    K Sigma( 3 ),
    Chart Col( :Acid,
        Individual Measurement( UCL( upper ), AVG( average ), LCL( lower ) )
    )
);
```

Result 10.4:

Figure 10.6 Control Chart with Specified Limits

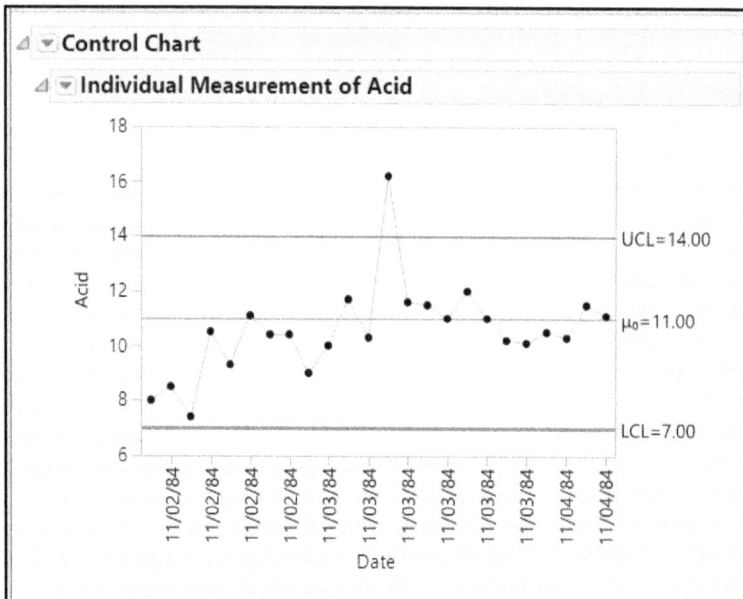

Question 10.5: For a control chart, how do I request that JMP open and use a table of saved limits rather than those limits calculated at run time?

Solution 10.5:

Use the **Get Limits()** option in the **Control Chart** platform object, as shown in the following code:

```
/* Generate the Control Chart using the Get Limits option with the file path as the
argument */
dt = Open( "$SAMPLE_DATA/Quality Control/Coating.jmp" );

cc = dt << Control Chart(
    Sample Size( :Sample ),
    Chart Col( :Weight, XBar, R ),
    Get Limits( "$SAMPLE_DATA/Quality Control/CoatingLimits.jmp" )
);
```

The argument for the **Get Limits()** option is the complete file path for the JMP table that contains the limits. The limits table is opened in JMP when this option is used.

Result 10.5:

Figure 10.7 Limits Table

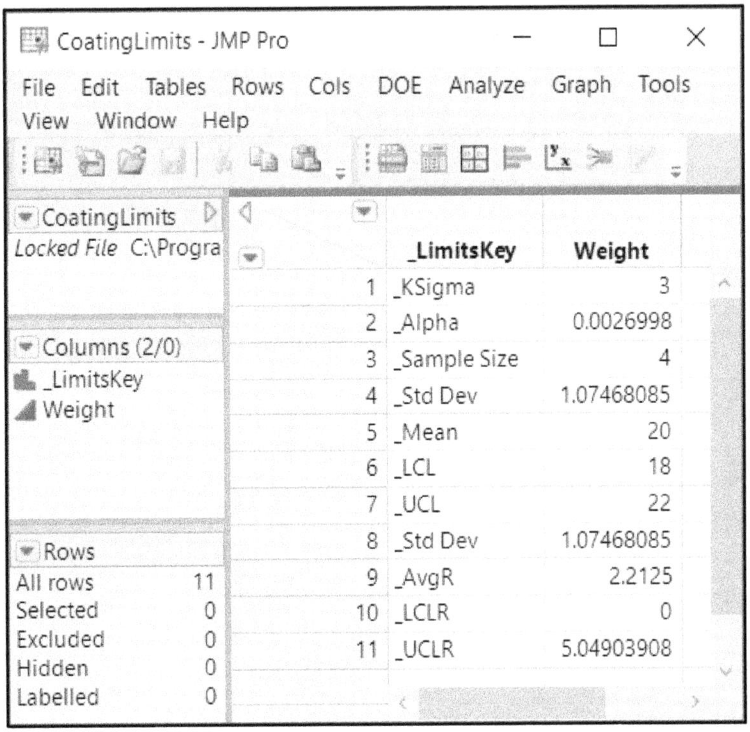

	_LimitsKey	Weight
1	_KSigma	3
2	_Alpha	0.0026998
3	_Sample Size	4
4	_Std Dev	1.07468085
5	_Mean	20
6	_LCL	18
7	_UCL	22
8	_Std Dev	1.07468085
9	_AvgR	2.2125
10	_LCLR	0
11	_UCLR	5.04903908

Figure 10.8 Control Chart with Specified Limits

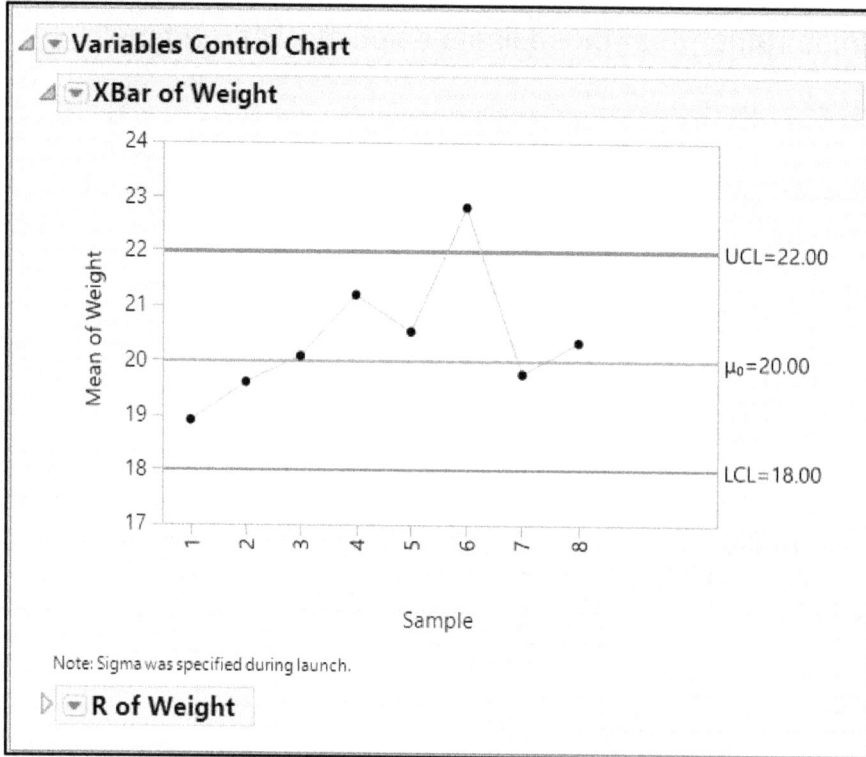

Question 10.6: How do you save limits from the Control Chart analysis into the column property?

Solution 10.6:

Send the **Save Limits(In Column)** message to the **Control Chart** object, or include the option in the Control Chart platform launch:

Option 1:

```
/* Open the Pickles sample data table */
dt = Open( "$SAMPLE_DATA/Quality Control/Pickles.jmp" );

/* Generate the Control Chart */
cc = dt << Control Chart(
    Sample Label( :Date ),
    K Sigma( 3 ),
    Chart Col( :Acid, Individual Measurement, Moving Range )
);

/* Save the limits in a new column */
cc << Save Limits( In Column );
```

Option 2:

```
/* Open the Pickles sample data table */
dt = Open( "$SAMPLE_DATA/Quality Control/Pickles.jmp" );

/* Generate the Control Chart using the Save Limits platform option with In Column as the
argument. */
cc = dt << Control Chart(
    Sample Label( :Date ),
    K Sigma( 3 ),
    Save Limits( In Column ),
    Chart Col( :Acid, Individual Measurement, Moving Range )
);
```

Option 1 demonstrates how to save the limits to the column property by sending the platform object reference a message. **Option 2** accomplishes the same goal but uses the option within the platform launch instead. Specifying an option within a platform or sending a platform object reference a message are methods available in all platforms.

Result 10.6:

Limits have been saved to the Control Limits column property of the process variable.

Figure 10.9 Saved Limits

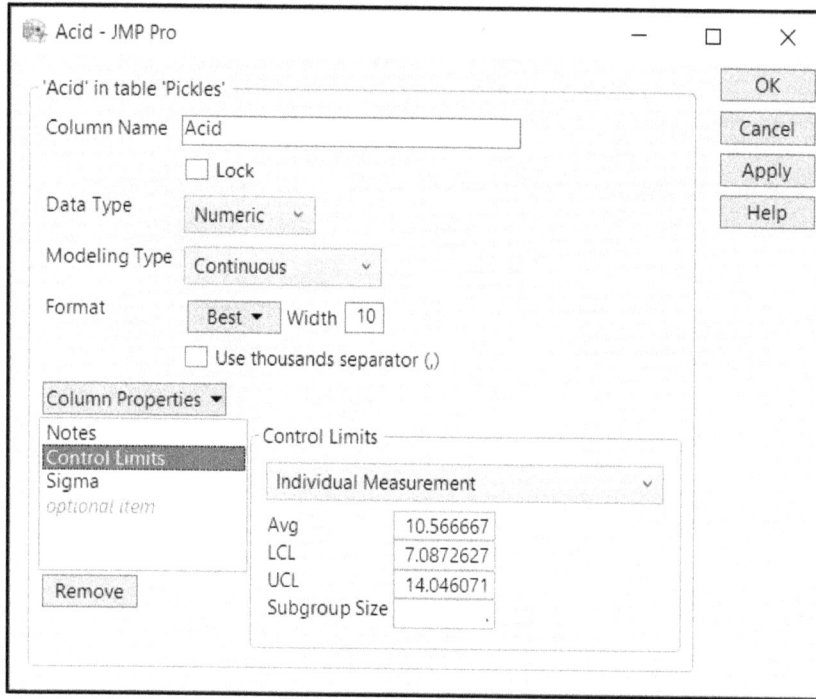

Question 10.7: How do you save limits from the Control Chart analysis into a new table?

Solution 10.7:

Send the **Save Limits** message to the platform reference using the **In New Table** argument, as shown in the following code:

```
/* Open the Pickles sample data table */
dt1 = Open( "$SAMPLE_DATA/Quality Control/Pickles.jmp" );

/* Generate the Control Chart */
cc = dt1 << Control Chart(
    Sample Label( :Date ),
    Group Size( 1 ),
    KSigma( 3 ),
    Chart Col( :Acid, Individual Measurement, Moving Range )
);

/* Send Save Limits message to platform object */
dt2 = cc << Save Limits( In New Table );

/* Save the new table */
dt2 << Save( "$DOCUMENTS/LimitsTable.jmp" );
```

The **Save Limits** option places the limits into a new table. The rest of the code shows the reference to the table, **dt2**, and then how to save it.

Result 10.7:

Figure 10.10 Saved Limits Table

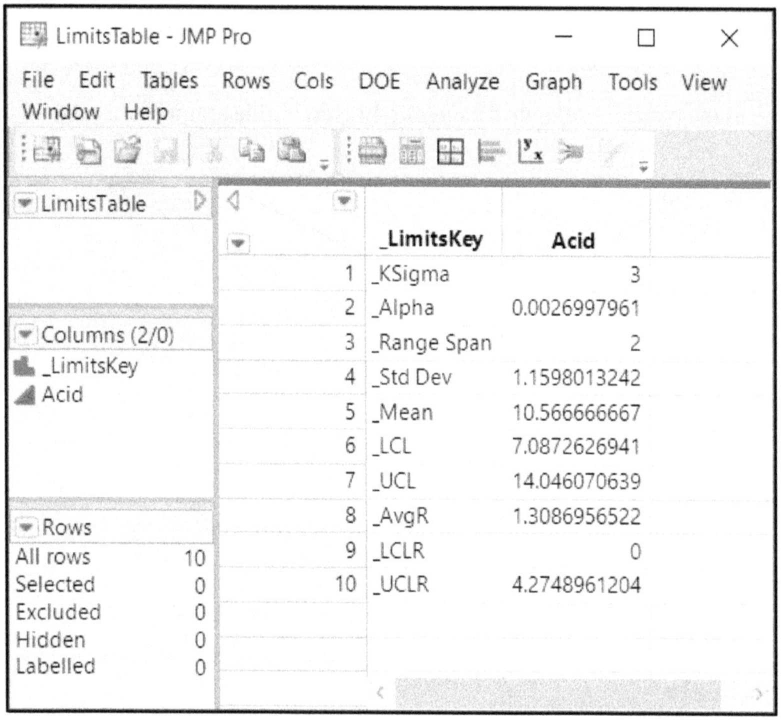

#	_LimitsKey	Acid
1	_KSigma	3
2	_Alpha	0.0026997961
3	_Range Span	2
4	_Std Dev	1.1598013242
5	_Mean	10.566666667
6	_LCL	7.0872626941
7	_UCL	14.046070639
8	_AvgR	1.3086956522
9	_LCLR	0
10	_UCLR	4.2748961204

LimitsTable - JMP Pro

File Edit Tables Rows Cols DOE Analyze Graph Tools View Window Help

LimitsTable

Columns (2/0)
_LimitsKey
Acid

Rows
All rows   10
Selected   0
Excluded   0
Hidden   0
Labelled   0

Question 10.8: How can I use spec limits that are stored in a separate data table?

Solution 10.8:

Obtain the spec limits stored in one data table, and assign the values to the Spec Limits column property of the desired column in the second table, as shown in the following code:

```
/* Create a limits table for demonstration purposes */
limitsDt = New Table( "Limits Table",
    Add Rows( 3 ),
    New Column( "Values", Numeric, Continuous, Format( "Best", 10 ), Set Values( [65, 50,
57] ) ),
    New Column( "Spec Limit", Character, Nominal, Set Values( {"Upper", "Lower", "Target"}
) )
);

/* Store the limits in global variables */
lowerSpec = Column( limitsDt, "Values" )[2];
upperSpec = Column( limitsDt, "Values" )[1];
targetSpec = Column( limitsDt, "Values" )[3];

/* Open table where limits will be placed as a column property */
dt = Open( "$SAMPLE_DATA/Big Class.jmp" );

/* Create an expression within an expression */
specExpr = Expr(
    Column( dt, "height" ) << Set Property(
        "Spec Limits",
        {LSL( Expr( lowerSpec ) ), USL( Expr( upperSpec ) ), Target( Expr( targetSpec ) )}
    )
);

/* Resolve the global variable, then evaluate the main expression */
Eval( Eval Expr( specExpr ) );

/* Perform a distribution that demonstrates that the desired spec limits were used */
dt << Distribution( Continuous Distribution( Column( :height ) ) );
```

Other options for spec limits can be found in the **Manage Spec Limits** utility, found at **Analyze ▶ Quality and Process ▶ Manage Spec Limits**.

Result 10.8:

Figure 10.11 Spec Limits Created in Column Property

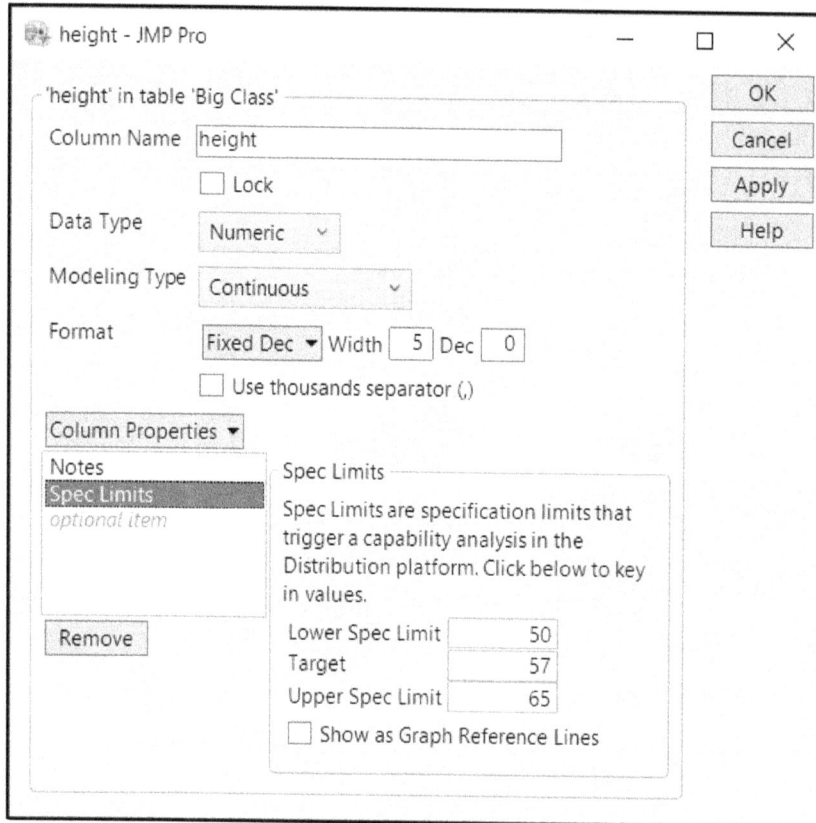

Figure 10.12 Distribution Report Result Showing Applied Spec Limits

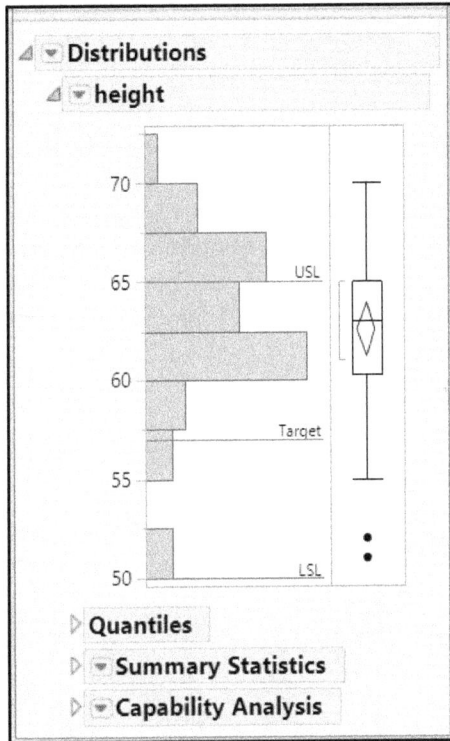

Question 10.9: I have many variables in my data table and want to perform a Stepwise regression analysis, and then run my new model. How do I script this?

Solution 10.9:

Specify the stepwise parameters in the **Run Model** arguments, and then send the **Finish** message to the platform object. A second Fit Model dialog window is created. Send the **Make Model** message to this dialog window as shown in the following code:

```
/* Open a sample data table for demonstration purposes */
dt = Open( "$SAMPLE_DATA/Fitness.jmp" );

/* Launch the Fit Model platform */
fit = dt << Fit Model(
    Y( :Oxy ),
    Effects( :Weight, :Runtime, :RunPulse, :RstPulse, :MaxPulse ),
    Personality( Stepwise ),
    Run Model( Prob to Enter( 0.2 ), Direction( Mixed ), Prob to Leave( 0.2 ) )
);

/* Force the stepwise to finish */
fit << Finish;

/* Create the stepped model dialog */
sm = fit << Make Model;

/* Execute the stepped model */
sm << Run Model;
```

To learn more about the options available for Stepwise Fit Model, go to **Help ▶ Scripting Index**, and search on "stepwise".

Result 10.9

Figure 10.13 Stepwise Report

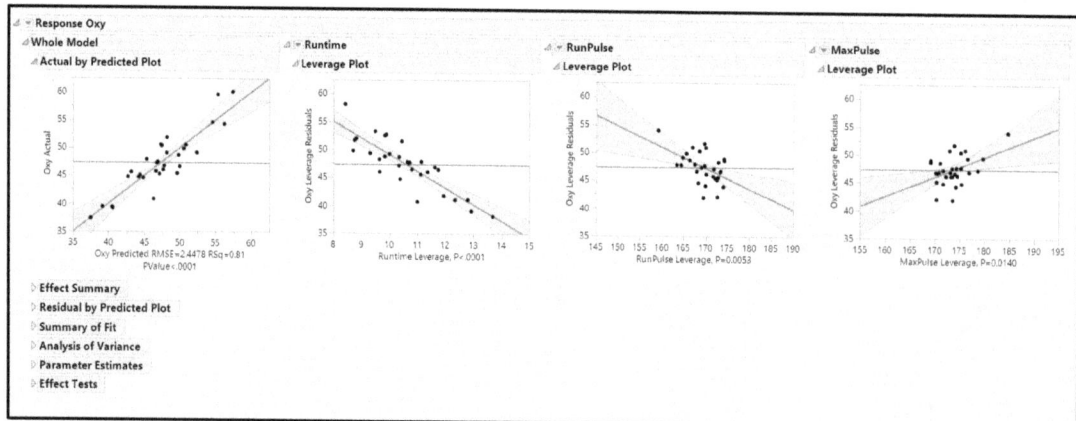

Question 10.10: I need to close the Fit Model dialog window. How do I reference it?

Solution 10.10:

Use **Model Dialog[n]** as reference, where n refers to the number of the particular dialog window, as shown in the following code:

```
Model Dialog[1] << Close Window;
```

Here's a tip for when there is more than one Model Dialog window to be closed.

If you have two Model Dialog windows open, you can close the first one with this command:

```
Model Dialog[1] << Close Window;
```

Use the same command to close the second Model Dialog window, as there will be just one model dialog window left:

```
Model Dialog[1] << Close Window;
```

Question 10.11: How can I use a list in place of the Fit Model effects?

Solution 10.11:

Use the **Eval()** function to evaluate the **myCols** variable, as shown in the following code:

```
/* Open the Big Class sample data table */
dt = Open( "$SAMPLE_DATA/Big Class.JMP" );

/* Assign a global variable to represent the list */
myCols = {:age, :sex, :height};

/* Create Fit Model and use Eval() function to evaluate myCols variable */
fm = dt << Fit Model(
    Y( :weight ),
    Effects( Eval( myCols ) ),
    Personality( Standard Least Squares ),
    Run Model(
        :weight << {Plot Actual by Predicted( 1 ),
            Plot Residual by Predicted( 1 ), Plot Effect Leverage( 1 )}
    )
);
```

Result 10.11:

Figure 10.14 Fit Model Dialog Window with Model Effects Added

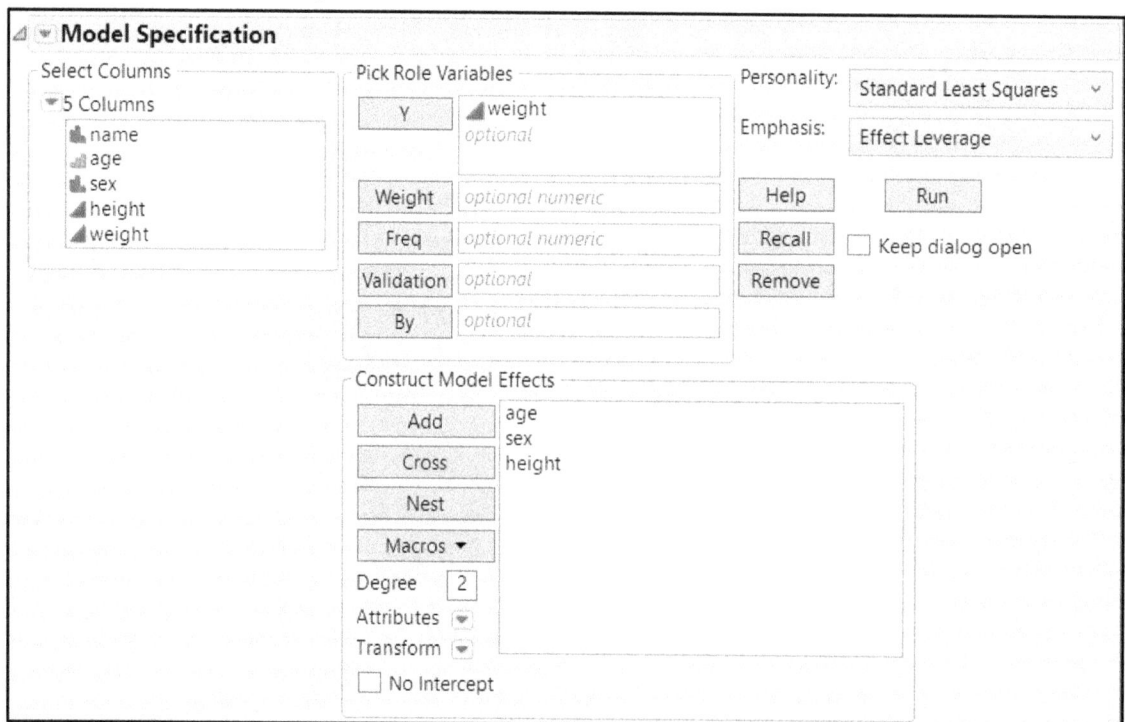

Question 10.12: How do I save X number of principal components of my multivariate analysis to the data table? I also want to include the eigenvectors in my report and save them into a new data table.

Solution 10.12:

Nest the **Save Principal Components** and **Eigenvectors** options inside the **Principal Components** option for the multivariate analysis. Specify the number of principal components to be saved to the data table as the argument for **Save Principal Components**.

```
/* Open the Solubility sample data table. */
dt = Open( "$SAMPLE_DATA/Solubility.jmp" );

/* Create multivariate analysis with Principal Components Arguments. */
mult = dt << Multivariate(
    Y( :Name( "1-Octanol" ), :Ether, :Chloroform, :Benzene, :Carbon Tetrachloride, :Hexane
),
    Correlations Multivariate( 0 ),
    Principal Components( on Correlations, Save Principal Components( 3 ), Eigenvectors )
);

/* Send message to EigenVectors table to create a data table */
newDt = Report( mult )["Eigenvectors"][Table Box( 1 )] << Make Into Data Table;

/* Name the new table. */
newDt << Set Name( "Eigenvectors" );
```

Result 10.12:

Figure 10.15 Eigenvectors Table

	Column 1	Column 2	Column 3	Column 4	Column 5	Column 6	Column 7
1	1-Octanol	0.37441	0.55987	-0.11070	-0.65842	0.31660	0.01874
2	Ether	0.34834	0.64314	0.11973	0.62764	-0.20890	0.11456
3	Chloroform	0.41940	-0.29864	-0.64850	0.30599	0.43061	0.18793
4	Benzene	0.44561	-0.14756	-0.21904	-0.09455	-0.49849	-0.68865
5	Carbon ...	0.43102	-0.29736	0.18487	-0.24135	-0.45965	0.64968
6	Hexane	0.42217	-0.27117	0.68608	0.10831	0.45926	-0.23426

Eigenvectors
- Make Into Data Table

Columns (7/0)
- Column 1
- Column 2
- Column 3
- Column 4
- Column 5
- Column 6
- Column 7

Question 10.13: How can I save the Mahalanobis outlier, Jackknife distances, and T-square values of the outlier analysis to the data table?

Solution 10.13:

Option 1:

```
/* Open the sample data table, Solubility.jmp */
dt = Open( "$SAMPLE_DATA/Solubility.jmp" );

/* Create multivariate analysis */
mult = dt << Multivariate(
    Y( :Ether, :Name( "1-Octanol" ), :Carbon Tetrachloride, :Benzene, :Hexane, :Chloroform
),
    Estimation Method( "REML" ),
    Scatterplot Matrix( Density Ellipses( 1 ), Shaded Ellipses( 0 ), Ellipse Color( 3 ) ),

  /* Set option for Mahalanobis and save values to table */
    Mahalanobis Distances( 1, Save Outlier Distances( 1 ) ),

  /* Set option for Jackknife and save values to table */
    Jackknife Distances( 1, Save Jackknife Distances( 1 ) ),

  /* Set option for T square and save values to table */
    Tsquare( 1, Save Tsquare( 1 ) )
);

/*** Alternate Method***/
/* Open the sample data table, Solubility.jmp */
dt = Open( "$SAMPLE_DATA/Solubility.jmp" );

/* Create multivariate analysis */
mult = dt << Multivariate(
    Y( :Ether, :Name( "1-Octanol" ), :Carbon Tetrachloride, :Benzene, :Hexane, :Chloroform
),
    Estimation Method( "REML" ),
    Scatterplot Matrix( Density Ellipses( 1 ), Shaded Ellipses( 0 ), Ellipse Color( 3 ) )
);

/* Set option for Mahalanobis and save values to table */
mult << Mahalanobis Distances( 1, Save Outlier Distances( 1 ) );

/* Set option for Jackknife and save values to table */
mult << Jackknife Distances( 1, Save Jackknife Distances( 1 ) );

/* Set option for T square and save values to table */
mult << Tsquare( 1, Save Tsquare( 1 ) );
```

Option 2:

```
/* Open the sample data table, Solubility.jmp */
dt = Open( "$SAMPLE_DATA/Solubility.jmp" );

/* Create multivariate analysis */
mult = dt << Multivariate(
    Y( :Ether, :Name( "1-Octanol" ), :Carbon Tetrachloride, :Benzene, :Hexane, :Chloroform
),
    Estimation Method( "REML" ),
    Scatterplot Matrix( Density Ellipses( 1 ), Shaded Ellipses( 0 ), Ellipse Color( 3 ) )
);

/* Set option for Mahalanobis and save values to table */
mult << Mahalanobis Distances( 1, Save Outlier Distances( 1 ) );

/* Set option for Jackknife and save values to table */
mult << Jackknife Distances( 1, Save Jackknife Distances( 1 ) );

/* Set option for T square and save values to table */
mult << Tsquare( 1, Save Tsquare( 1 ) );
```

Mahalanobis(1), **Jackknife(1)**, and **Tsquare(1)** are the messages to create these analyses in the multivariate report. To save the values that these reports generate as new columns in the data table, use the **Save** option nested within that argument.

You can use the terms Tsquare, T Square, or T^2 interchangeably.

Result 10.13:

Figure 10.16 Table with Mahalanobis, Jackknife, and T-Square Values Saved

	Carbon Tetrachloride	Hexane	Mahal. Distances	Jackknife Distances	T^2
1	-2.100	-2.800	2.6042700576	2.7593373407	6.782222533
2	-1.400	-2.100	2.5357704657	2.6793098469	6.4301318549
3	-0.820	-1.520	1.726823512	1.7770230348	2.9819194418
4	-0.400	-0.700	1.3085567369	1.3340229901	1.7123207338
5	0.400	-0.400	1.1277306116	1.1459878834	1.2717763323
6	0.990	0.460	1.3086846713	1.3341566845	1.712655569
7	1.670	1.010	1.992747757	2.0659772514	3.9710436231
8	-2.450	-3.060	2.3590771688	2.4758330151	5.5652450882
9	-1.600	-2.140	1.8134277495	1.8704274174	3.2885202025
10	-0.970	-1.760	1.8909118253	1.954555383	3.5755475309
11	0.570	-0.460	3.5224709475	3.9102031797	12.407801576
12	-0.420	-1.000	1.2778378474	1.30194925	1.6328695643
13	-1.660	-2.630	2.3925186571	2.5140307242	5.7241455246

Data table panel (left side):
- Solubility
- *Locked File* C:\Program Files\S
- Notes Chemical compounds
- Source Koehler, M. G., Grigora
- ▶ Distribution
- ▶ Scatterplot 3D
- ▶ Multivariate
- Columns (10/0)
- Labels
- 1-Octanol
- Ether
- Chloroform
- Benzene
- Carbon Tetrachloride
- Hexane
- Mahal. Distances
- Jackknife Distances

Chapter 11: Graph Components

Question 11.1: How do I replace the default axis label with a different label in Graph Builder?

Solution 11.1:

Updating axis labels in Graph Builder is a bit different from updating other graphs in JMP. For Graph Builder, it is best to perform the actions interactively, and then capture the report customizations by saving the script.

After generating Graph Builder, delete the axis labels interactively and save the script. Notice that in the **SendToReport** and **Dispatch** sections of the script, the current axis label text has been removed.

This code sample shows two options for changing the label for each axis, X and Y. For **Option 1**, send messages to the appropriate AxisBoxes to add your custom labels. For **Option 2**, simply replace the text in the **Set Text()** message with the desired label.

Option 1:

```
/* Open the Big Class sample data table */
dt = Open( "$SAMPLE_DATA/Big Class.jmp" );

/* Create the desired analysis and remove the default axis labels */
ov = dt << Graph Builder(
    Show Control Panel( 0 ),
    Variables( X( :height ), Y( :weight ) ),
    Elements( Points( X, Y, Legend( 1 ) ) ),
    SendToReport(
        Dispatch( {}, "X title", TextEditBox, {Set Text( "" )} ),
        Dispatch( {}, "Y title", TextEditBox, {Set Text( "" )} )
    )
);

/* Replace the X axis label */
Report( ov )[AxisBox( 1 )] << Add Axis Label( "Class Height" );

/* Replace the Y axis label */
Report( ov )[AxisBox( 2 )] << Add Axis Label( "Class Weight" );
```

Option 2:

```
/* Open the Big Class sample data table */
dt = Open( "$SAMPLE_DATA/Big Class.jmp" );

/* Create the desired analysis and remove the default axis labels */
ov = dt << Graph Builder(
    Show Control Panel( 0 ),
    Variables( X( :height ), Y( :weight ) ),
    Elements( Points( X, Y, Legend( 1 ) ) ),
    SendToReport(
        Dispatch( {}, "X title", TextEditBox, {Set Text( "Class Height" )} ),
        Dispatch( {}, "Y title", TextEditBox, {Set Text( "Class Weight" )} )
    )
);
```

Result 11.1:

Figure 11.1 Graph Builder Axis Labels Before

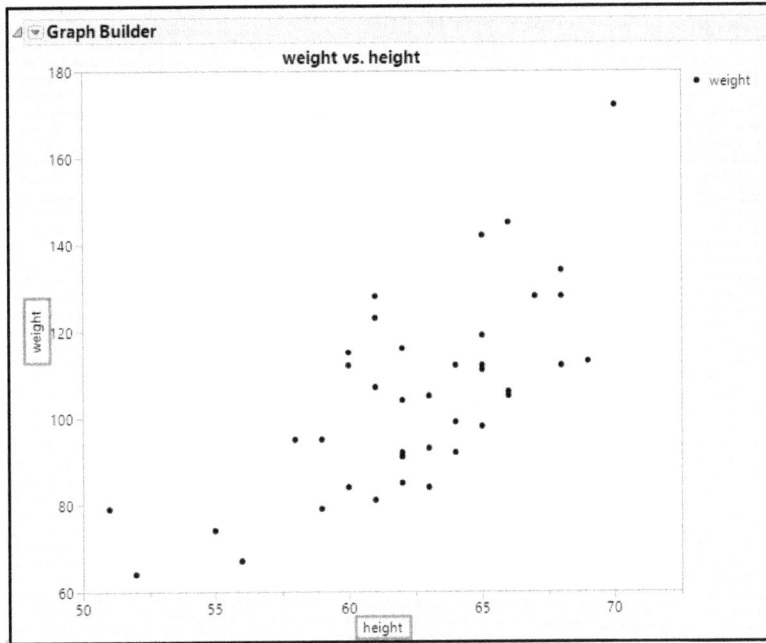

Figure 11.2 Graph Builder Axis Labels After

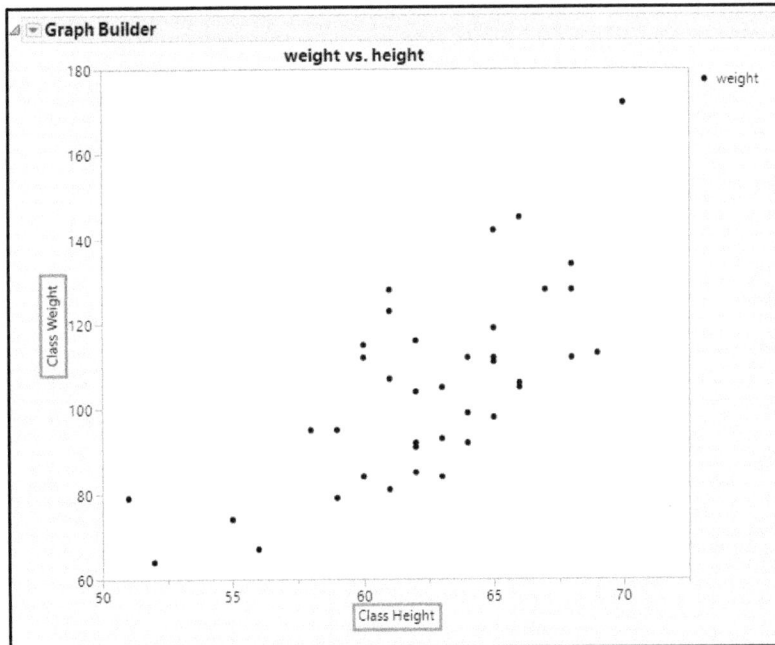

Note: For most other platforms, you can change the axis label by sending the **Remove Axis Label** message to the **AxisBox** followed by the **Add Axis Label()** message to establish the desired axis label. Here is one example to demonstrate:

```
biv = dt << Bivariate( Y( :weight ), X( :height ), Fit Line );

Report( biv )[AxisBox( 1 )] << Remove Axis Label;
Report( biv )[AxisBox( 1 )] << Add Axis Label( "Class Height" );

Report( biv )[AxisBox( 2 )] << Remove Axis Label;
Report( biv )[AxisBox( 2 )] << Add Axis Label( "Class Weight" );
```

Question 11.2: The font size, type, style, and color of the axis labels need to be changed in my report. How do I accomplish this?

Solution 11.2:

Send messages to the appropriate **Text Edit Box**, **1** for the Y axis and **2** for the X axis, to make the changes: **Set Font Size**, **Set Font Style**, and **Font Color,** as shown in the following code:

```
/* Open the Big Class sample data table */
dt = Open( "$SAMPLE_DATA/Big Class.jmp" );

/* Create the desired analysis */
ow = dt << Oneway(
    Y( :height ),
    X( :sex ),
    Means( 1 ),
    Box Plots( 1 ),
    Mean Diamonds( 1 )
);

/* Y axis label is Text Edit Box(1) in this example */
Report( ow )[Text Edit Box( 1 )] << Set Font Size( 14 )
    << Set Font( "Arial" )
    << Set Font Style( "Italic" )
    << Font Color( "Red" );

/* X axis label is Text Edit Box(2) in this example */
Report( ow )[Text Edit Box( 2 )] << Set Font Size( 14 )
    << Set Font( "Arial" )
    << Set Font Style( "Italic" )
    << Font Color( "Red" );
```

Result 11.2:

Figure 11.3 Oneway Axis Labels Before

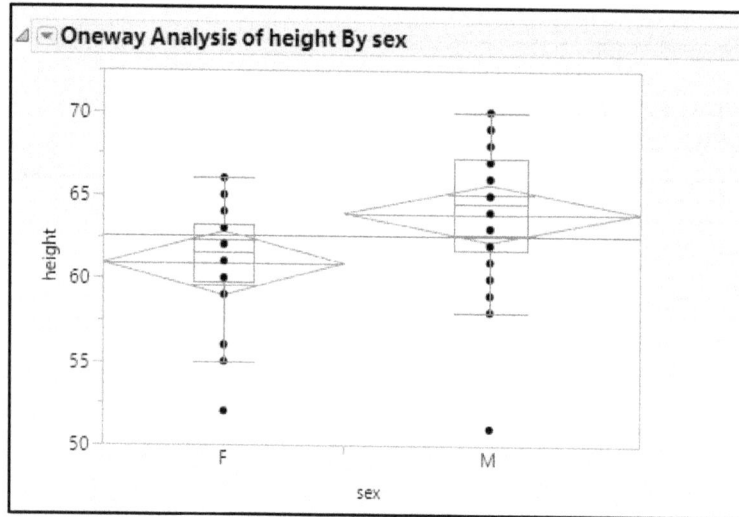

Figure 11.4 Oneway Axis Labels After

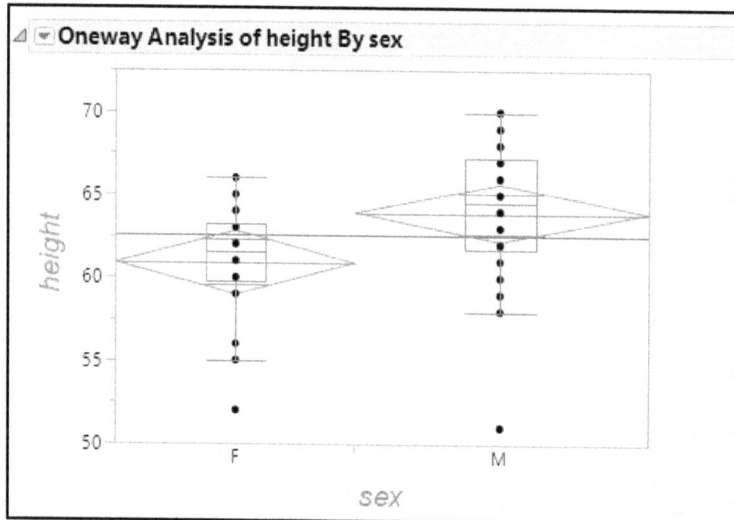

For information about JMP colors, see the *Scripting Guide*. To determine which fonts are available on your machine, right-click an axis, select the Axis Settings dialog window, and then click the **Font** button.

Figure 11.5 Font Settings

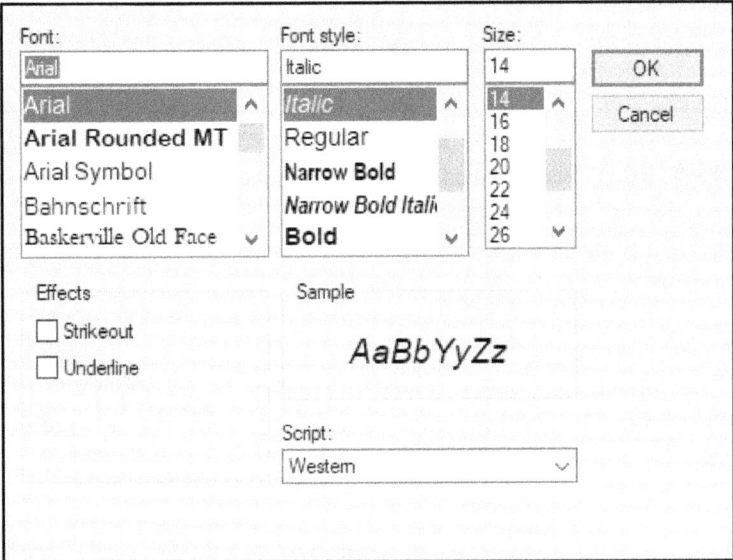

Question 11.3: How do I specify a different font for the tick labels on my graph?

Solution 11.3:

Use the **Tick Font()** message for the **AxisBox**, where you can specify font name, size, and style arguments, as shown in the following code:

```
/* Open the Big Class sample data table */
dt = Open( "$SAMPLE_DATA/Big Class.jmp" );

/* Create the desired analysis */
gb = dt << Graph Builder(
    Show Control Panel( 0 ),
    Variables( X( :height ), Y( :weight ), Overlay( :sex ) ),
    Elements( Points( X, Y, Legend( 1 ) ), Smoother( X, Y, Legend( 2 ) ) )
);

/* Create a report object */
repGB = gb << Report;

/* Set the style, size, and face using Tick Font */
repGB[AxisBox( 1 )] << Tick Font( "Arial", 12, "Bold Italic" );
repGB[AxisBox( 2 )] << Tick Font( "Arial", 12, "Bold Italic" );
```

To determine the fonts, font styles, and sizes that are available on a machine, right-click a plot axis, select the Axis Settings dialog window, and then click the **Font** button (see Figure 11.5).

Result 11.3:

Figure 11.6 Tick Font Changes

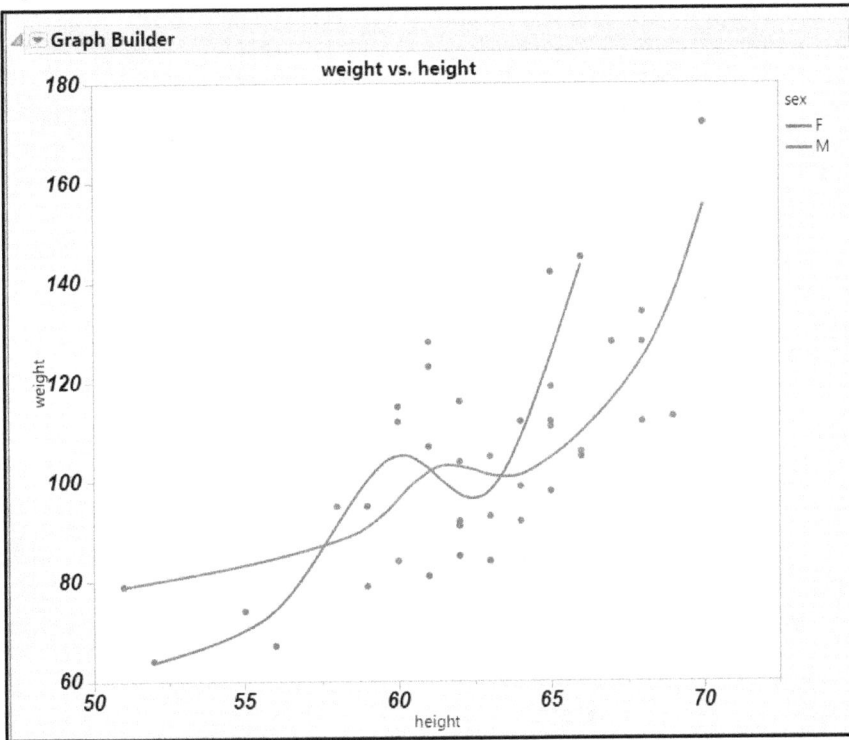

Question 11.4: The tick labels on an axis need to be rotated and formatted to two decimal places. How is this done?

Solution 11.4:

Rotating tick labels and specifying the format can be accomplished by sending the **Axis Settings()** message to the **AxisBox**. Rotate the labels using the **Label Orientation** setting, and use the **Format()** message to change the formatting of the labels. Both messages are sent to the **AxisBox**, as shown in the following code:

```
/* Open the Big Class sample data table */
dt = Open( "$SAMPLE_DATA/Big Class.jmp" );

/* Create the desired analysis */
biv = dt << Bivariate( Y( :height ), X( :weight ) );

/* Set tick label format to vertical with 2 decimal places */
Report( biv )[AxisBox( 2 )] << Axis Settings(
    {Format( "Fixed Dec", 12, 2 ), LabelRow( Label Orientation( "Vertical" ) )}
);
```

The **Axis Settings()** message accepts a list argument containing named arguments that correspond to the settings available in the Axis Settings dialog.

Result 11.4:

Figure 11.7 Tick Orientation and Format Changes

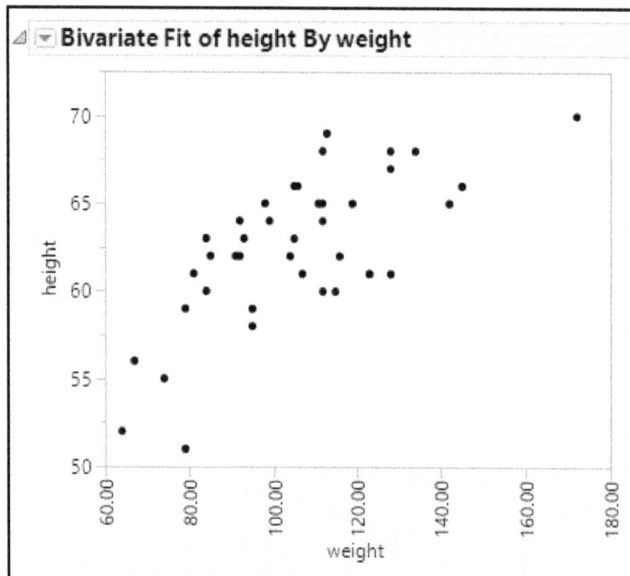

To see the available options for the **Format()** function, right-click an axis, select the Axis Settings dialog window, and then click the down arrow for **Format** to display the list. You can see the **Label Orientation** options in this dialog, as well.

Figure 11.8 Axis Setting Format Menu

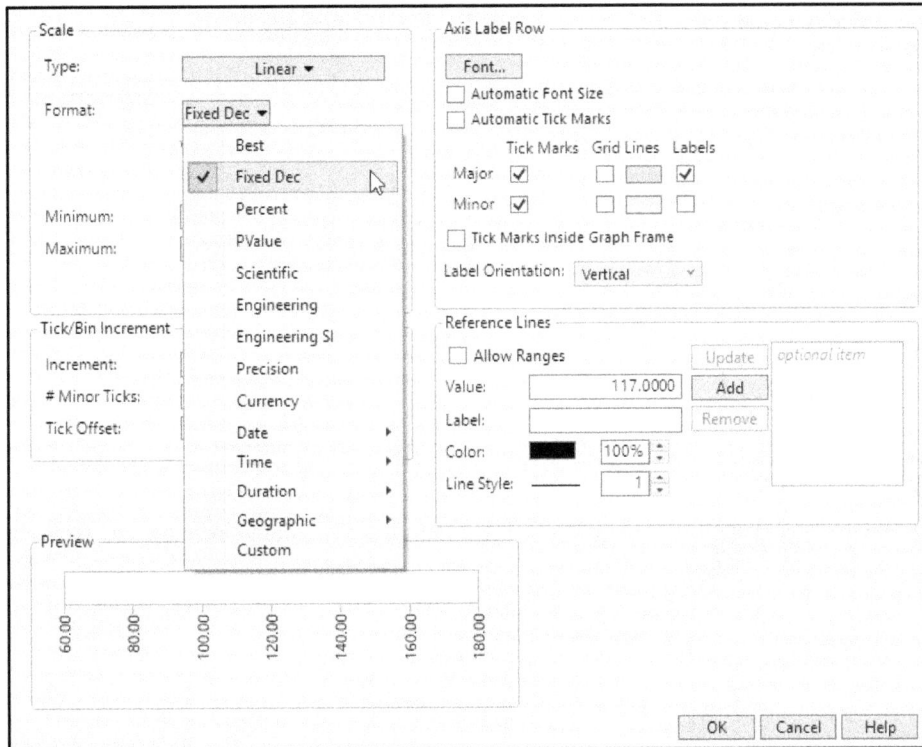

Question 11.5: How can I specify the order of values on an axis?

Solution 11.5:

Assign the Value Ordering column property using the **Set Property()** message for the column, as shown in the following code:

```
/* Open the Big Class sample data table */
dt = Open( "$SAMPLE_DATA/Big Class.jmp" );

/* Assign the Value Ordering column property */
Column( "age" ) << Set Property( "Value Ordering", {17, 15, 16, 12, 13, 14} );

/* Create a Bar Chart to see the effect */
gb = dt << Graph Builder(
    Size( 533, 448 ),
    Show Control Panel( 0 ),
    Variables( X( :age ), Y( :height ) ),
    Elements( Bar( X, Y, Legend( 6 ) ) )
);
```

Result 11.5:

To check the Value Ordering property for the column **age**, right-click the column heading, and then select **Column Info**.

Figure 11.9 New Value Ordering Property

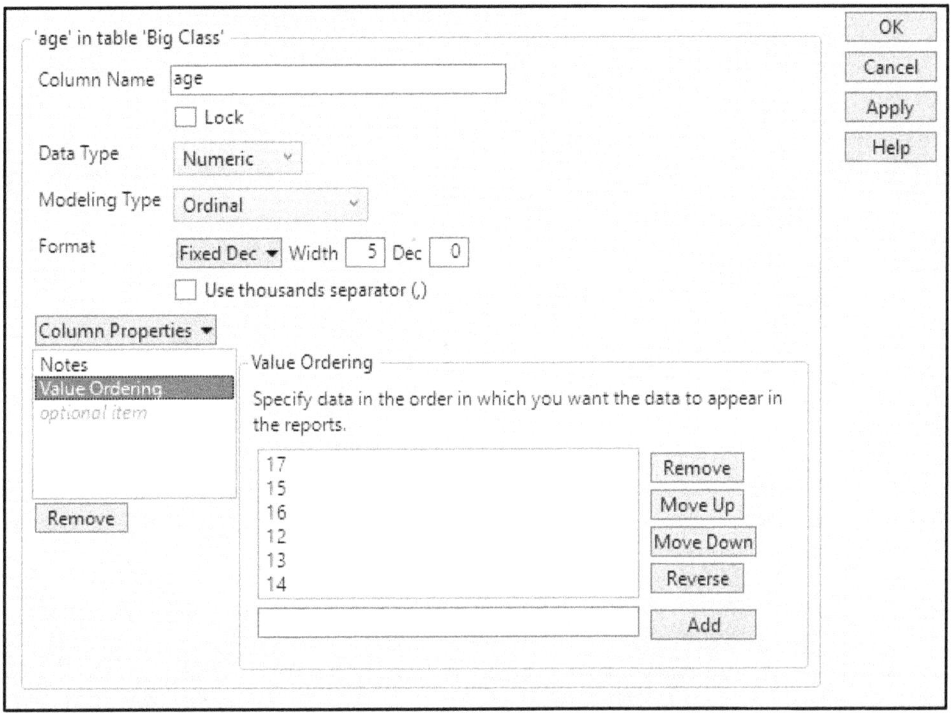

Figure 11.10 Bar Chart Demonstrates the New Axis Order

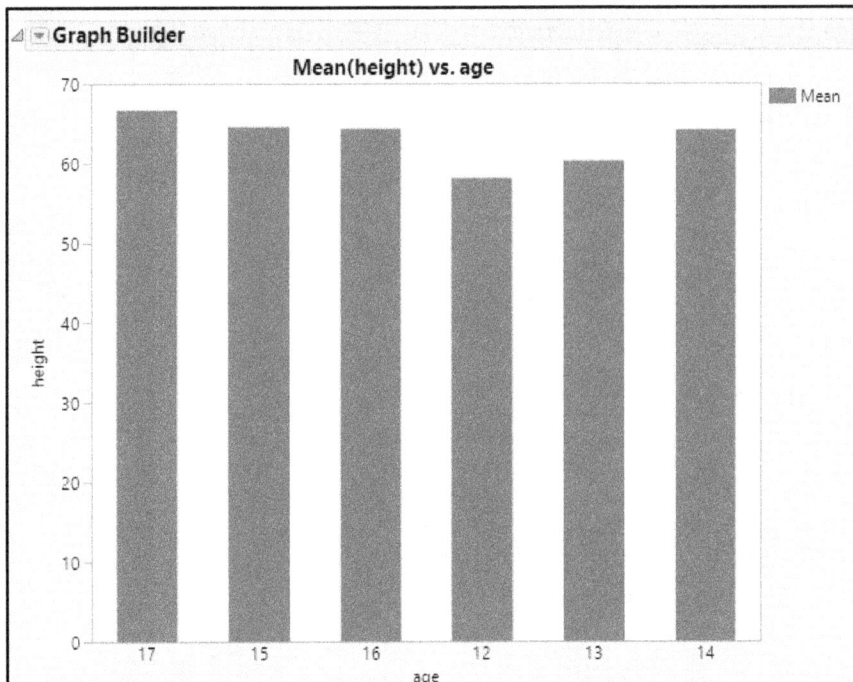

Question 11.6: How do I add a reference line on any graph?

Solution 11.6:

Send an **Add Ref Line()** message to the **AxisBox**, as shown in the following code:

```
/* Open the Big Class sample data table */
dt = Open( "$SAMPLE_DATA/Big Class.jmp" );

/* Create the desired analysis */
biv = dt << Bivariate( Y( :weight ), X( :height ) );

/* Add a reference line to the Y axis */
Report( biv )[Axisbox( 1 )] << Add Ref Line( 100, "Solid", "Red" );
/* Add a reference line to the X axis */
Report( biv )[Axisbox( 2 )] << Add Ref Line( 55, "Dashed", "Green" );
```

This example is for the Bivariate plot, but the concepts are the same for other graphs as well. The **Add Ref Line** message requires the number coordinate argument. Line style and color arguments might be included, as this example shows.

NOTE: For Graph Builder, it is best to perform the actions interactively, and then capture the report customizations with the **SendToReport** and **Dispatch** scripts.

Result 11.6:

Figure 11.11 Added Reference Lines

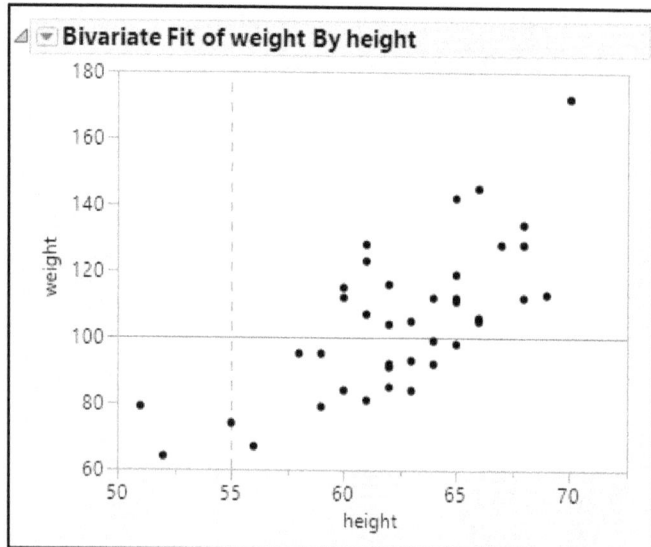

Question 11.7: How can I remove a reference line?

Solution 11.7:

Use the **Remove Ref Line()** message with the location of the line as its argument, as shown in the following code:

```
/* Open the Big Class sample data table */
dt = Open( "$SAMPLE_DATA/Big Class.jmp" );

/* Create the desired analysis */
biv = dt << Bivariate( Y( :weight ), X( :height ) );

/* Add a reference line to the Y axis */
Report( biv )[Axisbox( 1 )] << Add Ref Line( 100, "Solid", "Red" );

Wait( 2 );   /* Added for demonstration purposes only */

/* Remove the reference line. */
Report( biv )[AxisBox( 1 )] << Remove Ref Line( 100 );
```

Result 11.7:

Figure 11.12 Reference Line Before

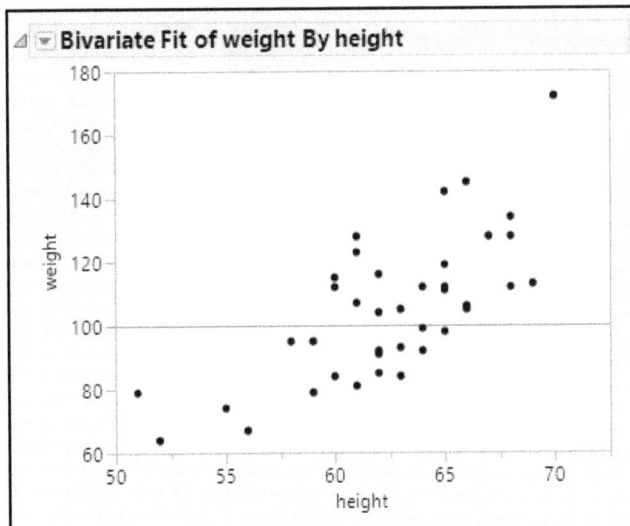

Figure 11.13 Reference Line Removed

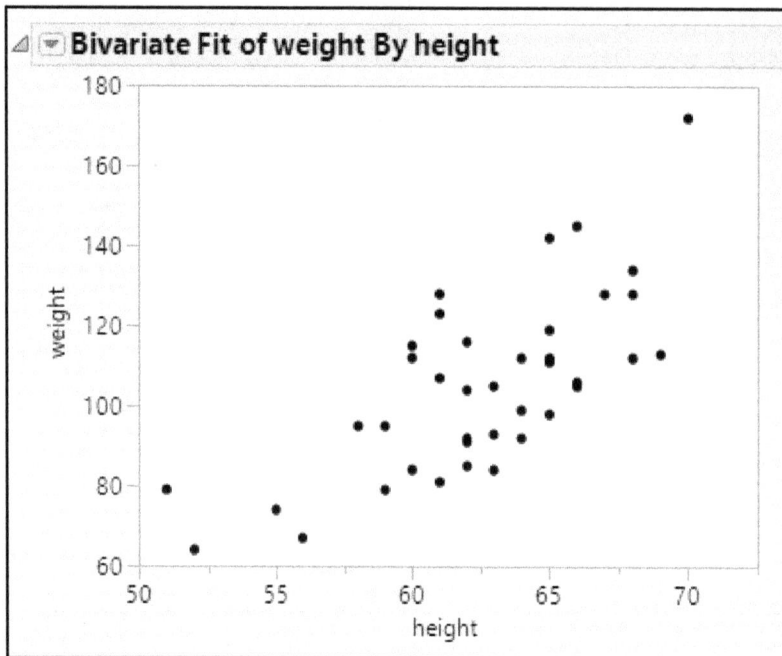

Question 11.8: How do I add annotations to my graph using a script?

Solution 11.8:

Use the **Text()** function within **Add Graphics Script()**, as shown in the following code:

```
/* Open the Big Class sample data table. */
dt = Open( "$SAMPLE_Data/Big Class.jmp" );

/* Generate the desired graph. */
cc = dt << Control Chart(
    Sample Label( :age ),
    KSigma( 3 ),
    Chart Col( :height, Individual Measurement )
);

/* Use the Text function within Add Graphics Script() to add the desired text to the
graph. */
Report( cc )[Framebox( 1 )] << Add Graphics Script(
    Text( right justified, {30, 55.0}, "ABC" );
    Text( right justified, {30, 70.0}, "XYZ" );
);
```

The **Add Graphics Script()** message enables running a script within a graph.

The *Scripting Guide* and the Scripting Index, under "Functions," provide information about the various options available for the **Text()** function, including color, font, position, and orientation.

Result 11.8:

Figure 11.14 Control Chart with Text Annotations

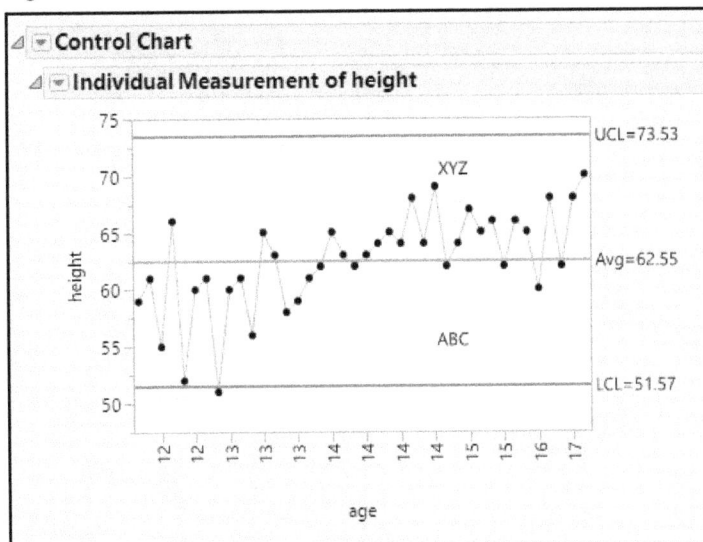

Question 11.9: I have a spec limits table with columns holding limits for each process variable. I want to plot these limits on Oneway plots. How can I do this?

Solution 11.9:

Use **Add Ref Line()** to add lines to the plot, and as the argument to the command, use column and row references to the specific cell containing that information in the spec limits table, as shown in the following code:

```
/* Open the sample data table, Big Class.jmp */
dt1 = Open( "$SAMPLE_DATA/Big Class.jmp" );

/* For demonstration purposes, create a table with spec limits */
dt2 = New Table( "Spec Limits Table",
    Add Rows( 2 ),
    New Column( "Process Column",
        Character, Nominal, Set Values( {"height", "weight"} ) ),
    New Column( "Lower Spec Limit",
        Numeric, Continuous, Format( "Best", 10 ), Set Values( [60, 90] ) ),
    New Column( "Upper Spec Limit",
        Numeric, Continuous, Format( "Best", 10 ), Set Values( [70, 150] ) )
);

/* Capture a list of variables to be used in Oneway analyses */
varList = dt1 << Get Column Names( "Continuous" );

/* Use a For loop to create a Oneway ANOVA for each member of the variable list */
For( i = 1, i <= N Items( varList ), i++,
    ow = dt1 << Oneway( Y( varList[i] ), X( :sex ),
        Means( 1 ), Box Plots( 0 ), Mean Diamonds( 1 )
    );

    /* Find the row in the data table that matches the column variable name */
    rownum = dt2 << Get Rows Where( :Process Column == Char( varList[i] ) );

    /* Assign the limit value from adjacent columns on that row, using the rownum
    variable value */
    lower = Column( dt2, "Lower Spec Limit" )[rownum[1]];
    upper = Column( dt2, "Upper Spec Limit" )[rownum[1]];

    /* Add reference lines to the Oneway plot, based on the spec limit values
    assigned */
    Report( ow )[Axisbox( 1 )] << Add Ref Line( lower, "Solid", "Red" );
    Report( ow )[Axisbox( 1 )] << Add Ref Line( upper, "Solid", "Red" );
);
```

Result 11.9:

Figure 11.15 Oneway Plots with Limit Lines Added

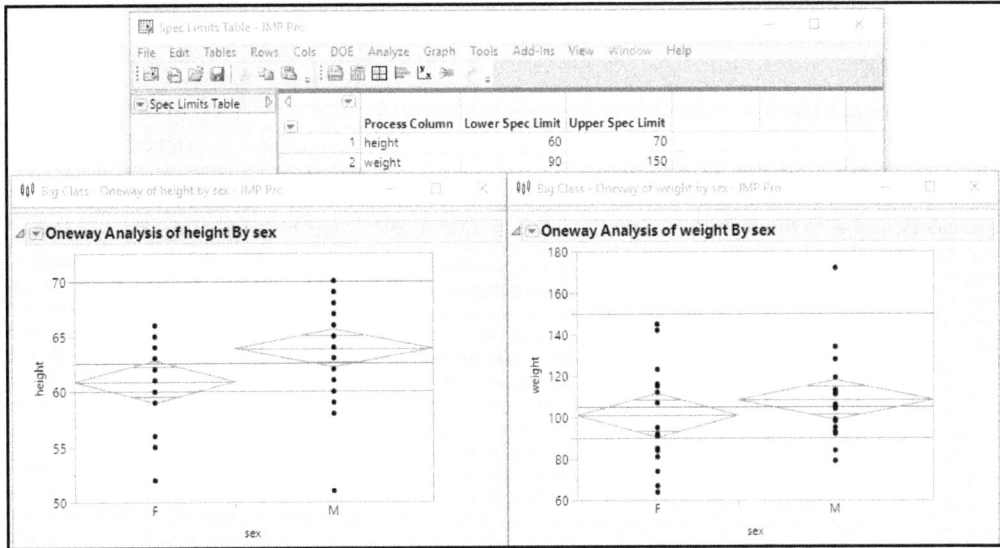

Question 11.10: How can I get consistent legend colors when using a local data filter with Graph Builder?

Solution 11.10:

When filtering a graph using a local data filter, it is possible to filter down to a subset of rows such that only some of the levels appear in the graph. When this occurs, the levels might be assigned different colors in the legend than when all the levels appeared.

To ensure that the items in the legend remain the same, create a new column called "Legend," or named as appropriate for your data, with a Value Colors column property. Assign categories to your grouping variable combinations in the Legend column. When creating your Graph Builder plot, cast the Legend column into the Overlay role:

```
/* Open the sample data table, Wine Sensory Data.jmp */
dt = Open( "$SAMPLE_DATA/Wine Sensory Data.jmp" );

/* Add a column to summarize data */
dt << New Column( "Summary Rating",
    Numeric,
    "Continuous",
    Format( "Best", 12 ),
    Formula(
      Sum( :Carolyn Tannic + :Carolyn Peppery + :Carolyn Aromatic + :Carolyn Berry Notes ))
);

/* Add a column to create categories for the legend */
dt << New Column( "Legend",
    Character,
    "Nominal",
    Formula(
        If(
                :Summary Rating < 17.5, "Low",
                17.5 <= :Summary Rating <= 21.5, "Good",
                21.5 < :Summary Rating <= 26, "Better",
                :Summary Rating > 26, "Best",
                "Unknown"
        )
    ),
    Set Property( "Value Colors",
        {"Best" = "Purple", "Better" = "Blue", "Good" = "Green", "Low" = "Red"} )
);

/* Create a list of all unique wine regions for the grouping variable */
/* The Summarize() function can be used as an alternative */
RegionList = Associative Array( :Region ) << Get Keys;

/* Create new window, which will show a report for each region, for demonstration purposes
*/
nw = New Window( "Legend Category Color Variation" );

/* Loop through each wine region and append Graph Builder to the window */
For( i = 1, i <= N Items( RegionList ), i++,
```

```
nw << Append(
    Outline Box( RegionList[i],
        gb = dt << Graph Builder(
            Size( 528, 477 ),
            Show Control Panel( 0 ),
            Variables( X( :Vineyard ), Y( :Summary Rating ), Overlay( :Legend ) ),
            Elements( Bar( X, Y, Legend( 6 ), Summary Statistic( "Sum" ) ) ),
            Local Data Filter(
                Add Filter( columns( :Region ), Where( :Region == RegionList[i]) ) ) )
    )
  )
);
```

This example uses the sample data table, Wine Sensory Data.jmp. Carolyn's wine sensory data columns are summed in the new column, Summary Rating. Another new column named Legend is created, where legend values are assigned into one of four categories based on the values from Summary Rating.

Result 11.10:

The data table with added columns is shown first, followed by the reports with the local data filters.

Figure 11.16 Wine Sensory Data Table with Added Columns

Summary Rating	Legend
31	Best
20	Good
30	Best
21	Good
21	Good
31	Best
25	Better
23	Better
26	Better
22	Better
10	Low
17	Low
16	Low
19	Good
13	Low
26	Better
23	Better
33	Best

Figure 11.17 Graph Builder Bar Charts with Local Data Filters (Excerpt)

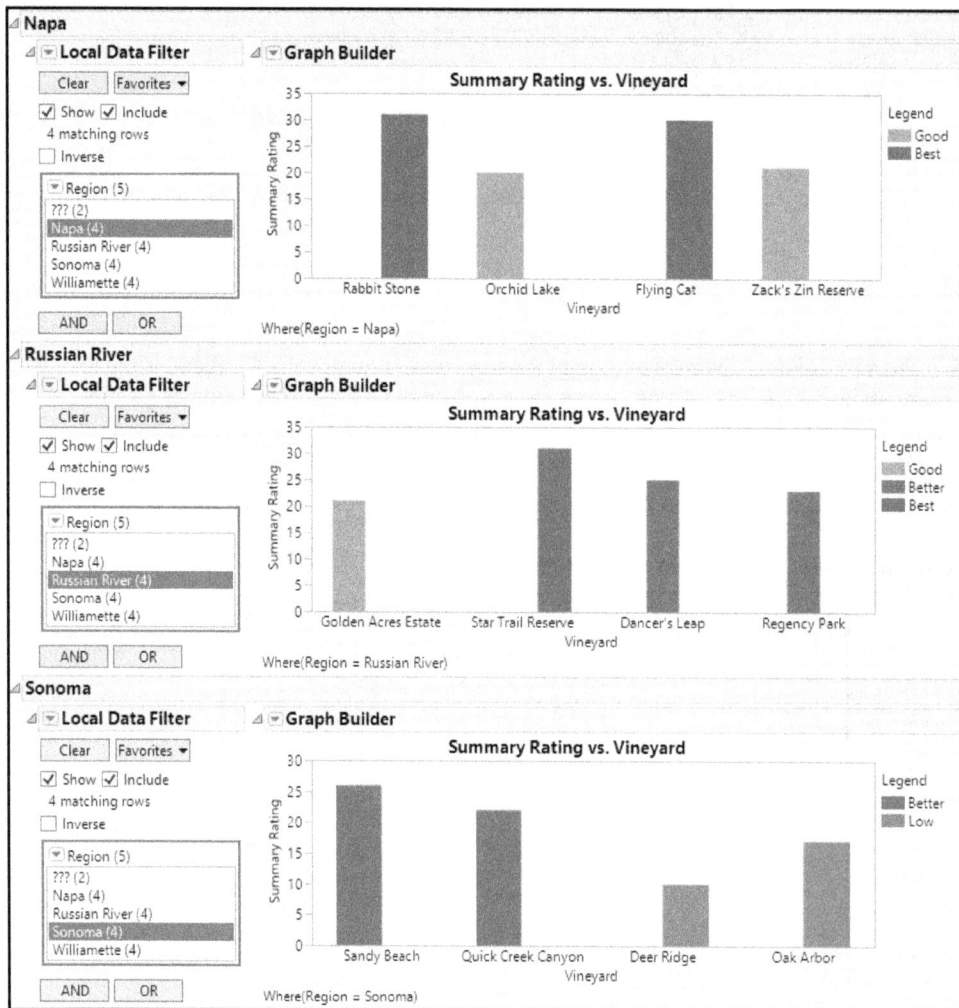

Chapter 12: Reports and Journals

Question 12.1: At the top of my report, there is a text string that begins "Where...". How can I remove this information from my report and instead show it in the top OutlineBox?

Figure 12.1 Where String in Bivariate Report

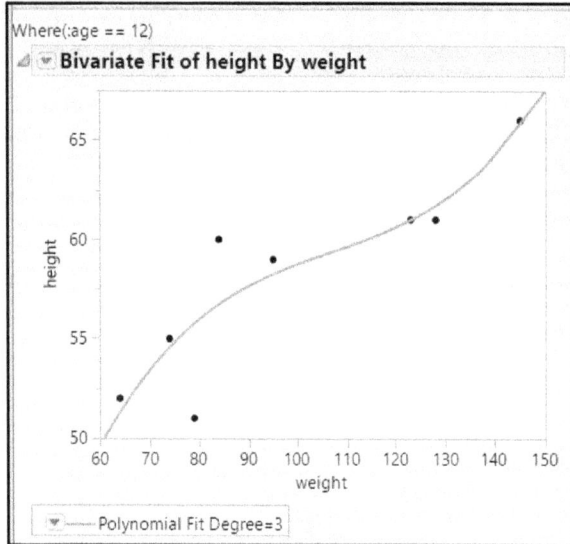

Solution 12.1:

The Where information appears as text above the OutlineBox. When you review the display tree, you will notice that the TextBox is at the same level as the OutlineBox (a previous sibling). One way to access this TextBox is to send the Parent message to the OutlineBox and then subscript to the first TextBox. Finally, the Where text can be removed from the report by changing the **Visibility** of the TextBox to **"Collapse"**.

The Where information can be added to the existing OutlineBox title by first extracting the current title. Then the new title can be assigned by concatenating the desired text to the original title.

NOTE: The number associated with the TextBox is **1** in this case. However, if the Report Preferences have been set for "Date Title on Output" or "Data Table Title on Output", the TextBox number for the Where information might be **2** or **3**. More information about parent and child relationships within reports can be found in the *Scripting Guide*.

```
/* Open the Big Class sample data table */
dt = Open( "$SAMPLE_DATA/Big Class.jmp" );

/* Create a few Bivariate plots to demonstrate
   the Where text */
For( i = 12, i <= 14, i++,
    biv = dt << Bivariate(
            Y( :height ),
            X( :weight ),
            Where( :age == i),
            Fit Polynomial( 3, {Line Color( "Green" ), Line Style( Smooth )} )
```

```
    );
    Wait( 1 );  //For demonstration purposes

    /* Hide the TextBox containing the Where text */
    (Report( biv ) << Parent)[Text Box( 1 )] << Visibility( "Collapse" );
    Wait( 1 );  //For demonstration purposes.

    /* Add Where information to first OutlineBox */
    currentText = Report( biv )[Outline Box( 1 )] << Get Title;
    Report( biv )[Outline Box( 1 )] << Set Title(
        currentText || ", age = " || Char( i )
    );
    Wait( 1 );  //For demonstration purposes, allowing time to view change
);
```

Result 12.1:

Figure 12.2 Where Text Removed and OutlineBox Title Updated

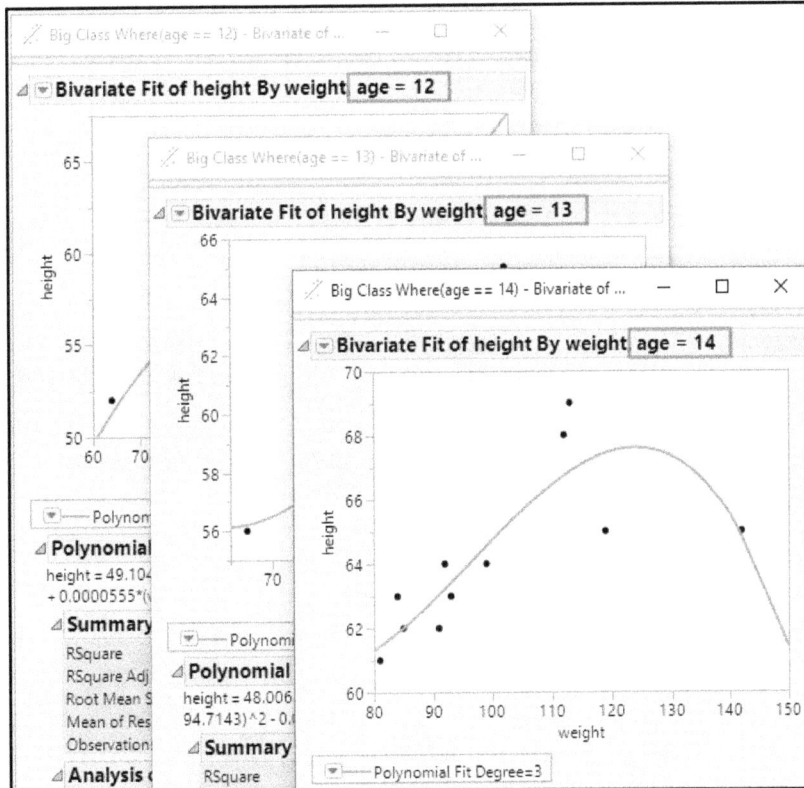

Question 12.2: How can I use a variable in a Where statement so that the window title and Where text show the actual variable values rather than the variable name?

Solution 12.2:

Build an expression, and then use **Eval Expr()** to resolve the global variable prior to evaluation of the expression:

```
/* Open the Fitness sample data table */
dt = Open( "$SAMPLE_DATA/Fitness.jmp" );

/* Assign the criteria to a global variable */
selVar = "M";

/* Build the main expression */
bivExpr = Expr(
    dt << Bivariate(
        Y( :MaxPulse ),
        X( :RstPulse ),
        /* Identify the global variable by wrapping it with the Expr function */
        Where( :sex == Expr( selVar ) )
    )
);

/* Resolve the variable expression first, then evaluate the main expression */
Eval( Eval Expr( bivExpr ) );
```

This solution illustrates how to use a global variable that contains a string, and how to place it in a Where clause in an analysis launch. First, an expression is built that contains a Where clause, which itself contains an expression.

In the last line of code, the **Eval Expr()** function evaluates the **Expr(selVar)** within the main expression, **bivExpr**. Finally, the **Eval()** function evaluates the main expression, **bivExpr**.

Result 12.2

Figure 12.3 Where Text Replaced

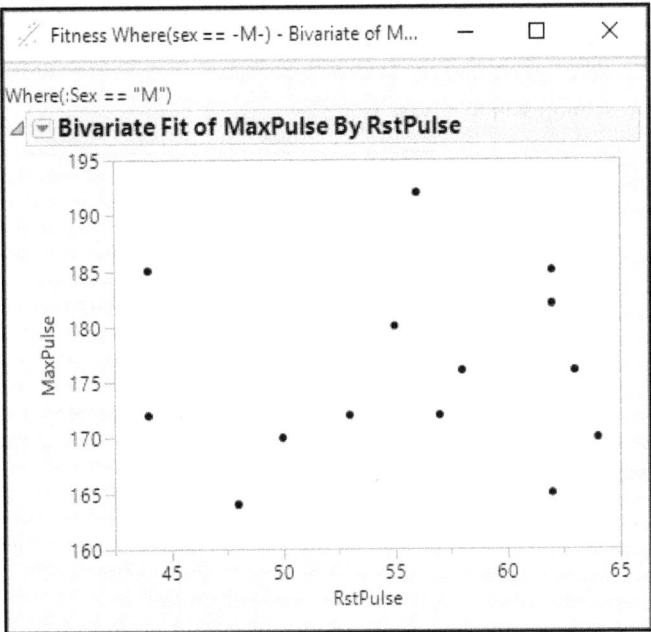

Question 12.3: How can I arrange my report so that I have two graphs per row?

Solution 12.3:

Use a **Lineup Box()** to arrange each By level report within a **New Window**:

```
/* Open the Big Class sample data table */
dt = Open( "$SAMPLE_DATA/Big Class.jmp" );

/* Use the Lineup Box with the N Col argument to arrange the By level plots */
nw = New Window( "Bivariate Report",
    Lineup Box( N Col( 2 ), Spacing( 10 ), dt << Bivariate( Y( :weight ), X( :height ), By(
:age ) ) )
);
```

Lineup Box() is a Display Box constructor that aids in the spatial arrangement of reports. The **N Col** argument in **Lineup Box()** establishes two columns for the By level display boxes. To learn more about **Lineup Box()** and its arguments, see the Scripting Index topic.

Result 12.3:

Figure 12.4 Bivariate Reports Arranged Two Graphs per Row

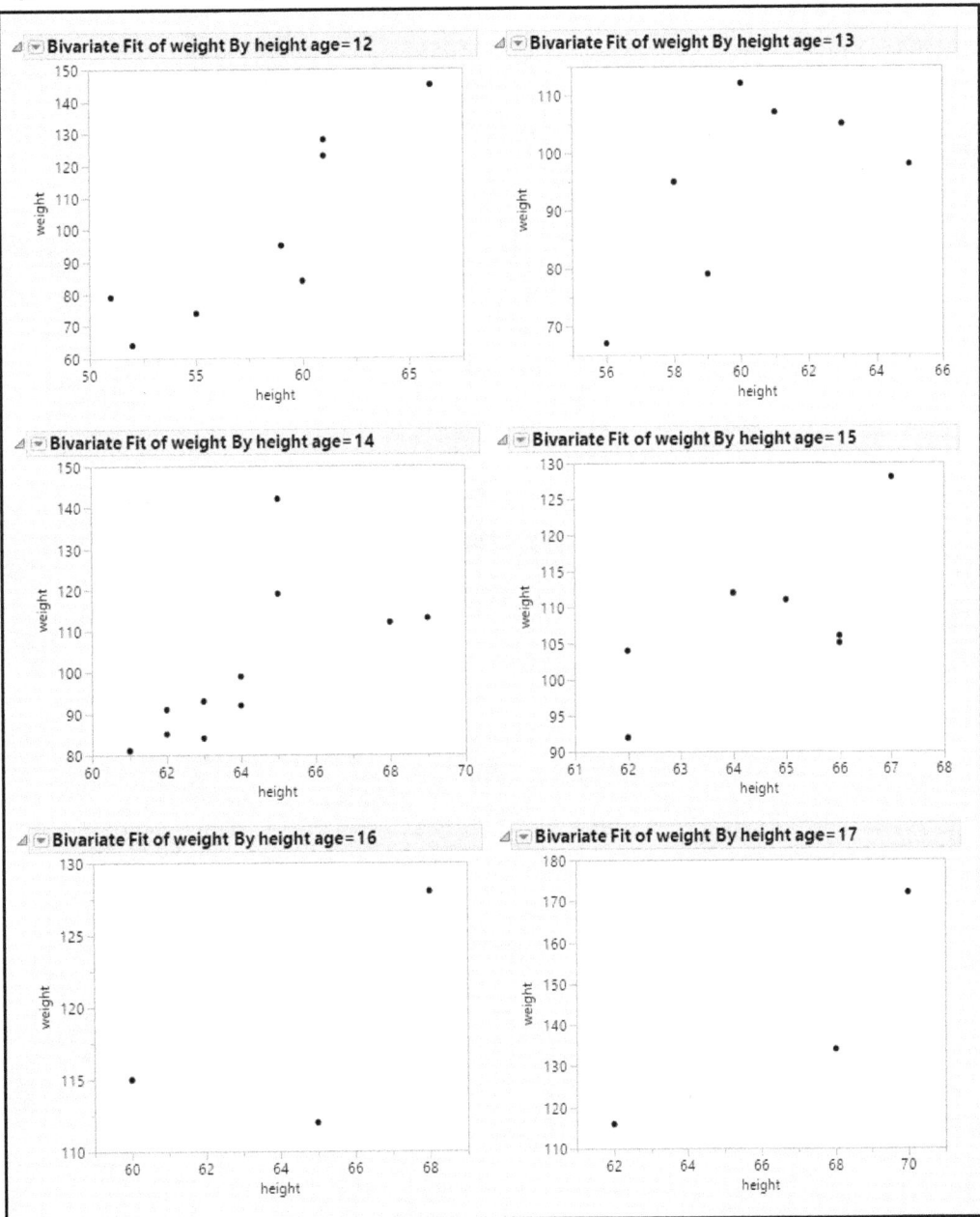

Question 12.4: How can I get a handle to the journal window so that I can save it?

Solution 12.4:

Use the **Current Journal()** function, as shown in the following code:

```
/* Open the Big Class sample data table */
dt = Open( "$SAMPLE_DATA/Big Class.jmp" );

/* Generate the desired analysis */
biv = dt << Bivariate( Y( :weight ), X( :height ), Fit Line );

/* Create a journal of the report */
Report( biv ) << Journal;

/* Obtain a handle to the current journal */
jrn = Current Journal();

/* Save the journal */
jrn << Save Journal( "$DOCUMENTS/DistJournal.jrn" );
```

The **Current Journal()** function returns a reference to the active journal that is open in the JMP application.

Result 12.5:

Figure 12.5 Journaled Report

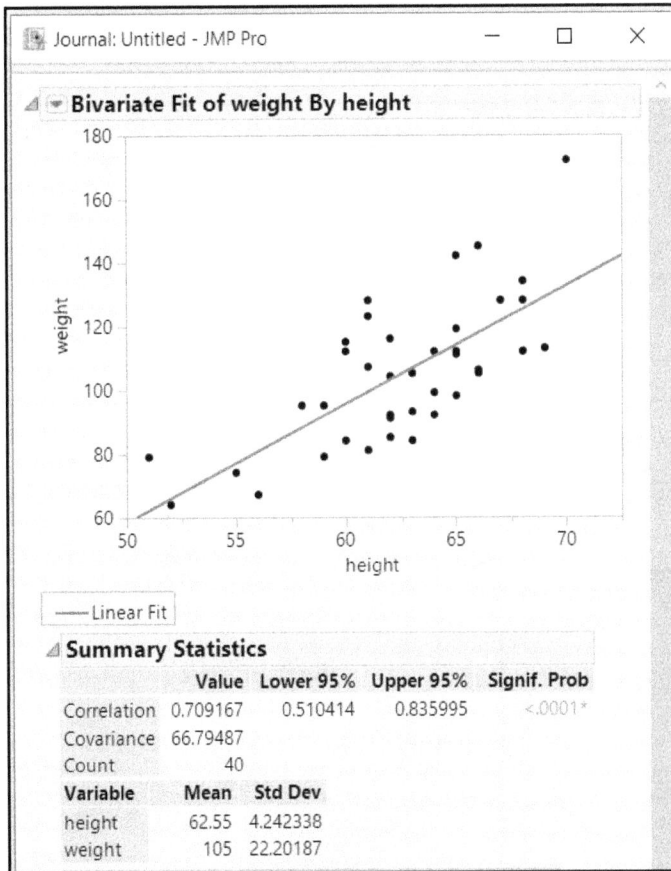

Figure 12.6 Journal Saved to Documents Folder

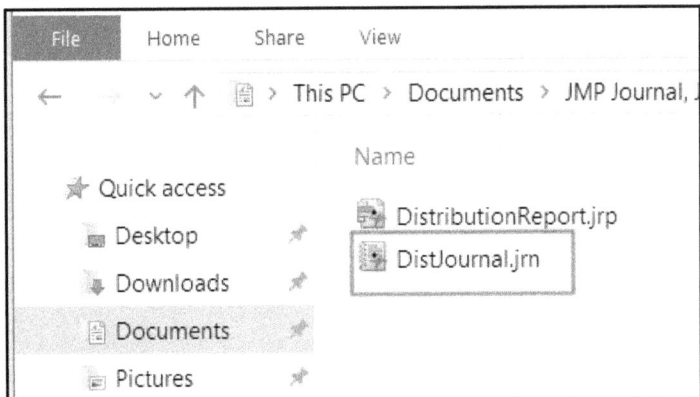

Question 12.5: How can I change the name of the journal window?

Solution 12.5:

Use **Set Window Title()** to set the title to the journal window, as shown in the following code:

```
/* Open the Big Class sample data table */
dt = Open( "$SAMPLE_DATA/Big Class.jmp" );

/* Create a journaled report using the New Window option */
jw = New Window( "Generic Journal Title",
    <<Journal,
    biv = dt << Bivariate( Y( :weight ), X( :height ), Fit Line )
);

/* Set the title of the journal window */
jw << Set Window Title( "My New Journal" );
```

The **Set Window Title()** message can be used to change any window titles.

Result 12.5:

Figure 12.7 Journal after Name Change

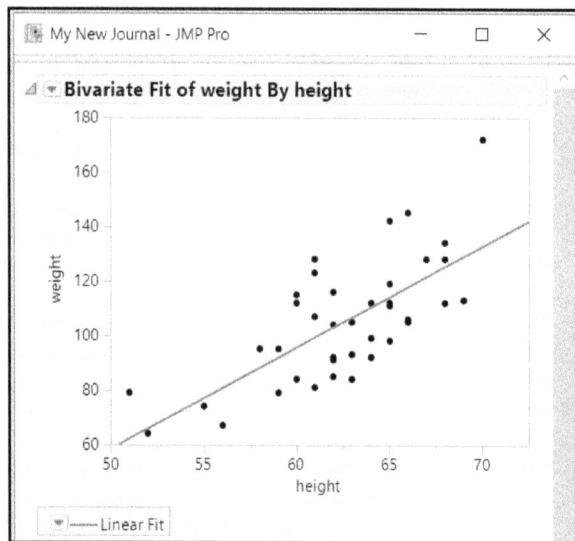

Question 12.6: How do I insert the contents of a data table into a journal, under a specific OutlineBox?

Solution 12.6:

The following example shows how to insert the sample data table, Big Class, under the Summary of Fit OutlineBox in a journal that contains a Bivariate report:

```
/* Open the Big Class sample data table */
dt = Open( "$SAMPLE_DATA/Big Class.jmp" );

/* Generate the desired analysis */
biv = dt << Bivariate( Y( :weight ), X( :height ), Fit Line );

/* Create a journal of the report */
Report( biv ) << Journal;

/* Obtain a handle to the current journal */
jrn = Current Journal();

/* Insert an OutlineBox containing the data table as a report object under the Summary of
Fit table */
jrn["Summary of Fit"] << Append(
    Outline Box( dt << Get Name || " Data Table", dt << Get As Report )
);
```

To append the data table as a report object under a particular OutlineBox in the main journal, send the **Append()** message to that OutlineBox.

Result 12.6:

Figure 12.8 Journal with Data Table Inserted

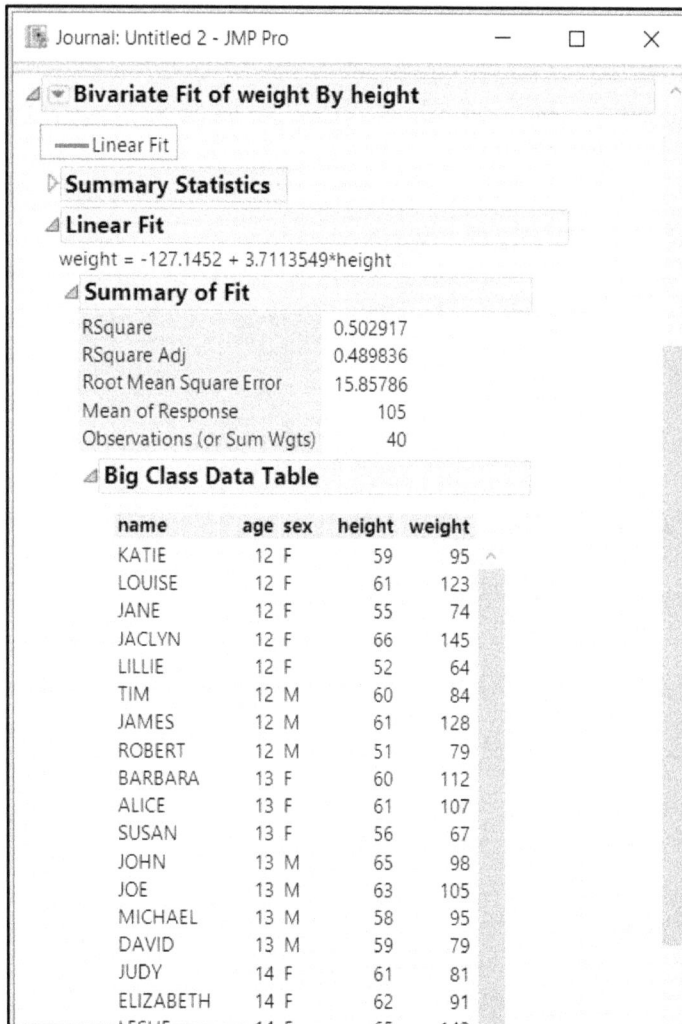

Question 12.7: I need to save my report as a .jrp file in my script. How is this done?

Solution 12.7:

There is no **Save()** option for the .jrp file type. The following method serves as a workaround.

Extract the script from the platform, and then use the **Save Text File()** command to save the file path and script as a text file, using the .jrp file extension:

```
/* Open the Big Class sample data table */
dt = Open( "$SAMPLE_DATA/Big Class.jmp" );

/* Create a distribution platform */
dist = dt << Distribution(
    Continuous Distribution( Column( :weight ) ),
    Nominal Distribution( Column( :age ) )
);

/* Get a script of the distribution platform */
distScript = dist << Get Script;

/* Save the file path and script as a text file, and specify .JRP as file type */
tfpath = Save Text File(
    "$DOCUMENTS/DistributionReport.jrp",
    "\[Open("$SAMPLE_DATA\Big Class.jmp");]\" || Char( Name Expr( distScript ) )
);
```

When creating a JMP report file (.jrp) in a script using the **Save Text File()** function, remember to specify the file path with the .jrp extension as the first argument. The second argument is the script that will be executed when opening the file. The first part of the script opens the data table. Notice how it is enclosed by a \[**string**]\ function, which enables you to use quotation marks or escape characters within the argument. This is concatenated to the platform script, which is wrapped in **Name Expr()** to return the script without evaluating and **Char()** to wrap the script in quotation marks for concatenation to the other parts of the script string.

Result 12.7:

Figure 12.9 Report is Saved as .jrp File Type

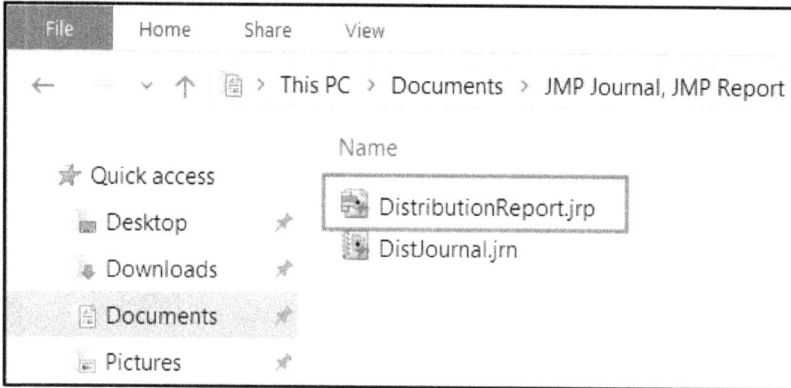

Figure 12.10 Report File Opened

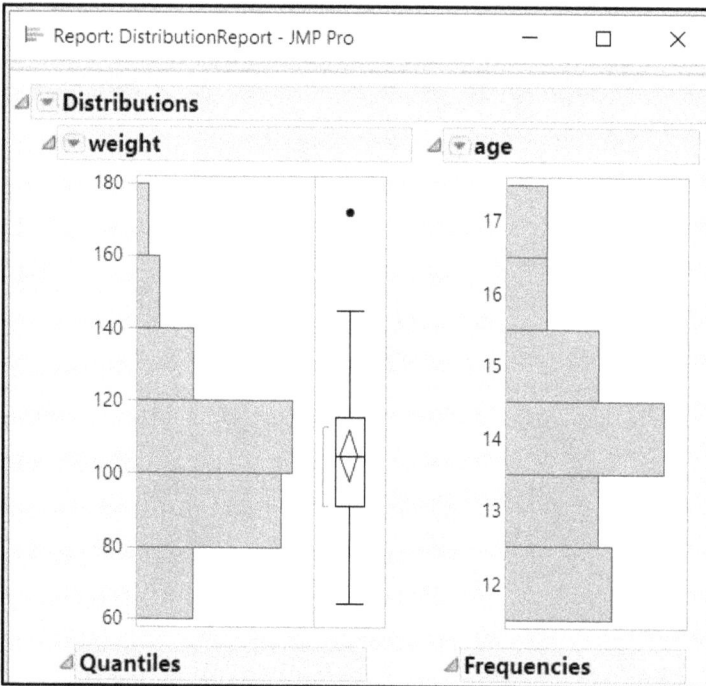

Question 12.8: How can I use a map as a filter?

Solution 12.8:

Use **Data Filter Context Box()** in conjunction with the **Data Filter Source Box()** to make a map plot the filter for a different plot within a report:

```
/* Open the SATByYear sample data table. */
dt = Open( "$SAMPLE_DATA/SATByYear.jmp" );

/* Create a New Window that will hold the filter(map) and the scatterplot to be filtered
*/
nw = New Window( "Use Map as Filter",
    /* Wraps both the source filter and the report being filtered */
    dfcb = Data Filter Context Box(
        H List Box(
            /* Wraps the map platform, which is the source filter */
            dfsb2 = Data Filter Source Box(
                gb1 = dt << Graph Builder(
                    Size( 273, 275 ),
                    Show Control Panel( 0 ),
                    Fit to Window( "Off" ),
                    Variables(
                        Color( :Name( "Expenditure (1997)" ) ), Shape( :State )
                    ),
                    Elements( Map Shapes( Legend( 2 ) ) ),
                    SendToReport(
                        Dispatch(
                            {},
                            "",
                            ScaleBox( 2 ),
                            {Min( 14.7815165876777 ), Max( 60.2184834123223 ),
                             Inc( 10 ), Minor Ticks( 1 ),
                            Label Row Nesting( 1 )}
                        ),
                        Dispatch(
                            {},
                            "400",
                            ScaleBox,
                            {Legend Model(
                                2,
                                Properties(
                                    0,
                                    {gradient(
                                        {Color Theme( "White to Green" ),
                                         Label Format( "Fixed Dec", 15, 0 )}
                                    )}
                                )
                            )}
                        )
                    )
                )
            ),
            /* Report that is being filtered */
```

```
            gb2 = dt << Graph Builder(
                Size( 534, 453 ),
                Show Control Panel( 0 ),
                Fit to Window( "Off" ),
                Variables( X( :SAT Verbal ), Y( :SAT Math ) ),
                Elements( Points( X, Y, Legend( 2 ) ),
                    Smoother( X, Y, Legend( 3 ) )
                )
            )
        )
    ) /* End of context box */
);
```

The **Data Filter Context Box()** and **Data Filter Source Box()** constructs enable you to create local data filters using graphs. In this example, we used a Graph Builder map plot as the designated filter for a scatter plot, but you can use a variety of graphs and reports to create your own hierarchy of filtering. Remember to wrap both the filtering display box and the display boxes to be filtered with the **Data Filter Context Box()**, and then wrap your filtering display with the **Data Filter Source Box()**.

Result 12.8

Figure 12.11 Map as Filter Report

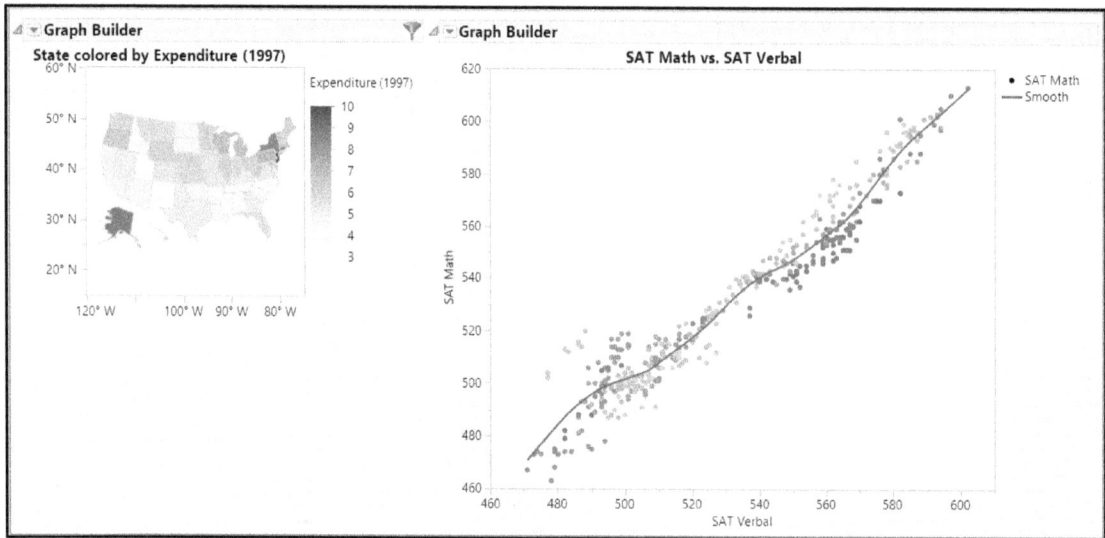

Question 12.9: How do I create a tabbed report?

Solution 12.9:

This example solution creates a tabbed report to hold three platforms: Distribution, Bivariate, and Oneway:

```
/* Open the Big Class sample data table */
dt = Open( "$SAMPLE_DATA/Big Class.jmp" );

/* Create a new window to hold three tab pages, one each for platform */
tabWin = New Window( "Fit Y by X Reports",
    /* The Tab Box is the container for the Tab Page Boxes */
    tb = Tab Box(
        /* Tab 1 */
            Tab Page Box(
                    Title( "Distribution" ),
                    dist = dt << Distribution(
                            Continuous Distribution( Column( :weight ) ),
                            Nominal Distribution( Column( :age ) )
                    )
            ),
        /* Tab 2 */
            Tab Page Box( Title( "Bivariate" ), biv = dt << Bivariate( Y( :weight ), X(
:height ), Fit Line ) ),
        /* Tab 3 */
            Tab Page Box(
                    Title( "Oneway" ),
                    ow = dt << Oneway( Y( :height ), X( :sex ), Means( 1 ), Mean Diamonds(
1 ) )
            )
    )
);
```

The Tab Box is a container for other display boxes, the Tab Page Boxes. Each Tab Page Box holds the title for the tabs and contents.

Another option for creating a tabbed report is to use the Application Builder. To see an example application that uses the Tab Box with Tab Page Boxes, go **to File ▶ New Application** and choose the Presentation sample.

Result 12.9:

Figure 12.12 Tabbed Report

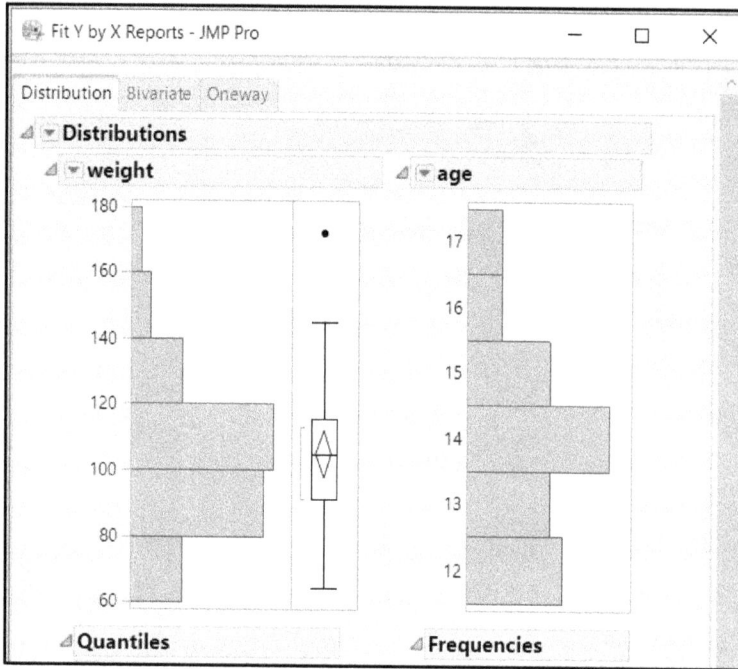

Question 12.10: My graph has a local data filter. How can I save both components as one interactive HTML file?

Solution 12.10:

Send the save message to the **Top Parent** of the report, which is a higher level in the display tree:

```
/* Open the sample data table, Big Class.jmp */
dt = Open( "$SAMPLE_DATA/Big Class.jmp" );

/* Create a graph builder plot with a local data filter */
gb = dt << Graph Builder(
    Size( 534, 454 ),
    Show Control Panel( 0 ),
    Variables( X( :height ), Y( :weight ) ),
    Elements( Points( X, Y, Legend( 10 ) ), Line Of Fit( X, Y, Legend( 13 ) ) ),
    Local Data Filter( Add Filter( columns( :sex ) ) )
);

/* Send message to Top Parent will include the Local Data Filter in saved HTML file*/
(gb << Top Parent) << Save Interactive HTML( "$DOCUMENTS/GraphBuilder_DataFilter.html" );
```

Result 12.10:

Figure 12.13 Report with Local Data Filter

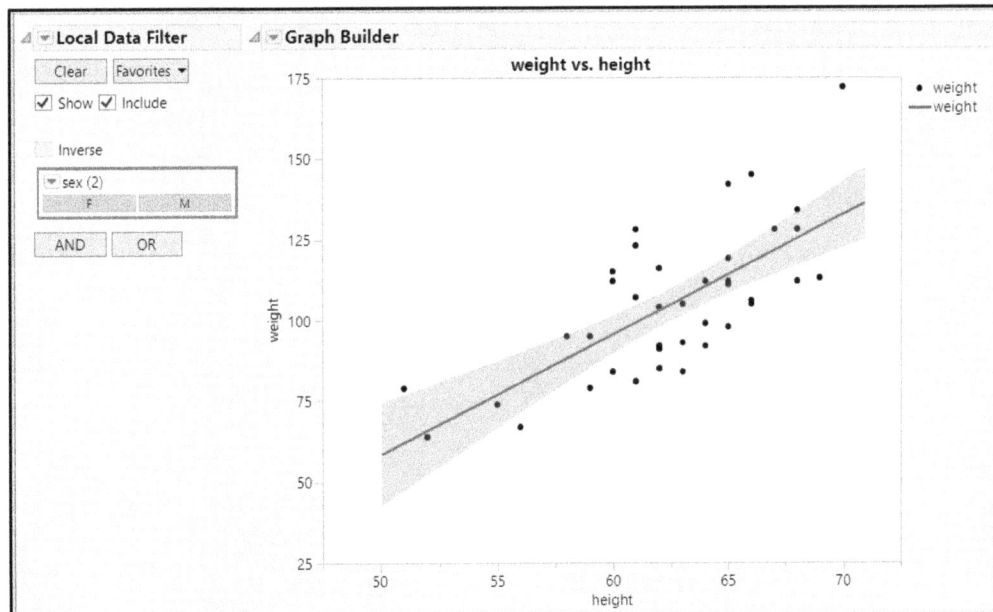

Figure 12.14 Saved Interactive HTML Report

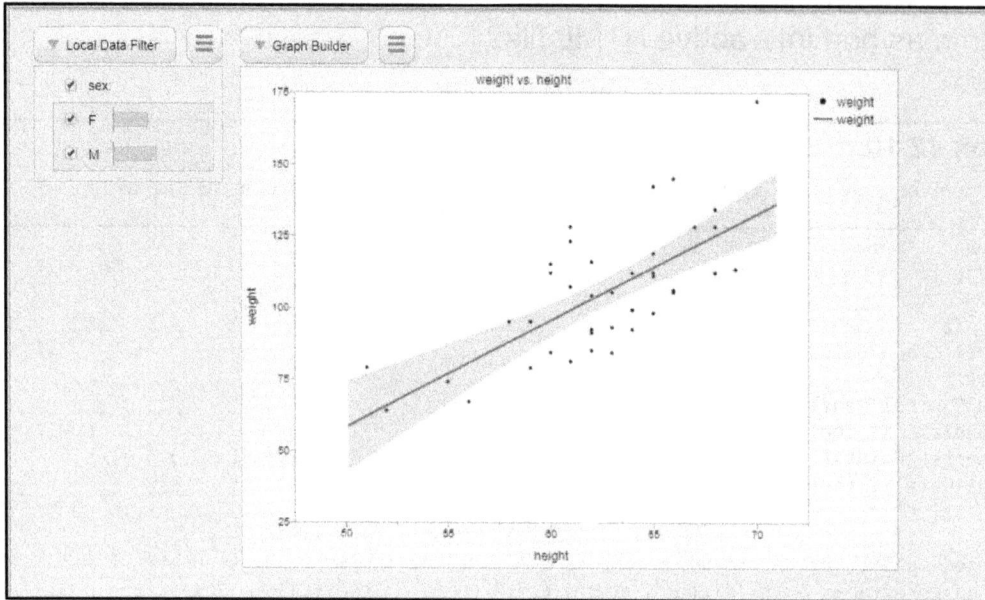

Index

Symbols and Numerics

A

B

www.ingramcontent.com/pod-product-compliance
Lightning Source LLC
Chambersburg PA
CBHW061924190326
41458CB00009B/2644